# CORPORATE SOCIAL IRRESPONSIBILITY: A CHALLENGING CONCEPT

# CRITICAL STUDIES ON CORPORATE RESPONSIBILITY, GOVERNANCE AND SUSTAINABILITY

Series Editor: William Sun

CRITICAL STUDIES ON CORPORATE RESPONSIBILITY,
GOVERNANCE AND SUSTAINABILITY   VOLUME 4

# CORPORATE SOCIAL IRRESPONSIBILITY: A CHALLENGING CONCEPT

EDITED BY

## RALPH TENCH
*Leeds Metropolitan University, UK*

## WILLIAM SUN
*Leeds Metropolitan University, UK*

## BRIAN JONES
*Leeds Metropolitan University, UK*

Emerald

United Kingdom – North America – Japan
India – Malaysia – China

Emerald Group Publishing Limited
Howard House, Wagon Lane, Bingley BD16 1WA, UK

First edition 2012

**British Library Cataloguing in Publication Data**
A catalogue record for this book is available from the British Library

ISBN: 978-1-78052-998-1
ISSN: 2043-9059 (Series)

ISOQAR certified
Management Systems,
awarded to Emerald for
adherence to Quality
and Environmental
standards ISO 9001:2008
and 14001:2004,
respectively

ISOQAR
REGISTERED

UKAS
MANAGEMENT
SYSTEMS

0026

Certificate Number 1985
ISO 9001
ISO 14001

INVESTOR IN PEOPLE

# CONTENTS

## PART I: INTRODUCTION

## PART II: CONCEPTUALISATION OF CSI

v

# LIST OF TABLES

# LIST OF FIGURES

# LIST OF CONTRIBUTORS

| | |
|---|---|
| *Victoria Olufunmilayo Ajala* | Department of Human Communications, Bowen University, Iwo, Nigeria |
| *Olusanmi C. Amujo* | Independent corporate marketing researcher/consultant, Nigerian Institute of Public Relations, Lagos, Nigeria |
| *Jennifer Bartlett* | School of Advertising, Marketing and Public Relations, Queensland University of Technology, Brisbane, Australia |
| *Clea Bourne* | Department of Media & Communications, Goldsmiths, University of London, UK |
| *Timothy S. Clark* | W. A. Franke College of Business, Northern Arizona University, Flagstaff, Arizona, USA |
| *Audra R. Diers* | Department PR & Journalism, Sheffield Hallam University, Sheffield, UK |
| *Trish Glazebrook* | Department of Philosophy & Religion Studies, University of North Texas, Denton, USA |
| *Kristen N. Grantham* | W. L. Gore & Associates, Inc., Flagstaff, AZ, USA |
| *Brian Jones* | School of Marketing and Public Relations, Faculty of Business and Law, Leeds Metropolitan University, Leeds, UK |
| *Äyvind Ihlen* | Department of Media and Communication, University of Oslo, Oslo, Norway |
| *Beatrice Adeyinka Laninhun* | Laninhun Department of Communication Arts, University of Ibadan, Ibadan, Nigeria |

| | |
|---|---|
| *Nicole Marie Lindsay* | School of Communication, Faculty of Communication, Art and Technology, Simon Fraser University, Burnaby, Canada |
| *Brad S. Long* | Department of Business Administration, Gerald Schwartz School of Business, St. Francis Xavier University, Antigonish, Nova Scotia, Canada |
| *Paul Manning* | Department of Organisation and Management, Management School, Liverpool University, Liverpool, UK |
| *Steve May* | Department of Communication Studies, University of North Carolina, Chapel Hill, NC, USA |
| *Alex Nunn* | School of Social, Psychological and Communication Sciences, Faculty of Health and Social Sciences, Leeds Metropolitan University, Leeds, UK |
| *Olutayo Otubanjo* | Lagos Business School, Pan-African University, Lagos, Nigeria |
| *Peter Stokes* | Chester Business School, University of Chester, Chester, UK |
| *Matt Story* | Department of Philosophy & Religion Studies, University of North Texas, Denton, TX, USA |
| *William Sun* | School of Strategy and Economics, Faculty of Business and Law, Leeds Metropolitan University, Leeds, UK |
| *N. A. J. Taylor* | Centre for Dialogue, La Trobe University and the School of Political Science and International Studies, University of Queensland, Australia |
| *Ralph Tench* | School of Marketing and Public Relations, Faculty of Business and Law, Leeds Metropolitan University, Leeds, UK |

# EDITORIAL ADVISORY AND REVIEW BOARD

# ABOUT THE EDITORS

**Ralph Tench** is Professor of Communication and Director of Research for the Faculty of Business and Law at Leeds Metropolitan University. He is a former Journalist and Communications Consultant. He was head of the UK's largest Public Relations and Communications academic department for 10 years at Leeds Business School until 2008. His research interests are in corporate communications, ethics, social responsibility and education. He is a member of the European Communication Monitor research team and is currently directing a pan European research team for the ECOPSI (European Communication Professionals Skills and Innovation pro-gramme), the largest EU-funded public relations research programme. Professor Tench is also managing research projects into communication strategies to tackle childhood obesity as well as communication dimensions of organisation's social and responsibility agendas. His work has been disseminated worldwide and translated in books and journals. He is a regular conference and keynote speaker at academic and practitioner conferences. During the last 12 months this includes keynotes and speaking at communication conferences in Istanbul, Chicago, Athens, Zagreb and Oslo.

**William Sun** is Reader in Corporate Governance and CSR, and Leader of Corporate Governance and Sustainability Research Group (CGSRG) at the Faculty of Business and Law, Leeds Metropolitan University, where he is also an Independent Chair for PhD Viva Voce Examinations and the Course leader of MSc Corporate Governance. Dr Sun has been a Co-Chair of the Finance and Sustainability Programme I & II initiated by research institutions in United Kingdom, France, Switzerland and two international academic associations since 2009. He is a member of the Management Committee of Corporate Governance Special Interest Group, British Academy of Management. Dr Sun received his PhD from Leeds Metropolitan University in 2002. His research interests include corporate governance, corporate social responsibility, sustainable business, business ethics, corporate strategy and process philosophy. He has published more than 50 journal papers and 16 academic books in corporate governance, corporate law, and transition economics. He is the author of the research monograph *How to Govern Corporations So They Serve the Public Good: A Theory of Corporate Governance Emergence* (Edwin Mellen, 2009) and lead editor of the book *Corporate Governance and the Global Financial Crisis: International Perspectives* (Cambridge University Press, 2011).

**Brian Jones** is Senior Lecturer at Leeds Business School, Leeds Metropolitan University. He has a BA (Honours) in Sociology from the University of Durham, an MA in Industrial Relations from the University of Warwick and a SERC/ESRC-funded PhD from the University of Bradford. He worked as a Research Officer for the Education and Skills Analysis Branch of the British Government's Employment Department, and previously lectured in Industrial Management at the University of Bradford. Prior to his current post he was Programme Director Vocational Education at Durham Business School, University of Durham, where he secured funding and managed a range of enterprise education programmes and projects locally, nationally and internationally. His research areas of interest are wide-ranging and cut across the business-management and social sciences.

# ABOUT THE AUTHORS

**Victoria Olufunmilayo Ajala** (PhD) is Reader at Department of Human Communications, Bowen University, Nigeria, holds a BSc (1st Class honours), two MScs in Advertising and PR and PhD in Communication. She has published books and several research articles in local and international journals, and is Fellow of the NIPR, a member of the ACCE and the APRA.

**Olusanmi C. Amujo** is independent corporate marketing Researcher/ Consultant. He holds an MA in Communication Art, a BA in History and Diploma in PR. He has published in *Tourist Studies, PRism, Journal of Product & Brand Management, Corporate Reputation Review*, etc. His research interests comprise corporate marketing and business history.

**Jennifer Bartlett** (PhD) is an Associate Professor at the Queensland University of Technology in Australia. Her work centres on the role of communication around corporate social responsibility and organisational legitimacy. She has published extensively on these topics including editing the award winning *Handbook of Communication and Corporate Social Responsibility* (2011).

**Clea Bourne** is Lecturer in Promotional Media at Goldsmiths, University of London. She worked in corporate communications for more than 20 years, latterly specialising in financial institutions. Her research focuses on the systemic production of trust/mistrust in financial markets, exploring communication strategies used by various market sectors.

**Timothy S. Clark** (PhD) is Assistant Professor of Management at The W. A. Franke College of Business at Northern Arizona University in Flagstaff, Arizona, USA. His research focuses on the reasons for or against firms' uptake of sustainability strategies, and his service work involves recognising the professionalism qualities sought by employers of business-school graduates.

**Audra R. Diers** (PhD) is Senior Lecturer in Public Relations at Sheffield Hallam University in Sheffield, UK and independent integrated Communication Consultant. Her work, both in practice and academia, focuses on multi-media strategy development and crisis communication.

xxi

**Trish Glazebrook** (PhD) received a PhD in Philosophy from the University of Toronto. She taught business ethics at Dalhousie University in Canada for several years, and currently chairs the Department of Philosophy & Religion Studies at the University of North Texas.

**Kristen N. Grantham** earned her bachelor's degree with a double major in Management and Finance from Northern Arizona University and plans to pursue a graduate degree in Business Studies in the future. Currently she is Inside Sales Representative for a medical device manufacturer in Flagstaff, Arizona, USA.

**Øyvind Ihlen** (PhD) is Professor at the Department of Media and Communication at the University of Oslo. He has published over 45 journal articles and book chapters, as well as seven books, including the award winning *Handbook of Communication and Corporate Social Responsibility* (2011).

**Beatrice Adeyinka Laninhun** (PhD) is Senior Lecturer in the Department of Communication Arts, University of Ibadan, Nigeria. She holds a BA English, an MA Language Arts and PhD Communication & Language Arts. Fellow of the Certified Marketing Communication Institute of Nigeria, she has published in local and international journals.

**Nicole Marie Lindsay** is a doctoral candidate in the School of Communication at Simon Fraser University. Her research is focused on the emergence and application of discourses of corporate social responsibility in the global mining industry, with an emphasis on Canadian mining companies operating in Latin America. She is co-editor of the book *Governance Ecosystems: CSR in the Latin American Mining Sector*.

**Brad S. Long** (PhD) is Associate Professor of Business Ethics and Leadership in the Gerald Schwartz School of Business, St. Francis Xavier University, Canada. Brad is a recipient of this university's Outstanding Teaching Award (2009) and his research appears in, amongst others, *Journal of Business Ethics* and *Journal of Organizational Change Management*.

**Paul Manning** (PhD) is Director of MSc programmes at Management School, Liverpool University. He previously worked as business school Lecturer at Northumbrian and Leeds Metropolitan universities. His research interest is focussed on the socially embedded nature of business and includes publications on social capital processes, business ethics and knowledge management.

**Steve May** (PhD, University of Utah, 1993) is Associate Professor in the Department of Communication Studies at the University of North Carolina at Chapel Hill. He has published numerous journal articles on work, ethics, and corporate social responsibility and has edited five award-winning books. His current book projects include *Corporate Social Responsibility: Virtue or Vice?* and *Working Identity*.

**Alex Nunn** (PhD) is Head of Politics and Applied Global Ethics at Leeds Metropolitan University and former Director of the Policy Research Institute at Leeds Metropolitan University. His academic work has a background in international political economy, crisis and global governance.

**Olutayo Otubanjo** (PhD) is Senior Lecturer at Lagos Business School, Pan-African University. He holds a PhD in Marketing with emphasis on corporate identity. He attended University of Hull (UK) and Brunel University, London. He has published in *Academy of Marketing Science Review, Tourist Studies, Management Decisions, Marketing Review, Corporate Reputation Review*, etc.

**Peter Stokes** (PhD) is Professor of Sustainable Management, Marketing and Tourism at Chester Business School, University of Chester, and is Editor-in-Chief of the *International Journal of Organizational Analysis*, EMRBI UK Country Director and UK Ambassador for the Association de Gestion des Ressources Humaines. He has published widely in journals and is the author of *Critical Concepts in Management and Organization Studies* (Palgrave Macmillan) and *Key Concepts in Business and Management Research Methods* (Palgrave Macmillan).

**Matt Story** is pursuing Philosophy at the University of North Texas and is the Founding Managing Editor of *Purlieu: A Philosophical Journal*.

**N. A. J. Taylor** is a research associate at La Trobe University's Centre for Dialogue, and a doctoral researcher in the School of Political Science and International Studies at the University of Queensland.

# ACKNOWLEDGEMENTS

We would like to thank all those who have engaged with and contributed to this volume. In particular individual chapter authors deserve praise and thanks for engaging so willingly with this project. All chapters were anonymously peer reviewed and we would like to thank all the reviewers for their time, effort and professionalism that have ensured the quality and consistency of the contributions. The reviewers of the volume chapters are:

- Ralph Bathurst, Senior Lecturer, School of Management (Albany), Massey University, New Zealand
- Barry Colbert, Reader & Director of CMA Centre for Business & Sustainability, Wilfrid Laurier University, Canada
- Gabriel Eweje, Senior Lecturer & Director of Sustainability & CSR Research Group, Department of Management & International Business, Massey University, New Zealand
- Tineke E. Lambooy, Associate Professor at Center for Sustainability, Nyenrode Business University, and at Law School, Utrecht University, The Netherlands
- Céline Louche, Assistant Professor, Vlerick Leuven Gent Management School, Belgium
- Paul Manning, Director of MSc Management Programmes, Management School, University of Liverpool, UK
- James McRitchie, Publisher of CorpGov.net (Corporate Governance), USA
- Simon Robinson, Professor of Global Ethics, Faculty of Business and Law, Leeds Metropolitan University, UK
- David Russell, Head of Department of Accounting & Finance, Leicester Business School, De Montfort University, UK
- Greg Shailer, Reader, School of Accounting and Business Information Systems, College of Business and Economics, the Australian National University, Australia
- John Shields, Professor & Associate Dean, Faculty of Economics and Business, the University of Sydney, Australia
- Peter Stokes, Professor of Sustainable Management, Marketing and Tourism, Chester Business School, University of Chester, UK

- Wayne Visser, Senior Associate, University of Cambridge Programme for Sustainability Leadership, UK; Adjunct Professor, La Trobe University, Australia
- Junjie Wu, Senior Lecturer, School of Accounting and Finance, Faculty of Business and Law, Leeds Metropolitan University, UK
- Suzanne Young, Associate Professor, La Trobe Business School, Faculty of Business, Economics and Law, La Trobe University, Australia

# PART I
# INTRODUCTION

# THE CHALLENGING CONCEPT OF CORPORATE SOCIAL IRRESPONSIBILITY: AN INTRODUCTION

Ralph Tench, William Sun and Brian Jones

## ABSTRACT

Purpose — *This chapter introduces this volume's topics, purpose and key themes.*

Methodology/approach — *This chapter reviews literature and chapters and offers conceptual development.*

Findings — *The difficulties of CSR in theory and practice are mainly due to its incomplete conceptualisation because its inseparable counterpart CSI has been eventually neglected or ignored in the CSR theorising process. The CSI concept is as equally important as CSR. CSI offers a theoretical platform to avoid the vagueness, ambiguity, arbitrariness and mysticism of CSR. CSI deserves to be a serious subject of inquiry and demands more scholarly attention.*

Practical/social implications — *With the aid of the CSI concept, CSR becomes more realistic and effective, as it is now more focused, practical and operational. While CSI is clear-cut, CSR is clearly meant, at the*

Corporate Social Irresponsibility: A Challenging Concept
Critical Studies on Corporate Responsibility, Governance and Sustainability, Volume 4, 3–20
ISSN: 2043-9059/doi:10.1108/S2043-9059(2012)0000004009

*very least, to do well by undoing CSI. It is easier to promote CSR by addressing CSI first. The concept of CSI may allow everyone, including business practitioners, to concentrate on resolving the most important and urgent issues of public concern. It also encourages people to address the root causes of CSI problems in a systematic way. Doing so undoubtedly expands and enriches the understanding of CSR.*

Originality/value of chapter − *The concept of CSI has been less developed in academic circles. While the contributors of this volume have made significant contributions to the understanding of CSI, this chapter adds fresh reasoning and explanations to the development of the CSI subject.*

**Keywords:** Corporate social responsibility; corporate social irresponsibility; concept; subject of inquiry

'Thoughts without content are empty; intuitions without concepts are blind'
— Immanuel Kant (1787)

At the time of writing (July of 2012), there have been three corporate scandals in Britain that have shocked the world: the phone hacking scandal of News International, involving serious misbehaviour by journalists, policemen and politicians with several arrests already made; Glaxo Smith Kline's mis-selling of drugs in the United States that resulted in $3 billion fine, the biggest ever sanction handed down; the inter-banking rate fixing of Barclays with a £290 million fine imposed by the US and UK governments. In the Barclays case, it has been reported that many other banks including a German one were also involved in the manipulation of inter-bank rates (Libor) from 2005 through to 2008. Investigations are still under way. The three scandals, among others over decades, have a common feature that such misbehaviours have not just occurred in a single company; rather, the 'reprehensible behaviour' (words of ex-Barclays CEO Bob Diamond) were often industry-wide. Indeed, according to George Osborne, the UK Chancellor of the Exchequer, we are in the 'age of irresponsibility'. Yet, strangely, the subject of Corporate Social Irresponsibility (CSI) has received little research attention so far. On the contrary, its counterpart Corporate Social Responsibility (CSR) has been the focus of business discussion and academic debate since the 1950s. In the last three decades CSR has increasingly become a subject area with intensive scholarly enquiry and research, along with various initiatives and programmes by governments, non-governmental organisations and companies throughout the world. But in the meanwhile, CSI has been continually neglected or ignored as a systematic research field. CSI has not been treated as a relatively independent subject of inquiry, probably because of its negative connotation. Clearly, CSI is a serious issue of our time, a time associated with both financial crisis and ecological crisis, and is an issue that management, governments and policy makers are by dint of circumstances increasingly being forced to address. CSI as a business and social phenomenon deserves more systematic studies and analysis.

This volume is not just to open more debates and discussions on CSI. The main task of the book is an attempt to establish CSI as an academic concept and subject of inquiry in its own right, which also helps to address the shortcomings of the CSR concept that has been criticised by many. We argue that CSR and CSI are logically inseparable. Without the concept of CSI, CSR is eventually empty. CSR and CSI coexist in practice and can be transformable to each other. By eliminating or reducing CSI, CSR will significantly increase and become more effective (of course, CSR and CSI are not a zero sum, and we will explain the logic in the second section below). The book serves to ignite the interest in this research direction and to promote CSR by clearly defining and containing CSI.

In the following sections, we first review the failure of CSR and the severe limitations of the CSR concept that are addressed in the literature. Then, we briefly analyse how the difficulties of CSR theorising can be overcome by the concept of CSI. We explain the logic and rationale for the establishment of the CSI subject based on, and also adding to, the reasoning of several chapters in this volume. Following this, we summarise key themes of the chapters in the book in line with the subject matter of CSI and finally conclude the Introduction chapter with some remarks.

## DIFFICULTIES OF THE CSR CONCEPT

In the first volume of the book series *Critical Studies on Corporate Responsibility, Governance and Sustainability*, the editors (Sun, Stewart & Pollard, 2010) note the overall and systemic failure of CSR in practice. This failure comes despite some micro aspects of improvement, evidenced by the fact that many of the long-time CSR campaigns and generated programmes did not in any sense prevent the 2008 global financial crisis; rather, the failure of CSR did actually (at least in part) contribute to the financial crisis. In that volume, several contributors used rich evidence to illustrate how CSR failed in practice and set out some of the reasons for that failure.

CSR has not seen any improvement post the financial crisis, as the CSR-related problems that caused the financial crisis remain largely untouched. In March 2011, Mervyn King, the Governor of the Bank of England, pointed out that Britain risks suffering another financial crisis because the banks' core issues are still there, such as the culture of short-term profits and excess bonuses, exploiting millions of customers, and living in a 'too big to fail' world (*The Telegraph*, 5 March 2011).

Thus, Wayne Visser (2011), among others, announced that CSR is dead. For Visser, the logic is simple: although there are specific CSR projects and practices at the micro level (with some improvements), however, at the macro level *almost* every indicator of social, environmental and ethical health is in decline. This decline is an obvious source of concern and almost inevitably raises the question: what is to be done?

The failure of CSR is seen to result from both theory and practice. Theoretically, the three core models of CSR, the shareholder value model, the stakeholder model and the business ethics model, are severely limited. The shareholder value model talks about business without ethics, the business ethics model talks about ethics without business, and the stakeholder model talks about business politically with a narrow-minded responsibility to few interest groups (for more detailed analysis, see Sun & Bellamy, 2010; Sun et al., 2010).

Furthermore, the concept of CSR is ambiguous. What is CSR? There is no clear-cut and concrete definition. For decades, the conceptualisation of CSR has been proliferating without a systematic conceptual framework (Carroll, 1999). And, of course, there is no easy way to arrive at a definitive definition of CSR, as CSR contains almost everything of public concern. Everyone has his/her own answer to and understanding of CSR. Van Oosterhout and Heugens (2008) note that from the beginning, the academic concept of CSR has been linked to ethics and tends to be overwhelmingly normative, which renders the definition of CSR more difficult.

Therefore, CSR in practice relies largely on managerial discretion to define and operate in the name of strategic choices (though their choices are subject to institutional conditions and constraints). This gives companies large room for selecting CSR programmes and initiatives arbitrarily in their own interests, for masking their socially irresponsible behaviour and actions, and for possibly accurate accusations of 'lip service' or 'green washing'. In their empirical analysis based on an extensive 15-year panel dataset that covers nearly 3,000 publicly traded companies in the

United States, Kotchen and Moon (2011) found that companies actually engaged in corporate social responsibility (CSR) in order to offset their corporate social irresponsibility (CSI). In its report 'Behind the Mask: The Real Face of CSR', the charity organisation Christian Aid (2004) suggests that 'CSR is a completely inadequate response to the sometimes devastating impact that multinational companies can have in an ever-more globalised world − and it is actually used to mask that impact'. In his article 'The Case against Corporate Social Responsibility' published in *The Wall Street Journal*, Karnani (2010) argues that the concept of CSR is logically flawed: if private profits and public interests are aligned, the idea of CSR is irrelevant; if profits and social welfare are conflicting, an appeal to CSR is ineffective, because executive managers are unlikely to act voluntarily in the public interest and against shareholder interests.

Moreover, if CSR is used as public campaigns to persuade companies towards social responsibility and as voluntary initiatives for companies to 'do good', such superficial work may divert attention from the damaging impact of corporate social irresponsibility and deflect concern about the underlying problem of corporate power (Corporate Watch, 2006). For years, Barclays has been presented as a good corporate citizen and it has spent millions of pounds on advertising and sponsorship, 'backing such as of football's Premier League, to bolster its PR credentials' (Treanor, 2012). The publication of GSK's annual corporate responsibility report with more than 100 pages, details its pledges to improve access to healthcare in the developing world and cut its carbon footprint (Macalister, 2012).But the public had known little about the serious CSI issues of both companies before they were discovered and reported.

Indeed, CSR has a danger of legitimising managers with more discretionary power at the expense of shareholders' and many other stakeholders' interests. It may delay or discourage more effective solutions to the root problems of corporate power and social welfare (Karnani, 2010).

## CSI AS A SUBJECT OF INQUIRY

We would argue that the above difficulties of CSR do not mean to deny the real intention and appeal of CSR; otherwise the idea and movement of CSR would not have been so popular. CSR is always a public concern when business exists. CSR represents the public hope and expectations towards a better world than the one we are living in. The core issue with

CSR lies in the academic conceptualisation of CSR that is both over-normative and non-operational. To overcome the limitations of CSR and promote the genuine agenda of CSR, we need a better conceptualisation of CSR. Many scholars use different concepts to replace CSR, such as stakeholder theory, corporate citizenship, corporate social responsiveness, corporate social performance, and corporate societal responsibility, which do not make any distinction from the concept of CSR and are thus subject to the same conceptual drawbacks. Instead, we propose an agenda of reframing CSR. In the first volume of the book series, titled *Reframing Corporate Social Responsibility: Lessons from the Global Financial Crisis*, an attempt is made to reframe CSR from Alienated CSR to Embedded CSR, an effort to concretise the contents of CSR in business and societal contexts, which enable CSR to be more understandable, definable and operational.

In this volume, we are going a further step to reframe CSR with the aid of its integrative component of CSI. We suggest that CSR cannot exist without the concept of CSI within its system of conceptual framework. CSR and CSI work as opposite forces in a systemic whole; just like in the Yin Yang dialectic, the seemingly contrary forces are interconnected and interdependent and they give rise to each other in turn. We may reasonably argue that the difficulties of CSR are largely a result of the incomplete conceptualisation of CSR, due to the lack of sufficient research on CSI and the neglect of CSI as a subject matter. When asking the question of what CSR is, we did not, from the beginning, ask the key question: what is not CSR? Without an opposite concept as a frame of reference, CSR is indefinable and confusing. Clearly, CSR would be more understandable by defining what it is not. Therefore, similar to the Yin Yang dialectic, CSI is an equally important or essential concept and subject in understanding CSR, and an equally important component in generating CSR (transforming CSI to CSR).

As a system of business behaviours, CSR and CSI can be depicted as a continuum, as Timothy S. Clark and Kristen N. Grantham display in this book (see also Jones, Tench, & Bowd, 2009). In the continuum, CSI stands at one extreme and CSR at another. But CSI has a finite endpoint (Clark and Grantham explain why) and CSR is infinitely scalable. CSI can be relatively easily and clearly defined in a societal context. For example, Armstrong (1977) has tried to define CSI with two criteria: 'where great harm is caused to the system, and where almost all unbiased observers are in agreement that an irresponsible act has occurred' (pp. 185). In general, we can identify two categories of business behaviours as CSI. First of all, it is beyond doubt that all illegal business behaviours are socially irresponsible. But, legal behaviours are not necessarily socially responsible. Certain legal behaviours can be defined as CSI in a society − this is why the concept of CSI is powerful and useful. Thus, we may define CSI as those business behaviours and actions that are:

- Illegal; or
- Legal but severely unsustainable and/or unethical and thus totally socially unacceptable.

What means legal but severely unsustainable and/or unethical and totally unacceptable is contextually dependent and can be clearly defined by collective agreements in a society through regulation (mostly compulsory), supervision (via governmental agencies, professional bodies, etc.) and tight monitoring (by pressure groups, media, whistle-blowing, etc.). This is a key area of CSI, which needs more profound research into it. The definition of CSI is always subject to societal norms, traditions, cultures, expectations, conditions and contingent factors. For example, whether we should define the currently very controversial industries like tobacco, alcohol and arms as CSI depends on how a society where those businesses are locating assesses and understands the impacts and consequences of the industries. Different societies may have different understandings, though their understandings are changing over time.

In the middle of the continuum, there is a 'grey area' where we may find something legal, but with minor unsustainable and/or unethical issues, which might be accepted in a society. In here, CSI may transform to CSR and there is no clear boundary between CSI and CSR. Its boundary is arbitrary, dynamic and shifting (see Fig. 1).

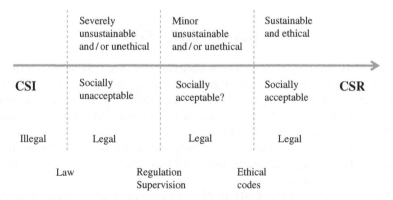

*Fig. 1.* The CSI and CSR Continuum.

On the other side, CSR is an open field without an end. This is why the CSR concept alone is difficult to be defined and specified. But with the concept of CSI as a frame of reference, we can define CSR easily by clearly defining CSI. What is CSR is, to the minimum extent, what is not CSI. While CSI is clear-cut with a concrete performance yardstick, CSR also becomes operational: at the very least do well by undoing CSI. Avoiding or reducing CSI is more compulsory than purely voluntary once a society determines what CSI is. Failing to address CSI can be very risky to business success and even survival. The indefinite end of CSR does not matter, as in theory it is only an evaluative norm and in practice it is not highly socially concerned. It is up to companies or pressure groups to define what the open field of CSR is, strategically or ethically.

With the aid of the CSI concept, CSR becomes more realistic and effective, as it is now more focused, practical and operational. Therefore, we may easily promote CSR by addressing CSI first. In a society, there are too many problems related to social and environmental welfares. Certainly, we cannot solve all the problems at once. We need a priority in social responsibility. Being responsible to everything is being responsible to nothing. Acting towards all responsibilities may divert our attention to fundamental or key problems in reality. CSI as a concept as well as a subject of inquiry may allow everyone (including business practitioners) to concentrate on resolving the most important and urgent issues of the public concern. It also encourages people to address the root causes of CSI problems in a systematic way. Doing so undoubtedly expands and enriches the understanding of CSR.

## THEMES OF THE VOLUME

This edited volume is collectively concentrated on CSI issues, with an intention to build CSI as an important subject of inquiry and research field. The total of 12 chapters is divided into three themes: the conceptualisation of CSI, the social construction of CSI versus CSR, and the systemic and structural issues of CSI in practice.

The first theme focuses on the conceptualisation of CSI with justifications for the conceptual establishment of CSI based on different angles of views and perspectives.

In the chapter 'What CSR Is Not: Corporate Social Irresponsibility', Timothy S. Clark and Kristen N. Grantham begin with a strong argument that while CSR has gained scholarly and public traction, the preponderance of study and advocacy focusing on pro-social business activity undermines intentions. The unresolvable debate on how to define CSR perpetuates ambiguity such that CSR can be claimed by virtually any corporation with an appealing cause and a marketing budget. Thus, by focusing on the affirmation of CSR, attention has been distracted from a more addressable concern: identification and denunciation of anti-social business behaviour. Clark and Grantham then go on to claim that focusing instead on the opposite, defined here as corporate social irresponsibility (CSI), avoids much of the ambiguity of CSR and presents a clarifying continuum between the two. In the chapter, they develop an argument against CSI as a contra-position of the traditional argument in favour of CSR, which is logically equivalent but potentially more effective because (1) injunctions provide clearer guidance than aspirational invitations, (2) a majority of business activity and social impacts may be concentrated on the CSI end of the continuum and (3) a broader range of both social activists and corporatists can align behind the mutual benefits of reducing CSI business behaviour. Clark and Grantham suggest that the alternative conceptualisation of CSI has significant implications for management practice, pedagogy, and research approaches. While promotion of CSR remains contentious, a broader range of business and thought leaders can find common ground by focusing on the CSI side of the continuum and uniting against it. Practitioners, academicians, and activists alike can agree that social benefits are greater from focusing on reduction of CSI rather than on promotion of CSR.

Nicholas A. J. Taylor's chapter 'A Rather Delicious Paradox: Social Responsibility and the Manufacture of Armaments' is tightly argued and rich in detail. Taylor points up a paradox which he captures in the question 'can arms makers be socially responsible?' Following the introduction the chapter thoughtfully and intelligently sets out the characteristics of the armaments industry. The limits of responsibility for institutional investors are then discussed and this is followed by a section which looks at the task of investing through the irresponsibility paradigm. The issues discussed are given context in the section which looks at 'The "cluster munitions dilemma" for Australian institutional investors' and then some overall conclusions are drawn to bring the chapter to a close. The central argument of this chapter is that, to quote Taylor, 'arms makers and their financers are not capable of being socially responsible'. This is an eminently sensible conclusion to reach but is not without controversy given the highly charged political nature of the debate around investment and the arms trade. The detailed examination of the investment practices and processes of Australian pension and sovereign wealth funds provide useful and rich data that are used to build and inform argument. With regards to the issue of CSI Taylor makes the very worthwhile point that it 'provides a degree of specificity not offered by the more nebulous concept of CSR' and further notes that it 'complements rather than competes with existing CSR programs and activities'. This chapter provides rich insight to the issues researched and reported and also engages in a constructive way with the debate on CSI.

Alex Nunn takes a controversial perspective on the irresponsibility debate and challenges many management theorists on the topic with his Marxist perspective chapter titled 'The Structural Contradictions and Constraints on Corporate Social Responsibility: Challenges for Corporate Social Irresponsibility'. In his chapter Nunn re-articulates the concept of 'CSR' as *Capitalist* Social Responsibility, showing how this is a much more productive analytical tool for understanding what is really at work when considering corporate 'responsibility' or 'irresponsibility'. In the chapter he argues *Capitalist* Social Responsibility refers not to the pursuit of 'social' goals per se, but of widely shared class-goals which reflect the common interest of the capitalist class, or at least significant sub-sections of it. In some places, and at some times, these will look like they align with the interests of other social groups, but ultimately this always masks (and most often further entrenches) competitive strategies and/or exploitative social relations.

After working through his arguments in the chapter Nunn attempts to summarise how inter-capitalist competition and capitalist social relations drive and constrain the agency of individual corporate actors to act 'responsibly' or 'irresponsibly'. He claims these limitations are important because policy makers at the local, national and even global level hope that CSR offers one means of overcoming the constraints that they themselves have placed on the ability of states to solve the complex problems they face in a world of globalisation. So too, they appeal to rules, norms and incentives in the hope of eradicating irresponsible behaviour on the part of capitalists. He argues that academic attempts to identify and expose CSI need to bear in mind the structural limits to the role of corporate agency in achieving progressive change. In concluding he makes a plea for attention to be focused on the socially and environmentally exploitative nature of capitalist social relations. But with that consideration in place, he says CSI could usefully form part of a broader based political project to identify and expose exploitation in an effort to transform those social relations.

The essence of Peter Stokes's chapter 'The Janus Dialectic of Corporate Social Irresponsibility and Corporate Social Responsibility − The Role of

Micro Moments' is captured in the title. The focus of this chapter is on micro-moments, that is the 'myriad micro-processes' that result in CSI. Stokes argues that organisational analysis can only do so much and cannot fully explain or account for individual acts and actions. He writes, '…micro-moments is the instant of choice – a choice between dialectics of good and bad positions, rights and wrongs, greater and lesser evils – which have ultimate implications for responsible and sustainable action. Individuals have to work to make the "right" choices in a given moment. To make the "wrong" choices mean that harm or damage may be caused as a consequence'. The focus on the macro-organisational level of analysis can detract from analysis at the micro-individual level and this is something that this chapter seeks to redress. People have choices and the decisions they make at the individual micro-level shape and influence those at the macro-organisational level. Stokes draws on an eclectic body of literature that includes Sartre, Levi, Aristotle, Machiavelli, Kant, Friedman, Crane and Matten, and Berger and Luckmann. This literature is used to inform discussion of a range of issues including culture and job design. Stokes argues that micro-moments help build 'the ultimate macro-picture, culture and environment'. Acts of CSR and CSI are in large part determined by 'micro-moments of choice'. Primary research data is used to inform and illustrate points raised in the literature. Observations about human behaviour in organisational contexts make for fascinating reading. Choices made and individual decisions taken at the micro level contribute to broader organisational culture.

The second theme of the volume attempts to understand how CSI is collectively defined, identified, or fostered and produced in theory and business practices, the mechanisms and strategies used in the constructing processes.

Paul Manning begins with a demonstration on how CSI has been fostered in 'Bad Management Theories' (Ghoshal, 2005). He observes that utility maximisation, taken from a narrow economic understanding of rationality, frames contemporary business school pedagogy and management theory. These framing rational notions foster a perspective that inclines towards excessive self-interest, as well as a concomitant lack of fellow feeling or morality, as students and business actors are influenced by the strictures of the economic way of looking at life in their economic interactions.

Manning illustrates this observation by detailing the rational framing assumptions in social capital literature and finds that social capital literature concerned with economic activity is framed by assumptions taken from rational choice theory. The rational choice perspective distorts and diminishes the role of moral behaviour and altruism in the market. Consequently, the framing rational choice assumptions in economic social capital tend towards an amoral, pessimistic view on human interaction, in which each individual is consistently striving to (selfishly) maximise their own utility, an outlook that inevitably encourages social irresponsibility. He argues that while rational choice assumptions are significant in social capital they nevertheless have narrow application, and the economic interpretation of rationality is over-extended in the social capital literature (and incidentally in most management literatures). Contrary to economic orthodoxy, as most influentially espoused by Samuelson (1983), rational self-interested utility maximisation does not offer either a universal method of analysis, or a universal description of motivation or behaviour. Because rational choice assumptions are limited, Manning's chapter concludes by offering an expanded understanding of social capital that presents a more accurate framework for understanding of how individuals accomplish − experience, interpret and shape − their social capital interactions. The expanded perspective also emphasises the role of social responsibility and its converse social irresponsibility, which has been under-reported in theoretical literature.

The chapter 'Rating Agencies as a Corporate Governance Mechanism: Power and Trust Production in Debt Capital Markets' by Clea Bourne describes, explains and analyses the complex nature of the relationship between system trust and credit rating agencies. The work of Giddens and Foucault provide the theoretical backdrop for the theorising of trust as 'trust production in capital markets'. Bourne asserts, 'System trust is a faceless, impersonal form of trust which we, the public, place in money, and increasingly in expert systems such as finance'. Foucault's work is used to theorise trust production and to better understand the knowledge-power controlling discourse that has grown up around credit rating agencies. Structured finance, credit rating agencies and debt capital markets inform discussion of system trust production. Corporate governance is argued to be a means of 'trust production in capital markets' and the chapter makes appropriate and informed reference to the 2007−2009 financial crisis. Financial mistrust is shown to become apparent when rating agencies downgrade financial products. Bourne's chapter is particularly topical. The issues discussed are theoretically informed and rigorous analysis is offered. The description and explanation has real world relevance as it has at its core an attempt to uncover, explain, detail and document. Theorising of trust production is outlined and has much to commend it.

In the chapter 'Organisations Behaving Badly − The Role of Communication in Understanding CSI and CSR' a communication perspective is brought to the irresponsibility debate. The authors from Australia,

United States and Norway, Jennifer Bartlett, Steve May and Øyvind Ihlen present a theoretical essay drawing on metaphors of communication as transmission and meaning-making to consider the communicative approaches to CSR. Through this approach the authors argue that while transmission models focus on highlighting responsibility, it is within the meaning-making approaches that opportunities for responsibility and irresponsibility emerge as organisations and society negotiate the boundaries of organisational behaviours. In doing so, the chapter develops arguments for how the meaning and criteria of ethical corporate behaviour are constructed and these arguments are exemplified through case examples of irresponsible behaviour worldwide.

The authors use these examples of irresponsibility to highlight that organisations take a strategic role in building, normalising and reshaping what is legitimate and not legitimate using existing structures and rationales within the broader society. As such they are actively involved in using communicative practices to shape meaning-making around what is responsible, and normalising or validating what might have otherwise been considered irresponsible. As such we believe that corporate social irresponsibility is more than a case of personal ethics.

Within the chapter the authors identify two significant areas within which irresponsibilities appear to occur. The first is in the internal management practices as noted by crisisexperts.com and the research that shows the majority of crises occur due to management decisions and internal practices. The other occurs at the macro level revealed through globalisation. It is here that shifting jurisdictions, weak governments, and economic imbalances provide fertile ground for irresponsibility to emerge as organisations seek to negotiate business in less familiar territory. The chapter concludes that it is within these spaces of contradictions that human praxis can engage and go beyond the behaviour that is institutionalised, legitimised and taken for granted.

Audra R. Diers chapter is summarised well by the title 'Reconstructing Stakeholder Relationships using "Corporate Social Responsibility" as a response strategy to cases of corporate irresponsibility: the case of the 2010 BP spill in the Gulf of Mexico'. BP's claim to CSR set out in its corporate strategy is looked at in the context of the image and reputational damage resulting from the 2010 Gulf of Mexico oil spill. Issues around crisis communication are discussed well and social construction provides some useful theoretical underpinning. The chapter is topical, current and reveals a lot about the aftermath and effects of communication crisis management. The role of language in shaping and determining public attitudes, views, perceptions and opinions informs discussion of social construction. After a brief introduction the chapter turns to an exploration and analysis of a relational model of corporate image assessment. It then outlines the methods of research, reports on and then discusses the results and offers some insightful concluding remarks. Stakeholder evaluation of crisis management response strategies is a subject that must surely be worthy of further investigation. This chapter provides a base from which future studies into stakeholder evaluation of crisis management by companies, other than BP, should make for useful points of comparison. From future comparative analysis general patterns and trends might be discerned and from this lesson learning might result. On this basis this chapter throws down an interesting challenge to researchers in the communication management, CSI and CSR areas.

The third theme of the book addresses the systemic issues and structural elements of CSI in mining and oil industries and in corporate downsizing practice.

Nicole Marie Lindsay's chapter 'The Structural Dynamics of Corporate Social Irresponsibility: The Case of The Canadian Mining Industry' examines how structural dynamics of the global mining industry condition and limit the positive impacts of corporate responsibility and sustainable development strategies, despite considerable efforts on the part of both the Canadian government and the global mining industry to promote the twin concepts of responsibility and sustainability. Her chapter takes the position that, given the complexities of the political economic context in which Canadian mining companies operate, mainstream policy approaches favouring voluntary self-regulation of the industry contribute to a 'recipe for irresponsibility' among industry laggards and a culture of complicity throughout the industry. Although rigid government command-and-control approaches to regulating business are clearly outdated, laissez-faire market solutions that have allowed corporations to define what constitutes 'responsibility' and encouraged them to monitor themselves have obvious limitations in an economic context defined by the imperative to maximise profit in a competitive global marketplace. The chapter argues that systemic limitations presented by the global economic context need to be understood and addressed in order to move beyond polarisations between hard and soft regulation of business and toward a more responsive, inclusive and robust mode of governing the business-society relationship in the mining industry. The chapter argues for a radical reconceptualisation of international governance in the mining industry based on four dimensions of responsibility (care, liability, accountability and responsiveness) and backed by a flexible and robust international legal framework.

In their chapter 'The Community Obligations of Canadian Oil Companies: A Case Study of Talisman in the Sudan', Trish Glazebrook and Matt

Story examine Talisman Energy's operations in the Sudan, as part of the Greater Nile Petroleum Operating Company (GNPOC).They employ this company case study to demonstrate that international corporate culture precludes ethical decision-making and practices by placing would-be ethical actors in untenable situations. Through an analysis of various lawsuits brought against Talisman by the Presbyterian Church of Sudan, who claim that Talisman aided and abetted the government of Sudan in genocide during the various protracted conflicts of a violent civil war, they argue for immediate application of the International Criminal Court in The Hague against corporate enablers of government violence against its peoples. Within the chapter they also go on to dissect Talisman's corporate social responsibility reports, and claim that placing corporate charters in the hands of nation-states results in an inherent tension that can only be resolved by either implementing an international corporate charter in the case of multinationals, or abandoning the corporate charter altogether. In the case of Talisman in the Sudan, they claim international corporate culture and a lack of support from its operating partners did more than discourage Talisman from implementing ethical practices; it prevented Talisman from acting ethically.

Another perspective of corporate irresponsibility is taken by Nigerian scholars Olusanmi C. Amujo, Beatrice Adeyinka Laninhun, Olutayo Otubanjo and Victoria Olufunmilayo Ajala who look at the impact of corporate social irresponsibility on the image/reputation of multinational oil corporations in Nigeria. The chapter examines how irresponsible corporate activities (*environmental pollution, human rights abuses, tax evasion, corruption and contract scandals*) of some multinational oil companies in the Niger Delta influence stakeholders' perception of their image/reputation in Nigeria. The chapter, the 'Impact of Corporate Social Irresponsibility on Corporate Image and Reputation of Multinational Oil Corporations in Nigeria', debates what it calls the 'rising menace of corporate social irresponsibility' in the Nigerian oil industry. The findings of the study point to the fact that corporate social irresponsibility affects corporate image/reputation of some oil corporations involved in unethical activities in the Niger Delta. They argue that a commitment to implementing corporate social responsibility will have a positive impact on a company's reputation: it will enable a corporation to establish favourable reputations among its stakeholders, attract socially responsible consumers, prevent the threat of harsh regulations, and reduce concern from the prying eyes of activists' organisations. Equally, corporate socially irresponsible behaviours leading to poor social and environmental ratings will detract substantially from a company's reputation and harm its performance. Using qualitative interviews the chapter study claims that socially irresponsible behaviours would have negative impact on a corporation's image/reputation. The authors argue that effective implementation of corporate social responsibility in the Niger Delta will cause a rise in reputation rating of some oil companies linked with irresponsible activities in the region, while socially irresponsible behaviours will cause a downslide in their reputation among stakeholders.

In the volume's final chapter 'The Irresponsible Enterprise: The Ethics of Corporate Downsizing', Brad S. Long argues that downsizing is an unethical and irresponsible business practice. The value of this chapter lies in its illustration of the 'application of principles that help guide business people to take morally right courses of action'. The chapter usefully quotes Marens (2010, p. 743) who points out that the literature on CSR has 'ignored an empirical record of corporate irresponsibility, especially in the area of employment relations'. However, the key argument posited by Long is that 'the prevalent business practice of downsizing raises prescriptive questions of ethics'. Downsizing is argued to result in a transfer of wealth from labour to capital. Ethics and morality run through this chapter. The chapter draws on a wide range of literature that is used to sustain and build a credible argument that takes in issues such as stakeholder theory, limited liability, ethics and morality. One section sets the context for and attempts to define downsizing and this makes for an informative and fascinating read. Reasons why companies downsize are then discussed. The consequences of downsizing are explored and the flawed nature of some of the justification given for downsizing is outlined. An argument is built that recasts 'downsizing as morally problematic' and at one point asserts that 'downsizing is ethically indefensible'. On a broader point Long argues that it is important to explore human activity within the social context in which it occurs. One thing that can be drawn from this chapter is that restructuring in whatever guise it takes is rarely easy and nearly always involves ethical and moral decisions.


# CONCLUSION

For decades corporate social responsibility has been a heated topic in media reports, public forums, academic debates, governmental policies and business practices. But the overall effects of CSR are poor or failed in practice. Many people have noted that the conceptualisation of CSR is problematic, as the concept is undefinable, confusing, non-operational and ineffective. We suggest that the difficulties of CSR are mainly due to its incomplete conceptualisation because its inseparable counterpart CSI has been eventually neglected or ignored in the CSR theorising process. We argue that the CSI concept is as equally important as CSR. CSI offers a theoretical platform to avoid the vagueness, ambiguity, arbitrariness and mysticism of CSR. CSI deserves to be a serious subject of inquiry that demands more scholarly attention. Systematic research on CSI is much needed and urgent, given the recent financial crisis and ecological crisis.

Contributed by leading scholars in the United Kingdom, United States, Canada, Australia, Norway and Nigeria, this volume sets up an initial theoretical framework for the subject of CSI and examines some core issues of irresponsibility in and beyond a corporate context. Rooted in theory and practice it seeks to understand how the boundaries of CSR and CSI have been constructed in society, and explores some systemic and structural issues of CSI. Offering theoretical developments and empirical studies, this volume is a significant contribution to the fierce debate on CSR/CSI and as such operates at the cutting-edge of knowledge.

# REFERENCES

Armstrong, J. S. (1977). Social irresponsibility in management. *Journal of Business Research*, 5(3), 185–213.

Bansal, P., & Kandola, S. (2003). Corporate social irresponsibility: Why good people behave badly in organizations. *Ivey Business Journal 67*(4), 1–5. March/April.

Carroll, A. (1999). Corporate social responsibility: Evolution of a definitional construct. *Business & Society, 38*(3), 268–295.

Christian Aid. (2004). *Behind the mask: The real face of CSR*. Retrieved from http://www. st-andrews.ac.uk/~csearweb/aptopractice/Behind-the-mask.pdf

Corporate Watch. (2006). *What is wrong with corporate social responsibility*. Corporate Watch CSR Report 2006. Retrieved from http://www.corporatewatch.org/download.php?id=55

Ghoshal, S. (2005). Bad management theories are destroying good management practices. *Academy of Management Learning & Education, 4*(1), 75–91.

Jones, B. (2010). Corporate social irresponsibility: The role of government and ideology. In W. Sun, J. Stewart & D. Pollard (Eds.), *Reframing corporate social responsibility: Lessons from the global financial crisis* (pp. 57–76). Bingley, UK: Emerald.

Jones, B, Tench, R., & Bowd, R. (2009). Corporate irresponsibility and corporate social responsibility: Competing realities. *Social Responsibility Journal, 5*(3), 300–310.

Kant, I. (1787/1965). *Critique of pure reason*. trans. N.K. Smith (Ed.), New York: St Martin's Press.

Karnani, A. (2010). The case against corporate social responsibility. *The Wall Street Journal*, 22 August.

Kotchen, M. J. and Moon, J. J. (2011). *Corporate social responsibility for irresponsibility*. National Bureau of Economic Research Working Paper 17254. Retrieved from http://www.nber.org/papers/w17254

Langel, D., & Washburn, N. T. (2012). Understanding attributions of corporate social irresponsibility. *Academy of Management Review, 37*(2), 300–326.

Macalister, T. (2012). Pharma overtakes arms industry to top the league of misbehaviour. *The Observer*, 8 July.

Marens, R. (2010). Destroying the village to save it: Corporate social responsibility, labour relations, and the rise and fall of American hegemony. *Organization, 17*(6), 743–766.

Mitchell, L. E. (2001). *Corporate irresponsibility: America's newest export*. New Haven, CT: Yale University Press.

Samuelson, P. A. (1983). *The foundations of economic analysis*. Harvard: Harvard University Press.

Sun, W., & Bellamy, L. (2010). Who is responsible for the financial crisis? Lessons from a separation thesis. In W. Sun, J. Stewart & D. Pollard (Eds.), *Reframing corporate social responsibility: Lessons from the global financial crisis*. Bingley, UK: Emerald.

Sun, W., Stewart, J., & Pollard, D. (2010). Reframing corporate social responsibility. In W. Sun, J. Stewart & D. Pollard (Eds.), *Reframing corporate social responsibility: Lessons from the global financial crisis*. Bingley, UK: Emerald.

Treanor, J. (2012). Barclays just the tip of the iceberg as banking braced for more scandals. *The Observer*, 8 July.

Van Oosterhout, J., & Heugens, P. P. M. A. R. (2008). Much ado about nothing: A critique of corporate social responsibility. In A. Crane, A. McWillaims, D. Matten, J. Moon & D. S. Siegel (Eds.), *The Oxford handbook of corporate social responsibility*. Oxford: Oxford University Press.

Visser, W. (2011). *The age of responsibility: CSR 2.0 and the new DNA of business*. London: Wiley.

# PART II
# CONCEPTUALISATION OF CSI

# WHAT CSR IS NOT: CORPORATE SOCIAL IRRESPONSIBILITY

Timothy S. Clark and Kristen N. Grantham

## ABSTRACT

Purpose — *By exploring what Corporate Social Responsibility (CSR) is not, its opposite termed Corporate Social Irresponsibility (CSI), we raise understanding and focus awareness on the material differences and associated arguments for and against.*

Approach — *Background, context, and theory introduce the concept of a continuum between CSI and CSR, which is illustrated in a progression of graphic figures.*

Findings — *Focus on the affirmation of CSR has distracted attention and resources from a more addressable concern: identification and denunciation of antisocial business behavior. Focusing instead on the opposite, defined here as CSI, avoids much of the ambiguity of CSR and presents a clarifying continuum between the two.*

Originality — *Using engaging logic, uncommon connections are made between such erstwhile polar-opposites as Friedman and Carroll to reveal broad agreement that CSI is destructive and can be universally opposed.*

Corporate Social Irresponsibility: A Challenging Concept
Critical Studies on Corporate Responsibility, Governance and Sustainability, Volume 4, 23–41
Copyright © 2012 by Emerald Group Publishing Limited
All rights of reproduction in any form reserved
ISSN: 2043-9059/doi:10.1108/S2043-9059(2012)0000004010

*Implications — While promotion of CSR remains contentious, a broader range of business and thought leaders can find common ground by focusing on the CSI side of the continuum and uniting against it. Practitioners, academicians, and activists alike can agree that social benefits are greater from focusing on reduction of CSI rather than on promotion of CSR.*

**Keywords:** Corporate social irresponsibility; corporate social responsibility; antisocial business behavior

Few topics in management science have generated as much polarized controversy in recent decades as the concept of corporate social responsibility (CSR), yet clarity remains elusive. Questions about what "responsibilities" businesses have and to whom have so fractured the debate that it is conceivable that certain parties have perpetuated the use of that charged word in order to palliate progress. Corporatists need not even engage in debate when those who argue for CSR cannot even agree how to define or apply it. Attempting to justify such an ambiguous ideal therefore becomes an uphill struggle for scholars and activists who seek to reason with corporatists that their business' responsibilities to society are broad. By pursuing this often fruitless path, many scholars and advocates who support more comprehensive responsibilities of business have unwittingly undermined their own cause. Worse, the unresolvable debate perpetuates ambiguity such that CSR can be claimed by virtually any corporation with an appealing cause and a marketing budget, which distracts attention from potentially harmful, thus far more important, aspects of their business operations.

This chapter introduces an alternative, parallel conceptualization of CSR meant to help distinguish the relevant factors in the relationship between business and society, and to help provide more effective channels for making progress for the greater good of both. While CSR may be critically ambiguous, exploration of its antithesis provides a more specifiable construct and a corresponding continuum between CSR and what will be called here corporate social irresponsibility (denoted as CSI). Exploration of the CSI aspects of business offers to shed light on undesirable business activities that may have been obscured by the focus on CSR. This shift in focus may help businesses to recognize and avoid CSI, rather than focusing on campaigns to achieve the perception of ambiguous responsibility or enacting shallow and disconcerted CSR efforts that have little positive impact on society or the bottom line.

Dozens of studies researching links between corporate social performance and financial performance have yielded "incomparable" results — in the unflattering sense (Griffin & Mahon, 1997) — leaving CSR a "tired, dead, and elusive construct" (Griffin, 2000, p. 482). Yet it is axiomatic that distinctly antisocial business behavior, at least when exposed and penalized in courts of law or public opinion, tends to have profoundly negative effects on corporations and their stakeholders (Frooman, 1997; Jones, 1995). Neither of these aspects of business activity can be as usefully considered in isolation from one another. Nor are CSR and CSI simple, binary attributes that any given business action plainly is or is not. Rather, by considering them as endpoints along a common continuum, gradations of business activity can be better distinguished, studied, and addressed.

Following a section on concept development, we outline our case and augment it with theory-based graphics to argue that redirecting focus to CSI offers more benefit for social outcomes and positive business change than the focus on CSR has proven heretofore. This is because (1) injunctions against specifiable negatives have tended to be more effective modulators of human behavior than general pressure to engage in positives, (2) business activity tends to be concentrated around legal-minimum requirements, which is argued to be more characteristic of the CSI end of the continuum, and (3) coalitions of social advocates and corporatists alike can rally around the broad, mutual benefits that come from reduction in CSI activity. Our chapter concludes with discussion of implications for management practice, pedagogy, and research approaches to develop the potential of this alternative conceptualization.

## BACKGROUND ON CSR

In the latter decades of the 20th century, the business-and-society field of management research addressed the challenge of ambiguities in CSR definitions by producing more theory and definitions rather than establishing a systematic conceptual framework (Carroll, 1999). Carroll's own model, published in 1979, integrated prior conceptions into a three-dimensional graphic that has been influential, though, like many mere approximations of a complex reality, it is difficult to defend and test. CSR's popularity as an empirical topic contributed to ongoing confusion, rather than reducing it, in part due to sometimes orthogonal variance in results (Griffin & Mahon, 1997; Margolis & Walsh, 2003) and possible researcher bias (Rowley & Berman, 2000). Also, research has been scattered by the evolution of related concepts, such as corporate social performance (Clarkson, 1995; Wood, 1991), corporate social responsiveness and rectitude (Frederick, 2006), and corporate citizenship (Gardberg & Fombrun, 2006).

The related concept of CSI partly overcomes such ambiguities by accepting them as unavoidable realities in the CSR construct rather than attempting to resolve them. While "The confusion that presently haunts the field is such that even the brightest minds succumb to the temptation of introducing new notions that substantially cover the same ground as the old ones without any additional or novel insight that would justify conceptual innovation" (van Oosterhout & Heugens, 2006, p. 7), it is argued here that CSI offers a fresh perspective of significantly clarifying utility − by explaining what CSR is not.

In a seminal publication that has mischaracterized much of the debate ever since, Friedman (1970) made a popular case against CSR that many have understood only as his article's title, "The social responsibility of business is to increase its profits." Of course, careful readers will know that Friedman's words went on to present a more sophisticated view than that oversimplification, including exhorting business conduct to "conform [with the] basic rules of society, both those embodied in the law and those embodied in ethical custom," with further explanation that not just the letter of the law but its spirit and intentions should also be followed (1970, p. 33). With this nuanced concept, even the libertarian economist confirms that "the law is not enough" (Stone, 1975), which stands to reason given Friedman's better known criticisms of the limitations of government as lawmaker and law enforcer. But the simplistic interpretation of Friedman's statement has become so pervasive that progress beyond that limited view has been slow. Perpetuation of this simplistic belief, with little clarification of underlying assumptions and caveats, remains embedded in much of contemporary business curricula (Mintzberg, 2004). This, in turn, perpetuates doubt by some that businesses hold any ancillary responsibilities to society beyond profits.

The more nuanced and complete interpretation of Friedman's corporatist view actually comports well with most of Carroll's (1979) model for CSR, which introduced four levels of social responsibilities of business to show that responsible activity is not merely a binary distinction. The bottom level of this model refers to firms' economic responsibilities to survive as a contributing economic unit by at least breaking even, followed by legal responsibilities to play by the rules as established by society. Above these levels Carroll (1979) places the category of "ethical responsibilities," which fits Friedman's accordance with "ethical custom" quoted above, showing these two supposedly divergent authors largely in agreement. (On Carroll's top level, discretionary responsibilities, he and Freidman's positions diverge, but that constitutes a minor fraction of the range of corporate responsibility.) While Friedman may exhort ethical practices because it is better for aggregate economic productivity, and Carroll may exhort them because it is better for broader sets of stakeholders, the point is there is agreement across the span of thought-leaders that mere profitability, or even legal compliance, is not sufficient for balancing the financial needs of business with the broader needs of society. Similarly, using logical contraposition, we can establish that those on both sides of the debate can agree that illegal and even unethical commerce is bad for both industry and society alike and therefore that a reduction in this sort of activity will positively impact both.

## INTRODUCTION OF CSI

Clear definitions or arguments about CSR are no easier to derive from one end of the literature's broad philosophical spectrum than the other. But the large overlap of agreement highlighted above shows utility in approaching business-responsibility questions not as a binary matter of black or white, but as a matter of degree across a range of gray. A binary distinction has left a large gap in understanding between activity that is illegal (presumed to be universally considered irresponsible) and activity that fits general standards of CSR. This is illustrated in Fig. 1, where the threshold of the Law (shown in a dashed line to reflect its approximations and imperfections) is far to the left along a continuum of business activity generally accepted to be CSR. This has perpetuated a large zone of equivocation between the two, which has likely factored into the unresolved debate. By recognizing that there are some types of business activity that could be legal, yet fall to the left of satisfying Friedman's "ethical custom" or Carroll's "ethical responsibilities," the equivocal zone and the range of debate is beneficially narrowed. This is illustrated as the portion of the continuum between the law and the right edge of what is being termed here CSI, which shrinks the equivocal zone from the dashed bracket to the narrower

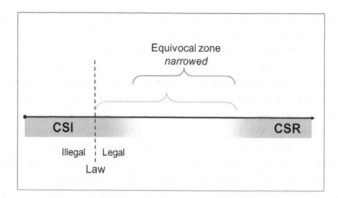

*Fig. 1.*   The Continuum of Business Behavior, from CSI to CSR.

solid bracket. The CSI concept, indicated in gray on the left-side of the continuum in Fig. 1, facilitates this distinction and can help to shift the debate in a constructive direction.

As the use of an illustrative continuum suggests, corporate responsibility is not categorical but infinitely scalable. This provides a more nuanced evaluation of business activity along a scale from one extreme to another, with ordinal rankings providing a distinct conceptual improvement over categorical limitations. Note that the CSI side is shown with a finite endpoint, while the CSR side is an arrow pointing off to infinity. This is because vice, for practical purposes, is finite (else customers or communities cease to exist), while forms and extents of virtue are virtually infinite and, therefore, impossible to specify (Boatright, 2000).

Since this open-endedness of CSR leaves it difficult to define, the utility of the CSI concept may be judged by its improved specificity. First, illegal activity is considered prima facie to be socially irresponsible. The law is a clear manifestation of the wishes, expectations, and prohibitions established by societies through representative governments. Lawmaking processes and enforcement are hardly perfect, including extensive influence from the business sector (Lehne, 2006). Laws and lawmaking bodies are reactive in nature, and therefore cannot be expected to encompass all that is unacceptable in behavior. This creates a lag between the recognition that certain behaviors are undesirable and the creation or updating of laws. CSI, in part, is that behavior that is presently legal but will eventually be sanctioned by government. Deliberate exploitation of weaknesses in the law fall short of the aforementioned ethical custom and responsibilities, so are considered here to be among the characteristics of CSI.

The ambiguity of CSR also led Armstrong (1977) to explore the effectiveness of considering its opposite in the normative managerial context:

"Social responsibility" is difficult to define. What *should* a manager do? It is easier to look at the problem in terms of what he should *not* do – i.e., at "social irresponsibility." A socially irresponsible act is a decision to accept an alternative that is *thought by the decision maker to be inferior to another alternative when the effects upon all parties are considered.* Generally this involves a gain by one party at the expense of the total system. (Armstrong, 1977, p. 185, emphasis in the original)

As Armstrong (1977) suggests, a key element of CSI is the exploitation of negative externalities. An externality is defined as "the impact of an economic agent's actions on the well-being of a bystander" (McWilliams, Siegel, & Wright, 2006), and can be either positive or negative. Innovation is an example of a positive externality, fitting within notions of CSR that focus on benefits of commercial activity accruing to society. But negative externalities are also an inevitable reality of commercial activity which corporate taxation is designed to help offset at least partially. Jensen acknowledges the role of externalities in his argument that "profit maximization leads to an efficient social outcome" with merely a corresponding footnote that reads "provided there are no externalities" (2001, p. 12), despite widespread rejection of the use of such simplistic assumptions in neoclassical economics models.

Negative externalities effectively transfer firm costs to unwilling or unwitting recipients, benefiting the firm "at the expense of the total system" (Armstrong, p. 185) which in this case is the overall social system. Key to this is the concept of sustainability, where activities that are exploitative of vulnerable stakeholders or resources, even if profitable in the short run, could not be continued, unabated, indefinitely. Sustainability applies to the "triple bottom line" (Norman & MacDonald, 2004) of economic, social, and environmental contexts (Crane & Matten, 2004). Businesses that continue unsustainable practices, whether intentionally or unintentionally, risk losing the ability to attract employees, investors, and customers, which provides substantial prerogative for proactive identification and management of such practices. Where basic resources, labor or customers themselves are degraded or exhausted in the manufacture or consumption of certain goods or services, their production and marketing constitute business practices which are unsustainable and, by this definition therefore, designated as CSI.

In a meta-analysis of event studies, Frooman disaggregated illegal activity from irresponsible activity in concluding that "socially irresponsible and illegal corporate acts result in substantial unrecovered decreases in shareholder wealth" (1997, p. 222). More recent cases of spectacular corporate frauds and failures provide further evidence that shareholder wealth destruction awaits violators who get caught, even before convictions are finally handed down. These findings effectively nullify the idea that shareholder wealth maximization is best achieved through profit maximization alone. But this overlooks what likely is the far more numerous and economically important class of businesses: those who act with irresponsibility but are not exposed, let alone indicted, convicted, and punished (in courts of law nor in the courts of public opinion). It is this type of legal-but-irresponsible business that goes relatively unaddressed, persisting in part because attention is diverted to the standard CSR arguments and spectacular cases of blatantly irresponsible corporate behavior.

Irresponsible corporate behavior has been described as being reflected in negative scores in the social performance database managed by KLD Analytics, and was labeled "CSI" by Strike, Gao, and Bansal (2006). In that study, Strike et al. focus on the seven categories of KLD evaluations that range from +2 to −2, summing the positive scores and negative scores separately and assigning them to each company's scores for CSR and CSI, respectively. While the KLD data are acknowledged to be the best quantitative information available (Mattingly & Berman, 2006), negative scores in these dimensions constitute a simplistic representation. One nuance it fails to account for regards trade-offs implicit in company actions, such as cases where CSI behavior that negatively impacts some stakeholders also benefits others.

CSI activity is defined here to be all illegal activity as well as that which is unsustainable for the overall system due to the exploitation of negative externalities. Such behaviors can be seen as anticompetitive between firms, which also lead to counter-productive outcomes for social welfare. Another criterion of net benefits or costs from externalities is judgment of particular activities using basic frameworks of ethics. The positive and negative Golden Rules, discussed below, offer an approach for this, as does the Rawlsian test for fairness from the objective perspective of "original position" (Boatright, 2000). CSI, therefore, includes behavior that would generate net-negative externalities and be judged unethical by such tests.

A familiar example of irresponsible corporate behavior is found in the tobacco industry, where information about the products' harmful and fatal consequences was withheld and intentionally obfuscated. Consumers' personal freedom of choice is deliberately compromised when harmful products are aggressively marketed specifically to overcome people's better judgment. Another net-cost-to-society results from the major oil and automobile companies' decades of resistance to conservation and alternative-fuels technology. Ever larger and less efficient vehicles have been extensively marketed to Americans, with social costs ranging from long-term, environmental effects to degraded national security from persistent dependence on foreign oil. Both of these types of lawful practices depend on extracting gains from a customer base that is systematically led to overlook the long-term ramifications of such consumption, deriving unsustainable, exploitative profits at the expense of the larger societal system. Another example can be seen in the recent wave of predatory lending and "creative" mortgages, with unsustainable gimmicks like nothing-down loans and balloon payments. The resulting rise in foreclosures and bankruptcies, which harms individuals greatly, also degrades economic well-being generally, generating fleeting profits for some while negatively impacting the rest of society.

More subtle, and perhaps most illustrative, is considering the range of business behavior between tax evasion (definitely illegal) and tax seeking (very rare) which is known as the vast field of tax avoidance − the gray area in which armies of accountants and lawyers help their clients to outsmart their governments and stay steps ahead of the law, such that they can avoid paying any more tax than the presently stipulated legal minimum. Where tax breaks are put to use in the spirit of their intentions, directing investment to areas of policy priorities, that activity aligns with society's larger interests. But where loopholes and "creativity" are exploited, the negative externality of companies that do not pay their fair share is a decrease in the amount of funds available to government programs that hurts society. Additionally, for those businesses that pay their taxes appropriately, competition with less scrupulous firms is made more difficult since they are essentially shirking their financial responsibilities and gaining an unfair advantage, leaving an increased tax burden to others. As explained further below, it is less effective a communicative device, leading to less benefit for society, to expose these business activities as *not* CSR than it would be to specify and proactively censure what they *are*: CSI.

## BUILDING AN ARGUMENT AGAINST CSI

Arguments in favor of CSR can be non-starters, especially when no social stigma is necessarily connected to CSR opposition. For instance, to say that a statement is not quite accurate carries much less negative connotation than to say that it is dishonest. To say that a business is not pursuing CSR activities is vague and of debatable importance, whereas the identification and condemnation of specifically irresponsible behaviors will likely carry more weight and therefore have more impact.

Enter the logic of contra-position (Hurley, 1997), which can help clarify arguments by examining what CSR is not. This tool of logic enables clarifications and conclusions about the accuracy of a statement such as "If X then Y" by examining "If not Y, then not X." For example, the statement "All sophomores are undergraduates" can be expressed "If a person is a sophomore, he or she must be an undergraduate." If there were any debate about this, the contra-positive would allow us to see that "If a person is not an undergraduate, then he or she must not be a sophomore," allowing another angle for possible resolution. This logic tool can be applied to the more vexing questions regarding CSR by similarly switching the order of the object and predicate terms and replacing each with their antithesis.

The traditional mainstream argument of corporatist pundits, along the lines of "If businesses have no responsibility to society beyond meeting legal minima, then meeting legal minima is adequate for fulfilling social interests," can be reexamined with contra-position. The statement "If meeting legal minima is not adequate for fulfilling social interests, then businesses have a responsibility to society in excess of meeting legal minima," shifts the query to whether businesses that merely meet legal obligations are, in aggregate, fulfilling their duties to society. Friedman's (1970) comments discussed above suggest that he would answer "no" to this last question, since he holds that adhering to "ethical custom" requires actions beyond legal minima. As this is in opposition to the common position of pundits who evoke him, the reordered question can be seen to probe nuances and expose gaps of logic more effectively than one approach alone.

While few pundits would attempt to defend or argue a case condoning illegal behavior, the broad range between that legal frontier (vertical dashed line in Fig. 1) and the ambiguous threshold of the CSR designation leaves room for much equivocation, stalling progress. Introducing CSI on the continuum narrows the gulf of equivocation, at least inasmuch as CSI can be widely acknowledged as being detrimental to overall social welfare. Illegal business activity is almost universally considered irresponsible, but it does not follow that doing something irresponsible is certainly illegal.

Therefore, the focus of CSI should be directed at that category of business activity that is not illegal (yet) but is irresponsible according to the criteria set forth above. It follows that, to the extent that no one would condone CSI either, the frontier of equivocation in the debate narrows. In a debate characterized by stalemates and intransigence, this figurative shift could catalyze renewed progress.

Shifting the focus in this way recalls an approach of Hobbes in *Leviathan* (Labiano, 2000), where he proposed something of a contra-positive version of the Golden Rule to create a more compelling and defensible argument. Turning around the traditional rule, *do unto others what you would wish done unto you*, his approach exhorts people *NOT to do unto others what you would NOT wish done unto you*. Gensler (1996) refers to this approach as the Negative Golden Rule. This line of reasoning transforms the debate from specifying and defending positive actions one should take in order to have favors returned, which has been associated with traditional CSR advocacy, and which is vulnerable to broad interpretation and criticism. The adjusted debate shifts to delineating what should not be done in order to avoid reciprocated harm, which can solidify argumentation and agreement.

Focusing on what should not be allowed may present a more defensible and relevant argument, especially with those who are disinclined to subscribe to the affirmative action implications of the conventional rule. As with any rulemaking regarding human behavior, from that directed at children to that regulating entire industries' executives, clarity about what *not* to do may be at least as effective as guidance for what *to* do. Efforts to convince businesses to take action to establish and publicize CSR activities comprise a prescriptive approach that represents only one aspect of the regulation of moral behavior. Creating aspirations and inspiring action to overcome inertia − which characterize the intentions of pro-CSR initiatives − can be extremely difficult, since core influences are social norms, rather than legal imperatives, as some sort of "moral regulation" (Janoff-Bulman, Sheikh, & Hepp, 2009). The second aspect is proscription, which entails defining what is undesirable behavior and what consequences will be experienced upon demonstration of such behavior. Well-documented psychological phenomena, namely the negativity bias and moral asymmetry, explain that acts which involve negative consequences are much more salient than acts which result in positive rewards (Janoff-Bulman et al., 2009). This makes proscription of CSI activities particularly important, as acknowledged across time and cultures through the creation of legal systems. As would be expected, cultural norms do impact what is considered to be irresponsible both legally and socially. For example, Google evidently found their famous internal mantra "Don't Be Evil" (Google, 2008) to be a more effective than its contra-positive equivalent, "Be Good," would have been.


# FOCUSING ON THE CSI SIDE OF THE CONTINUUM

Beyond communicative clarity, the value of shifting research attention — from apparently irresolvable questions surrounding the merits of promoting CSR to the specific arguments condemning CSI — may be a function of volume. This refers to the hypothetical concentration of business activity on the y-axis across the CSI-CSR continuum on the x-axis, as presented in Fig. 2.

Whether volume of business activity is measured in terms of number of transactions, value of trading, profitability, or virtually any other metric, its distribution across the continuum of social responsibility is unlikely to be a perfectly level line. So Fig. 2's "a" line is easy to reject, but of the four remaining options (all of which are meant to have the same area under the line), which one is best? Does business activity tend to be heavily concentrated in CSI activity (line "b") or in CSR activity (line "c")? Neither seems likely, but nor does a normal "bell-curve" distribution (line "d"). This is because the threshold of the law is likely to have significant impact

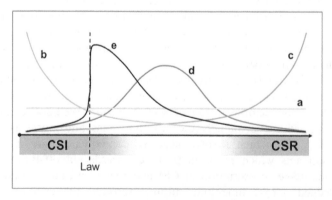

*Fig. 2.*   Five Hypothetical Distributions of Business Activity.

on the concentration of business activity, especially in industries without retail customers where there is comparatively little "reward for virtue" (Vogel, 2005). Rather, it is at least as reasonable to suppose that business activity tends to be concentrated just within the stipulations of the legal threshold, with relatively few activities in the illegal zone and asymptotically decreasing volumes toward the CSR side of the continuum. This is graphically represented in the line labeled "e" in Fig. 2. Therefore, the first proposition here is stated as follows:

**Proposition 1.** Business activity is concentrated just within the threshold of lawfulness.

If Proposition 1 were upheld, it would lend credence to the notion that a focus on CSI could have more effectiveness (beyond the communicative device discussed above) than the recent prevalence of focus on CSR in academic research. The question of which side of the continuum lends itself to more effective focus is graphically represented in Fig. 3.

In the field of business management, the focus of academicians and practitioners seem to have been focused disproportionately on the CSR side of the continuum. While journalists and bloggers seem more focused on exposing negative stories and acts of irresponsibility, the business establishment tends to avoid the negative perspective. For example, an Internet-search-based estimate of the number of scholarly publications discussing CSR and its benefits, relative to the volume and effects of CSI, reveals an approximately twelve-to-one ratio. But if Proposition 1 were upheld, such

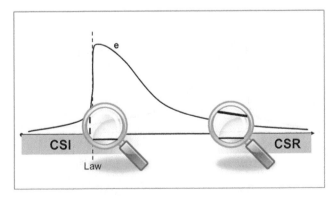

*Fig. 3.* On Which Side of the Continuum to Focus Attention?

that it was evident that far more business activity is concentrated on the CSI side of the continuum (the "e" line's y-value near the left-side of the continuum), then it could be established that redirecting focus here would at least bring relevance to a higher portion of the extant business activity. Fig. 4 illustrates the focal point being directed to the CSR side of the continuum.

Attention focused on the CSR side of the continuum is presumed to be motivated by an objective to promote the adoption of CSR, as represented graphically in Fig. 4. Increasing awareness, definitions, or evident benefits of CSR would tend to increase y-axis concentrations of CSR-type activity, as shown by the "e'$_1$" line's increased height over the "e" line in the vicinity of the magnifying glass. But, assuming business activity is finite in any given period, where will that increase draw from? The suggestion here is that those firms who were positively predisposed toward to concept of CSR, such as those whose business models or product offerings enable some sort of "reward for virtue" (Vogel, 2005), are those most likely to shift incrementally to the right. So, theoretically, firms would be drawn mainly from the equivocal middle toward the right. This would tend to shift the overall average to the right, and would provide a distinct social benefit, but it would leave untouched the bulk of business activity. Fig. 5 illustrates turning attention to the CSI end of the spectrum.

Shifting focus to the left would be better suited to the objective of reducing the incidence of CSI. Increased attention directed to this side of the continuum of business activity would expose a portion of those firms performing just within the stipulated constraints of the law. Where these

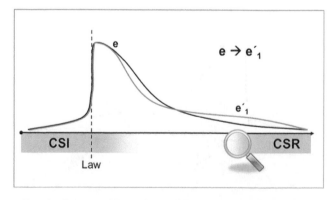

*Fig. 4.*   Presumed Intentions of Focus on Promoting CSR.

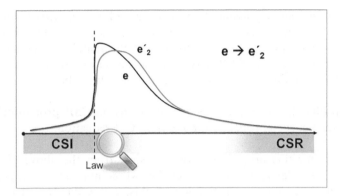

*Fig. 5.* Possible Outcome from Directing Focus to Condemning CSI.

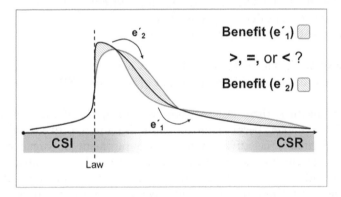

*Fig. 6.* Relative Social Benefit of the Different Focal Points.

firms and, moreover, their influential stakeholders could be helped to see their behavior fits the definition of CSI, in that it is exploitative and a net-cost to larger social systems, the likelihood of behavioral changes rises. As opposed to the focus on CSR, here the difference is expected to manifest among the firms practicing the left-most activity that shift rightward into the equivocal zone.

Having considered the theoretical outcomes of adjusting focus along the continuum, a larger question arises: is the chief objective to promote CSR or to reduce CSI? But the normative answer seems straightforward: attention and effort should be invested where the greater social benefit lies. Fig. 6 presents these two hypothetical shifts concurrently.

With a simplifying assumption that the volume of activity displaced would be the same under both scenarios, Fig. 6 illustrates the direct comparison of movement from CSI to toward the middle versus movement from the middle toward CSR. Expressed as a proposition, one presumptive answer to the question posed within the graphic would be:

**Proposition 2**. Net social benefit from focus on CSR promotion is less than the net social benefit from focus on CSI reduction.

Support for this proposition comes mainly from the above discussion regarding the relative effectiveness of the two communicative approaches. Inasmuch as the contra-positive logic holds, where the Negative Golden Rule proves more effective at specifying, condemning, and changing human behavior than its opposite, focus on the CSI side of this continuum will prove more effective. To express this concept, it would lead to the larger point to consider effectiveness per unit of input of focus or attention. In these terms, this body of logic holds that:

**Proposition 3**. The volume of business activity displaced per unit of attention focused on CSI exceeds that of focus on CSR.

Taken together, these last two propositions arrive at the central argument of this chapter: because human nature is more sensitive to injunctions against specifiable negatives than to encouragement of vague positives, efforts to present both sides of the continuum will be more effective than focus on either side alone. Furthermore, increased social benefits will accrue not just from this more effective communicative approach, but because even if the quantity of shifted business activity were the same, the net benefits of reduced harms are likely to exceed those of increased goods.

## CONCLUSION

If the logic and argument in this chapter holds, then why has so much academic attention been focused on the CSR side of the topic? Why is more written about corporations moving their activities from "good to great" rather than from "poor to mediocre"?

Part of the explanation may lie in advantages of the status quo debate for powerful corporatist interests that see threats in the progress of the

CSR movement. Where their influence could be applied, these interests would seek to retain the focal point right where it has been stuck. Further, many powerful business interests are already reaping competitive advantages by "greening" (or "green-washing") themselves in ways that appear better than rivals, such that these firms would resist losing the spotlight that the CSR debate extends. In these ways, CSR has become a mere palliative, sating the need for a sense of advancing debate and providing leverage for creative marketing, but actually stymieing real progress for society. The status quo situation is one which logic alone will not be enough to shift and one where there is a real social cost to its persistence. Ultimately, all social interests − including big business, in the long run − stand to benefit from progress.

This still does not explain why such a high proportion of academic attention has tended to focus on the CSR side. Clearly, journalists focus more often on stories of irresponsibility, largely because such stories constitute breaking news, with sensational interest that helps sell their products. But academicians have more complicated interests in their pushing of the frontier of knowledge. On the basic level of mainstream business books, a title like "Poor to Mediocre" would not advance the careers of author(s) so much as "Good to Great" (Collins, 2001) certainly did. And as alluded to several paragraphs above, perhaps business schools have been constrained or co-opted to some degree by the business interests that serve as important supporters and stakeholders of the industry of management education. It seems unlikely that a business school that becomes known for producing research or hosting lectures that focus on the social harms from mainstream business activity would rise in the good graces of critical portions of its stakeholders. Other authors have explored this line of reasoning, and fill an important role of critical reflection by continuing to do so.

Other contributions by more skilled authors could be made with respect to the underlying logic and philosophy outlined in this chapter. Gaps could be bridged, rough edges could be smoothed, and either the general idea could be invalidated or it could be advanced with a much stronger case than this. Theoreticians could establish clearer definitions of what constitutes CSI, especially in that novel gray area between the threshold of the law and zone with neutral or net-beneficial social outcomes. Empiricists could shift study from elusive connections between CSR practices and profitability, to look for connections between CSI and not profitability (because profits likely underlie the cause) but more important metrics tracking overall social outcomes.

Even without such advances to polish this approach, the CSI and continuum concepts are significant contributions. Already, the communicative device has proven effective in pedagogical settings. In the classroom, a visual aid like the continuum can stir thinking and facilitate discussions to arrive at insights from alternative perspectives. After all, with classically nay-saying students, or even at cocktail parties with irritating conversationalists (corporatists, perhaps), it can be quite effective to reply to indifference or opposition with a simple "okay, if you are against CSR, then what are you for?" The shift can be catalytic, opening up a fresh approach to get to the point.

Rather than introducing a nominally tangential paradigm that only splinters the field, the concept of CSI is intended to introduce an orthogonal stream of thought that could clarify and advance the overall cause by establishing what CSR is not. Effectively, it modifies and turns back onto corporatists the words of their most-quoted libertarian economist: "the social responsibility of business is to not be irresponsible."

# REFERENCES

Armstrong, J. S. (1977). Social irresponsibility in management. *Journal of Business Research*, *5*, 185–213.

Boatright, J. R. (2000). *Ethics and the Conduct of Business* (3rd ed.). Upper Saddle River, NJ: Prentice Hall.

Carroll, A. B. (1979). A three-dimensional conceptual model of corporate performance. *Academy of Management Review*, *4*(4), 497–505.

Carroll, A. B. (1999). Corporate social responsibility: evolution of a definitional construct. *Business & Society*, *38*(3), 268–295.

Clarkson, M. B. E. (1995). A stakeholder framework for analyzing and evaluating corporate social performance. *Academy of Management Review*, *20*(1), 92–117.

Collins, J. C. (2001). *Good to great: Why some companies make the leap... and others don't.* New York, NY: HarperCollins.

Crane, A., & Matten, D. W. (2004). *Business ethics: A European perspective. Managing corporate citizenship and sustainability in the age of globalization*Oxford, UK: Oxford University Press.

Frederick, W. C. (2006). *Corporation be good.* Indianapolis, IN: Dog Ear Publishing.

Friedman, M. (1970). The social responsibility of business is to increase its profits. *The New York Times Magazine*. September 13, pp. 32–33, 122–126.

Frooman, J. (1997). Socially irresponsible and illegal behavior and shareholder wealth. *Business & Society*, *36*(3), 221–249.

Gardberg, N. A., & Fombrun, C. J. (2006). Corporate citizenship: Creating intangible assets across institutional environments. *Academy of Management Review*, *31*(2), 329–346.

Gensler, H. J. (1996). *Formal ethics.* Oxford, UK: Routledge.

Google. 2008. Google code of conduct. Retrieved from http://investor.google.com/conduct. html. Accessed on September 5, 2008.

Griffin, J. J. (2000). Corporate social performance: Research directions for the 21st century. *Business & Society*, *39*(4), 479–491.

Griffin, J. J., & Mahon, J. F. (1997). The corporate social performance and corporate financial performance debate: twenty-five years of incomparable research. *Business & Society*, *36*(1), 5–31.

Hurley, P. J. (1997). *A concise introduction to logic* (6th ed.). Belmont, CA: Wadsworth.

Janoff-Bulman, R., Sheikh, S., & Hepp, S. (2009). Proscriptive versus prescriptive morality: Two faces of moral regulation. *Journal of Personality and Social Psychology*, *96*(3), 521–537.

Jensen, M. C. (2001). Value maximization, stakeholder theory, and the corporate objective function. *Journal of Applied Corporate Finance*, *14*(3), 8–21.

Jones, T. M. (1995). Instrumental stakeholder theory: A synthesis of ethics and economics. *Academy of Management Review*, *20*, 404–437.

Labiano, J. M. Z. (2000). A reading of Hobbes' Leviathan with economists' glasses. *International Journal of Social Economics*, *27*(2), 134–146.

Lehne, R. (2006). *Government and business: American political economy in comparative perspective*. Washington, DC: CQ Press.

Margolis, J. D., & Walsh, J. P. (2003). Misery loves companies: Rethinking social initiatives by business. *Administrative Science Quarterly*, *48*, 268–305.

Mattingly, J. E., & Berman, S. L. (2006). Measurement of social action: Discovering taxonomy in the Kinder Lydenburg Domini ratings data. *Business & Society*, *45*(1), 20–46.

McWilliams, A., Siegel, D. S., & Wright, P. M. (2006). Corporate social responsibility: Strategic implications. *Journal of Management Studies*, *43*(1), 1–18.

Mintzberg, H. (2004). *Managers not MBAs: A hard look at the soft practice of managing and management development*. San Francisco, CA: Berrett-Koehler.

Norman, W., & MacDonald, C. (2004). Getting to the bottom of "Triple Bottom Line". *Business Ethics Quarterly, March*, 243–262.

Rowley, T. J., & Berman, S. (2000). A brand new brand of corporate social performance. *Business & Society*, *39*(4), 397–418.

Stone, C. D. (1991). *Where the law ends: The social control of corporate behavior*. Prospect Heights, IL: Waveland Press.

Strike, V. M., Gao, J., & Bansal, P. (2006). Being good while being bad: Social responsibility and the international diversification of US firms. *Journal of International Business Studies*, *37*, 850–862.

van Oosterhout, J. & Heugens, P. (2006). Much ado about nothing: A conceptual critique of CSR. Research paper available at http://www.hdl.handle.net/1765/7894. Accessed on March 14, 2007.

Vogel, D. (2005). *The market for virtue: The potential and limits of corporate social responsibility*. Washington, DC: Brookings Institution Press.

Wood, D. J. (1991). Corporate social performance revisited. *Academy of Management Review*, *16*(4), 691–718.

# A RATHER DELICIOUS PARADOX: SOCIAL RESPONSIBILITY AND THE MANUFACTURE OF ARMAMENTS

N. A. J. Taylor

## ABSTRACT

Purpose — *To argue for the use of corporate social irresponsibility (CSI) proves far more useful in assessing arms makers' limits of responsibility in a different way altogether. By focusing on the negative 'externalities' — that is impact on society — we are able to examine the practice in the context of constitutive and regulatory norms (i.e. the accepted rules), as opposed to norms that are merely evaluative (i.e. moral) or practical (i.e. what's possible).*

Methodology/approach — *This chapter examines the investment policies, practices and procedures of a handful of Australian pension and sovereign wealth funds in relation to investment in the development and production of cluster munitions — a class of weapon banned under international law since August 2010.*

Findings — *The chapter finds that the negative externalities inherent in armaments manufacturing demand that institutional investors view such*

Corporate Social Irresponsibility: A Challenging Concept
Critical Studies on Corporate Responsibility, Governance and Sustainability, Volume 4, 43–62
ISSN: 2043-9059/doi:10.1108/S2043-9059(2012)0000004011

*firms through a 'CSI lens', especially when tasked with identifying and developing strategies to account for emerging social norms such as the prohibition of cluster munitions.*

Practical implications — *The investor is advantaged by having at its disposal a roadmap for managing — though not necessarily predicting — emerging social norms. This is so for ethical, responsible and mainstream investment approaches, although is most readily compatible with investors who have pre-established exclusionary policies as well as effective implementation procedures.*

Social implications — *A CSI approach to investment in cluster munitions as outlined in this chapter benefits society by inducing economic actors, such as pension and sovereign wealth funds, to direct their capital in such a way as to minimize humanitarian and environmental harm.*

Originality/value of chapter — *Proponents of the social responsibility of business and investment have seldom assessed the makers of conventional armaments such as machine guns, attack helicopters and battle tanks. Fewer still have attempted to devise and implement such programs within firms. Simply put, the prevailing argument is that arms makers and their financers are not capable of being socially responsible.*

**Keywords:** Arms makers; cluster munitions; conventional armaments; violent harm; international humanitarian law; corporate social irresponsibility

War, mechanization, mining and finance played into each other's hands. Mining was the key industry that furnished the sinews of war and increased the metallic contents of the original capital hoard, the war chest; on the other hand, it furthered the industrialization of arms, and enriched the financier by both processes. The uncertainty of both warfare and mining increased the possibilities for speculative gains: this provided a rich broth for the bacteria of finance to thrive on. (Lewis Mumford, Technics and Civilization, 1934)

Proponents of the social responsibility of business and investment have seldom assessed the makers of conventional armaments such as machine guns, attack helicopters and battle tanks. Fewer still have attempted to devise and implement such programs within firms, although a growing number of civil society groups have begun to identify those entities involved — both directly and indirectly — in the development, production and investment of 'controversial' weapons such as landmines and cluster bombs (IKV Pax Christi and Handicap International and Netwerk Vlaanderen, 2010). Simply put, the prevailing argument is that arms makers[1] and their financers are not capable of being socially responsible due to three unique characteristics. First, the producers of arms are commonly viewed as *agents of the state* due to its importance to maintaining national sovereignty, rather than independent actors with liability to manage the harm resulting from its products. Second, there is a belief that the manufacture of arms *necessitates a higher degree of opaqueness* than other industry groups due to national defence considerations. Third, the state plays a dual – and at times, conflicting – role as principal customer and regulator.

Whilst these three rocks in the road may be pushed aside,[2] I argue that the emerging concept of corporate social irresponsibility (CSI) proves far more useful in assessing arms makers' limits of responsibility in a different way altogether. By focusing on the negative 'externalities' – that is impact on society – we are able to examine the practice in the context of constitutive and regulatory norms (i.e. the accepted rules), as opposed to norms that are merely evaluative (i.e. moral) or practical (i.e. what's possible). Put another way, CSI effectively confines analysis to a relatively precise set of considerations, whilst a more traditional corporate social responsibility (CSR) approach necessitates choosing from a raft of potential implementation strategies and activities. Thus CSI provides a degree of specificity not offered by the more nebulous concept of CSR, as well as one that complements rather than competes with existing CSR programs and activities.

In arguing for the usefulness of CSI to institutional investors, I come to address a seemingly large paradox in the form of a small question: can arms makers be socially responsible? This chapter takes a small step toward answering that question by examining the investment policies, practices and procedures of a handful of Australian pension and sovereign wealth funds in relation to investment in the development and production of cluster munitions – a class of weapon banned under international law since August 2010. The case selection is especially significant since the international *Cluster Munitions Convention* is the most ambitious disarmament and humanitarian treaty of the last ten years, and the Australian investment industry – with A\$1.4 trillion in assets – is the fourth largest in the world. Whilst no Australian firm is in the top 100 manufacturers of conventional weapons globally (Jackson, 2010), Australian banking and financial institutions are among the largest investors in such companies overseas. By focusing on the Australian experience, this chapter explores the 'dilemma' institutional investors face when the positions of domestic governments do not explicitly prohibit direct and indirect investment as has been done in other markets such as New Zealand, United Kingdom, Germany, France, Ireland, Holland, Luxembourg, Belgium, Switzerland, Lebanon, Mexico, Norway and Rwanda.

Drawing on theoretical discussions in international relations as well as critical studies of CSR, I find that the negative externalities inherent in armaments manufacturing demand that institutional investors view such firms through a 'CSI lens', especially when tasked with identifying and developing strategies to account for emerging social norms.


## CHARACTERISTICS OF THE ARMAMENTS INDUSTRY

The phrase 'armaments industry' is a misnomer: it is not a distinct industrial sector,[3] but rather a loose collection of firms operating in a number of disparate industry and sub-industry groups such as: aerospace and defence, electronics, semiconductors, information technology and shipbuilding. In addition, very few companies operate solely for military purposes, either deriving a significant proportion of their revenue from civilian goods, or producing 'dual-use' components that have both a military and civilian application. Despite widespread arguments to the contrary, the marriage of the military and industry was, in fact, an observed phenomena as early as 1897, when founder of the modern human rights movement Jean Henri Dunant, predicted that:

> Everything that makes up the pride of our civilisation will be at the service of war. Your electric railroads, your dirigibles, your submarines ... telephones ... and so many other wonderful inventions, will perform splendid service for war. (Wallbank 1970, p. 343)

Today there are thousands of companies that may be classified as being in the 'armaments industry', albeit to varying degrees and in any number of ways. For example, Boeing is widely known as makers of commercial aircraft, however the firm also derive around half of its A\$60 billion revenue from military contracts. The structure of these businesses is such that any individual firm's suppliers, operations and functions are likely to be located in different states. For this reason, it remains especially difficult for investors to precisely identify and implement policies that require the targeting − either through exclusion or engagement − of specific stocks or sectors as is common in responsible business and investment programs.

A number of national governments have begun disclosing high-level information on their domestic activity in this area, however significant gaps in publicly available information remain. For instance, there is no single document published by the US government on its development and production of conventional armaments, despite having the highest level of government expenditure, the greatest volume and value of exports, and the largest number of private companies of any state in the world. Instead, some basic information about the scale and scope of the arms production is made available along with other major sectors in the Annual Industrial Capabilities Report to Congress that has been published annually since 1996. Disclosure is slightly more forthcoming in parts of Europe, with the British and French publishing comprehensive stand-alone financial and employment data from 1992 to 1997 respectively. In the absence of regular reporting cycles, prior to a review of defence procurement in 2010, the Australian government last commissioned a bespoke survey of domestic activity in the mid-1990s as part of a broader strategic review.

In response, civil society groups and scholars have increasingly called for greater governmental and intergovernmental transparency through voluntary reporting instruments such as the Stockholm International Peace Research Institute's (SIPRI) Arms Industry Database or the UN Register of Conventional Arms. However, the information contained in these databases is incomplete and unverified. There is therefore a high degree of complexity and opaqueness that must be overcome when assessing the limits of responsibility of arms makers.

## THE LIMITS OF RESPONSIBILITY FOR INSTITUTIONAL INVESTORS

At \$1.4 trillion, Australia has the fourth-largest investment market in the world — thanks largely to the 9 per cent employee superannuation (pension) guarantee. Pension funds control about 75 per cent of Australia's investment capital and will do so while this compulsory system remains. And so despite employing a number of external service providers to advise, implement and assess the performance of the fund, pension funds are quite literally at the heart of the investment markets, and their actions are carefully and deliberately governed by a system of trust law.[4]

Historically, investment approaches that attempt to marry socially responsible principles — whether they have been 'morally', 'religiously' or 'sustainability' based — have been thought to contradict pension fund trustees' fiduciary responsibility to act in the 'best interests' of its members (Kinder, 2005). The courts in Australia (as well as in the United Kingdom, which has the most similar legal system) by trustees have been adamantly opposed to the application of so-called 'non-financial' criteria to investment decisions.[5] This derives from the fundamental principle of trust law that states trustees must exercise their powers for a proper purpose (i.e. the purpose for which the power was granted).[6] In a trust whose purpose is to provide financial benefits to its beneficiaries, the purpose of the investment power can be none other than to augment, if possible, the value of the financial benefits to those members.[7]

The courts have been particularly intent on recognizing the moral plurality of Anglo-Australian society, counselling strongly against the incorporation of moral prejudice into fiduciary decision-making.[8] Collateral benefits, such as may satisfy some form of moral imperative, may accrue, but trustees must first and foremost pursue the purpose of the trust. Some links in this chain of logic are enshrined in statute in Australia. Section 52(2)(c) of *Superannuation Industry (Supervision) Act 1993* (SIS) provides that trustees must act in the 'best interests' of their members, which is interpreted to mean their best financial interests. Section 62 of SIS requires that the 'sole purpose' of a superannuation fund is to be the provision of benefits to members upon their retirement. Finally, section 52(2)(b) requires that a trustee exercise 'the same degree of care, skill and diligence as an ordinary prudent person would exercise in dealing with property of another for whom the person felt morally bound to provide'.

There is however a broader range of factors that must affect the quality of the decision process and those that relate to the motives of the trustee. As regards to the motivation for the decision, there are five central considerations. First, the investment power must be exercised in the 'best interests' of the members, which is interpreted to mean their financial best interests.[9] Second, trustees cannot permit consequential, collateral benefits to prejudice their pursuit of the trust's purpose. Third, the connection between the purpose and the benefit to the beneficiary must be material and direct. 'Speculative and remote' benefits, such as the impact of a single superannuation fund on the economy, will not suffice. Fourth, trustees are required to act impartially in balancing the interests of different members of their fund. And fifth, the trustee may be required to rebut an assertion that the decision to pursue a socially responsible approach was motivated by some improper purpose, such as the furtherance of union policy (as in *Cowan v Scargill*) or some personal moral or ethical ground (as in *Harries v Church Commissioners*).

Commensurately, the quality of the decision process may be affected by a further three factors. First, Section 52(2)(b) of the SIS Act restates the general law principle that trustees must be able to demonstrate that they took due care and exercised appropriate levels of skill and diligence in coming to their decisions.[10] This means that any investment strategy chosen by a trustee must be founded on objective evidence, which has been rigorously analysed and carefully considered by the trustee. Second, trustees are required to give explicit consideration to whether their decisions are in the interests of their beneficiaries.[11] Third, the courts are highly unlikely, therefore, to participate in a determination of the relative merits of different investment strategies, so long they possess some basic level of plausibility and the procedural elements (independence, impartiality, loyalty, prudence, objectivity, care/skill/diligence etc.) are satisfied.

Hence Australian trust law is unlikely to impugn an investor which adopts a, broadly defined, 'socially responsible' investment approach, so long as the strategy is: carefully considered, designed and implemented; not expected by the trustees to prejudice the financial outcomes for members on retirement; and not polluted by outside motivations. Thus a strategy that is based on legal and financial theory norms will satisfy an Australian court. Examinations of the legal constraints on trustees in regards to socially responsible investment approaches are well developed and many, suffice to say, there are two predominant financial constraints on institutional investors. First, it is difficult to empirically prove the effect of CSR programs, and at best evidence suggests the impact on investment performance is statistically insignificant. Second, the ability to pursue a CSR policy may signal certain things about the company (stability, long term focus etc.) that may be the actual drivers of corporate performance. That is, CSR may be the result, not the cause of any above average corporate performance (Camejo, 2002). Less explored in the literature are those strategies based on irresponsible action, as defined by illegality. I now review the critical studies of CSR and traditional CSR literature that does address arms makers, followed by an examination of the 'cluster munitions dilemma' in Australia.

# APPROACHING THE TASK OF INVESTING THROUGH THE IRRESPONSIBILITY PARADIGM

An alternate strategy that the above analysis did not assess against the demands of the court is the inverse yet complementary concept of CSI. Based not on moral or practical norms, but rather constitutive and regulatory ones, strategies and practices based on CSI offer institutional investors specificity rather than an open-ended raft of environmental, social and governance concerns (Armstrong, 1977). This is because what is considered illegal is also likely socially irresponsible, or put another way: vice is finite, whilst the means and ends of virtue are infinite (Boatright, 2000). According to some research, the threshold of the law is likely to have significant impact on the concentration of business activity, especially in industries without retail customers where there is comparatively little 'reward for virtue' (Vogel, 2005). A number of meta-analysis into socially responsible and ethical investment approaches (Donald & Taylor, 2008), as well as traditional CSR strategies (Griffin & Mahon, 1997), demonstrates statistically insignificant returns. And yet a similar study of illegal and socially irresponsible corporate behaviour found a significant economic performance penalty (Frooman, 1997).

In one of the very few attempts to apply CSR criteria to arms makers, Byrne inadvertently comes close to advocating for a CSI approach when he suggests that there is a 'need to reconsider the justification for assigning limited liability to any corporation regardless of its products negative externalities' (Byrne, 2007, p. 213). Traditionally, CSR programs and frameworks have focused on aspirational and moral virtues of human rights and society. For instance, the UN Global Compact, formed in 1999, draws on a range of international conventions regarding environmental, social and governance issues such as the United Nations Declaration of Human Rights (1948) that is a set of aspirational goals rather than a defined set of laws. Similarly, both the Interfaith Centre for Corporate Responsibility (ICCR) formed in 1971 and the 1993 Interfaith Declaration on Business Ethics attempted to codify 'the shared moral, ethical and spiritual values' that must be imbued within business according to the three Abrahamic traditions: Judaism, Christianity and Islam. Yet arguably these initiatives have lead to lasting and meaningful change in business behaviour.

Since the 2003 War in Iraq, there have been additional efforts to address the role of business in society, especially as it relates to human rights. Taking a distinctly legalistic view, the Business & Human Rights Resource Centre was formed as a collaborative partnership between Amnesty International and various academic institutions and practitioners around the world, and which has come to house the work of the United Nations Special Representative of the Secretary-General on Business & Human Rights, Professor John Ruggie, who was appointed in 2005 following the failure of the 2003 *Norms on the responsibilities of transnational corporations and other business enterprises with regard to human rights*, in part as a result of its normative 'privatisation' of corporate responsibilities under international law in which the classical view of legal personality – that being state-centric – was questioned. However the discussions that took place proceeding the failed norm were significant: it was the first time that States – which bear the primary obligation for the realization of human rights – recognized that business must also play its part.

The issue of state sovereignty and responsibility are the very basis of public international law; international law is primarily concerned with the rights and duties of states, not of market actors in their jurisdiction (Malanczuk, 1997). Although there exists public and private international law, the applicability of international laws to market actors such as corporations and investment capital providers is highly contested. In general, the responsibility falls with the state for the behaviour of all actors within its jurisdiction (i.e. state boundaries). However the application of that responsibility, between different issues and different nations varies widely as does the duty to ensure compliance in the instance of extraterritoriality. One of the central issues of international law as it relates to non-state actors is the fact that there exist 192 nation states and over 80,000 multinational corporations, which in turn have commercial relationships with millions of affiliates and suppliers all over the world.

However the 'solution' presented by CSI is incomplete: it explicitly relies upon the formation of domestic legislation (which, by its very nature varies between states) and the acceptance of international laws and principles. Therein lies another gap. At present no international law exists that places obligations on market actors directly – to do so would require the formation of a treaty. The UN Secretary-General Special Representative on Business and Human Rights John Ruggie reasons that there are four drivers why such a development is unlikely to materialise.[12] First, there exist a raft of cultural, religious and civilizational differences between states that have not been resolved in order to establish a truly universal set of human rights, and therefore it is unlikely this will occur based on the initiative of market actors such as corporations and investors. Second, in order to reach agreement, the standards of such a treaty are likely to be lower than the standards set in the myriad of existing treaties concerning humanitarian or human rights standards. Third, enforcement would likely be left to nation states and result in variable standards between them. Forth, such significant treaties are complex matters to resolve, and the diversified and global structure of modern economic actors further exacerbates the prospect of formulating a binding instrument. Indeed, as United Nations Special Representative of the Secretary-General for Business & Human Rights, Professor John Ruggie stated previously:

> ... the root cause of the business and human rights predicament today lies in the governance gaps created by globalization − between the scope and impact of economic forces and actors, and the capacity of societies to manage their adverse consequences. (Ruggie, 2009, p. 3)

## THE 'CLUSTER MUNITIONS DILEMMA' FOR AUSTRALIAN INSTITUTIONAL INVESTORS

A cluster bomb is a weapon that has inside multiple − often hundreds − of small explosive sub-munitions or 'bomblets' that are dispersed over an area the size of several football fields from either the air or ground. As a result, the final location of each bomblet is impossible to control for those deploying them, and so whom they maim or kill is both unknown and indiscriminate. Some bomblets are even designed to look like soft drink cans, hockey pucks or tennis balls. As a result, the victim of a cluster munition could equally be a soldier, an innocent woman or a small child − later that day, in a week, or ten years. In Laos an estimated 50−70 million bomblets are still killing people over 35 years after they were dropped. In fact, research conducted by Handicap International (2006) found that as many as 98 per cent of the victims of unexploded cluster munitions are civilians, a third of which are children.

In December 2008 the Australian Government was among those norm entrepreneurs that signed the internationally agreed *Cluster Munitions Convention*. Repeated statements by the Australian Government since have conceded that the use of cluster munitions presents the risk of 'unacceptable harm to civilians' and must therefore be subject to an internationally binding ban. When the Convention came into effect in August 2010, there appeared a chorus of NGOs and governments that sought 'an end for all time' of the use of cluster munitions by prohibiting their production, use, stockpiling and transfer. It is widely believed that Article 1c of the

Convention further prohibits investment in companies that either develop or produce cluster munitions by also prohibiting signatories from any activity that may 'assist and encourage' any other countries to do so.

However for the Convention to be binding, the mere signing of a treaty by a government is not enough. In addition it must be ratified, which is achieved by introducing domestic legislation that makes it a criminal offence under Australia law to act in anyway contrary to the international Convention. In late March 2011, the Senate Committee on Foreign Affairs, Defence and Trade tabled its report to the Australian Senate on the proposed *Cluster Munitions Prohibition Bill,* some provisions of which violently differ from the commitments made by the Australian Government to the international community when it signed the Convention in 2008. In particular, there are two related loopholes in the bill that the Senate Committee responsible for reviewing the bill chose not to tighten.

First, the bill undermines that part of the Convention that requires Australia to 'never under any circumstances' act contrary to the Convention by adding phrases that explicitly allow those of our military allies that are not party to the Convention unfettered access to stockpile, retain and transit cluster munitions within Australia. No other signatory country in the world has expressly permitted such unfettered free access to its territories as this. It is unprecedented. The legislation further allows Australian military personnel to actively assist in cluster munitions-related activities during joint military operations with our non-signatory allies to the extent where, according to Human Rights Watch, Australian troops would be permitted to develop strategies, direct attacks, and assist in the deployment of cluster bombs − basically, to operate to the point where they can do anything bar pull the trigger.

Second, the legislation does not explicitly prohibit investment in companies that produce cluster munitions. Indeed the respective governments of New Zealand, Ireland, Holland, Luxembourg and Belgium have in their domestic legislation included statements specifically banning investment and provision of other financial services − such as banking, loans and equity − to companies that either develop or produce cluster munitions. Other governments, including those of United Kingdom, Germany, France, Switzerland, Lebanon, Mexico, Norway and Rwanda, have all publicly stated that they interpret the Convention as including a prohibition of direct and indirect investment. So the bill that is currently in front of the Australian parliament is clearly out of line with international standards and expectations.

Indications are that the investment community in Australia also wants this issue addressed with more adequate legislation. For instance, the Australian Council of Super Investors (ACSI) − a body that represents over A

$300 billion of domestic retirement savings – has been especially vocal in its opposition to the proposed bill. In its latest submission to the *Senate Foreign Affairs, Defence and Trade Committee* dated 8 March 2011, ACSI states 'the current drafting will have no practical effect on the financing of cluster bomb production'. In an earlier submission, ACSI called for amendment to 'prohibit the direct and indirect financing of companies involved in the production of cluster munitions' in order to ensure the Australian legislation does not 'go against the spirit of the [Convention]'.

In its 2009 report recommending that the Australian Government ratify the Convention, the *Parliamentary Joint Standing Committee on Treaties* recommended that any bill prevent 'investment by Australian entities in the development or production of cluster munitions, either directly, or through the provision of funds to companies that may develop or produce cluster munitions'. And yet, in research I began to publish in 2009 explained how two Australian pension funds and the Australia's principal sovereign wealth fund are likely to have investments in companies that produce cluster munitions – in the absence of publicly available exclusion policies – despite the international Convention generally being read as seeking to prohibit such activity from August 2010. In addition, a significant number of the hired investment managers are also known to provide bank loans, investment banking, or other financial services to makers of cluster munitions which, whilst not as direct an issue for Australian institutional investors who employ the services of the investment manager, does demonstrate the complexity of some of the financial relationships involved. Nor is there any publicly available information suggesting that any of the three funds engage with the firms that are involved in cluster munitions production (See Table 1).

Advice from the Attorney-General's department on the bill has pointed out that it presently 'does not include an investment offence' in its provisions adequate enough to prohibit investment in companies involved in the production of cluster munitions if that financing was not provided for the express purposes of developing or producing cluster munitions (Australian Department of Foreign Affairs and Trade 2011, p. 11). The issue is that of the six companies known to be presently involved in such business, none do so exclusively – they make other civilian and/or military products.

Investment theory contends that the exclusion of the six companies would limit the investment returns available to members. This widely held logic applies to all sorts of companies, regardless of the reason for limiting the number of stocks available to invest in (i.e. whether it be

*Table 1.* Australian Exposure to Cluster Munitions Manufacturers Based Overseas.

| | Australian Super | Health Super | Future Fund |
|---|---|---|---|
| Type | Pension Fund | Pension Fund | Sovereign Wealth Fund |
| Size | A$32 billion (large fund) | A$8 billion (small-mid fund) | A$75 billion (primary government fund) |
| Publicly declared exclusion policy | No | No | No |
| Hired investment managers known to invest in cluster munitions manufacturers (relevant arms manufacturers) | Acadian Asset Management (US): *Poongsan Corp (South Korea).* LSV Capital Management (US): *Textron (US).* T. Rowe Price Group (US): *Alliant Techsystems (US), Lockheed-Martin (US).* Vanguard (US): *Textron(US), Poongsan Corp (South Korea), Singapore Technologies Engineering (Singapore), Alliant Techsystems (US), Hanwha Corp (South Korea).* Blackrock (US): *Singapore Technologies Engineering (Singapore), Textron(US), Hanwha Corp (South Korea), Alliant Techsystems (US), Lockheed-Martin (US).* | Blackrock (US): *Singapore Technologies Engineering (Singapore), Textron(US), Hanwha Corp (South Korea), Alliant Techsystems (US), Lockheed-Martin (US).* JP Morgan Chase (US): *Alliant Techsystems(US).* Goldman Sachs (US): *Alliant Techsystems(US), Textron (US), Lockheed-Martin (US).* Société Générale (France): *Alliant Techsystems(US).* Credit Suisse (Switzerland): *Singapore Technologies Engineering (Singapore), Alliant Techsystems (US).* General Electric (US): *Alliant Techsystems(US), Textron (US).* | State Street (US): *Textron(US), Poongsan Corp (South Korea), Singapore Technologies Engineering (Singapore), Alliant Techsystems(US).* Vanguard (US): *Textron(US), Poongsan Corp (South Korea), Singapore Technologies Engineering (Singapore), Alliant Techsystems(US),Hanwha Corp (South Korea).* Goldman Sachs (US): *Alliant Techsystems(US).* Blackrock (US): *Singapore Technologies Engineering (Singapore), Textron(US), Hanwha Corp (South Korea), Alliant Techsystems(US), Lockheed-Martin (US).* |

**Table 1.** (*Continued*)

| | Australian Super | Health Super | Future Fund |
|---|---|---|---|
| Hired investment managers known to provide loans and investment banking services to cluster munitions manufacturers (relevant arms manufacturers) | State Street (US): *Textron(US)*, *Poongsan Corp (South Korea)*, *Singapore Technologies Engineering (Singapore)*, *Alliant Techsystems(US)*. Credit Suisse (Switzerland): *Singapore Technologies Engineering (Singapore)*, *Alliant Techsystems(US)*. State Street (US): *Lockheed-Martin (US)*. Morgan Stanley (US): *Textron (US)*, *Lockheed-Martin (US)*, *Singapore Technologies Engineering (Singapore)*. Credit Suisse (Switzerland): *Textron(US)*. | Morgan Stanley (US): *Textron (US)*, *Lockheed-Martin (US)*, *Singapore Technologies Engineering (Singapore)*. AXA (Switzerland): *Singapore Technologies Engineering (Singapore)*, *Lockheed-Martin (US)*, *Textron(US)*. Regions Financial Corp. (US): *Alliant Techsystems (US)*. Société Générale (France): *Textron(US)*. BNP Paribas (France): *Textron (US)*, *Lockheed-Martin (US)*. | State Street (US): *Lockheed-Martin (US)*. Goldman Sachs (US): *Alliant Techsystems(US)*, *Textron (US)*, *Lockheed-Martin (US)*. Canyon Capital Advisers (US): *Alliant Techsystems(US)*. |

Goldman Sachs (US): *Alliant Techsystems(US)*.

General Electric (US): *Alliant Techsystems(US)*.

Barclays (UK): *Textron(US)*, *Lockheed-Martin (US)*.

Prudential Bank (UK): *Singapore Technologies Engineering (Singapore)*.

Mizuho Bank (Japan): *Lockheed-Martin (US)*, *Alliant Techsystems(US)*.

Sumitomo Mitsui Financial Group (Japan): *Lockheed-Martin (US)*.

JP Morgan Chase (US): *Textron (US)*, *Lockheed-Martin (US)*, *Alliant Techsystems (US)*.

HSBC Holdings (UK): *Textron (US)*.

Credit Suisse (Switzerland): *Textron(US)*.

*Note:* Due to the nature of modern investment management, the level of transparency in stock holdings and mandate contracts, as well as turnover of portfolios, it remains unclear whether the individual mandates between the aforementioned funds and their service providers (investment managers) either directs or results in the exclusion of cluster munitions manufacturers.

environmental grounds or climate change). However I am unaware of any investor specifically arguing for the bill to permit Australian entities to continue investing in companies involved in the production of cluster munitions overseas. The argument that is made is done so to strictly adhere to financial theory, not to oppose any emerging or established norm of behaviour. In the absence of legislation dictating for investors what they can and can't invest in, it will remain difficult for investors to identify and act on emerging norms such as the banning of cluster munitions. Given Australia has the fourth-largest investment market in the world arguably the extent to which the international Convention is successful rests on how institutional investors address such norms within their day-to-day operations and strategic policies.

## CONCLUSION

By focusing on the experience of institutional investors in Australia regarding the makers of cluster munitions, I have demonstrated how pension funds are faced with a 'dilemma': accept the Federal Government's restrictive application of the international Convention within its domestic legislation, or adopt a more expansive reading and cease investing directly and indirectly in cluster munitions over and above its stated obligations. An analysis of stock holdings of several Australian pension funds and the government's principal sovereign wealth fund indicates that, as yet, it is common for investors to wait for legislative direction before excluding particular stocks and sectors. This is so for investors who adopt either a mainstream or responsible investment approach, and is due, in part, to difficulties in implementation as well as compatibility with widely held investment principles such as the efficient market hypothesis.

The concept of CSI was offered as a practical and theoretically compelling solution for investors seeking to reconcile their fiduciary duties and investment objectives (i.e. mainstream or responsible investment approach) with the demands of both identifying and satisfying emerging social norms such as the prohibition of cluster munitions. In contrast to traditional CSR strategies and activities, CSI accepts as an intrinsic feature of armaments manufacturing the existence of certain 'negative externalities' that result from standard use of its products and services. This precise formulation limits the investor's responsibility considerations to constitutive and regulatory norms, as opposed to norms that are merely evaluative or practical.

In so doing, the institutional investor may better resolve what I have termed the 'cluster munitions dilemma' with suitable strategies and programs.

The mechanics of implementation options have been explored more fully elsewhere, but may broadly include both exclusion and engagement strategies. A pre-defined exclusionary policy ensures that identified stocks and sectors are 'negatively screened-out' (divested) from the investible universe as well as 'blacklisted' from any future investment. So-called 'ethical investors' such as Christian Super (2008) commonly exclude controversial weapons such as cluster munitions, which they view as being intrinsically 'indiscriminate' in design as well as 'inhumane and cruel'. The vast proportion of mainstream and responsible investors, however, adopt an engagement approach, with no exclusionary mechanism on certain stocks and sectors. Signatory members of the UN Principles for Responsible Investment (UNPRI) — whose asset owners and service providers marshal over A\$22 trillion in assets — instead advocate for 'responsible' and 'sustainable investment' strategies which take environmental, social and corporate governance (ESG) factors into account, in so far as they are material (i.e. statistically significant) to investment performance. A small number of funds attempt to switch between being responsible (engagement) and ethical (exclusion) investment strategies, such that where engagement fails to achieve the desired change in company behaviour, investors have a pre-defined process for excluding the stocks from the portfolio. Alternatively, engagement and exclusionary approaches may be used more interchangeably depending on the issue that arises from the asset — such as in the case of an emerging international and domestic norm proscribing cluster munitions.

The benefits of the CSI approach are significant and many. The investor is advantaged by having at its disposal a roadmap for managing — though not necessarily predicting — emerging social norms. This is so for ethical, responsible and mainstream investment approaches, although is most readily compatible with investors who have pre-established exclusionary policies as well as effective implementation procedures. Society is benefited as a result of increasingly significant economic actors, such as pension and sovereign wealth funds, directing their capital in such a way as to minimize humanitarian and environmental harm. I have argued how the use of cluster munitions demonstrates in places like Laos demonstrate how corporate activity may impact broader social objectives. Given the severity of the problem in Laos, it recently added a ninth Millennium Development Goal on its road to economic development, which requires it clear its land of

unexploded ordnance. And both processes arguably better serve the beneficiaries' 'best interests', which is, after all, the sole purpose of the institutional investment industry.

# NOTES

1. For the purposes of this chapter, the terms "arms maker", "producer" and
"manufacturer" will be used interchangeably to refer to all firms involved in the
development and production of conventional armaments, including mere component suppliers.

2. For instance, E.F. Byrne (2007) challenges the Westphalian notion of state
sovereignty and the importance of armaments production for national defence in
order to assess arms makers against four corporate social responsibility criteria:
environmental performance, social equity, profitability, and use of political power.

3. A widely accepted standard developed by the financial industry for classifying
listed companies is the Global Industry Classification Standards (GICS) which
include ten key sectors (each with their own industry groups and sub-industries):
energy, materials, industrials, consumer discretionary, consumer staples, health
care, financials, information technology, telecommunications services, and utilities.

4. For a more thorough legal analysis than the one that follows, see: Donald and
Taylor (2008).

5. See most notably Megarry V-C in *Cowan v Scargill* (1985) Ch 270. The principles in that case were affirmed in Australia in *Buckland v AG for Victoria* (unre-
ported judgment of the Supreme Court of Victoria, No.10536 of 1992), and more
recently in *Asea Brown Boveri Superannuation Fund v Asea Brown Boveri* [1999] 1
VR 144, *Knudsen v Kara Kar* (2000) NSWSC 715, *Crowe v SERF* (2003) VSC 316
and *Invensys v Austrac Investments* (2006) 198 FLR 302.

6. *Balls v Strutt* (1841) 1 Hare 146 at 149; 66 ER 984 at 985.

7. This principle was clearly expressed in *Harries v Church Commissioners* [1992]
1 WLR 1241, a case involving a charity associated with the Church of England, a
situation where one might have expected ethical considerations to have some influence. In that case Sir Donald Nicholls V-C held that: 'investments are held by trustees to aid the work of the charity in a particular way; by generating money. That
is the purpose for which they are held. That is their raison d'être. Trustees cannot
use assets held as an investment for other, viz, non-investment, purposes. To the
extent that they do they are not properly exercising their powers of investment.'

8. See for instance see: *Harries v Church Commissioners, re Wyvern Developments*
[1974] 1 WLR 1097; *Martin v City of Edinburgh District Council* [1989] 2 PBLR 8.

9. Cowan v Scargill [1985] 1 Ch 270. The principle was first endorsed in Australia in Crowe v SERF (2003) VSC 316. Earlier Australian cases cite Cowan v Scargill in support of other principles, or in obiter dicta.

10. Although not specifically stated in the legislation, the care, skill and diligence
benchmarks are likely to be higher for professionals than for volunteers, and higher
for experts than for lay-people; *ASC v AS Nominees* (1995) 133 ALR 1 at 14.

11. This is most clearly stated in *Martin v City of Edinburgh* (1988) SCT 329,
which reviewed the adoption of an anti Apartheid investment policy in trusts

administered by a local council. Although a Scottish case, the principle is good law in Australia and the U.K. generally.

12. In 2003 the United Nations Social & Economic Council attempted an attempted normative re-conceptualisation of corporate responsibilities under international law such that "transnational corporations and other business enterprises have a responsibility to respect human rights" (Resolution 8/7) which was vehemently opposed by key industry lobby groups such as the IOE and ICC (2004).

# REFERENCES

Armstrong, J. S. (1977). Social irresponsibility in management. *Journal of Business Research*, *5*, 185–213.

Australian Council of Super Investors. (2011). *Criminal Code Amendment (Cluster Munitions Prohibition) Bill 2010. Submission to the Senate Foreign Affairs, Defence and Trade Committee*. Retrieved from https://senate.aph.gov.au/submissions/comittees/view document.aspx?id = bc0a53b6-7c13-47a0-93e4-1a97108c4dd8. Accessed on 8 March 2011.

Australian Department of Foreign Affairs and Trade. (2011). *Criminal Code Amendment (Cluster Munitions Prohibition) Bill 2010. Department of Foreign Affairs and Trade – Additional information*. Retrieved from https://senate.aph.gov.au/submissions/comittees/viewdocument.aspx?id = 43e95584-3973-4435-813c-6fe31c3ba064. Accessed on 1 March 2011.

Boatright, J. R. (2000). *Ethics and the conduct of business*. Upper Saddle River, NJ: Prentice Hall.

Byrne, E. F. (2007). Assessing arms makers' corporate social responsibility. *Journal of Business Ethics*, *74*(3), 201–217.

Camejo, P. (2002). *The SRI advantage: Why socially responsible investing has outperformed financially*. Altona: Friesens Inc.

Christian Super. (2008). *Weapons: Ethics position paper*. Retrieved from http://www.christian-super.com.au/ethic-statements-resources/ethic-statements/weapons. Accessed on 1 March 2011.

Clark, T. S. (2008). What CSR is not: CSI. Conference paper for Critical Management Studies Conference, University of Southern California, 7–8 August 2008.

Donald, M. S., & Taylor, N. A. J. (2008). Does 'sustainable' investing compromise the obligations owed by superannuation trustees. *Australian Business Law Review*, *36*(1), 47–61.

Frooman, J. (1997). Socially irresponsible and illegal behaviour and shareholder wealth. *Business & Society*, *36*(3), 221–249.

Griffin, J. J., & Mahon, J. F. (1997). The corporate social performance and corporate financial performance debate: Twenty-five years of incomparable research. *Business & Society*, *36*(1), 5–31.

Jackson, S. T. (2010, April). *The SIPRI Top 100 arms-producing companies 2008*. Stockholm International Peace Research Institute Fact Sheet.

Handicap International. (2006). *Fatal footprint: The global human impact of cluster munitions*. Retrieved from http://www.mineaction.org/downloads/1/Fatal_Footprint_HI_report_on_CM_casualties.1.pdf. Accessed on 1 March 2011.

IKV Pax Christi and Handicap International and Netwerk Vlaanderen. (2010, April). *Worldwide investments in cluster munitions: A shared responsibility*. Cluster Munitions Coalition Report. Brussels, Belgium, April 2010.

Kinder, P. D. (2005). New Fiduciary duties in a changing social environment. *Journal of Investing, 14*(Fall), 324–338.

Malanczuk, P. (1997). *Akehurst's modern introduction to international law*. New York, NY: Routledge.

Ruggie, J. (2009, June 9). Submission to Australian National Human Rights Consultation Committee, Cambridge, MA, 3.

Vogel, D. (2005). *The market for virtue: The potential and limits of corporate social responsibility*. Washington, DC: Brookings Institution Press.

Wallbank, T. W (1970). *Civilisation past and present*. Glenview, IL: Scott, Foresham and Company.

# THE STRUCTURAL CONTRADICTIONS AND CONSTRAINTS ON CORPORATE SOCIAL RESPONSIBILITY: CHALLENGES FOR CORPORATE SOCIAL IRRESPONSIBILITY

Alex Nunn

## ABSTRACT

Purpose – *This chapter engages critically with the ideas of corporate social responsibility (CSR) and irresponsibility (CSI) in order to examine their utility for the purposes of realizing more socially just and environmentally sustainable social and economic practices.*

Methodology/approach – *The chapter develops Marx's understanding of the twin pressures of class struggle and inter-capitalist competition in setting the limits of agency for corporate actors. It is thus theoretical and discursive in nature.*

Findings – *The findings of the chapter suggest that the scope for corporate agency in relation to responsibility/irresponsibility is severely*

Corporate Social Irresponsibility: A Challenging Concept
Critical Studies on Corporate Responsibility, Governance and Sustainability, Volume 4, 63–82
ISSN: 2043-9059/doi:10.1108/S2043-9059(2012)0000004012

*limited by inter-capitalist competition and capitalist social relations. It therefore argues that those interested in social justice and environmental sustainability should focus on these structural pressures rather than theorizing corporate agency.*

Social implications − *The research suggests that the focus of academic and government attention should be on resolving the contradictions and exploitative social relations inherent in capitalism. Without this emphasis activism, corporate agency and government action will not eradicate the types of problem that advocates of CSR/CSI are concerned about.*

Originality/value of paper − *The value of the paper is that it contests and engages critically with the utility of the notion of CSR and the emergent concept of CSI. It asks proponents of these concepts to think seriously about the structural pressures and constraints within which business and policy makers act.*

**Keywords:** Corporate social responsibility; corporate social irresponsibility; class struggle; inter-capitalist competition; capitalist social relations; social justice

Interest in corporate social responsibility (CSR) has grown markedly over recent decades and more recently still has been accompanied by a concern with corporate social irresponsibility (CSI). This is not just an academic interest but a practical and policy matter too. In a world of complex social problems, in which the dominant political and economic values suggest that the state and its agencies should promote free market capitalism, CSR apparently offers the potential for states to absolve themselves of policy responsibility while ensuring that public and social goods are privately produced. However, in the wake of the financial crisis that emerged from 2007/2008 onward, there is increasing concern that CSR has failed to live up to its potential. CSI suggests that problematic behavior among some firms can be explained as the result of agency on the part of individuals and corporations. Understanding it in this way suggests that there is the potential for policy measures to "design out" irresponsibility and maximize responsibility through legislation or soft governance. It also implies that firms are in a position to choose the extent to which they act "responsibly." These are laudable aims, but this chapter argues that the degree of agency available to firms is in fact severely constrained by the structural features of global capitalism. It draws attention to the role of inter-capitalist competition and social struggle in determining the limits of corporate agency in this regard. The implication of this analysis is that attention is more usefully focused at the system level rather than the level of individual corporate actors.

By shifting attention to structural constraints in capitalism, the incentives and motivations for firms attempting strategies of CSR or being accused of CSI might also be understood differently. First, it suggests that a significant degree of "irresponsible" behavior will always exist, regardless of the handwringing of politicians or academics. That does not rule out socially altruistic or "responsible" behavior on the part of corporate actors. Indeed, there are several very specific conditions in which this type of behavior is likely to be realized. The problem is that, for the most part, these are associated either with competitive strategies or with circumstances that are harmful to the continuity of capitalism as a social system.

The chapter rearticulates the concept of "CSR" as *capitalist* social responsibility, showing how this is a much more productive analytical tool for understanding what is really at work when considering corporate "responsibility" or "irresponsibility." Here *capitalist* social responsibility refers not to the pursuit of "social" goals *per se* but of widely shared class goals that reflect the common interest of the capitalist class, or at least significant subsections of it. In some places, and at some times, these will look like they align with the interests of other social groups, but ultimately this always masks (and most often further entrenches) competitive strategies and/or exploitative social relations.

In this context, irresponsibility can also be understood differently. In the first instance, irresponsibility should be understood as behavior that transgresses the bounds of the social norms of capitalist production. Of course, these norms are not the same across either time or space; so what was acceptable in the 19th century London is not in the 21st century London and is different again from the 21st century Shanghai. Competition, especially at the margins, will always push individuals and firms to push the bounds of those norms, and sometimes exceed them. This is irresponsible in another sense though; in the sense of *capitalist* social irresponsibility. Here transgressing the social norms of capitalism in a particular place is "irresponsible" in class terms because it threatens to undermine capitalist legitimacy.

Finally, the chapter argues that the concept of CSI can be put to powerful political use. However, for this power to be realized, it needs to be placed in the context of the structural analysis set out below. When this is in place, CSI could be seen as one component of a wider social struggle to rearticulate social relations in ways that are supportive of principles of equality, social justice, and sustainability.

## THE PROMISE OF CORPORATE SOCIAL RESPONSIBILITY AND THE PERSISTENT PROBLEM OF IRRESPONSIBILITY

CSR has attracted much attention since its emergence in the 1950s (e.g., Bowen, 1953; Carroll, 1999; Davis, 1960). Dominant themes in the literature include moral arguments about the responsibility that accompanies power and influence and the alignment between business and the dominant values of the society in which it operates. This alignment is important because it reflects the socially acceptable trade-off between the production of private and social goods at any one point in time and space. This is frequently expressed as a rather mechanistic concern that business operates within the law (Carroll, 1979b), which is itself the socially constructed codification of the social relations of capitalism. In an age of transnational production, this has led to an extended concern, driven in part by consumer and shareholder activism, that the standards expected in one part of a business operation are upheld throughout, regardless of whether formal legal obligations assert this (Hudson & Hudson, 2003; Hale, 2008). Others draw attention to the importance of business producing the goods and services that society wants and sustaining this through profits (Carroll, 1979a; Matten & Moon, 2008), with still others suggesting that the prospect for diluting this makes CSR a "fundamentally subversive doctrine" (Friedman, 1970). Drucker sought to move beyond the apparent tension between social and private responsibility here by suggesting that they are compatible to the extent that business is not only able to reconcile social responsibilities with profit seeking but also to turn the provision of social goods into profit-seeking opportunities (Drucker, 1984). Despite repeated attempts, however, it is not entirely clear that contemporary writing on CSR has fully resolved some of the tensions inherent in these various definitions (Dahlsrud, 2008; Matten & Moon, 2008).

Nevertheless the promise of CSR is so attractive because it appears to offer one means by which complex social problems might be addressed in an era of globalization where the capacity of the state to do this alone is routinely questioned (Rosenau, 1995; Rosenau, 2002). CSR is seen as one mechanism by which a range of different actors can be engaged in a network of organizations helping to deal with complex problems such as service delivery, poverty alleviation, or combating environmental problems. There are prominent examples of this at both global and national level (Cameron, 2011; Ruggie, 2004).

For their part, firms have been keen to adopt the CSR mantra for a variety of reasons, including consumer and shareholder activism. In the 1990s and 2000s, concern with the exploitative production practices adopted by the decentralized suppliers of Multinational Corporations (MNCs) motivated several high-profile activist campaigns to boycott particular brands. Acting first to defend themselves from direct criticism, or the potential for it, several high-profile MNCs adopted labor codes of conduct and other statements of CSR. Firms quickly realized that the value embedded in brand fetishism could be exploited by adopting and promoting their CSR credentials and therefore CSR became a part of the competitive strategies of an increasing number of corporations (Hudson & Hudson, 2003; Taylor, 2011; Yu, 2008).

If CSR exists at one end of a spectrum, however, at the other end must exist CSI (Clark & Grantham, 2012; Jones et al., 2009, 2010). It is claimed that CSI can help to recognize that business is not always "responsible" and also to theoretically account for that empirical reality. In the context of the financial crisis — dubious lending practices, clearly negative social externalities from practices such as short selling in the financial markets, tax avoidance, and the current scandal engulfing News International[1] — it seems as if the concept of CSI might have found its time. CSI apparently offers the promise of naming and shaming corporate actors to adopt more ethical, socially just, and environmentally sustainable behavior (Clark & Grantham, 2012; Taylor, 2012).

A focus on corporate irresponsibility as well as responsibility might be said to appeal more to critics of capitalism and there are several notable examples in the literature (Banerjee, 2008; Chatterji & Listokin, 2007; Shaw, 2009). Shaw (2009) attempts to unify the study of business ethics with Marxist critiques of capitalism. However, his argument demonstrates an inadequate understanding of Marx's critique and specifically equates Marx's identification of the structural pressures of capitalism (though Shaw, rather tellingly, fails to spell out his understanding of these) with the rather different assertion that this must mean that there are no ethics in business. His failure to fully develop Marx's analysis of the structural features of capitalist development leads him to erroneous conclusions, not just about the nature of Marx's critique but also about the scope for corporate and individual agency. By caricaturing Marx, Shaw is able to claim that the empirical observation that corporate actors often do adopt ethical codes of conduct disproves the Marxist case, though as the discussion below suggests, this is not the case. Chaterji and Listokin (2007) present a rather atheoretical argument that advocates of CSR simply overstate the scope to persuade rather than force corporate actors to modify their behavior to take into account social and environmental concerns. For his part, Banerjee (2008) develops Foucault's analysis of the structural power of discursive knowledge to present a largely successful critique of CSR as at best misplaced optimism and at worst legitimation of capitalist exploitation. However, his analysis would be considerably strengthened by linking it to an understanding of inter-capitalist competition and capitalist social relations.

This chapter seeks to go beyond these existing critiques by demonstrating the relationship of CSR to Marx's analysis of capitalist competition and social relations. In doing so, it advances the arguments of those who are skeptical about the prospects of CSR to realize more socially and environmentally just outcomes. It also therefore appraises the utility of the emerging concept of CSI, and suggests that its proponents need to take seriously the structural constraints of capitalism. The first section starts with a brief summary of Marx's critique of capitalism before outlining the role of inter-capitalist competition as a precursor to identifying the implications that this has for understanding CSR and CSI.

## Capitalist Social Relations

Marx's analysis of capitalism is based on the premise that the key feature of any mode of production is the social relations between individuals and social groups that it generates. In a capitalist society, a particular form of social relations is produced between those who must sell their labor power to survive and reproduce themselves in "every day" life and generationally (i.e., the working class) and those who own or control the means of production (i.e., the bourgeoisie or capitalists) and therefore purchase the labor power of the working class (Wood, 1995, pp. 31–36). At the heart of capitalist social relations is a process of class struggle and inter-capitalist competition, rather than one of free agency on the part of either seller or purchaser (Morton, 2006, pp. 63–65; Wood, 2002, pp. 96–98).

Value is generated from the application of labor power in the production process. The amount of labor power embodied in the production of a commodity determines its ultimate value, though confusingly this does not always equal its price. The price of a commodity may fluctuate due to conditions of demand and supply, but once these are stripped away the "equilibrium" price will reveal the value of the "socially-necessary" average labor time embodied in its production (Marx, 1867, Ch. 19). "Socially-necessary" here is crucial to understand the role of labor time in generating value because it introduces the notion of both abstract average labor (i.e., excluding the variation in productivity, skill, and speed of individual workers) and the idea that what is "necessary" is not a given, but it is socially constructed in any one place or time by a complex range of cultural, social, and material factors. The socially necessary labor time embodied, for instance, in the production of a car will vary over time and space to reflect the balance of social relations between capital and labor, social and legal norms about working hours and conditions, the level of technology applied, socially acceptable standards of living, the degree of sophistication of the car as an end product, and so on.

Of course, there are other determinants of the degree of surplus value generation. Marx is famous for the line in the *Communist Manifesto* that all history is "...the history of class struggles" (Marx & Engels, 1848, Ch. 1). One of the ways in which the distribution of surpluses can be shaped is through the balance of power in the social relations between capital and labor in any particular place (country/region, etc.), economic sector, and time. Social struggles, industrial relations, and the like are therefore part of the process of determining how much surplus is generated (e.g., the pace and intensity of work, the amount of labor power employed, and the technology used in production) and who it is distributed to (e.g., wages, profits, and taxes). In most capitalist countries, strong legal statutes limit the scope of these struggles from being social and political to the atomized enterprise level of industrial relations. Again the extent to which this is achieved is dependent on the nature and dynamics (and therefore path dependency) of class struggle in any one particular place at a point in time. Historically rooted social struggles between capital and labor, often articulated through the state, will lead to a particular manifestation of those relations (Marx & Engels, 1848, Ch. 1). Some of these norms will become codified in legal statute while others will be more implicit and customary.

The employment of the labor power of the working class results in the production of "surplus value" that accrues to the capitalist. The capitalist can opt to increase surplus value by increasing the amount of labor power employed by increasing the number of workers employed or lengthening the working day (absolute surplus value). Alternatively, they can increase it by reorganizing production to make it more productive, through innovations in the organization or technology of production (relative surplus value) (Marx, 1867, Ch. 16). To this extent, the degree of surplus value generated by capitalist enterprises as profits is dependent on a combination of class struggle and management strategies.

The role of wages in determining surplus value is also connected to a range of factors associated with capitalist social relations but which are exogenous to the industrial relations of individual enterprises. For example, one of the determinants of wages is the cost of the reproduction of labor power (Marx, 1867, Chs. 12, 19). If costs of living increase, then wages must also rise to enable labor power to be reproduced and surplus generation to continue. Conversely, if the cost of living falls, then wages can also fall, and the proportion of the working day that is spent generating output to cover the costs of reproducing labor power can be reduced. Consequently, a greater part of the time that labor power is employed can be devoted to generating surplus value. In this sense, all capitalists benefit from innovations that result in reductions in the costs of reproducing labor power. Innovation then provides not just a private and excludable good for one capitalist but a social good for all, so long as it relates to products consumed in the regeneration of labor power. As we shall see below, this introduces one way in which "social responsibility" might be seen under capitalism in quite different terms to the CSR literature.

### Inter-Capitalist Competition

Alongside class struggle, inter-capitalist competition is also a key structural feature of capitalist social relations. So far we have only shown how innovation and organizational change impact on the general or average rate of surplus value in any particular sector. However, of course, the enterprise or firm that implements successful innovations has an advantage over its competitors. This is because products trade at the average price. As such, those firms that can take advantage of successful innovations can gain additional relative surplus value compared with their competitors.

> The real value of a commodity is, however, not its individual value but its social value; that is to say, the real value is not measured by the labor-time socially required for its production. If therefore, the capitalist who applies the new method sells his commodity at its social value of one shilling, he sells it for three pence above its individual value, and thus realizes an extra surplus-vale of three pence. (Marx, 1867, Ch. 12)

This can generate advantages in several ways: firms with this competitive form of surplus value will find it easier to generate additional investment; they may choose to share the benefits of the additional relative surplus value with key workers, thereby attracting the best talent and enhancing future productivity; or they may choose also to increase market share by foregoing some of the increase in additional relative surplus value by lowering their prices below the average rate; and finally they may choose to reinvest part of the additional surplus value in further product or process innovations.

Without responding to these kinds of innovations, it is easy to see that other firms in the same market will quickly go out of business. Therefore, they are spurred either to replicate or leapfrog these innovations in their own processes. As such, the additional relative surplus value that is generated by innovations in the organization and technology of production in a single firm is short lived:

> ...this extra surplus-value vanishes, so soon as the new method of production has become general, and has consequently caused the difference between the individual value of the cheapened commodity and its social value to vanish. The law of the determination of value by labor-time, a law which brings under its determination the individual capitalist who applies the new method of production, by compelling him to sell his goods under their social value, this same law, acting as coercive law of competition, forces his competitors to adopt the new method. (Marx, 1867, Ch. 12)

Inter-capitalist competition provides the role of explaining why individual capitalists and their cadres are so concerned with these sorts of organizational and technological innovations. Incidentally, it also means that innovation is in fact risky. It is not always bound to be successful. Even successful ideas can fail due to poor implementation. It is this that leads to the recognition of the importance of "soft skills" and the cult of "leadership" in ensuring that the implementation of innovation and change are widely supported in the workforce so that they have a better chance of success. It also explains the emphasis in economic development policy in virtually all countries on the role of competition, innovation, risk taking, and entrepreneurship: all are absolutely central to a capitalist economy (Cammack, 2006; Cammack, 2008). Without them, growth stalls and crisis emerges. Indeed they are so central that the balance of social struggle, codified in legal statute, is frequently such that corporations are legally compelled to follow the imperative of competition. The famous 1919 ruling against Henry Ford's plans to subsume the short-term profit motive under longer-term plans for embedding a particular industrial and social model demonstrate this point ably (Banerjee, 2008, pp. 58−59).

These laws of competition do not just generate innovation but also expansion. Unless a capitalist, faced by competition, acts to expand the scale of their production, then others will do so and drive them out of business. Competition drives expansion in the commodification of labor power, use of raw materials, and fixed capital − itself the product of expansionary competitive pressures. As such, a preoccupation with growth is inbuilt to capitalism as a social system.

There are, though, important problems associated with this pattern of expansion and competitive innovation. The generation of surpluses, and the ability of capitalists to capture these as profits, tends toward the polarization of society with increasing amounts of surpluses accruing at one end and increasing amounts of unemployed or underemployed labor power at the other (Harvey, 1982, p. 195; Marx, 1894, Ch. 13). Inter-capitalist competition also generates a pressure toward centralization in the credit system and sectoral monopolies as some firms are successful at producing innovations that generate competitive advantage and are therefore able to exclude their competitors from the market.

These problems can be offset, for a time. Surpluses can be invested in increasing the scope of capitalist production − such as by investing in production in areas of the world economy that were previously outside of capitalist social relations (part of what we currently call "globalization"). This is what might be called a *spatial strategy* of offsetting overaccumulation. *Temporal strategies* involve the "sinking" of surpluses into long-term fixed investments, usually in infrastructure but sometimes also fixed capital investment (Harvey, 1982; Harvey, 2003, pp. 109−121).

Both temporal and spatial strategies involve further expansion, however, and involve ever greater consumption of economic, social, and environmental resources and narrowing the scope for future expansion, delaying but not eradicating the onset of crisis. Periodic crises of overaccumulation, including the emergence of speculative bubbles, devaluation, and the resulting social and political upheaval, are an inbuilt component of capitalist development. So too, expansion clearly has bi-products: for example, the globalization of capitalist social relations, resource depletion, and ecological and environmental degradation. In short, capital comes up against limitations in its social relations and also its relationship to the natural world, which can be offset for a time but not for ever.

## THE LIMITS TO CORPORATE SOCIAL RESPONSIBILITY AND THE ROLE OF POLITICAL AGENCY

The role of competition in capitalist development places strict limits on the extent of CSR and shapes the way in which we should understand examples of socially "responsible" and "irresponsible" behavior on the part of corporate actors. Inter-capitalist competition means that a successful capitalist enterprise must constantly redirect the surplus value it generates into investments which will increase its future productivity. This means cutting costs, increasing productivity, and expanding production. This naturally places limits on the extent to which any firm in a competitive market can redirect its focus away from profit maximization.

Of course, this does not eliminate the possibility of "socially responsible" behavior entirely. Strategically, well-positioned managers might exploit the autonomy afforded to them to pursue their own personal altruistic interests by sponsoring local sports teams, implementing pro-bono work schemes, or giving charitable donations to local causes. The scale, reach, and extent of these activities will clearly depend on the scale of their organization and their position in the hierarchy. Relatively low-level managers may pursue these objectives at a local level; high-level managers in nationally significant industries may launch nationally significant initiatives. Likewise, businesses may pursue "socially responsible" activity as a means to promote their image or increase their sales, in the way suggested by the "business case" emphasis in the CSR literature.

Both these examples though are clearly constrained in terms of the extent to which CSR can really take hold in a capitalist economy. They rely on either exceptions to the norms of capitalist competition or the subsumption of the idea of social responsibility under the real objective of competitiveness (the Drucker–Friedman logic).

The first example – the altruistic and opportunistic individual – is in fact the perversion of the normal objectives of a capitalist enterprise. If the scale of that activity got too large, the individual firm would succumb to the pressures of capitalist competition. The examples of Ben and Jerry's; Body Shop; and Green and Blacks are all illustrative here, having initially forged a competitive niche on the basis of the value added to their brand by their socially responsible image they have subsequently been swallowed up by larger more profit-seeking competitors. If socially responsible activity got too widespread, thereby alleviating the impact on the competitive pressures facing the individual firm, capitalism itself would slow down and start to atrophy — just the concern that led Friedman (1970) to be so vituperative in his critique of CSR.

Clearly, CSR activity and the autonomy to pursue it might expand where an individual firm faces less competitive pressure in the first place — that is, in a monopoly situation. But once again, this is both an exception to the normative values[2] of capitalism and a serious problem for the health of capitalism as a social system. The empirical evidence about the impact of monopolies also tells us that they are as least as likely to use that position for their own gain as they are for wider social good. There appear at least as many robber barons as there are philanthropists. Indeed, sometimes the two go together and the social objectives of philanthropists can at times be seriously questioned.

The second example of how socially responsible activity might blossom is more in line with the normal operation of capitalism both at the firm and at the social level. Many firms have in fact attempted to engage with CSR as a means of embellishing their brand image with additional value by appealing to the ethical concerns of consumers. However, this is not in fact CSR at all but a carefully implemented strategy to enhance firm competitiveness while offsetting consumer or investor critique by appearing to abide by codes of responsible behavior (Chatterji & Listokin, 2007). This does not mean that "social benefit" is absent. However, to label competitive strategy as *driven by* social rather than private gains is simply to misunderstand the motivation at play. Moreover, careful empirical work on CSR, for example, in the adoption of labor codes of conduct in transnational supply chains, shows how they can be used to maintain uneven geographical development by catching suppliers between twin pressures of compliance with codes of conduct and maintaining cost competition. The outcome is to maintain unequal power relations between western consumer brands and their low-value-added manufacturing suppliers in the developing world, while at the same time meaning that many of those suppliers actually invest heavily in strategies of minimal compliance, evasion, and falsification (Taylor, 2011). It might be tempting to see this as merely irresponsible behavior on the part of individual firms, but that would be to misunderstand the structural pressures at work.

# CAPITALIST SOCIAL RESPONSIBILITY

These structural constraints on corporate agency also suggest that the idea of the social responsibilities of capitalists might be cast in a rather different light: as the shared responsibilities of capitalists as a social class. First, competition and innovation are essential shared responsibilities of all capitalists. As we have seen, without them growth stalls and crises emerge. Rather paradoxically, a Marxist analysis suggests that Friedman is right – the imperative to compete is the first responsibility of capitalists.

Second, since capitalist growth is dependent on the unequal and exploitative nature of the production of surplus value, it is dependent on obscuring and securing this class relation. The next shared responsibility of capitalists, it follows, is to sustain this class relation through a combination of material and ideological action to obscure the exploitative character of capitalist social relations (Banerjee, 2008).

Both these, and additional (see below), elements of capitalist responsibility are sometimes difficult to realize through individual corporate agency. As such, the social interests of capital as a class are often pursued through collective institutions. Membership and representative groups are one means of achieving this, but the modern state was founded on through the requirement to assert the class interests of capital. It simultaneously embodies the codification of private property rights (in legal codes), the development of the coercive capacity (jurisprudence and policing) (Gill, 1998) to uphold these, and the ideological capacity to defend and justify these as natural (through a variety of means, including control of the education system (Gramsci, 1971, pp. 3–43). Whether the state is captured by the capitalist class or subsections of it or is able to exercise "relative autonomy" is largely defined by the balance of class struggle and the nature of inter-capitalist competition (Poulantzas, 2000).

A final element of capitalist responsibility lays in offsetting crisis tendencies. Crisis tendencies in capitalist development are manyfold. They include the agglomeration of capital such that it is hoarded and can no longer find profitable investment opportunities (overaccumulation crises) (Marx, 1867, pp. 762–794; Marx, 1894, pp. 359–368, Ch. 13), the extension of workplace discipline to such an extent that workers are no longer able to purchase final consumer goods (underconsumption crises) (Baran et al., 1966; Luxemburg, 2003) or to regenerate their labor power on a daily or intergenerational basis (reproduction crises) (Gill, 2003) and problems in the sequence of demand for goods between different parts of the economy such that inventories build up, credit markets seize up, or cash-flow problems emerge (disproportionality) (Clarke, 1990; Clarke, 1994). To these might be added a further category of crisis tendencies associated with negative environmental externalities and resource depletion (ecological and raw materials crises). Capitalists and their collective agencies thus have a responsibility to offset these. Again the primary agent of such off-setting is the state and other public agencies. Historical examples of the state playing these roles include the regulation of externalities, the creation of welfare states to assist with social reproduction, or offsetting overaccumulation by investing a portion of the surplus value taken in taxes or lending to the state in long-term projects which only release their productivity benefits over the long term (e.g., housing and infrastructure projects) (Harvey, 1982, p. 427; Harvey, 2003, pp. 109−111). But individual capitalists often undertake these roles also, particularly where the balance of social relations leads to a weak state infrastructure. This is part of the explanation, for example, for the large philanthropic foundations in the United States and their role in offsetting crisis tendencies by providing public goods.

## WHAT PROSPECTS FOR THE CONCEPT OF CORPORATE SOCIAL IRRESPONSIBILITY?

The purpose of this volume is to put forward and elaborate the concept of CSI as an alternative analytical and political tool for the realization of progressive social change. This is motivated by a recognition that CSR has failed to motivate the degree of change in business practices that many of its proponents would like to see. The discussion above shows why CSR has failed: its proponents and academic discussants, ironically save for Milton Friedman, never recognized the severe constraints that hem in corporate agency.

CSI is a relatively recent concept and begins from the premise that there is a spectrum of capitalist agency ranging from the socially responsible at one end to the illegal and irresponsible at the other. Rather than exhort those in the middle of this distribution to ape those at the most virtuous end of the spectrum, the argument is that naming and shaming those at the irresponsible end of the spectrum might have more persuasive power and likelihood of realizing increased social benefit. In this spectrum, CSI is shown as spanning the boundary between legal and illegal practice, and the suggestion is that at least part of what ought to be defined as irresponsible is behavior that falls short of being illegal but is either against the "spirit" of the law or is widely regarded as unethical and in as much might become illegal in the future. Here, the example of tax avoidance (not illegal but about exploiting loopholes and weaknesses in tax law) is illustrative of irresponsible behavior. So too is the exploitation of negative externalities (pollution, etc.) for competitive advantage (Clark & Grantham, 2012).

In one sense, the idea of CSI is appealing in that it is rather like motherhood and apple pie: there is little scope to be against it. Who could be against working to reduce illegal or blatantly exploitative business practices with substantial negative externalities? To that extent, then it is clear that it should be supported. However, the discussion above suggests that proponents of CSI need to bear in mind a series of important features of capitalist growth that will shape their success in shifting the "equivocal zone" of behavior to realize progressive social and economic change.

First, proponents of CSI need to remember that capitalism *per se* is an exploitative social system. Sure it is true that some business practices are more exploitative than others, but the production of surplus value is essentially an exploitative process and therefore even the most "virtuous" business practice is of questionable morality. Marx famously elaborates this in relation to the genesis of capital in the first instance − that is, the accumulation of a mass of money commodities for investment requires unjustifiable dispossession as an *a priori* condition. Historically, this process was bloody and violent (Marx, 1867, Chs. 26−33) and still continues today (Harvey, 2003). Second, since surplus value comes from labor power, it belongs to those whose labor is used in its creation. The argument that capitalists as a social class are owed a portion of this because of their initial investment is not just dismissed on the grounds of the original dispossession but because the consumption of surplus value in the form of profits effectively writes off the initial investment:

> If a capital of £1,000 beget yearly a surplus value of £200, and if this surplus value be consumed every year, it is clear that at the end of 5 years the surplus value consumed will amount to 5 × £200 or the £1,000 originally advanced. If only a part, say one half, were consumed, the same result would follow at the end of 10 years, since 10 × £100 = £1,000…the capitalist; when he has consumed the equivalent of his original capital, the value of his present capital represents nothing but the total amount of the surplus value appropriated by him without payment. Not a single atom of the value of his old capital continues to exist. (Marx, 1867, p. 396)

Third, in capitalism there are both universal and specific elements to the "business ethic." Capitalism always requires a business ethic that supports and upholds contracts and agreements, praises and rewards a certain degree of integrity, and suggests to workers that personal responsibility (a large part of what are currently defined as employability skills – see Nunn et al., 2009) is essential to support their success in selling their labor power. However, the precise nature of these obligations will vary over time and space according to the contours of class struggle and inter-capitalist competition. For example, at one place and time, the balance of inter-capitalist and capitalist working class social relations may support child labor, sweat shops, and environmental degradation, and the predominant business ethic will support, justify, and regulate the norms of interaction around this. In another context, an emphasis on financial services and high-value-added production would lead to a relevant but different business ethic. In yet another social context, the predominant business ethic will support long-term manufacturing, through fostering long-term relationships between manufacturing and finance capital and stable relationships with large-scale organized labor. Varieties in capitalist social relations therefore explain variation in the predominant business ethic.

While it is not surprising that for the most part corporate actors will try to live within the law and the business ethic, the competitive pressures at work mean that there will always be examples of firms and managers that live at the edge of these: toward the left hand side of Clark and Grantham's spectrum. As such, capitalist "irresponsibility" is to be expected – it is the product of inter-capitalist competition and the search for advantage at the margins of "acceptable" competitive strategy. Just as players in a game push the limits of rules and norms and occasionally transgress them, so too it is to be expected that inter-capitalist competition will lead to similar behaviors. Further, just as sports players will often go furthest in this transgression when not in the normal field of play where it is least visible (e.g., by using performance-enhancing drugs in private), then so too it is to be expected that corporate actors will be more likely to transgress social norms when outside of the most visible arena in which they do business.

This irresponsibility at the individual level has system-level implications. Just as *capitalist* social responsibility may manifest itself in actions designed to secure and embed capitalism as a social system, irresponsible behavior can be seen in some contexts to undermine its legitimacy. Transgressions of the law or the rules and norms of capitalist behavior can occasionally undermine the legitimacy of business and capitalism more broadly. Political agency here is clearly important because such transgressions take place within the context of both inter-capitalist competition and class-based social struggle. As such, some capitalists will seek to use irresponsible behavior by others as a means to secure their own position, perhaps by promoting legislation or similar to harm competitors.

This suggests several important considerations for the proponents of CSI. It certainly suggests that CSI is a more appropriate focus than is CSR on the grounds that it avoids falling into the trap of simply supporting the competitive strategy of some firms over others or endorsing superficial window dressing activities which have little or no purchase in reality. It might also form one part of a political strategy to identify symbolically powerful examples of exploitative or unsustainable practice as a means of building support for a progressive transformation of social relations. Indeed, it is just such a "war of position" that Gramsci advocated as a means of bringing about progressive social change (Gramsci, 1971). Such a strategy requires scrutiny of CSI to be part of a political movement as well as an abstract academic concept.

# CONCLUSION

This chapter shows how inter-capitalist competition and capitalist social relations drive and constrain the agency of individual corporate actors to act "responsibly" or "irresponsibly." These limitations are important because policy makers at the local, national, and even global level hope that CSR offers one means of overcoming the constraints that they themselves have placed on the ability of states to solve the complex problems they face in a world of globalization. So too, they appeal to rules, norms, and incentives in the hope of eradicating irresponsible behavior on the part of capitalists.

The limitations on corporate agency generated by inter-capitalist competition and class struggle arise from the need to constantly redirect corporate resources into innovation and to suppress the claims of the working class to realize increases in relative surplus value. These pressures do not eliminate the possibility of "socially responsible" behavior, but they do ensure that it can only emerge in very specific circumstances. Put simply, it is just not possible for CSR to resolve the systemic social and environmental problems generated by capitalism itself. Where it does come to the fore it is usually because there is a fit between some sort of social objective (often superficially pursued) and the profit motive. In these cases though, this is just the pursuit of a market niche, brand value, or sectional interests within capitalism. In such instances, this is simply the normal operation of structural pressures toward competition. It thus follows that there is no need to invent concepts like CSR to describe or understand it. Indeed, doing so may lead to significant misunderstanding.

With these considerations in place, we can think of a different meaning for CSR – as *capitalist* social responsibility. *Capitalist* social responsibility focuses attention on the objectives capitalists must pursue if they are to be successful individually and if capitalism is to flourish. These competitive pressures reveal a positive relationship between the private gains associated with competition and the social gains of capitalists as a class. This is manifested in multiple ways from the general pursuit of competitiveness (*alá* Friedman) to the imposition of discipline on society in general. The common theme that unites the different aspects of *capitalist* social responsibility is the pursuit of the general interests of the capitalist class or its subsections, rather than the interests of society more generally. In this context, CSI might also be understood in a specific way: as behavior that transgresses the social norms associated with capitalism in any particular context. Such transgressions should be expected as the product of the pressures generated by inter-capitalist competition, but in certain contexts, they can undermine the legitimacy of capitalism as a social system, or at least variants of it.

Academic attempts to identify and expose CSI need to bear in mind the structural limits to the role of corporate agency in achieving progressive change. Attention needs to be focused on the socially and environmentally exploitative nature of capitalist social relations. But with that consideration in place, CSI could usefully form part of a broader based political project to identify and expose exploitation in an effort to transform those social relations.

# NOTES

1. At the time of writing this chapter in July 2011, News International was engulfed in criminal and parliamentary inquiries into the role of major newspapers in tapping the phones of prominent politicians, celebrities, and victims of crime. The scandal associated with this followed the line that journalists and editors responsible for this had acted irresponsibly and in so doing had led to a crisis of legitimacy in the privately owned print media and the political influence of news organizations like News International.

2. It is a subversion of the rhetorical ideal of capitalism – but as Marx comprehensively shows there are distinct and powerful pressures toward both centralization and monopoly present in capitalist development. Unfortunately, a full discussion of these is beyond the scope of this chapter.

# REFERENCES

Banerjee, S. B. (2008). Corporate social responsibility: The good, the bad and the ugly. *Critical Sociology, 34*(1), 51–79.

Baran, P. A., Sweezy, P., et al. (1966). *Monopoly capital. An essay on the American economic and social order,* pp. ix. 402. New York & London: Monthly Review Press.

Bowen, H. R. (1953). *Social responsibilities of the businessman.* New York: Harper.

Cameron, D. (2011). Speech on the big society. Milton Keynes, Number 10 Downing Street.

Cammack, P. (2006). The politics of global competitiveness. Papers in the Politics of Global Competitiveness, 1.

Cammack, P. (2008). *Building BRICs for global competitiveness: The OECD and the emerging market economies.* Papers in the Politics of Global Competitiveness.

Carroll, A. (1979a). A three-dimensional conceptual model of corporate performance. *Academy of Management. The Academy of Management Review, 4,* 497–505.

Carroll, A. B. (1979b). A three-dimensional conceptual model of corporate performance. *The Academy of Management Review, 4*(4), 497–505.

Carroll, A. B. (1999). Corporate social responsibility. *Business & Society, 38*(3), 268–295.

Chatterji, A. & Listokin, S. (2007). Corporate social irresponsibility. DemocracyJournal.Org. Winter.

Clark, T. S., & Grantham, K. N. (2012). What CSR is not: Corporate social irresponsibility. In W. Sun, R. Tench & B. Jones (Eds.), *Corporate social irresponsibility: A challenging concept emerging from the shadow of corporate social responsibility.* Leeds: Emerald.

Clarke, S. (1990). The Marxist theory of overaccumulation and crisis. *Science & Society, 54*(4), 442–467.

Clarke, S. (1994). *Marx's theory of crisis.* Basingstoke: Macmillan.

Dahlsrud, A. (2008). How corporate social responsibility is defined: An analysis of 37 definitions. *Corporate Social Responsibility and Environmental Management, 15,* 1–13.

Davis, K. (1960). Can business afford to ignore social responsibilities. *California Business Review, 2,* 70–76.

Drucker, P. (1984). The new meaning of corporate social responsibility. *The California Business Review, 26,* 53–63.

Friedman, M. (1970). The social responsibility of business is to increase its profits. *The New York Times Magazine.*

Gill, S. (1998). New constitutionalism, democratisation and global political economy. *Pacifica Review, 10*(1), 23–38.

Gill, S. (2003). Social reproduction of affluence and human in/security. In S. Gill & I. Bakker (Eds.), *Power, production and social reproduction.* Basingstoke: Palgrave Macmillan.

Gramsci, A. (1971). *Selections from the prison notebooks of Antonio Gramsci.* London: Lawrence and Wishart.

Hale, A. (2008). *Organising and networking in support of garment workers: Why we researched subcontracting chains* (pp. 40–68). *Threads of labour,* Angela Hale: Blackwell Publishing Ltd, pp. 40–68.

Harvey, D. (1982). *The limits to capital.* London: Verso.

Harvey, D. (2003). *The new imperialism.* Oxford: Oxford University Press.

Hudson, I., & Hudson, M. (2003). Removing the veil? *Organization & Environment, 16*(4), 413–430.

Jones, B. (2010). *Corporate social irresponsibility: The role of government and ideology. Reframing corporate social responsibility: Lessons from the global financial crisis.* Bingley: Emerald.

Jones, B., Bowd, R., et al. (2009). Corporate social responsibility and corporate social irresponsibility: Competing realities. *Corporate Social Responsibility Journal, 5*(3), 300–310.

Luxemburg, R. (2003). *The accumulation of capital.* London: Routledge.

Marx, K. (1867). *Capital: A critique of political economy.* Moscow Progress Publishers.

Marx, K. (1894). *Capital volume 3: The process of capitalist production as a whole.* New York: International Publishers.

Marx, K., & Engels, F. (1848). *The manifesto of the communist party.* Moscow: Progress Publishers.

Matten, D., & Moon, J. (2008). "Implicit" and "Explicit" CSR: A conceptual framework for a comparative understanding of corporate social responsibility. *Academy of Management Review, Academy of Management, 33,* 404–424.

Morton, A. D. (2006). The Grimly comic riddle of Hegemony in IPE: Where is class struggle? *Politics, 26*(1), 62–72.

Nunn, A., Bickerstaffe, T., et al. (2009). *The employability skills project.* Wath-upon-Dearne, UK: Commission for Employment and Skills.

Poulantzas, N. (2000). *State, power, socialism.* London: Verso Classics.

Rosenau, J. (1995). Governance in the 21st century. In R. Wilkinson (Ed.), *The global governance reader. Oxon.* Routledge.

Rosenau, J. (2002). Governance in a new global order. In D. Held & A. Mcgrew. (Eds.), *Governing globalization* (pp. 70–86). Cambridge: Polity.

Ruggie, J. G. (2004). Reconstituting the global public domain – issues, actors, and practices. *European Journal of International Relations, 10,* 499–531.

Shaw, W. (2009). Marxism, business ethics, and corporate social responsibility. *Journal of Business Ethics, 84*(4), 565–576.

Taylor, M. (2011). Race you to the bottom ... and back again? The Uneven development of labour codes of conduct. *New Political Economy, 16*(4), 445–462.

Taylor, N. A. J. (2012). A rather delicious paradox: Social responsibility and the manufacture of armaments. In W. Sun, R. Tench & B. Jones (Eds.), *Corporate social irresponsibility: A challenging concept emerging from the shadow of corporate social responsibility.* Leeds: Emerald.

Wood, E. M. (1995). *Democracy against capitalism: Renewing historical Materialism.* Cambridge: Cambridge University Press.

Wood, E. M. (2002). *Empire of capital.* London: Verso.

Yu, X. (2008). Impacts of corporate code of conduct on labor standards: A case study of Reebok's athletic footwear supplier factory in China. *Journal of Business Ethics, 81*(3), 513–529.

# THE JANUS DIALECTIC OF CORPORATE SOCIAL IRRESPONSIBILITY AND CORPORATE SOCIAL RESPONSIBILITY – THE ROLE OF MICRO-MOMENTS

Peter Stokes

## ABSTRACT

Purpose – *This chapter examines the central and potent role of 'micro-moments' in relation to the development and construction of corporately responsible cultures and environments.*

Methodology/approach – *The chapter engages a participant observational method set within an interpretivist methodology. The data generated take the form of vignettes which are used to explore the issues.*

Findings – *The discussion and argument demonstrate that while much worthwhile attention has been paid to the macro aspects and dimensions of corporate social responsibility, less scrutiny has been focused on the myriad micro-moments that operate to ultimately create macro-settings.*

Corporate Social Irresponsibility: A Challenging Concept
Critical Studies on Corporate Responsibility, Governance and Sustainability, Volume 4, 83–108
Copyright © 2012 by Emerald Group Publishing Limited
All rights of reproduction in any form reserved
ISSN: 2043-9059/doi:10.1108/S2043-9059(2012)0000004013

*The chapter illustrates the nature of micro-moments and shows their interactive nature combined with their consequences and implications for building corporately social irresponsible or corporately social responsible environments.*

Research limitations/implications − *The chapter underlines the vital role of micro-moments for corporate social responsibility. The data consist of a number of vignettes which illustrate a particular circumscribed setting. As is commonly the case with inductive research, further work, mindful of on-going reliability and validity measures, will be required to assess the generalisability of the findings across other sectors and organisations.*

Practical implications − *The chapter affords people working in organisations the opportunity to reflect on their actions in the micro-moment and scale them towards corporately social responsible outcomes.*

Social implications − *Improvement of micro-moment interactions should work to improve corporate social responsibility across a range of organisational settings.*

Originality/value − *The chapter constructs a novel argument in relation to micro-moments and demonstrates through original vignette data the impact and interplay of micro-moments for corporate social responsibility/irresponsibility.*

**Keywords:** Micro-moments; corporate social responsibility/irresponsibility; ethics

In the twenty-first century, the idea of corporate social responsibility (CSR) has come to form an accepted part of both corporate and public discourses (CSR Europe, 2011; Friedman, 1970; Marens, 2010; Newton, Englehardt, & Pritchard, 2010; Principles for Responsible Management Education (PRME), 2011; Roberts, 2003; Tams & Marshall, 2010). In terms of understanding CSR, it is widely acknowledged that corporate boardrooms and organisational directorates, in recognition of growing public consciousness and activism, should undertake responsibilities towards bodies, entities and communities that go beyond simply 'producing goods and services within the law' (Hartman & DesJardins, 2008, p. 306). As a consequence, the debate on CSR now plays out across a span of governmental, commercial, academic and third sector (Scherer & Palazzo, 2007; Knights & Willmott, 2011, pp. 285–304). However, while much progress has been made, and CSR processes can be seen as having evolved substantially, it is nevertheless self-evident that we are still a long way from inhabiting utopian societal and organisational realms. Well-publicised reports of various corporate debacles and dilemmas evidence the fact that undesirable and negative practices of corporate social irresponsibility (here-after termed CSI) seem as prevalent as much as those of the desired and positive CSR.

Much of the focus on CSR has tended to concentrate on actions and contexts at the *organisational* rather than the *individual* level. This organisational activity generally manifests itself in the form of edicts and policy formulation regarding, for example, values and mission statements combined with CSR initiatives and responsible postures. On the other hand, the focus on the individual level has commonly been addressed through the discipline of business ethics which feed into corporate structures and policies (Chryssides & Kaler, 1993; Lawrence, Weber, & Post, 2010; Crane & Matten, 2010; Griseri & Seppala, 2010). We have already indicated that organisations sometimes 'get things badly wrong', however, what is less considered are the myriad micro-processes that bring this about. Business ethics has assisted to some degree in bridging this gap, but its focus has often been as much on philosophical frameworks and larger critical incidents or *major* moments of choice. In fact, more crucial perhaps are the often neglected or overlooked myriad *micro-moments* of both 'good' (sic: responsible) and 'bad' (sic: irresponsible) behaviour in everyday organisational lives. Good and bad *micro-moments* provide an indication that the domains of responsible and irresponsible behaviour cohabit in a closer, or more conjoined, spatial and temporal manner than is often presented in CSR or business ethics writings. This chapter, through the use of empirical field data, and the application of the metaphor of the ancient world mythical two-headed Janus, explores the cohabitation between responsible and irresponsible behaviour in micro-moments and, in particular, proposes positive stances in which responsible and irresponsible acts might be considered.

# CORPORATE SOCIAL RESPONSIBILITY AND IRRESPONSIBILITY – MICRO-MOMENTS AND THE JANUS DIALECTIC

*A Consideration of the Micro-Moment in Relation to CSR–CSI*

In the late twentieth century and early twenty-first century, CSR has emerged as a domain in its own right. The area is now underpinned by

extensive bodies of academic and practitioner commentary and incorpo-
rates and broaches notions of, *inter alia*, organisational justice, corporate
governance and responsible management. Moreover, the concept and operation of CSR has been rolled out across the sphere of human activity and
CSR now forms an unavoidable part of the *zeitgeist* of our era. Nevertheless, achieving an all-encompassing definition of CSR is a challenging task.
Daft, Murphy, and Willmott (2010, p. 134) provide a basic but useful
departure point for defining CSR as

> management's obligation to make choices and take actions that will contribute to the
> welfare and interests of society as well as the organization.

In expanding his definition, Daft et al. introduces the central issue of
'stakeholders' in relation to CSR. This is important to the current discussion and it is interesting that in his *a priori* definition, Daft et al., while
acknowledging the impact of CSR-related issues on a wide range of individuals and groups, nevertheless stresses the role of *managers* as the key
agents in ensuring CSR compliance.

Moreover, CSR is kindred with the realms of sustainability and business
ethics and the proposition that behaving in a socially and ethically responsible manner will engender sustainable businesses together with the environments in which they operate. A key proponent of the inclusion of
sustainable and responsible aspects into business planning was Elkington
(1997) who introduced the notion of the 'triple bottom line' (*TBL*) of
*profit, people, planet*. Elkington asserted that a business which does not
develop a TBL cannot be properly mindful of the full costs of its operations. Within the twists and turns of the overall CSR debate, the tension
between efficiency and profit metrics, ethically 'good' corporate citizenship
and conduct has been an enduring one. With this in mind, sustainability
has been variously translated into, for example, green, environmental, self-
sufficiency, ecopreneurship, energy-efficiency and carbon footprint policies
(Dixon & Clifford, 2007; Berners-Lee, 2010). Within the present argument,
the discussion sees *responsible choices* and *behaviour* in micro-moments (the
myriad everyday fleeting encounters, exchanges and glances that occur in
life including work settings) as leading to *sustainable situations and environments* and *irresponsible behaviour and poor choices* as leading to *unsustainable conditions* and settings.

We have introduced above the idea of the 'micro-moment' in relation to
organisational cultures and it is also worthy of note that it is one that has
received attention in wider aspects of the literature as well as the media.
Typical of this latter reportage is a heading from *The Los Angeles Times*

(Roan, 2009) – 'The key to happiness is living in the micro-moment'. The article catches the spirit of much of the popular commentary on micro-moments which is the idea of 'carpe diem' (seize the day) and the enjoyment of the 'now' rather than the unrelenting pursuit of hectic and busy modern lives that postpones the savouring of the small and simple pleasure of everyday life, interactions and routines. From these writings, it is also possible to take the important idea of the crucial nature of the concept and experience of the moment – it is not merely fleeting and ephemeral but also simultaneously potentially seminal. However, the idea of focusing on the micro and moments in various guises has also been discussed within management and organisation writing. The idea of, for example, 'Moments of Truth' is associated with Jan Carlzon, former CEO of SAS Airlines (Carlzon & Peters, 1989). Carlzon points up the crucial nature of treating every moment of interaction with customers correctly and appropriately from the outset. Reflecting 'The Ten Commandments', he proposes illustrations of 'Moments of Truth':

When we talk to a customer on the phone

When a customer walks through the door

When a customer asks a question

When a customer purchases a product

When a customer returns a product

When a customer enters of leaves the parking lot (area).

Carlzon shows that when a passenger boards a plane, sits down and then, for example, notices litter on the floor, stains on the seats and the pull-down table, this represents a 'moment of truth'. Carlzon states that the customer might rightly ask if this is the state of the cabin what level of attention is being accorded to other, for example, technical aspects of the flight and service? Carlzon and Peters' (1989) commentary is concerned with *customer* interaction; however, clearly, their work also indicates the essential importance of the concept and reality of the 'moment'. This might exhibit managerialistic, jingoistic and rhetorical tones common to management edicts such as 'Making people feel like they are really needed' and 'people are our most important resource', but it is nevertheless valuable in drawing attention to the criticality of the notion of 'moment'. Furthermore, allusions and commentaries on moments can also be located in, for example, leadership and coaching literatures. For example, Shaw (2010) builds a thesis around the concept of the 'Defining Moments' in peoples' lives. He usefully explores this theme through examination of notions of, for example, 'light-going on moments', 'surprising moments', standing-back moments', 'joyful moments', 'crisis moments', 'moments of anger' and so on and so forth. Although he does not pursue it, he lays the foundations for the possible development of typology, or at very least a framework, of 'moments' for change environments.

## A Contribution from Business Ethics to Understanding the Micro-Moment

As was alluded to above, business ethics also has a potentially interconnected and important role to play in an understanding of CSR and CSI moments (Chryssides & Kaler, 1993; Lawrence, Weber, & Post, 2010; Crane & Matten, 2010; Griseri & Seppala, 2010). It is significant to note that the much of this literature is commonly structured around presentations and considerations of well-rehearsed philosophical frames of reference that invoke and address various deliberations on deontology, utilitarianism, egoism and so on an so forth. These provide long-standing and valuable theory in relation to which individuals or collectives might make sense of choices between seemingly 'good' and 'bad' situations and ethical dilemmas. Both macro- and especially micro-behaviour are potentially informed by a range of ethical frameworks because sense making begins at the level of the individual (Weick, 1995, 2001). From within the field of business ethics, 'good' and 'bad' behaviour, in relation to responsible and sustainable conduct in organisations, illustrates the manners in which individuals continue to behave in ways that might be generally be judged 'bad' or 'good' by others in daily organisational life. Clearly, as indicated above, what is 'good' and 'bad' rapidly becomes, to a greater or lesser extent (and certainly at the margins of any decision), a subjective moral and ethical debate. On this point, in discussing ethical behaviour in the micro-moment, it is useful to consider the work on 'virtue ethics' conducted by the ancient Greek philosopher Aristotle (384–322 BC). In his exploration of the nature of a desirable human condition to the ethical challenges of life, Aristotle stated that the key was the development of 'character'. This was seen as being in contrast to dedicating extensive energies to the development of prescriptive bodies of rules and codes. In other words, by developing personality and character of the individual, Aristotle contended that he or she would innately *be*, or have, a nature of a certain positive manner. This, in turn, is seen as being conducive to an individual, *de facto*, conducting him or herself in an appropriate manner in the situations and contexts that arise. This, therefore, is Aristotle's appeal for the 'ethical individual' rather than aiming to control behaviour through a set of rules or codes, externally developed and imposed (MacIntyre, 1981; Fisher & Lovell, 2008).

Aristotle's postulation can be seen in partial contrast to the position developed by, for example, deontological perspectives and the work of the Immanuel Kant (1724–1804). Kant argued that the path towards 'good' ethical behaviour is through the progressive, experiential and evolutionary development of the notion of the *categorical imperative* (Chryssides & Kaler, 1999; Hartman & DesJardins, 2008). This imperative would consist of the development of rules for appropriate conduct that could be accepted and added to the overall canon of ethical behaviour. In other words, rules so devised could be established as broadly acceptable and universally applicable principles. Kant's position is commonly summarised as 'do unto others as you would have done unto yourself' or equally illustrated by all embracing religious codes such as, for example, The Ten Commandments. Thus, deontology offers a code to guide behaviour and steer choice – *what we should do*, whereas pursuit of virtue ethics tells us *how we should be* – and this in turn is seen as likely to engender the appropriate 'doing' or behaviour. It can be argued, of course, that both have a role to play in personal and professional individual and organisational life. On the one hand, we would hope for people to have a disposition that is inherently 'good' and yet at the same time we may also acknowledge that we need to make rules that guide people to behave well or responsibly. The crux, then, for the present argument is that the micro-moment is the instant of choice – a choice between dialectics of good and bad positions, rights and wrongs, greater and lesser evils – which have ultimate implications for responsible and sustainable action. Individuals have to work to make the 'right' choices in a given moment. To make the 'wrong' choices mean that harm or damage may be caused as a consequence. This in turn works to engender 'remembered pain' in the individual living the experience of the harm whereby the individual builds up a memory of things that have happened and does not necessarily forget them. The implication, therefore, seems to be that a combination of a virtue ethics and deontological approach may provide a basis for actions that avoid the creation of 'remembered pain'. Moreover, in relation to choice, the idea that sometimes individuals do not have a choice is roundly rejected as disingenuous by, for example, the French philosopher, Jean-Paul Sartre and his notion of *mauvaise foi* (i.e. disingenuous or bad faith)(1943/2003). Sartre suggested that it is inauthentic for a person to suggest that he or she does not have a choice in

any given set of circumstances — that is even in seemingly impossible settings there is always choice and in taking it we move away from slipping
into a normative CSI mode of operating:

> Every day, every hour, offered the opportunity to make a decision, a decision which
> determined whether or not you would become the *plaything of circumstance, renouncing*
> *freedom and dignity to become moulded into the form of the typical inmate.* (Frankl,
> 1946) [Emphasis added]

In many ways, many extant commentaries from business ethics may also
be seen as providing forms of idealistic stances which might be viewed as
dislocated from a 'lived experience' of handling and dealing with ethical
moments (Knights & Willmott, 1999; Stokes, 2011). The notion of 'lived
experience' is concerned with attempts to elaborate richer understandings
of how an individual or group make sense of life and the events, structures
and relationships that constitute their experiences (Weick, 1995, 2001).
Lived experience's desire to portray life with all its emotion and perception
and in this way, it offers something in stark contrast to many of the often
dry, sterile and anodyne representations offered in normative and mainstream textbooks. Knights and Willmott's (1999) work *Management Lives:*
*Power and Identity in Work Organizations* has been an important landmark
study in this regard. They employ the resource of novels to elaborate 'lived
experience' life. This aspect of the discussion also underscores the important point that micro-moments can be understood through myriad textual
lenses. Although it may seem stark and remote in comparison to many
experiences in everyday life — 'lived experience' — also draws upon a range
of *extreme* organisational contexts and micro-moments. In relation to this
point, Stokes and Gabriel (2010) even identify organisational parallels with
genocidal contexts. Thus, business ethics makes an important contribution
to understanding individual situations, but it frequently achieves this in a
manner that seems remote from everyday experience. Moreover, business
ethics has frequently been charged as constituting a 'bolt-on' to management courses and organisational procedures and policies rather than being
an innate way of thinking and behaving within and around corporations
and organisations (Locke & Spender, 2011; MacVeigh & Norton, 2011).

### Surfacing the Character of CSR–CSI: Culture, Micro-Moments and the Janus-Dialectic

In a similar problematising vein, in spite of the appeals of Elkington
(1997) and others noted above, much of the debate on CSR, and its

associated sustainability, has also been couched in terms of corporate *ends*, or, alternatively expressed, as something delivering, *inter alia*, greater reputation, competitive advantage, cost savings or enhanced profits rather than a purely altruistic or idealistic purpose (see, e.g. EFMD, 2010). Moreover, the predominance of this corporate-focused performativity imperative aspect is commonly aligned with strong inclinations towards, for instance, organisational 'continuity' and sustainability (Parada & Viladás, 2010) or, more bluntly expressed, *corporate survival*. Recognising this, Milne, Kearins, and Walton (2006) satirise corporate reports as a journey, dressed up in a particular discourse and language which 'paradoxically, serves to further reinforce business-as-usual' rather than any genuine enlightened approach to sustainable and responsible action. In spite of the many positive developments in the realms of CSR, it remains valid to say that the multiple and recurrent issues of conflict, scandals, crises and disingenuous action and words continue to be evidenced in organisational life and that it might be possible to characterise this as a form of *failed CSR* or alternatively as CSI.

Within much of the extant commentary on CSR, the 'unit of action and analysis' (and hence sense making) (Weick, 1995, 2001) is focused on the macro-level of the firm or organisation rather individual or one-to-one, micro-interactions or micro-moments. In other words, it is the firm, company or organisation which is seen as the *prima facie* sense-making unit for any meaningful action and outcomes. Whereas, in fact, it might be argued that responsibility at the individual level pre-dates and pre-determines outcomes and collective responsibility at the macro-level. While the role of the individual manager or employee is clearly recognised as important, the CSR literature *de facto* seems to have a predilection to focus predominantly on the corporate, or *macro*, level. As such the corporate entity (albeit under managerial control) is, so to speak, the 'unit' of analysis and action. While the CSR literature does indeed embrace a wide concept of 'stakeholders', there is nevertheless a sense that the relative power of non-managerial stakeholders (both within and outside the organisation) is on occasion limited. On the other hand, within management literature, one of the arenas where such issues are often addressed is the notion of 'managing (corporate/organizational) culture'. Culture and micro-moments are inextricably linked. It can be suggested that any given culture is the product of multifarious micro-moments and repetitions of behaviours (Berger & Luckmann, 1966; Weick, 1995, 2001). Culture embraces a vast sphere of influences and commentaries, encompassing notions of judgement in conjunction with matters of intellectual, artistic and social development. It is not the purpose of the present discussion to examine culture as its central focus; nevertheless, it will be valuable to develop a background under-standing of how cultures can be cultivated in relation to ethics and micro-moment choice of individual action as it is in this amalgam that CSR or CSI can occur. Culture is most frequently explained as shared values, beliefs, atmospheres, customs and practices, goals and missions present in an organisation (Clegg, Kornberger, & Pitsis, 2011, pp. 263–298). In mainstream managerialistic texts, which can be characterised as broadly embracing a perspective grounded in rationalism, objectification, as opposed to a more subjectivised, 'lived experience' (Knights & Willmott, 1999; Stokes, 2011), corporate culture is discussed as something that managers need to control and direct with the aim of higher production and performativity. Therein, resistance, or alternatively expressed the exercising of choice, is more often than not represented as problematic and something to be marginalised or overcome (Linstead, Fulop, & Lilley, 2009, pp. 93–122; Stokes, 2011).

In contrast, a critical perspectives approach questions whether it is appropriate or helpful to attempt to construct and perceive culture as something that is predominantly coherent, fixed, structured and stable. From a critical perspective, culture in organisations is more likely to be viewed as organic and evolving patterns of behaviour, shifting power alli-ances and evolving discourses, narratives and identities rather than being fixed in nature (Alvesson, 2002; Badham, Garrety, Morrigan, & Zanko, 2003; Buchanan & Badham, 2009; Parker, 2000; Rhodes & Parker, 2008; Stokes, 2011). A critical stance resonates with the argument of the present discussion and provides an insight into the variously CSR or CSI-prone organisation. The organisation at the macro-level is fundamentally depen-dent on the micro-behaviours, attitudes and, of paramount importance, the *choices* that people make at the micro-level of everyday organisational life and culture (Kira, Eijnatten, & Balkin, 2010). This implies that it is vital to examine and be mindful of the multifarious micro-events and encounters of organisational everyday life and places importance, not just on trying to behave responsibly at some critical incidents or key moments, but also in the myriad micro-moments − every glance, exchange, action and interac-tion. Moreover, this echoes Popper's (1945) challenge, in the domain of science, against generalised macro-historicist approaches and his call for greater attention to be paid to the micro-processes that underpin scientific decision and sense making.

The juncture of the individual and the collective culture, or alternatively phrased the micro and the macro, turns our gaze of the debate firmly towards this micro-level. Central to ideas of responsibility and choice within a given culture are the *attitudes, values and mindsets* that underpin attempts to engender desirable sustainable and responsible activity and behaviour. Implicitly, herein we are thinking of the notion of sustainability as being as equally germane to values and behaviour as to, for example, environmental and carbon foot print concerns. If an organisation is to have a culture that is sustainable (which in turn will mean that the organisation, *per se*, is sustainable) then it must factor in not only ethical ethos but also job-related processes. Kira, Van Eijnatten, and Balkin (2010) develop the idea of crafting sustainable work through the development of 'personal resources'. They make a case that it is vital to appreciate this and factor sustainability into *job design* of individuals. In addition, Marcum (2009) introduces the notion of 'sustainability by engagement' and highlights the role of the manager in engendering motivation and staff commitment in employees. These are useful insights; however, overall, they appear rooted in a mainstream frame of reference — a predilection to taking actions that will ensure corporate survival rather than adherence necessarily to any particular ideals. By this it is meant that the literature on CSR has a tendency to exude a *modernistic, teleological and managerialist* tone, whereby it is managers and directors rather than other employees who are picked out as having the function, rights, power, responsibility and authority to set targets in order to bring to fruition agendas and actions on sustainability (Stokes, 2011). Of course, managers *are* invested with authority to direct organisational affairs; however, this does not remove the fact that in executing their roles, managers might also on occasion conduct their responsibilities in a poorly judged, unethical or irresponsible manner. Moreover, a placing of the spotlight primarily on managers ignores the crucial contribution and role played by other, majority, organisational employees. There is therefore scope to reconsider approaches to choice and responsibility within cultures in a manner that moves beyond its current macro, rhetorical and normative representations. Here, 'normative' can be characterised as generally espousing mono-dimensional, rationalistic, objectified, quasi-scientific approaches rather than subjectivised, 'lived experience' rich and multi-perspective orientated appreciations or organisation and management (Knights & Willmott, 1999; McCabe, 2007; Stokes, 2011). By developing a deeper understanding of micro-moments of responsible behaviour, it is contended that the foundations for more effective change and transformatory processes in organisations may be developed.

Drawing on the above overall discussion of comments on 'moments', it can therefore be seen that 'micro-moments' crystallise into the macro-situations and events that manifest into cultures, situations and atmospheres. More specifically, and empirically, micro-moments consist of, variously, for example, the dialectics and dualities of individual dubious and honourable conduct, choice and responsibility embracing, for example, a potentially potent cocktail of Machiavellian-style (to use the term in its modern idiom) gossip, lies, naivety, deceit, political manoeuvring and misrepresentation jostle for position and interplay with aspirations of hope integrity, honesty, directness, reputation and wisdom − often simultaneously in any given moment or incident (Machiavelli, 1532/2008; Michelson, van Iterson, & Waddington, 2010). Within these incidental moments, how managers, leaders and other organisational members and employees respond to issues of choice and responsibility, often in a series of multiple and contiguous fleeting moments, is paramount. This is not simply a question of organisational politics or micro-political survival in the organisational 'jungle'. Rather it should also be underpinned by a Kantian or Aristotelian form of ethical human desire for satisfaction, happiness, well-being and to live and cohabit in an environment that exudes a sense, albeit often highly subjective, of being decent, honourable and, in essence, meaningful and worthwhile. This then would constitute an approach towards an idealist posture of a responsible and sustainable organisation seen through the micro-lens.

Thus, it can be seen that the development of responsible and sustainable organisational life is accomplished through the building of responsible values and principles in the myriad micro-situations. This is not something that can be adhered to in one moment and conveniently or expediently overlooked in the next. Rather, it must be adhered to assiduously and maintained through the multifarious choices and situations of everyday 'lived experience'. The work environment does not always present 'clean' and clear-cut situations and choices and there will be constant invitation and temptation to enter what Levi (1958/1987, 1986/1988) calls the 'grey zone' (sic: ambivalent, amoral and ambiguous) of situations and behaviour. These challenging and seemingly paradoxical choices live potentially side by side and it is the choice by the individual towards the Aristotelian and Kantian-style responsible (as opposed to irresponsible) actions and postures that can determine the success of the micro-moment of lived experience. On this depend the sustainability and accomplishment of the overall gradual processes of organisational change at macro-levels and the achievement of CSR overall. In this way, the micro-moment becomes the 'thin end of the wedge' for the macro-moment.

Therefore, it is possible to view a CSR−CSI dialectic as presenting itself in a *Janus-like* manner. In Roman mythology, Janus was represented by a two-headed god symbolising 'gateways' and 'doorways' and therefore spatial and temporal transition. In association with this, he also embodied notions of 'beginnings' and 'endings' in relation to time. Thus, in the same-way that CSR and CSI seem to point, prima facie in opposing directions so too do the two heads of Janus. However, therein resides a metaphorical tension and a paradox. As in the case of Janus, CSR and CSI dwell on, and form part of, the *same body*, entity or *same organisation*. Here, it is meant body both of the individual person and body as organisation. The potential for CSR and CSI incidents or moments therefore reside in the *same domain*. It is not, in fact, the case that we should look at CSR as some form of normative aspirational or operational situation and, alternatively, on CSI as the problematic exception. At the instance of choice in the micro-moment, individuals have the chance to make choices about employing seemingly unimportant, but nevertheless crucial, micro-behaviours involving, for example, 'white-lies', 'economy of truths', gossip, glossing facts, spin-doctoring and politicking and so on and so forth. These moments are in fact vital. Each moment contributes towards building the ultimate macro-picture, culture and environment. Done wrongly, it will create remembered pain. Done well, it will facilitate the building of a 'good' and worthwhile culture. In so doing, and in alignment with a Janus-faced notion, people and organisations have the possibility of moving through contrasting portals and gateways leading to potentially very distinct and contrasting destinations and outcomes. In sum, the segregation of CSR and CSI is less distinct than at first may seem to be the case and, in fact, they cohabit the same micro-moment of choice. The discussion now moves on to examine these phenomena in the field.

# A METHODOLOGY FOR CONSIDERING CSI MICRO-MOMENTS

The research data are gathered through longitudinal ethnographic interpretive methodological approaches (Van Maanen, 1988, 2010). The research involved everyday participant observation and document analysis (e.g. including email content) research methods within a quasi-public organisation setting concerned (Waddington, 2004). The observations were conducted over a three-year period and involved access to a range of meetings and everyday interactions. Data were recorded in notebooks and took the form of story-style accounts, vignettes and email extracts.

The research setting constituted a study of a business unit comprising some 25 professionals working in a department within a larger entity of some 100–120 colleagues. For reasons of research ethics and respondent confidentiality, it is not possible to provide more extensive detail on the context. The group was made up equally of male and females and 60% of them had worked in the organisation for more than 12 years. The remaining individuals had generally worked in the setting for less than five years.

The observation was necessarily conducted covertly and implicitly, and as a consequence it was neither appropriate nor possible to seek positive consent from the many respondents. Moreover, a further reason for this approach was that the intention was not to directly or deliberately influence behaviours and quasi-Hawthorne effects (Roethlisberger & Dickson, 1939). However, with regard to reflexivity, it was recognised that the researcher–respondent relationship implies a joint role in sense-making process which is unavoidable and inevitable (Alvesson & Sköldberg, 2009). In relation to the narratives, and as a consequence of the above access issues, all participants and organisations have been anonymised in order to protect confidentiality.

The data analysis employed critical moment analysis linked to storytelling and sense-making approaches in order to develop a thematic analysis of the patterns of behaviour and attendant consequences (Berger & Luckmann, 1966; Czarniawska, 1998; Gabriel, 2000; Watson & Harris, 1999; Weick, 1995, 2001). In selecting data for the chosen micro-moments, the focus was on CSI-linked (rather than CSR building) moments. It was felt that such moments offer insights on instances that show how a micro-moment of irresponsible behaviour gradually contributes to the overall building of a CSI culture. It would, of course, also be possible to choose from the data other myriad micro-moments to discuss, but in general they would serve to replicate and reinforce the illustrative data presented here in the available space. Nevertheless, in the section that follows the data and comments on the experiences, there is the necessary attempt to show the CSI–CSR Janus like dimensions and consequences of the situations presented.

These moments operated in conjunction with an acknowledgement of the role of 'lived experience' within the tradition of critical perspectives (Knights & Willmott, 1999; Clegg, Kornberger, & Pitsis, 2011; McCabe, 2007; Stokes & Gabriel, 2010). Methodologically, the amalgam of the notion of lived experience, narratives and stories attempts to elaborate richer understandings of how an individual or group make sense of life and the events, structures and relationships that constitute their experiences (Weick, 1995, 2001). Therefore, methodologically, lived experience is a valuable device for identifying, describing and examining corporately socially irresponsible and responsible micro-moments in closer detail.

## BACKGROUND TO THE CSI FIELD MICRO-MOMENTS

The researched department, and indeed the overall setting, had experienced substantial change in recent years against an industry sector context of on-going transformation. Within the group, there were a range of tensions as people sought to develop team projects and new projects for client delivery. The newly appointed manager was not readily accepted by a small number of the senior members of the team. This therefore constituted a significant task with the objective being to change and transform the culture and behaviour of the department at the same time as modernising and enhancing the product portfolio and performance.

Prior to the arrival of the new manager, these particular members had held the position of manager but, after a relatively short period of time, and, for various motives and reasons had decided not to continue in the role (generally believed in the organisation to be grounded on selfish reasons because they had stayed in the role only long enough to secure and confirm promotion grades for themselves). A majority of the remaining staff had welcomed the new manager as a 'breath of fresh air' and for not being part of the old 'mafia' or 'pasta club'. It was termed this based on the predilection of the overall controlling group in the organisation to invite 'the chosen acolytes' (including the former managers) to the occasional informal social/business talk dinners at a local Italian restaurant. This 'club' also variously drew in the occasional senior members and 'friends' from lower graded staff. Gossip and reports in relation to 'Pasta Club' indicted that all manner of confidential matters were often openly discussed which many people residing 'outside' the Club felt blurred lines of confidentiality and partiality in trying to conduct everyday business.

There was also evidence of bullying and manipulation taking place by this 'unofficial' plutarchy towards other members of the team and indeed wider members of the organisation. This would manifest itself in a range of forms including sinister emails containing veiled threats, forwarding emails from managers that when investigated had been strangely doctored and amended so as to give the impression that something different had been said. The intention of this act was to wrong foot the recipient and make him or her carry out an action that the unofficial lower echelon sender would wish.

Further actions included various forms of resistance and organisational misbehaviour to the actions that had been democratically discussed and agreed
by a majority of the team (Collinson, 1994; Ackroyd & Thompson, 1999).
This had led to verbal abuse and even questions of financial irregularities.

Overall, it constituted an intense and fraught environment. Respondents
employed a range of popular allusions and metaphors to describe it including 'jungle', 'mad house' and so on and so forth. Senior figures in the organisation were generally considered to have achieved their posts through
personal connections rather than possessing the prerequisite qualifications
or experience. It was noted that a range of posts seemed to have taken
place from the 'Pasta Club' attendees or their associates.

## MICRO-MOMENTS IN A CSI-STYLE CULTURE –
## FINDINGS, ANALYSIS AND DISCUSSION

The findings take the form of micro-moment narratives that portray a
moment or situation (Czarniawska, 1998; Gabriel, 2000, 2004). These
enable the portrayal of 'lived experience' or, in other words, an alternative
way of showing the micro-moments and actions that can play a role in creating sustainable CSR values, behaviour and attitudes.

The micro-moments selected focus on moments that offer Janus-like
potential for 'bad' CSI-forming moments of behaviour to be handled in a
manner that involves a potentially poor or good choice and response. The
micro-moments shown are therefore predominantly negative in nature. The
reason for this is to show how irresponsible micro-behaviour can go
towards building cultures of CSI. The discussion that follows the presentation of micro-illustrations and vignettes explores the Janus dialectic dimensions of the situations to a greater extent.

The presentation of data takes two forms: first, a number of rapid
micro-illustrations of micro-moments are illustrated. The purpose of the-
seis to provide a sense of the fleeting nature of micro-moments and how,
in a second, it can leave a damaging 'remembered pain' impression.

*Initial Micro-Illustrations from Micro-Moment Data*

1. A smile of complicity across a meeting room between two 'Pasta Club'
   members as yet another privilege is accorded to them by the person in
   authority.

2. A 'Pasta Club' employee receives a full-time contract due to favouritism and without due procedure being shown.
3. One employee thinks it is okay to be short tempered and impatient with another employee on a regular basis.
4. One employee congratulated employee A on a promotion then goes straight to employee B and said what a 'b*****d employee A was'. Employee B felt obliged to report to employee A what had just happened.

### Extended Vignettes of Micro-Moments

1. A person repeatedly, or even inconsistently, not replying to an email.

This was not an uncommon instance. When people did not reply to an email, colleagues found this very discourteous and irritating. There was often the mutual realisation that a reply might involve taking a stance on a matter and this might close down the options of person who was not responding. However, at the same, non-response conveyed the message that the sender of the message was not being treated with respect or considered 'sufficiently important' to merit a response. The sender reported being slighted and said it had a powerful and lasting effect on the sender.

2. A senior colleague being caught picking up his step in order to avoid bumping into a colleague.

A respondent reported that he had been working hard to rebuild a relationship with a particular senior colleague. Part of this process involved the increased sharing of thoughts and confidences, often informally, for example, dropping by to each other's office or in the corridor. One day, the respondent had walked towards the senior colleague's office and noticed that coincidentally he was just leaving in the other direction. He also noticed that the manager had half-noticed the respondent's approach and had put a little spring in his step which enabled him to disappear round the corner and not be caught up with. The respondent felt this was unfriendly and disingenuous. This micro-moment put the thought in the respondent's mind that perhaps the manager was not really sincere towards him and was even using him.

3. A person taking credit for a report by putting his name on it when it was mainly produced by another person.

A senior colleague suggested collaborating with a colleague (the respondent) on a report. The respondent conceived the idea, wrote the report and sent it to the senior colleague for input as part of the team effort. As expected the senior colleague contributed nothing to the report. As agreed the report was sent through to the external audience to which it related. When it arrived at that destination, it transpired that the senior colleague had changed the names round and put hers in front of the respondent who had written the report. Although the respondent was aware that other colleagues had indicated that the senior colleague was capable of this sort of behaviour, he still felt as if he had been taken advantage of and 'robbed' of what was rightly his. Given the power relationship between himself and the senior colleague, he elected not to raise the matter with her as she had a reputation of becoming very defensive and even unpleasant.

4. Providing opportunities for one person that do not seem to be available to others.

A given female senior colleague was well known for constantly supporting the career of another woman who was her best friend. This involved the granting of additional time allowances for parts of her job and generous seminar travel allowances. In addition, the manager arranged for a 'temporary, partial' promotion to be arranged because of some 'special responsibilities' that had allegedly been taken on. Many respondents sensed that in a relatively small period of time, this would turn out to be permanent which was in fact the case. Although the person receiving the 'grace and favour' of the manager, together with the senior colleague, were in fact a member of unofficially termed ' Pasta Club', this nevertheless caused gossip and comment among other 'Club' members as well as evidently the wider staff.

5. Discovering that some staff are receiving privileges that others are not.

It was publically accepted, although not overtly stipulated, that all staff in the department used to buy cartridges from their own income for printers at home even though many colleagues did a substantial amount of printing for work purposes because of the professional nature of their roles. Through an inadvertent 'slip', it became apparent that the senior colleague and a small group of acolyte, favoured staff had over a number of years been charging the department for their home cartridge consumption. This caused a great sense of unfairness in the department and led to some ugly exchanges that drew in other unrelated issues of behaviour and fairness.

6. The Classic 'Friday Evening' or the 'Day before Going on Holiday' Email.

In the midst of a particularly busy period for reports and updating on the change management programme that was being progressed, the team manager was working at home trying to get on top of paperwork. The home telephone rang at 2.30 pm and it was a member of the team, indicating that, yet another (for this had recently become a recurrent phenomenon), unpleasant and worrying email had just been received from another team member indicating that there were supposedly a range of issues and problems in a project for which the person receiving the email was responsible.

Dear X

Given recent issues reported by the clients in relation to the project X I have discussed this with the clients and they would like to organise a meeting on XX/XX/XX to discuss possible changes to the project. I hope you will be able to attend as project leader as it will be valuable to have your input and experience. If, however, you are unable to attend please do not hesitate to let me know and I will forward your apologies.

Regards, Employee Y

This had clearly genuinely unnerved the recipient of the email who was trying to finalise some other documents for a different deadline and did not have time to address the alleged matter. Based on past record and behaviour of employee Y, it was evident that the sender of the email had no real right or business sending the email and was deliberately trying to cause problems at a point at the end of a week when nobody would be able to address them satisfactorily before the following Monday. This form of 'sabotage' came to be known as the 'buggaration' factor in the team – a piece of sabotage that would impede or delay progress of other team members. Consequently, the email recipient and associated colleagues affected would be preoccupied by this over the weekend.

The manager receiving the call requested that the caller/person who was the recipient of the email reply only in brief to acknowledge the email and to indicate that the matter would be dealt with. The manager then sent an email to the sender of the email indicating that what had been sent was entirely inappropriate and that the matter would be addressed through the proper management and team meeting procedures in due course. He also informed the nominal senior line manager even though there would be the concern that the senior manager would probably shy away from getting involved or dealing with the matter in full.

# REFLECTIONS AND DISCUSSION ON
# MICRO-MOMENTS

The above micro-moment illustrations and vignettes provide a concise but insightful indication handful of the overall sample. While some of the moments might, by their very nature, seem minor, trivial, mean, small-minded and ultimately demeaning, they will perhaps be clearly recognised as not atypical of some everyday workplaces (Knights & Willmott, 1999). More importantly, all of the above micro-moments have contributed to the generation in some way or other to the engendering of a wider CSI-prone culture in that they made a negative addition to building up some notion of 'remembered pain' — the physical or, especially, the psychological pain that has not gone away from an earlier psychological event or trauma.

In the data illustrations above, Janus dialectical moments occurred in which people had a choice in which they elected, for whatever motive or reason to do a 'bad' thing. An implicit and constructed part of that is, when questioned on their behaviour, the individuals who were perpetrating the actions were frequently defensive and sought to justify their actions. Very rarely did a perpetrator of a 'bad' act apologise or renounce their actions as being wrong. This raises an interesting issue around the choice in relation to the Janus dialectic — when people are doing 'bad' things or making CSI-prone choices, does the person think or believe they are doing 'bad' things or acting for the 'good' or some higher purpose or goal? This social constructive aspect of the dialectic creates considerable challenges for managers charged with building CSR-focused cultures because it cannot be assumed that people who are perpetrating so-called bad acts will necessarily see them in this light.

Perhaps one seemingly automatic response is that some form of ethical code or system should normatively be in operation within any given organisation, whether notionally or actively (or indeed both) (e.g. see illustrations of this in McEwan, 2001; Fisher & Lovell, 2008; Hartman & DesJardins, 2008; DesJardins, 2011; Fraedrich, Ferrell, & Ferrell, 2011). This would at least seem to provide some standard against which behaviour and actions could be interpreted, understand and classified. This echoes the Kantian deontological approach to guiding and building what might be considered appropriate behaviour. These codes, formal and informal, did, of course, exist within the field setting studied and therefore this still begs the question — how does 'bad' behaviour get policed, monitored or controlled, in relation to such codes? One partial response to this issue, as an alternative to codes of ethical conduct and practice, might be the idea that engaging in counter-politicking or 'sharp practice', in other words 'fighting fire with fire' might be seen as a way forward to tackle such behaviours. While some respondents were tempted to respond in this manner, in many instances this was felt that such responses led only to the protagonist lowering him or herself to the same level as the person committing the unjust act in the first instance. This was not an opening or a pathway of the Janus dialectic that many respondents wanted to consider, as it would see a departure from their own choice of way of being and values. Respondents made sense of the situation through reverting to everyday sayings and wisdoms as a form of narrative and 'lived experience' tradition. Respondents used expressions such as 'he who lives by the sword, shall die by the sword', and 'what goes around, come around' and so on and so forth. Uttering such sentences seemed to assist respondents in helping people to remain controlled and offered some form of postponed justice in their mind. As a corollary to the guiding effect of this canon of popular wisdom, it was also noted that the idea of 'good manners' was deemed important by many respondents. The notion of being polite was something that seemed to be considered a building block for responsible behaviour and a counterbalance to unreasonable or irresponsible behaviour.

Furthermore, these data cameos could be used, for example, to throw up issues of courage, integrity, wisdom and principles. As discussed above, these are characteristics that would be likely to work towards building a CSR-oriented culture. Rather than relying solely on a deontological styled code, there may well be scope for aspiring and encouraging an Aristotelian 'character' approach to prepare people for the choices of the Janus dialectic. If people have an inherent and internal set of generally believed 'good' values that guide their choice, then this means that they are more likely to take actions that will work towards a CSR rather than a CSI culture and environment. Given the limitations of space in the chapter, the data presented here focused primarily on CSI-destined incidents and micro-moments. However, a closer illustration of the interplay of CSI−CSR behaviour is provided in Vignette 6. In this vein, it can be seen the challenges for people, and especially managers, to make difficult decisions and take difficult choices in relation to action in the micro-moment. In most of the above instances presented, allowing a situation to perpetuate or pass within some form of comment or action was a step towards contributing the construction of a corporately irresponsible future – one in which the many micro-actions would produce a culture capable of a more series and damaging event. Within the data set and time span, such events did occur. Indeed in the research setting, there were instances of substantial financial and procedural irregularities when employees, not checked enough, had followed a pattern of micro-moments of behaviour and this had grown into a flagrant abuse of position. Equally, there were a number of embarrassing moments where employees behaved towards external audiences and guests in a similar manner to that which they had treated their colleagues. All of these instances were calmed down and addressed over time, but damage was done to the image of the organisation and, in many instances, careers of managers responsible for the employees involved. It has to be said that this latter consequence was often not conducted out of a sense of 'putting things in order' but rather akin to punishing people for allowing the 'lid to be lifted off Pandora's Box'.

In building a response to the Janus dialectic dilemma of the micro-moment, *choice*, and the acceptance of being responsible for choice, is therefore a key aspect to consider. In the micro-moments presented in the data above, it might appear that these are just isolated incidents, particular to a specific spatial, temporal moment. However, the argument suggests that these are readily recognised by wider audiences. Moreover, the multiplicity and compound nature of such cumulating events means that, ultimately, they gravitate towards constructing a macro-context and environment. It is frequently the case, and this was borne out by the observational data, that sometimes people believed, or on occasion and, more disturbingly, elect to believe that it was the case that they did not have a choice. The issue of choice is a pivotal aspect of the micro-moment. Referring again to the lexicon of popular expressions and clichés, it can metaphorically be seen to represent something of a 'thin end of a wedge'. If issues occurring in the micro-moment are not dealt with early on, then they risk growing into a dominant and recurrent way of being. As such they become, sooner or later, the 'thick end of the wedge' leading to macro-events of CSI. And, as indicated by Sartre (1943, 2003) and Frankl (1946), choice always exists. Choice, therefore, linked to the notion of striving for responsible action in the micro-moment takes us to the heart of the Janus dialectic. As stated above, 'good' and 'bad' choices, similar to the two heads, reside within the same body of the individual and indeed the same body of the organisation. The potential and risk of responsible and irresponsible behaviour and consequences is a product of cultures built up through myriad micro-moments.

# CONCLUSION

The argument presented above has duly recognised that CSR has come to be seen as important, even imperative, activity for organisations in the contemporary era. However, as noted, much of the extant commentary on CSR has been conducted with the sub-narrative of a rationalistic and managerialistic paradigm that ultimately seeks to use CSR as another tool to heighten competitive position and corporate standing and performance. Equally, much of the analysis has had a propensity to focus on the 'macro' aspect of CSR, in other words at the company or organisational level. The introduction of CSI into the debate provides the lens necessary to begin to better understand the recurrent failures of purported CSR projects in organisations. The present chapter has sought to move away from the macro-focus and to introduce the idea of micro-moments to CSR–CSI contexts. Central to micro-moments are the ideas of recognition and the constant presence and option of 'choice' linked to responsibility. Poor choices and decisions create remembered pain from multifarious negative micro-moments. In contrast, wise, 'good' choices can work to build a responsible culture and avoid CSI incidents. The metaphor of Janus and the doorway and beginnings and endings imagery it represents provides a vivid device to portray and illustrate this dialectical situation. In conjunction with this, approaches and frameworks such as lived experience, narrative and critical perspectives serve to facilitate a richer and more insightful understanding of the micro-moment. Managers, and those who lead or have formal authority, clearly have a powerful role to play in relation to overseeing and getting involved, rather than ignoring, the micro-moment and its ultimate journey to either CSR or CSI. Aristotelian virtue ethics and Kantian deontology can play a central role in guiding choice with the Janus dialectic. However, to think that it is uniquely this group that has the potential solutions is to overlook that ultimately the responsibility resides with all organisational members to consider the micro-moment choices and actions that they make on a daily basis.

# REFERENCES

Ackroyd, S., & Thompson, P. (1999). *Organizational misbehaviour*. London: Sage Publications.
Alvesson, M. (2002). *Understanding organizational culture*. London: Sage Publications.
Alvesson, M., & Sköldberg, K. (2009). *Reflexive methodology, new vistas in qualitative research*. London: Sage Publications.

Badham, R., Garrety, K., Morrigan, V., & Zanko, M. (2003). Designer deviance: Enterprise and deviance in culture change programmes. *Organization, 10*(4), 707–730.

Buchanan, D., & Badham, R. (2009). *Power, politics and organizational change: Winning the turf game.* London: Sage Publications.

Berger, P., & Luckmann, T. (1966). *The social construction of reality: A treatise in the sociology of knowledge.* London: Penguin.

Berners-Lee, M. (2010). *How bad are bananas? The carbon footprint of everything.* London: Profile Books Ltd.

Carlzon, J., & Peters, T. (1989). *The moment of truth.* New York: Harper Row.

Chryssides, G. D. C., & Kaler, J. H. (1993). *An introduction to business ethics.* London: Cengage Learning.

Clegg, S., Kornberger, M., & Pitsis, T. (2011). *Managing and organizations: An introduction to theory and practice.* London: Sage Publications.

Collinson, D. (1994). Strategies of resistance: Power, knowledge and subjectivity in the workplace. In J. Jermier, D. Knights & W. Nord (Eds.), *Resistance and power in organizations* (pp. 25–68). New York: Routledge.

Crane, A., & Matten, D. (2010). *Business ethics: Managing corporate citizenship and sustainability in an age of globalization.* Oxford: OUP.

CSR Europe (2011). http://www.csreurope.org. Accessed 2nd June.

Czarniawska, B. (1998). *A narrative approach to organization studies.* London: Sage Publications.

Daft, R., Murphy, J., & Willmott, H. (2010). *Organization theory and design.* Andover, UK: Southwestern Cengage Learning.

DesJardins, J. (2011). *An introduction to business ethics.* New York: McGraw-Hill.

Dixon, S., & Clifford, A. (2007). Ecopreneurship – A new approach to managing the triple bottom line. *Journal of Organizational Change Management, 20*(3), 326–345.

Elkington, J. (1997). *Cannibals with forks: The triple bottom line of 21st century business.* London: Capstone.

EFMD. (2010). *The sustainable business.* Brussels: European Foundation for Management Development.

Fisher, C., & Lovell, A. (2008). *Business ethics and values: Individual, corporate and international perspectives.* Harlow, FT: Prentice Hall.

Frankl, V. (1959). *Man's search for meaning.* London: Beacon Press.

Fraedrich, J., Ferrell, O., & Ferrell, L. (2011). *Ethical decision making for business.* Andover, UK: South Western Cengage Learning.

Friedman, M. (1970). The social responsibility of business is to increase profits. New York Times Magazine, 13 September.

Gabriel, Y. (2000). *Storytelling in organizations: Facts, fictions and fantasies.* Oxford: Oxford University Press.

Gabriel, Y. (2004). *Myths, stories and organizations: Pre-modern narratives for our times.* Oxford: Oxford University Press.

Griseri, P., & Seppala, N. (2010). *Business ethics and corporate social responsibility.* Andover, UK: Cengage Learning.

Hartman, L., & DesJardins, J. (2008). *Business ethics: Decision making for personal integrity and social responsibility.* New York: McGraw-Hill.

Kira, M., Van Eijnatten, F., & Balkin, D. (2010). Crafting sustainable work: Development of personal resources. *Journal of Organizational Change Management, 23*(5), 616–632.

Knights, D., & Willmott, H. (1999). *Management lives.* London: Sage Publications.

Knights, D., & Willmott, H. (2011). *Organizational analysis: Essential readings.* Andover: Southwestern Cengage Learning.

Lawrence, A, Weber, J., & Post, J. (2010). *Business and society: Stakeholders, ethics and public policy.* London: McGraw-Hill.

Levi, P. (1987). *If this is a Man.* London: Abacus.

Levi, P. (1988). *The drowned and the saved.* London: Abacus.

Linstead, S., Fulop, L., & Lilley, S. (2009). *Management and organization: A critical text.* Basingstoke: Palgrave Macmillan.

Locke, R., & Spender, J. (2011). *Confronting managerialism: How the business elite and their schools threw our lives out of balance.* London: Zed Books.

Machiavelli, N. (2008). *The Prince.* Oxford: Oxford University Press.

MacIntyre, A. (1981/2007). *After virtue: A study in moral theory.* London: Gerald Duckworth and Co Ltd.

MacVeigh, J., & Norton, M. (2011). Introducing sustainability into business education contexts using active learning. *Higher Education Policy, 24,* 439–457.

Marcum, J. (2009). Sustainability by engagement. *The Bottom Line: Managing Library Finances, 22*(3), 76–78.

Marens, R. (2010). Destroying the village to save it: Corporate social responsibility, labour relations and the rise and fall of American hegemony. *Organization, 17*(6), 743–766.

McCabe, D. (2007). Individualization at work? Subjectivity, teamworking and anti-unionism. *Organization, 14*(2), 243–266.

McEwan, T. (2001). *Managing values and belief in organizations.* Harlow, FT: Prentice Hall.

Milne, M., Kearins, K., & Walton, S. (2006). Creating adventures in wonderland: The journey metaphor and environmental sustainability. *Organization, 13*(6), 801–839.

Michelson, G., van Iterson, A., & Waddington, K. (2010). Gossip in organizations: Contexts, consequences and controversies. *Group and Organization Management, 35*(4), 371–390.

Newton, L., Englehardt, E., & Pritchard, M. (2010). *Taking sides: Clashing views in business ethics and society.* New York: McGraw-Hill.

Parada, M. J., & Viladás, V. (2010). Narratives: A powerful device for values transmission in family businesses. *Journal of Change Management, 23*(2), 166–172.

Parker, M. (2000). *Organizational Culture and Identity.* London: Sage Publications.

Popper, K. (1945). *The Open Society and its Enemies.* London: Routledge.

Principles for Responsible Management Education (PRME) (2011). http://www.unprme.org. Accessed 23 May.

Rhodes, C., & Parker, M. (2008). Images of organizing in popular culture. *Organization, 15*(5), 627–637.

Roan, S. (2009) The key to happiness is living in the micro-moment. *Los Angeles Times,* Retrieved from http://latimesblogs.latimes.com/booster%20_shots/2009/07/happiness. html. Accessed on 23 May 2011.

Roberts, J. (2003). The manufacture of corporate social responsibility: Constructing corporate sensibility. *Organization, 10*(2), 249–265.

Roethlisberger, F., & Dickson, W. (1939). *Management and the worker.* Cambridge, MA: Harvard University Press.

Sartre, J.-P. (2003). *Being and nothingness.* Paris/London: Gallimard/Routledge.

Scherer, A., & Palazzo, G. (2007). Towards a political conception of corporate responsibility: Business and society seen from a Habermasian perspective. *Academy of Management Review, 32,* 1096–1120.

Shaw, P. (2010). *Defining moments: Navigating through business and organizational life.* Basingstoke: Palgrave Macmillan.

Stokes, P. (2011). *Critical concepts in management and organization studies.* Basingstoke: Palgrave Macmillan.

Stokes, P., & Gabriel, Y. (2010). Engaging with genocide – Challenges for organization and management studies. *Organization, 17*(4), 461–480.

Tams, S., & Marshall, J. (2010). Responsible careers: Systematic reflexivity in shifting land-scapes. *Human Relations, 64*(1), 109–131.

Van Maanen, J. (1988). *Tales of the field: On writing ethnography.* Chicago: University of Chicago Press.

Van Maanen, J. (2010). A song for my support: More tales of the field. *Organizational Research Methods, 13*(2), 240–255.

Waddington, D. (2004). Participant observation. In C. Cassell & G. Symon (Eds.), *Essential guide to qualitative methods in organizational research* (pp. 165–179). London: Sage Publications.

Watson, T., & Harris, P. (1999). *The emergent manager.* London: Sage Publications.

Weick, K. (1995). *Sensemaking in organizations.* London: Sage Publications.

Weick, K. (2001). *Making sense of the organization.* Oxford: Blackwell Publishing.

# PART III
# UNDERSTANDING CSI: A SOCIAL CONSTRUCTIONIST PERSPECTIVE

# ECONOMIC RATIONALITY AND CORPORATE SOCIAL IRRESPONSIBILITY: AN ILLUSTRATIVE REVIEW OF SOCIAL CAPITAL THEORY

Paul Manning

## ABSTRACT

Purpose – *The purpose of this chapter is to argue that utility maximisation, taken from a narrow economic understanding of rationality, frames contemporary business school pedagogy and management theory. The chapter will illustrate this observation by detailing the rational framing assumptions in social capital literature. The chapter will argue that these framing rational notions foster a perspective that inclines towards excessive self-interest as well as a concomitant lack of fellow feeling or morality.*

Methodology – *Literature review of Social Capital theory.*

Findings – *The chapter demonstrates that the narrow economic understanding of rationality that predominates as the framing notion in management theory tends towards amorality as it privileges individual*

Corporate Social Irresponsibility: A Challenging Concept
Critical Studies on Corporate Responsibility, Governance and Sustainability, Volume 4, 111–134
Copyright © 2012 by Emerald Group Publishing Limited
All rights of reproduction in any form reserved
ISSN: 2043-9059/doi:10.1108/S2043-9059(2012)0000004014

*self-interest. In consequence, the significance of ethics and cooperation are under-reported and under-emphasised which leads to Corporate Social Irresponsibility (CSI). These observations are discussed with reference to social capital theory.*

Research implications − *To consider the significance of the under-acknowledged rational background or framing perspectives in distorting theory and empirical research in social capital literature, and more generally in contemporary management literatures and business school pedagogy.*

Social implication − *There is a need to re-examine and challenge the validity and application of rational notions in contemporary management literatures and pedagogy.*

Originality − *The chapter identifies that a narrow utility maximising understanding of rationality frames and therefore inhibits current management literatures and pedagogy, including social capital literature.*

**Keywords:** General review; social capital; economic rationality

Prompted by the business scandals that exemplified social irresponsibility, Sumantra Ghoshal has recently argued that '... by propagating ideologically inspired amoral theories, business schools have actively freed their students from any sense of moral responsibility' (2005, p. 76). The purpose of this chapter is to illustrate this observation by reviewing social capital literature concerned with economic activity, which is a recently prominent area of research that typifies the rational choice assumptions evident in current management theory. The chapter will argue that this literature, along with other management literatures,[1] is framed by assumptions taken from rational choice theory that tend towards amorality, and in consequence implicitly endorse social irresponsibility. This is an important observation, as these framing assumptions also incline towards self-fulfilment as '... a management theory − if it gains sufficient currency − changes the behaviours of managers who start to act in accordance with the theory' (*ibid.*, p. 77). For illustration, it has been observed that individuals who study economics invariably act in accordance with the dictates of economical rationality:

> ... the only group for which the strong free rider hypothesis received even minimal support in the vast experimental literature turns out to be a group of economics graduate students (Frank, 1988, pp. 226−227).

In short, the chapter will demonstrate that social capital literature concerned with economic activity is framed by notions of self-interested amoral utility maximisation, notions which are contagious for those who have studied the theory. Accordingly, after studying social capital, literature students will be inclined towards amorality and social irresponsibility, as they are influenced by the strictures of the economic way of looking at life in their economic interactions. Moreover, this process is illustrative of other 'Bad Management Theories' (Ghoshal, 2005).

The economic social capital literatures are also worthy of a review from an ethical or responsibility perspective as it presents a contemporary area of research which have achieved prominence or 'stagflation' (Adam & Roncevic, 2003, p. 157) since the 'rational nineties' (Kay, 2010, p. 81). Moreover, this chapter will demonstrate that the economic form of social capital is framed by background/framing assumptions taken from rational choice theory, influenced by James Coleman's instrumental theory of teleology (1990, 2000). Further, the contention of this review is that the rational choice perspective distorts and diminishes the role of moral behaviour and altruism in the market (Lane, 1995, pp. 107–126). Consequently, the chapter will highlight that the framing rational choice assumptions in economic social capital tend towards an amoral, pessimistic view on human interaction, in which each individual is consistently striving to (selfishly) maximise their own utility, an outlook that inevitably encourages social irresponsibility.

Conversely, this chapter will demonstrate that while rational choice assumptions are significant in social capital, they nevertheless have narrow application, and it follows therefore that the economic interpretation of rationality is over-extended in the social capital literature (and incidentally in most management literatures).Thus, contrary to economic orthodoxy, as most influentially espoused by Samuelson,[2] rational self-interested utility maximisation does not offer either a universal method of analysis or a universal description of motivation or behaviour, in this instance for understanding social capital interactions (networking in more common parlance). Furthermore, because rational choice assumptions are limited, both as a method of analysis and as a description of motivations and behaviour, the chapter will conclude by offering an expanded understanding of social capital that presents a more accurate framework for understanding of how individuals accomplish – experience, interpret and shape – their social capital interactions. This expanded perspective will also emphasise the role of social responsibility, and its converse social irresponsibility, which hitherto has been under-reported in theoretical literature.

In addition, this chapter interprets social irresponsibility synoptically, with reference to the following understanding, with CSI being the negative side of corporate social responsibility:

> Ethics is clearly linked to moral philosophy and commonly a prescription of what behaviour ought to be (although this varies according to the theoretical perspective taken). CSR is a term more embedded in societal expectations on corporations, and has wider currency in the corporate world and with business elites (Blundel, Spence & Zerbinati, 2008, p. 4).

In overview, this chapter will review economically focussed social capital literature to highlight its rational choice framing assumptions, which the chapter contends under-report the significance of humanistic and embedded sociological factors, including the importance of social responsibility and irresponsibility, as well as instincts, the urge to create, risk taking, emotions and the sub-conscious. Thus, cultivating connection is a more complicated process than the linear cost/benefit utility maximisation model posited in rational choice theory. For instance, Frank has contended that 'Being known to experience certain emotions enables us to make commitments which otherwise would not be credible. The clear irony here is that this ability, which springs from a *failure* to pursue self interest, confers certain advantages...confronted with the commitment problem an opportunistic person fares poorly' (1988, p. 5). An illustration of the efficacy of forgoing opportunistic behaviour can be observed in the common fusion of business and social and leisure pursuits: many deals are struck at the nineteenth hole based on bonding over an emotional attachment to golf, rather than being predicated on instrumentalising relations.

The argument of this chapter therefore is that management theories framed by the economic understanding of rationality have a propensity towards social irresponsibility, as they present an under-socialised view of economic activity in which individuals consistently maximise their utility in terms of costs and benefits, without regard to more humanistic factors, which are dismissed in economic rationality as mere impediments to competition.

## CONTEXT OF REVIEW

This review is timely for two reasons. First, the economic interpretation of rationality (most commonly sometimes referred to as rational choice theory) is one of a number of contemporary 'egoist doctrines,' which have been described as the orthodoxy of the age (Midgely, 2010, p. 39). However, these egoist doctrines have of late been questioned, following the financial crisis of 2008. Further the chapter's view is that the economic rational perspective can be understood as integral to a triumph of economic ideology justifying a particular set of (neo-liberal) economic views that dominate (or arguably dominated) contemporary economic thought and practice. In Lane's words: 'I think rationality is inserted to justify not explain the market' (1996, p. 112). Economic rationality can be understood therefore as a legitimising rhetoric to vindicate economic orthodoxies. Accordingly, this review is timely as these economic orthodoxies have been subject to intense criticisms following the 2008 financial crash, which has led to direct challenges to neoliberal assumptions, that is of deregulated markets inevitably leading to efficient outcomes. For example, Nicholas Taleb has just enjoyed a best-seller, *The Black Swan*, which analysed economic orthodoxies, arguing that rationality has become a 'strait-jacket' and that optimisation has, '... no practical (or even theoretical) use' (2007, p. 184). In sum, economic rationality can be understood as a doctrine justifying the prevailing socio-economic and political viewpoints and ideological choices, including the market doctrine of self-reliance, frugal self-discipline and the maximising of profits.

Second, the focus on social capital can be justified as this theory has grown in prominence since the 1990s to the point that 'One of the main virtues of social capital is that it is close to becoming a joint concept for all social sciences' (Paldam, 2000, p. 631). Accordingly, its rise to importance is worth considering, especially as this chapter will subsequently demonstrate that this theory is framed by rational assumptions that pervade orthodox economic thinking and contemporary management literatures. For instance, there are a number of scholars who have argued that social capital complements and nourishes the 'Colonization of the Social Sciences by Economics' in which areas of the social sciences are claimed for economics' individualistic traditions (Fine & Green, 2000, pp. 78–93). Fine and Green also contend that social capital allows the perspective of the utility maximising individual to be introduced into the social sciences, and consequently they label the theory as an intellectual: 'Trojan horse...in which more and more areas of social science are claimed for economics' (2000, p. 91). Wallis, Killerby and Dollery concur: 'The recent interest in governmental effectiveness reflects an effective 'capture' of social capital by mainstream economists' (2004, p. 243). In sum, there are a number of scholars who have identified Coleman's social capital treatment as the moving force in the rise of rational choice theory in the social sciences (Field, 2003, p. 21).

To conclude, the rational choice understanding of social capital focuses on greater productivity returns. Accordingly, it is taken as desirable to nurture interactions and to develop a collective social structure, as these will lead to positive utility outcomes. From this rational choice theoretical perspective, it also follows that it is rational to develop social capital for maximising returns on utility: an understanding which is consistent with the utility maximising 'Homo Economicus' of the 'formalist school'. However, consideration of the significance of business ethics or levels of responsibility is absent in the reasoning of this extremely abstracted 'Homo Economicus'.

## UNDERSTANDING THE RATIONAL PERSPECTIVE

The contention of this review is that management theories framed by rational assumptions will lead to greater social irresponsibility because they disregard business ethics and encourage a self-interested understanding of the economy, and indeed of the wider universe. However, pinning down the precise meaning of the rationality is difficult as: 'There are almost as many definitions of rationality as there are people who have written on the subject' (Frank 1988, p. 2). In broad terms, rationalist believe that human reason is the primary source of knowledge of the world. In consequence, the theory, or more accurately, 'body of ideas' (Kelly, 1995, p. 96, 97), origins are diverse, stretching from the Ancient Epicureans, to the French Enlightenment (often called the 'Age of Reason'), and later to the utilitarian philosophy of Jeremy Bentham. In synopsis, rational choice theory belongs to a set of theories that emphasise the reason-based character of the human personality. Further, given its multiple origins together with its claims to be a grand or meta-theory, it is best to consider rational choice as a term for a family of sometimes conflicting theories, which nevertheless share a common assumption on the importance of reason (Kelly, 1995, pp. 96, 97).[3]

Rational choice sociology assumes that actors act rationally (based on reason) in terms of calculating the costs and benefits of actions (Coleman & Fararo, 1992; Friedman, 1995; Green, 2002; Hedstrom & Stern 2008; Scott, 2000). Rational choice theory (termed the neo-classical paradigm in Economics) is also based on the materialist assumption that individuals are self-interested and deliberate utility maximisers. Moreover, according to

Lin while rational choice has multiple motives regarding valued resources, two are fundamental: 'the minimization of loss and the maximisation of gain' (2001, p. 128).

In sociology the pioneers of the rational approach were Blau (1964) – associated with contract theory – and George Homas (1961), who contended that sociological theories should be grounded in behavioural psychology. It also has been argued that James Coleman's rational choice sociology should also be viewed as a direct extension of the Homas framework of exchange theory (Scott, 2000). Thus, there is a lineage for Coleman's rational perspective, which is significant as he has been described as

> ...the single most important person to influence rational-choice sociology...In Foundations, he shows how a range of traditional sociological concerns such as norms, authority systems, trust and collective action can be addressed from a rational choice perspective' (Hedstrom & Stern, 2008, pp. 4, 5).

Swedburg also argues for the importance of Coleman's methodological individualism, which he claims is responsible for, '...trying to recast sociology on the basis of rational choice' (1990, p. 6). In summary, there are a number of scholars who have identified Coleman's social capital treatment as the moving force in the rise of rational choice theory in the social sciences (Field, 2003, p. 21).

Further, Coleman (1972, 1973) developed his rational choice sociology, from an understanding that social interaction was a form of trade: the core assumption of social exchange theory is that individuals are engaged in a market of social exchanges (Fine, 2001, p. 72). In this interpretation Coleman developed his conceptualisation of interactions as a marketplace (driven by self-interested, cost/benefit notions of maximisation), as an extension of social exchange theory. Therefore, one interpretation is that Coleman's developed his views on interaction as an off-shoot or variant of social exchange theory, in terms of emphasising self-interestedness, opportunism and bounded rationality.

However, to take Coleman at his own words: 'If we begin with a theory of rational action, in which each actor has control over certain resources and interests and events, then social capital constitutes a particular type of resource available to an actor' (Coleman, 2000, p. 20). The key features of Coleman's rational approach can be listed as follows:

• Macro phenomena can be explained with reference to micro behavior.
• Utility maximisation (optimisation) serves as an explanatory theory of motivation and as a method of analysis to explain all purposeful action.

- All action is rational from the perspective of the individual, who examine their environment, weigh possible courses of action and choose what they view as the most expedient path to their preferences.
- Macro-level norms (accepted and standardised ways of accomplishing goals) are also significant in making certain choices more likely while restricting other choices.

It has also been noted that Coleman worked closely with fellow Chicago University Professor Gary Becker, winner of the Nobel Economics Prize in 1962 for his human capital theories and Coleman stated he understood social capital as '...paralleling the concepts of financial capital, physical capital and human capital, but embodied in relations among persons' (1990: 30). Therefore, it is reasonable to assume that Coleman's sociology was grounded in a rational/materialist view of social interaction, an approach with universal claims that it could be applied to any social interaction. For illustration of the breadth of this economic approach to rationality, Becker's *A Treatise on the Family* examines the efficiencies in a marriage market in which '...people with stable well-defined preferences act in purposeful ways to choose a mate that best promoted their material interests' (Frank, 1988, p. 185).

In summary, for Coleman the purpose of social capital was as an explanatory theory of cooperative behaviour and group level behaviour within the framework of rational choice theory. Coleman's social capital was also an attempt to explain systematic cooperative behaviour within a meta-theory of 'methodological individualism' in which the interaction of the individual level rational pursuit of utility, leads to 'emergent phenomena at the system level' (1990, pp. 1–23). For example, Coleman's contended that by forgoing immediate advantage individual actors could gain greater utility by being part of a collective structure/network.

# THE RATIONAL UNDERSTANDING OF SOCIAL CAPITAL

This review understands social capital as being 'situational', with different forms in different contexts (Coleman, 1990, p. 302; Woolcock 2001, p. 194), and that in its economic form social capital has been framed by background assumptions originating in James Coleman's rational utility optimisation modelling (1990 and 2000). Coleman pioneered the application of economic concepts in sociology, and his theoretical legacy is evident in the prevalence of rational choice suppositions in social capital literature. For example, Ahn and Ostrom (2008); Commin (2008); Fine and Green (2000); Fine, (2001); Lin (2001) have all discussed the significance of rational choice theory in framing understandings of social capital. However, *The Economic Way of Looking at Life* with its method of analysis which assumes individuals 'maximize welfare as they conceive it', as well as displaying a consistency in forward looking behaviour (Becker, 1992), has been subject to forceful criticism (see below). Further, it is also worth emphasising that criticisms of rational choice theory, which is based on a paradigm of self-interest, and arguably posits a gloomy view of the human personality, are more acute when the utility maximising method is extended beyond its established field of economics. Thus, it is deeply controversial to apply the economic understanding of rationality, as a method of analysis, to sociological/humanistic phenomena that have not hitherto fallen within the cost/benefit optimisation approach.[4]

To illustrate this pervasive framing perspective on social capital, Table 1 references the extent of rational thinking in the leading scholars of social capital theory. In addition, Table 2 illustrates the significance of rational choice theory in the key scholar of social network analysis, Mark Granovetter (1973, 1985, and 1992, 2005). This table has been included because social network analysis closely related to social capital theory. The purpose of these two tables is to illustrate therefore the prevalence of economic rationality in framing the theoretical treatment of the major scholars of social capital.

# THE LIMITS OF RATIONALITY

This section will discuss the limitation of the economic interpretation of rationality, which in social capital's case is derived from Coleman's instrumental theory of teleology (1990, 2000). The review will contend that rational choice offers a penetrating, but partial lens for understanding social capital processes. Therefore economic rationality's explanatory power is restricted to a significant but nevertheless narrow area of social capital processes. It follows that the explanatory power of rational choice is over-extended in social capital, as it is in other management literatures.

***Table 1.***   Rational Choice Theory and Social Capital.

| Scholar | Rational Choice Understanding of Social Capital | Commentary |
|---|---|---|
| James Coleman | '...aspects of social structure that enhance opportunities of actors within that structure' (Coleman, 1990, p. 302) | Sociological and ego-centric, Communitarian – political/ sociological understanding Both internal and external |
| Robert Putnam | '...social contacts affect the productivity of individuals and groups' (Putnam, 2000, p. 19) | Political approach that understands social capital as a property of a group, either as regions in Italy (1993) or at the level of the nation state (2000) |
| | In terms of generalised reciprocity quotes approvingly of de Tocqueville's: 'Self-interest rightly understood' (2000, p. 135) | Socio-centric, whole network, internal |
| Nan Lin | '...the notion of social capital-capital captured through social relations. In this approach, capital is seen as a social asset by virtue of actors' connections and access to resources in the network or group of which they are members' (Lin 2001, p. 19) | Sociological and ego-centric |
| | Investment in social relations with expected returns in the market-place.' (2001, p. 19) '...investment by individuals in interpersonal relations useful in the markets.' (*ibid.*, p. 25) | External |
| | '...an elementary exchange, evoking a relationship between two actors and a transaction of resource(s), contains both social and economic elements' (*ibid.*, p. 144). | |
| Ron Burt | To provide, 'access, timing and referrals' (Burt, 1990, p. 62). | Ego-centric |
| | 'The advantage created by a person's location in a structure of relationships is known as | External |

***Table 1.*** (*Continued*)

| Scholar | Rational Choice Understanding of Social Capital | Commentary |
|---|---|---|
| | social capital.... Social capital is the contextual complement to human capital in explaining advantage...social structure defines a kind of capital that can create for individuals or groups an advantage in pursuing their end. People and groups who do better are somehow better connected' (Burt 2005, pp. 4, 5). | |
| Henry Flap | '...an entity consisting of all future benefits from connections with other persons' (Flap, 1994, p. 136). | Utility maximisation of connections<br>External |
| Ben Fine | 'Essentially social capital is nepotism-you have to use the ones you know, but at least you know them' (Fine, 2001 p. 157). | Utility maximisation of social connections<br>External and internal |
| Portes describes Coleman and Putnam's social capital treatments | 'An approach closer to the under-socialised view of human nature in modern economics sees social capital as primarily the accumulation of obligations from other according to the norms of reciprocity' (Portes, 1998, pp. 48, 49). | Economic notions of rationality of instrumentalising social connections for personal advantage<br>External |
| Flavio Comin | Commented on the social capital focus on the 'instrumentalisation of social relations' (2008, p. 629) | Sociological and ego-centric, instrumentalises social interactions and relations |

Moreover, even among cheerleaders for free markets there have always been cautions over the extent that rational choice and the economic way of looking at life can be universally applied, for example:

> We can think of neoclassical economics as being, say, eighty per cent right'.... But there is a missing twenty per cent of human behavior about which neoclassical economics can give only a poor account (Fukuyama, 1995, p. 1).

*Table 2.*   Rational Choice Theory and Social Network Analysis.

| Scholar | Rational Choice Understanding | Commentary |
|---|---|---|
| Mark Granovetter | 'Insofar as rational choice arguments are narrowly construed as referring to atomised individual and economic goals, they are inconsistent with the embeddedness position presented here. In a broader formulation of rational choice, however, the two views have much in common...while the assumptions of rational choice must always be problematic; it is a good working hypothesis that should not easily be abandoned. What looks to the analyst non-rationalist behaviour may be quite sensible when situational constraints, especially those of embeddedness, are fully appreciated' (Granovetter, 1985, pp. 505, 506). | In Granovetter's view personal relations engender trust, which in turn creates vulnerability and 'enhanced opportunity for malfeasance', as reflected in the saying about personal relations that 'you always hurt the one you love' (1985, p. 491). Granovetter argues that rationality needs to be considered with reference to social structure (1985, p. 506). External and internal |

*Source*: Paul Manning.

Fukuyama also asserts:

> ... the totality of the intellectual victory of free market economic theory in recent years
> has been accompanied by a considerable degree of hubris. Not being content to rest on
> their laurels, many neo-classical economists have come to believe that the economic
> method they have discovered provides them with the tools for constructing something
> approaching a universal science of man. The laws of economics, they argue, apply
> everywhere.... These economists believe in a deeper epistemological sense as well;
> through their economic methodology, they have unlocked a fundamental truth about
> human nature that will allow them to explain virtually all aspects of human behaviour
> (1996, p. 17).

Consistent with these cautions, more strident critics of the baleful influence of economic rationality have also come to the fore since the onset of the financial meltdown. For example, the philosopher Mary Midgely has recently argued for an alternative zeitgeist, spirit of the age, to reflect the '...recent widespread interest in the social brain: that is, of natural human cooperation and mutual suggestibility' (2010, p. 39). Thus there needs to be a shift away from the model of the self-interested atomised individual, in favour of an understanding that emphasizes the significance of cooperation in economic life. This understanding also challenges the simplistic rational approach to motivation, which is based on an Hobbesian extreme account, in contrast offering a more synoptic that attempts to capture the different wellsprings of action.

Reflecting this view that the economic view of rationality has been over-extended, Midgely has also written about our age being obsessed by individual competition, with social atomism as the prevailing myth of the time. For illustration of her views:

> Today, as in the nineteenth century, individualist propaganda is phrased in economics terms drawn from the spectacular financial gyrations of the time. The fantastic idea of 'the bottom line' —money as the final arbiter of reality- grew up then and is prevalent again today (2010, p. 115).

Moreover, based on the limitations of economic rationality there is a need to present an expanded perspective for framing social capital, which will also reinstate earlier assumptions concerning the nature of economic behaviour. For illustration:

> Even before Darwin, the scholars of the Scottish Enlightenment and thoughtful conservatives such as Edmund Burke had sensed that social organisation emerged through iteration and adaptation and was not the product of a serene or lucid mind (Kay, 2010, p. 152).

This expanded perspective is additionally consistent with Fukuyama's emphasis on the importance of culture in determining economic outcomes:

> The problem with neoclassical economics is that it has forgotten certain key foundations on which classical economics was based. Adam Smith, the premier classical economist, believed that people are driven by a selfish desire to 'better their conditions' but he would never have subscribed to the notion that economic activity could be reduced to rational utility maximisation. Indeed, his other major work besides 'The Wealth of Nations' was 'The Theory of Moral Sentiments' , which portrays economic motivations as being highly complex and embedded in broader social habits and mores (1996, pp. 17, 18).

Thus, social capital and networking literature needs to be framed by assumptions that expand the economic rational perspective beyond the extant market doctrine of heroic independence, at its extreme of 'Randian individualism', 'laissez-faire' capitalism and an absolute faith in the market to produce efficiencies out of disorder, without any regard to social responsibility or irresponsibility.

To conclude, the economic perspective on rationality has been summarised as emphasising: 'Material self-interest, usually financial, [tending] to be a privileged justification' (Abelson, 1995, p. 32). One consequence is that the rational perspective inhibits explanations of real-world behaviour (including social responsibility and irresponsibility) by virtue of its claims for universality.

## THE LIMITATIONS OF RATIONAL CHOICE

There are numerous alternatives to the rational choice paradigm, including the Austrian, Post-Keynesian, Marxist and behavioural constructions of reality: rational choice therefore has competing theoretical paradigms. Further, Coleman was acutely aware of the alternatives to rational choice theory and sought to delineate and defend the rational vantage, for instance in a co-edited book he wrote with Thomas J. Fararo entitled *Rational Choice Theory: Advocacy and Critique*, with chapters arguing for and against the merits of 'using optimization as a criterion at all points' (1992, p. xi). However, for the sake of brevity this section will limit its discussion to a number of the key limitations of rational choice theory as relevant for this review into the levels of social responsibility in social capital processes.

The first limitation of Coleman's understanding of social capital is the broad conclusion that rational choice assumptions do not offer a comprehensive (and consequently accurate) method of analysis for understanding the viewpoints and inter-subjective experience of managing social capital. For example, the accuracy of economic rationality's consistency of self-interestedness can be questioned for positing an overly materialist and perhaps misanthropic (driven by greed) understanding of motivations and behaviour. Further, beyond economics the inherent flaws of economic rationality's assumptions are long held and not controversial. For example, ancient scholars such as Cleon noted the lack of rationality that people '...despise those who treat them well and look up to those who make no concession' (Burrows, 2007, p. 41), and philosophers such as Thomas Hobbes, John Locke, Spinoza and John Hume have also noted that impulses make people choose irrationally, being led by passions and desires instead of by the dictates of reason (Frank, 1988, pp. 84, 85). Additional well-known examples of irrationality in the economy are detailed in Charles Mackey's the *Extraordinary Popular Delusions and the Madness of*

*Crowds* which gives a convincing account of irrational, 'National Delusions', 'Peculiar Follies' and 'Philosophical Delusions' (1841/1995). For instance during the 'South Sea Bubble' of 1720 investors clamoured to pour money into various strangely titled schemes, the strangest being 'A Company for carrying on an Undertaking of Great Advantage, but nobody to Know what it is'. Market based booms, such as 'Tulipmania' in seventeen-century Holland, are further recurring examples of the non-rational side of market behaviour. Thus, there are numerous examples of non-rational behaviour, and consequently rational choice theory can be questioned for its claims to be a comprehensive descriptive and explanatory model of behaviour and motivation.

Second, it can be contended that the rational approach has been over-extended from its still contentious, but arguably more natural domain in economics. Thus, the marketplace is the area of activity where rational materialist, instrumental behaviour is acceptable (at least in the West), whereas in other spheres of activity or social interaction a cost/benefit optimisation approach would not hitherto have been taken as legitimate. For example, in law notions of justice will often over-ride a strictly cost/benefit approach, and in medicine rationality is tempered by views on the intrinsic worth of individuals, against rational utilitarian or eugenic approaches that exclusively focus on the costs and potential outcomes of treatment. Further, even within the market sphere rational choice theory is controversial: Lane for instance offers a succinct summary of the rational choice as an inadequate theory of behaviour in the market (1995, pp. 108–114). For this chapter the rational approach to social capital key limitation is that though the focus is on economic activity, the theory also examines humanistic phenomena that are not readily reduced to a rational analysis. For example, approaching social relations from a cost/benefit angle ignores the intuitive aspect of social interaction: people possess instincts that make them recoil from such (charmless) self-serving networking and excessive instrumentalism of social connections. In sum, the rational/economic approach can lead to insights that are at variance with conclusions from other disciplines, as well as being at odds from conventional non-economic wisdom and observed behaviour. For illustration, it is not rational to rely on gut instincts or take high risks, but no market has ever functioned without these low or non-rational motivations and behaviours.

Third, Coleman took a very broad interpretation of rationality (1990, p. 18) which is arguably tautological. For example, according to Coleman any action can be termed rational as the manifestation of the individual's preferences. Accordingly, drug addiction can be interpreted as rational behaviour as the expression of the addict's preferences.[5] Thus, '... the essentially tautological nature of the wide version' (Dunham, 2009, p. 102) is that it defines rationality too broadly, so that any action is deemed rational, if understood from the individual's perspective. Etzioni's comments are therefore apt: 'Once a concept is defined so that it encompasses all that incidents that are members of a given category (in the case at hand, the motives for all human activities) it ceases to enhance one's ability to explain' (1988, p. 27). In sum the rational approach can be criticised for over-extension in its claims for universalism.

Fourth, Granovetter has questioned rational choice theory in terms of the assumption that

> ...one's economic interest is pursued only by comparatively gentlemanly means. The Hobbesian question-how can it be that those who pursue their own interests do not do so mainly by force and fraud-is finessed by this conception. Yet as Hobbes saw so clearly there is nothing in the intrinsic meaning of 'self-interest' that excludes force of fraud (1985, p. 488).

It can be argued therefore that there is no reason for a rationalist to exclude force or fraud, other than the risk of being apprehended and punished. In the real world though there are many instances when individuals could use force or fraud with little chance of being caught, but choose not to: hence the 'policing mechanism' does not explain their actions.[6] An alternative understanding is that the markets need shared values to function, Fukuyama for example stresses the importance of trust and 'ingrained ethical habit' (1995) for 'lubricating' market based transactions. It could also be argued that the most transparent examples of rationalists in the market place are criminals and fraudsters who pursue a Machiavellian 'realpolitik', self-interested approach: Bernie Maddoff, for example, can be understood as an extreme rationalist who ruthlessly worked at promoting his own interests (self-interested utility optimisation) without regard to any non-rational (moral) frameworks (Manning, 2010).

## LAS VEGAS WOULDN'T EXIST IN A RATIONAL ECONOMY

The rational perspective on social relations in social capital has flourished, driven by the understanding that this method of analysis has extensive explanatory and predictive power. Coleman's variant of methodological individualism can also be interpreted as a 'wide version' of rational choice that aims to expand rational assumptions, within neo-classical economics to include beliefs, altruisms norms and social sanctions in explaining behaviour (Dunham, 2009, p. 101). However, this review has discussed a number of key limitations of the rational understanding of motivations and behaviour and also its limited value as a method of analysis. For instance social cooperation may be based on emotional motivations, as Coleman acknowledges when he attempts to elucidate the 'rationality of free-riding and zeal' (1990, pp. 273–276): an impossible task because zeal is not rational. Further, rational choice theory cannot fully explain outcomes that are by-products of other activities, or the result of addictive, habitual or moral imperatives. The 'selfish' utility maximisation understanding of individual motivation and method of analysis can also result in an idealised emotionless 'rational fool' who does not acknowledge the importance of humanistic factors, such as cultural and custom based constraints and 'moral sentiments' in social interactions.

## IMPLICATIONS

Given the limitations of the economic understanding of rationality, there is a need to re-frame social capital (and other management theories) so that they more accurately describe and analyse economic behaviour, the corollary is that they will also be able to more accurately describe and analyse levels of social responsibility and irresponsibility. Further, the view of this chapter is a good starting point is to expand the theoretical lens to include a socio-economic 'embedded' perspective in social capital and other management literatures. This economic understanding originated in Karl Polanyi's embedded understanding of the economy (1944/2001), and was subsequently developed in socio-economic literature by Mark Granovetter. In Granovetter's view the embedded view of the economy is associated with, 'the 'substantivist' school in anthropology, identified especially with the afore-mentioned Karl Polanyi...and the idea of moral economy in history and political science' (1985, p. 482). However, there is a considerable difference from Polanyi's 'fictitious commodities' hankering after a pre-capitalist age that valued social cohesiveness and the social contract, and Granovetter's social network analysis.

Granovetter has also examined *Economic Action and Social Structure: The Problem of Embeddedness* to consider the origins of the under- and over-socialised conceptions of action to contend that '...purposive actions are embedded in concrete, ongoing systems of social relations'

(1985, p. 487). In Granovetter's embedded logic of exchange market performance can be enhanced via intra-firm resource pooling and commercial cooperation, as well as by social connections coordinating adaptation processes. Conversely, social and structural over-embeddedness can undermine economic performance by locking firms into downward levelling networks that seal firms from non-redundant information, thereby reducing the opportunities for brokerage. Over-embeddedness can thus create inertia that undermines the firm's 'creative abrasion' that creates entrepreneurial risk taking necessary for survival in competitive markets. For example, Uzzi has concluded, from a study of New York garment manufacturers, that both over- and under-embeddedness has a negative effect on economic performance; that is, very weak and very strong embeddedness were detrimental to firm survival (1996). A conclusion confirmed in recent research into the effects of 'network redundancy' for start-ups (Westerlund, & Savhn, 2008, pp. 492–501).

For an additional illustration of the embedded view of the economy, Granovetter has also noted that supplier relationships are not driven both by economic motives and also by embedded personal relationships (business friendships). He reached this conclusion by observing that purely economic motives would cause firms to switch suppliers far more commonly than is the case: he also notes that firms required a shock to jolt them out of their buying patterns (1985, p. 496). Moreover, his comments on personal embeddedness limiting opportunism and encouraging expectations of trust are relevant:

> That is, I may deal fairly with you because it is in my interest, or because I have assimilated your interest to my own (the approach of interdependent utility functions) but because we have been close for so long that we expect this of one another, and I would be mortified and distressed to have cheated on you even if you did not find out (though all the more so if you did) (1992, p. 42).

In overview, Granovetter's social network approach subscribes to the embedded understanding of the economy in which individuals do not act individually, goals are not independently arrived at, and interests are not wholly selfish. This understanding of the economy has been summarised as follows: '...the economy should not be identified with the market ('the economist fallacy') and that, indeed the market itself is a system embedded in society.' (Smelser & Swedberg, 2005, p. 19) Moreover, Granovetter's 'embedded' understanding also accords with Polanyi's insight that 'Cooperation for a joint material advantage is the predominant feature of society as an economic system' (1958, p. 212). Thus, Granovetter's embedded view argues that the economy is one branch of human activity alongside many others: it is not a semi-detached area of activity where society's rules and mores do not apply. Thus, in the embedded perspective there are limits to markets and not everything of value can be captured in the pricing mechanism.

In summary, understanding of the economic form of social capital could be enhanced with the inclusion of a socio-economic perspective that takes the market as being embedded in the broader economy, which in turn is embedded in broader society. In addition, an essential aspect of the embedded, socio-economic perspective of the economy is that it offers a sociological and humanistic view of market activity, and rejects the 'obsolete market mentality', with its 'crass materialism' and 'motive of gain' as an inaccurate lens for viewing business interactions (Polanyi, 2001[1944], p. 31). The implication of this literature stream is that social capital research will become sensitive to the significance of sociological and humanistic factors in the data. These factors include social responsibility and irresponsibility.

## CONCLUDING REMARKS

Rationality of any stripe is at least in part learned, and therefore not an expression of an innate human proclivity to self-interest, rather rationality is a social construction. In consequence the chapter refutes the view that economists are realists, whose theories are 'Not recommending selfishness just recognising it' (Ridley, 1996, p. 145).

The chapter's theoretical contribution is to propose expanding the framing notions in social capital, and more generally in management theory, beyond their current rational theory assumptions. Moreover, this is not a new method of analysis, but rather argues for a reinstatement of previous perspectives on economic activity which have been forgotten or jettisoned in the recent 'rational' past. This expanded perspective is therefore consistent with the views that economic rationality has been over-extended in contemporary analysis. Frank, for instance has drawn attention to the significance of compassion and morality in Smith's view of the market, which is absent from contemporary understandings of economic rationality (1988, pp. 21–23). Fukuyama further elaborated this observation by contending that social capital requires a 'moral community' that can't be acquired through, '...a rational investment decision' (*ibid.*, p. 26).

This chapter's conclusion is that self-interested, opportunistic, ends-means rationality offers a penetrating but narrow lens for understanding purposive economic action. Thus, rational choice theory with its utility maximisation has the potential to explain, and to an extent predict, certain motivations and behaviours in the economy. However, rational choice theory is not a comprehensive method of analysis or a universal theory of motivation and action. In consequence, the problem is that the universal claims for the rational method of analysis inhibit the development of insights that more accurately depict and explain social capital and other economic phenomenon. Further, this understanding is consistent with recent literature into second generation theories of collective knowledge which argue that 'Unlike first generation theories of collective action that presuppose universal selfishness, second generation collective action theories acknowledge the existence of multiple types of individuals as a core principle of modelling human behaviour'.

It is also worth noting that both Granovetter (1992, p. 27) and Coleman (1990, pp. 300, 301) identify the Scottish Enlightenment's market liberalism (and its organising principle of subordinating society to the economy) as the origin of an under-socialised view of the market. Conversely, it is worth noting that a number of authors disagree and consider that the notion of the self-serving, self-interested, calculating individual to be a misreading of Adam Smith's morality and commitment to mutual obligation (Fukuyama, 1995, p. 13; Paterson, 2000, pp. 39–55).

In general terms the implication of this conclusion is to challenge the core precepts of leading management and strategic scholars. For example, Igor Ansoff's (1985) method with its defined analysis and objectives assumes more knowledge about the world, and greater predictive power than humans possess. It also assumes a level of consistency which is highly improbable. Porter's positional approach to strategy (1980) also assumes a science of decision making that fails to acknowledge the vastly unpredictable and complicated essence of the human condition, including the economic condition. In terms of this paper's focus on social capital, the implication of this conclusion is that the sharp focus on self-interest, which is the theoretical orthodoxy, is not the optimum approach for cultivating social capital processes. For example, an influential article by Nahapiet and Ghoshal declares that it is centrally concerned, '...with the significance of social relations as a resource for social action' (1998, p. 120). However, thinking about, and approaching social relations as merely a resource is to strip relationships of their humanity, and consequently is likely to be counter-productive. For illustration, experienced business people will be on their guard against relationships that are not based on mutual advantages, and hence would avoid connections in which they were a 'resource'. Running the risk of sounding too idealistic, one alternative approach is to view economic connections as friendships. The developing literature in this area could therefore inform social capital theory and practical measures to develop this resource. For example, Jonathan Schonsheck has taken Aristotle's classic analysis to argue that business friendships are an example of 'incomplete friendships for utility' (2000, pp. 897–910). Laura Spence has also concluded that business friendships offer a positive contribution to the well-being of actors (2004). Network literature, which is extensive,[7] has also considered business friendships, with a substantial sub-set of network research focussing on entrepreneurial processes from a social network viewpoint[8]. For instance, Mark Granovetter's seminal article 'The Strength of Weak Ties' (1973) can be thought of as theorising business friendships in network terms.

In conclusion, the surfeit of contemporary management theories framed by notions from elegant models of optimisation modelling (originating in Paul Samuelson's, 'Foundations of Economic Analysis', 1983), stressing egoistic ends-means, forward looking consistency, have either been learnt or accepted as the dominant orthodoxy, though often at an unconscious level. However, these notions are over-extended and inaccurate, not least because they fail to give due weight to morality and culture, and consequently severely under-report the significance of social responsibility and irresponsibility.

## NOTES

1. Sumantra Ghoshal, (2005: p. 75) describes these amoral theories to include agency theory, transaction cost economics (Williamson, 1985) and Porter's five forces framework (1980).

2. Paul Samuelson has been credited with the rise to prominence of economics, based on his promotion of the rational consistency approach to mathematical optimisation, with maximisation equalling consistency (Kay, 2010, p. 157; Taleb, 2007, pp. 184–185). It is also worth noting that Samuelson is much quoted as asserting that '...many economists would separate economics from sociology upon the basis of rational or irrational behaviour' (quoted in Granovetter, 1985, p. 506).

3. For example, rational choice has been described as '...one variant of a much larger research programme of nineteenth century energy mechanics .... Indeed, virtually every discipline that aspires to the mantle of science does so by adopting the paradigm of classical mechanics' (Murphy, 1995, p. 157).

4. For a general criticism of the over-extension of rational choice theory, see Bohmam (1992).

5. Abelson (1995, p. 34) has criticised the article 'Rational addiction and the effect of price on consumption' by Becker, Grossman and Murphy (1993) for gross theoretical over-reach.

6. Granovetter further discussed how clever institutional arrangements, such as implicit and explicit contracts, including deferred payment, had evolved to discourage the problem of malfeasance. However, Granovetter considered that these arrangements, '...do not produce trust but are a functional substitute for it'. (1985, 4p. 89) Further, he noted that conceptions that have an exclusive focus on institutional arrangements are '...undersocialized in that they do not allow for the extent to which concrete personal relations and the obligations inherent in them discourage malfeasance' (*ibid.*, p. 489). He also cautioned that if malfeasance was controlled entirely by clever institutional arrangement then a malign cycle could develop in which economic life would '... be poisoned by ever more ingenious attempts at deceit' (*ibid.*, p. 489)

7. For an introduction to network theory, see Nohria and Eccles (1992).

8. There are a number of understandings of SMEs and entrepreneurial networking, including Blundel and Smith (2001), O'Donnel (2004), and Shaw and Conway (2000, pp. 367–383).

# REFERENCES

Abelson, R. P. (1995). The secret existence of expressive behaviour. In J. Friedman (Ed.), *The rational choice controversy*. Yale: Yale University Press.

Adam, F., & Roncevic, B. (2003). Social capital: Recent debates and research trends. *Social Science Information, 42*(2), 155–183.

Ahn, T. K., & Ostrom, E. (2008). Social capital and collective action. In D. Castiglione, J. W., Van Deth & G. Wolleb (Eds.), *The handbook of social capital* (pp. 70–100). New York, NY: Oxford University Press.

Ansoff, H. I. (1985). *Corporate strategy*. London: Penguin.

Becker, G. S. (1992). *The economic way of looking at life*. Nobel lecture, December 9. Retrieved from http://home.uchicago.edu/-gbecker/Nobel/nobellecture

Becker, G. S., Grossman, M., & Murphy, K. M. (1993). Rational addiction and the effect of price on consumption. In G. Loewenstein & J. Elster (Eds.), *Choice over time*. New York, NY: Sage.

Blau, P. (1964). *Exchange and power in social Life*. New York, NY: Wiley.

Blundel, R. K., Smith, D. (2001) *Business networking: SMEs and inter-firm collaboration: a review of the literature*. Research Report RR003/01. Small Business Service, Sheffield. Retrieved from http://www.sbs.gov.uk/research

Bohmam, J. (1992). The limits of rational choice explanation. In J. S. Coleman & T. S. Farraro (Eds.), *Rational choice theory, advocacy and critique* (pp. 207–227). London: Sage.

Burrows, J. (2007). *A history of histories*. London: Penguin.

Burt, R. S. (1990). The social structure of competition. In N. Nitin & R. G. Eccles (Eds.), *Networks and organisations: Structure, form, and action* (pp. 57–91). Boston, MA: Harvard Business School Press.

Burt, R. S. (2005). *Brokerage and closure*. Oxford: Oxford University Press.

Coleman, J. S. (1972). Systems of social exchange. *Journal of Mathematical Sociology, 2*, 145–163.

Coleman, J. S. (1973). *The mathematics of collective action.* Chicago: Alder.

Coleman, J. S. (1990). *Foundations of social theory.* Cambridge: Bellknap Press of Harvard University Press.

Coleman, J. S. (2000). Social capital in the creation of human capital. In E. L. Lesser (Ed.), *Knowledge and social capital: Foundations and applications* (pp. 17–41). Oxford: Butterworth and Heinemann.

Coleman, J. S., & Fararo, T. S. (Eds.). (1992). *Rational choice theory: Advocacy and critique.* London: Sage.

Commin, F. (2008). Social capital and the capability approach. In D. Castiglione, J. W. Van Deth & G. Wolleb (Eds.), *The handbook of social capital* (pp. 624–651). Oxford: Oxford University Press.

Dunham, L. C. (2009). From rational to wise action: Recasting our theories of entrepreneurship. *Journal of Business Ethics, 46,* 99–110.

Field, J. (2003). *Social capital.* London: Routledge.

Fine., B. (2001). *Social capital versus social theory: Political economy social science at the turn of the millenium.* London: Routledge.

Fine, B., & Green, F. (2000). Economics, social capital and the colonization of the social sciences. In S., Baron, J., Field & Schuller (Eds.), *Social capital: Critical perspectives* (pp. 78–93). Oxford: Oxford University Press.

Flap, H. D. (1994). *No man is an island: The research program of a social capital theory.* Presented at the European Consortium of Political Research on Social Capital and Democracy, October 3–6, Milan, pp. 29–59.

Frank, R. H. (1988). *Passions within reason: The strategic role of the emotions.* New York, NY: W.W. Norton.

Friedman, J. (1995). Economic approaches to politics. In J. Friedman (Ed.), *The rational choice controversy* (pp. 1–24). New Haven, CT: Yale University Press.

Fukuyama, F. (1995). *Trust: The social virtues and the creation of prosperity.* New York, NY: Simon & Schuster.

Ghoshal, S. (2005). Bad management theories are destroying good management practices. *Academy of Management Learning & Education, 4*(1), 75–91.

Granovetter, M. (1973). The strength of weak ties. *American Journal of Sociology, 78,* 1360–1380.

Granovetter, M. (1985). Economic action and social structure: The problem of embeddedness. *American Journal of Sociology, 91*(3), 481–510.

Granovetter, M. (1992). Problems of explanation in economic sociology. In Nitin, N. & Granovetter, M. (2005). The impact of social structure on economic outcomes. *Journal of Economic Perspectives, 19*(1), 33–55.

Granovetter, M. (2005). The impact of social structure on economic outcomes. *Journal of Economic Perspectives, 19*(1), 33–55.

Green, S. L. (2002). *Rational choice theory: An overview.* Baylor University Seminar on Rational Choice Theory, May. Retrieved from http://business.baylor.edu/steve_green/green1

Hedstrom, P., & Stern, C. (2008). Rational choice and sociology. In S. N. Durlauf & L. E. Blume (Eds.), *The new Plagrave dictionary of economics.* London: Palgrave Macmillan.

Homas, G. (1961). *Social behaviour: Its elementary forms.* London: Routledge.

Kay, J. (2010). *Obliquity.* London: Profile Books.

Kelly, S. (1995). The promise and limitations of rational choice theory. In J. Friendman (Ed.), *The rational choice controversy* (pp. 95–106). New Haven, CT: Yale University Press.

Lane, R. E. (1995). What rational choice explains. In J. Friedman (Ed.), *The rational choice controversy* (pp. 107–126). New Haven, CT: Yale University Press.

Lin, N. (2001). *Social capital: A theory of social structure and action.* Cambridge: Cambridge University Press.

Manning, P. (2010). The dark side of social capital: Lessons from the Madoff case. In W. Sun, J. Stewart & D. Pollard (Eds.), *Reframing corporate social responsibility: Lessons from the global financial crisis* (pp. 207–228). Bingley: Emerald Publishing.

Midgley, M. (2010). *The solitary self: Darwin and the selfish gene.* Durham: Acumen.

Nahapiet, J., & Ghoshal, S. (1998). Social capital, intellectual capital and the organizational advantage. *Academy of Management Review, 23*(2), 242–266.

Nohria, N., & Eccles, R. G. (Eds.). (1992). *Networks and organizations.* Harvard: Harvard Business School Press.

O'Donnel, A. (2004). The nature of networking in small firms. *Qualitative Market Research: An International Journal, 7*(3), 206–217.

Paldam, M. (2000). Social capital: One or many? Definition and measurement. *Journal of Economic Surveys, 14*(5), 629–653.

Patterson, L. (2000). Civil society and democratic renewal. In S. Baron, J. Field, & T. Schuller (Eds.), *Social capital: Critical perspectives* (pp. 39–55). Oxford.

Polanyi, K. (2001[1944]). *The great transformation* (2nd ed.). Boston, MA: Beacon Press.

Portes, A. (1998). Social capital: Its origins and applications in modern sociology. *Annual Review of Sociology, 24*, 1–24.

Putnam, R. D. (2000). *Bowling alone.* New York, NY: Simon & Schuster.

Ridley, M. (1996). *The origins of virtue.* London: Penguin.

Scott, J. (2000). Rational choice theory. In G. Browning, A. Halcli & F. Webster (Eds.), *Understanding contemporary society: Theories of the present.* London: Sage. Retrieved from http://privatewww.essex.ac.uk/~scottj/socscot7.htm

Schonsheck, J. (2000). Business friends: Aristotle, Kant and other management theorists on the practice of networking. *Business Ethics Quarterly, 10*(4), 897–910.

Smelser, N. J., & Swedberg, R. (2005). The sociological perspective on the economy. In N. Smelser & R Swedberg (Eds.), *Handbook of economic sociology* (pp. 3–26). New York, NY: Russell Sage Foundation.

Swedburg, R. (Ed.). (1990). *Economics and sociology, redefining their boundaries: Conversations with economists and sociologists.* Princeton, NJ: Princeton University Press.

Taleb, N. N. (2007). *The black swan.* London: Penguin Books.

Uzzi, B. (1996). The sources and consequences of economic embeddedness for the economic performance of organizations: The network effect. *American Sociological Review, 61*(4), 674–698.

Westerlund,, M., & Savhn,, S. (2008). Social capital in networks of software SME's: A relationship value perspective. *Helsinki School of Economics Research Papers, 37*(5), 492–501.

Williamson, O. E. (1985). *The economic institutions of capitalism.* Free Press.

Woolcock, M. (2001). Microenterprise and social capital: A framework for theory, research, and policy. *Journal of Socio-Economics, 30*, 193–198.

# RATING AGENCIES AS A CORPORATE GOVERNANCE MECHANISM: POWER AND TRUST PRODUCTION IN DEBT CAPITAL MARKETS

Clea Bourne

## ABSTRACT

Purpose — *The purpose of this chapter is to explore the voluntary corporate governance role played by credit rating agencies, closing the 'trust at a distance' gap which might otherwise hinder fundraising in debt capital markets.*

Methodology/approach — *The chapter draws on Giddens' system trust theory and Foucauldian perspectives of knowledge/power to unpack trust production as a discursive process in financial markets. Foucauldian discourse analytic techniques are used to examine texts deployed by or about Standard & Poor's, the global credit rating agency, leading up to the 2007 credit crunch.*

Findings — *The texts analysed illustrate the influence of rating agencies in producing trust as well as mistrust in debt instruments.*

Corporate Social Irresponsibility: A Challenging Concept
Critical Studies on Corporate Responsibility, Governance and Sustainability, Volume 4, 135–156
ISSN: 2043-9059/doi:10.1108/S2043-9059(2012)0000004015

Research limitations/implications — *Rating agencies produce trust by aligning with state regulatory systems, simplifying complex debt instruments with 'AAA' and other well-known mnemonics, as well as offering apparent transparency and guarantees.*

Practical implications — *While influential, rating agencies can only produce trust by proxy. Their contribution to the actual protection of investments is minimal.*

Social implications — *The analysis highlights the flawed nature of trust relations in debt capital markets as rating agencies' primary customers are the arrangers and issuers of debt rather than the investors who seek protection from risk.*

Originality/value — *The chapter sheds light on the deliberate nature of trust production in financial markets. Five trust/mistrust production practices are introduced — protecting, guaranteeing, aligning, making visible and simplifying. Strategic trust production is established as part of corporate governance ideology in financial markets.*

**Keywords:** Corporate governance; debt markets; power; rating agencies; trust

Like priests in the medieval church, ratings agencies representatives spoke the equivalent of financial Latin, which few in their investor congregation actually understood. Nevertheless, the congregation was comforted by the fact that the priests appeared to confer guidance and blessings. Such blessings, after all, made the whole system work: the AAA anointment enabled SIVs to raise funds, banks to extend loans, and investors to purchase complex instruments that paid great returns, all without anyone worrying too much... (Tett, 2009, p. 118)

In today's global markets, companies are engaged in an increased search for legitimacy, building trust among key stakeholders in order to reap greater profits. Credit rating agencies have come to play an increasing role in providing this legitimacy in the form of voluntary corporate governance, closing the 'trust at a distance' gap which might otherwise hinder fundraising in debt capital markets. One of the most complex and obscure corners of debt capital markets is the field of structured finance, where one might be forgiven for thinking that 'financial Latin' *is* spoken. Structured finance involves the construction of debt products for companies that have unique financing needs, which do not match conventional financial products such as a loan. The essence of structured finance involves the pooling of assets such as loans, bonds and mortgages. Lenders are then attracted by the prioritised structure of claims or tranches issued against these assets (Coval, Jurek, & Stafford, 2008), but more particularly by the prospect of high returns.

Before structured finance evolved, credit rating agencies were already an integral part of debt capital markets. However, they gained further influence by providing a formal trust mechanism for high-risk debt. The world's 'big three' credit rating agencies – Standard & Poor's (S&P), Moody's and Fitch – aided the massive growth of debt capital markets, and particularly structured finance, by acting as voluntary 'trust guardians' (Shapiro, 1987). Rating agencies charge fees to interpret and assess the creditworthiness of borrowers, then discursively assign and publish the resulting credit ratings for all to see. In order to establish themselves as market-wide governance mechanisms, rating agencies employ specific means of trust production; translating complex debt products into simple mnemonic symbols known as credit ratings, while receiving the backing of state institutions for their voluntary governance activities. For several years, the 'big three' rating agencies issued Triple A ratings on a wide range of structured finance instruments. In 2007, the rating agencies revised and downgraded many of these ratings, helping to trigger the global financial crisis which followed. Borrowers and lenders in debt capital markets were unsure of whom or what to trust. As a result, the 2007–2009 crisis became the first global financial crisis to result from a breakdown of assurance mechanisms, or generators of trust (Yandle, 2008).

In the analyses that followed, rating agencies came in for much of the blame for the crisis (Deutsche Welle, 2010). However, this view seems somewhat skewed: In reality, credit ratings as a corporate governance mechanism represented aspects of both Corporate Responsibility and Corporate Irresponsibility (Jones, Bowd, & Tench, 2009). At one end of the spectrum, credit rating agencies certainly aided the flow of information and therefore greater transparency in capital markets. At the other end of the spectrum, however, their voluntary system of governance ultimately shielded powerful financial actors, including global investment banks which arrange high-risk debt issues, and hedge funds and institutional investors seeking high return. Moreover, rating agencies' voluntary governance mechanisms allowed states to 'take a back seat' in financial markets, reducing market surveillance costs, while simultaneously stipulating that pension and insurance funds around the world should only or primarily invest in Triple A debt (Partnoy, 1999).

In this chapter, it is argued that rating agencies were able to gain the influence they did as a corporate governance mechanism, in part, because of the particular form of trust which flows through financial markets, namely, system trust. The purpose of this chapter, therefore, is to reconsider corporate governance as a means of deliberate trust production in capital markets, driving profits. The profit motive means that corporate governance practices often underscore the forms of Corporate Irresponsibility which led to events such as the 2007–2009 crisis and subsequent financial instability. The chapter examines the role of rating agencies as a shield for powerful actors seeking legitimacy for new discourses of structured finance (Hanlon & Fleming, 2009). These powerful actors – investment banks and large investors aided and abetted by state systems – employed the voluntary governance mechanism of credit ratings in order to translate complex structured finance discourses into trust discourses. From this perspective, corporate governance is read as both an ideology produced to mask corporate interests (Pesqueux, 2005), and an arena of political contestation between dominant actors in financial markets (Hanlon & Fleming, 2009; Prieto-Carron, Lund-Thomsen, Chan, & Bhushan, 2006).

The chapter begins with a brief description of debt capital markets and the role of credit rating agencies. The next section reviews the relevant literature, initially to uncover links between corporate governance and trust. From a critical perspective, trust is theorised as trust production in capital markets drawing on the work of Giddens (1990) and Foucault (1969, 1976) to suggest that the corporate governance mechanisms enacted by rating agencies are primarily a set of discursive trust practices. A trust practice framework is introduced through which to understand how system trust was produced in structured finance, backed by the discursive power of rating agencies. System trust then broke down, accelerated when rating agencies revoked their Triple A ratings, helping to spread and crystallise *mis*trust. Rating agencies' trust and mistrust production is illustrated through a discursive analysis of documents published by or about S&P, one of the 'big three' rating agencies, in the years leading up to the global financial crisis.

# CAPITAL MARKETS AND CREDIT RATINGS

Much of the literature on corporate governance concerns equities markets as an arena of political contestation between company management and shareholders. Yet, leading up to the 2007–2009 financial crisis, debt capital markets far exceeded the size of equity capital markets. In 2006, just prior to the crisis, total market capitalisation of the world's equity markets reached US$54.2 trillion. In debt capital markets, by contrast, the face value of outstanding bonds totalled US$67.4 trillion, while the derivatives market accounted for an additional US$12 trillion in gross market value (SIFMA, 2007).

In debt capital markets, one might expect political contestation to take place between the borrowers/issuers and lenders/investors, with lenders wielding much of the power. However, this arena of political contestation is more complex than may first appear: Firstly, the investment bankers and other arrangers who intermediate the flow of capital from investors to debt issuers are dominant actors in capital markets, though somewhat hidden from view (see Fig. 1). Secondly, many of the companies that issue high-risk debt instruments are unregulated, off-balance sheet vehicles, existing only to hold such instruments. As a result, the creators of these off-balance sheet vehicles — banks and other financial institutions — form part of a 'shadow banking system' (McCulley, 2009). The role of rating agencies, meanwhile, is to research, analyse and rate debt issued by companies, cities and states. While offering governance by proxy, rating agencies feign

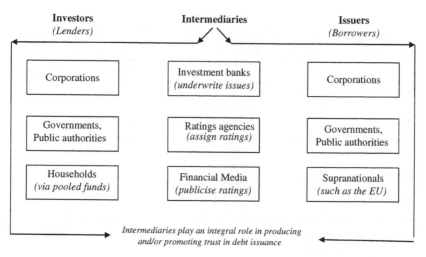

*Fig. 1.* Trust in Debt Issuance — Main Actors. *Source*: Author.

benign influence by positioning their role as nothing more than financial publishers promoting market opinions. In the words of S&P:

> Credit ratings are opinions about credit risk published by a rating agency. They express opinions about the ability and willingness of an issuer, such as a corporation, state or city government, to meet its financial obligations in accordance with the terms of those obligations. Credit ratings are also opinions about the credit quality of an issue, such as a bond or other debt obligation, and the relative likelihood that it may default.
>
> Ratings should not be viewed as assurances of credit quality or exact measures of the likelihood of default. Rather, ratings denote a relative level of credit risk that reflects a rating agency's carefully considered and analytically informed opinion as to the credit-worthiness of an issuer or the credit quality of a particular debt issue. (2011a)

The quality of a debt issue is translated to investors via symbols taken from a ratings scale that is simple enough for all market actors to understand (see Table 1). If something is Triple A (AAA) it has minimal probability of default. If it is Triple B or Triple C it has far more risk and is therefore less trustworthy. When a rating agency assigns a debt instrument a Triple A rating, it is considered a 'prime' rating with virtually no chance of loan default. Such clear-cut designations were comforting to all market actors (Tett, 2009). Since institutions tend to invest more in companies with high bond ratings (Bhojraj & Sengupta, 2001), the highly desirable Triple A 'anointment' in structured finance enabled unregulated, offshore 'shadow' vehicles to raise funds and arrange loans with mainstream lenders (Tett, 2009).

*Table 1.*  Credit Ratings and Trust Production.

| Most trusted | Credit Ratings[a] Risk Scale | | Market Perception |
|---|---|---|---|
| | AAA (Aaa) | Minimal Credit Risk | Highest Investment Grade |
| | AA (Aa) | Very low credit risk | |
| | A | Low credit risk | |
| | BBB (Baa) | Moderate credit risk | Lowest investment grade |
| Least trusted | BB (Ba) | Substantial credit risk | Highest non-investment grade |
| | B | High credit risk | |
| | CCC (Caa) | Very high credit risk | |
| | CC (Ca) | Vulnerable, near default | |
| | C | Near or in default | |
| | D | Payment default | |

[a]Ratings listed above represent a cross-section of general ratings designations employed by global credit rating agencies.
*Source*: Author.

Credit ratings therefore contributed to a corporate governance ideology, allowing investors to trust and believe in the transparency and efficiency of financial markets (Pesqueux, 2005). Through a set of internationally recognised symbols, rating agencies converted trust into a saleable product, automatically creating an active trust market (Zucker, 1986). Credit ratings therefore came to act as mnemonics for trustworthiness in the form of credit quality; put simply, "AAA-rated companies don't default" (Partnoy, 1999, pp. 635–636). Since credit ratings are the most visible form of corporate governance in debt capital markets, ratings symbols became the primary means of separating out companies that are trustworthy from those that are untrustworthy, thus linking corporate governance and trust.

## CORPORATE GOVERNANCE AND TRUST

Normative views of Corporate Responsibility establish strong links between corporate governance and trust (Child & Rodrigues, 2004). Corporate governance mechanisms are not only put forward as a means of addressing persistent mistrust, they are also proffered as a means of restoring trust once lost. Normative literature also makes the link between corporate governance and *mis*trust, suggesting that prevailing mistrust between board directors and shareholders in equity markets led to the level of controls we have come to understand as corporate governance and accountability, such that trust and control have a symbiotic relationship in corporate governance (Skinner & Spira, 2003; Todd, 2006). Todd (2006) goes further by identifying an inextricable link between corporate governance and trust, suggesting that 'good' corporate governance is defined by its ability to build trust with shareholders/stakeholders. This link is established in more detail in the following definition:

> Good corporate governance is all about trust; shareholders must trust that the board of directors will exercise their fiduciary duties of care and loyalty to the corporation when monitoring, ratifying and sanctioning (reward and punishment) management ... decisions. As well, directors must trust that corporate officers are managing the affairs of the corporation competently and with integrity. Investor confidence in capital markets depends on the soundness of the chain of trust. The sole measure, and the definition for 'good corporate governance', should be the level of trust and confidence shareholders have in the board's effectiveness to establish and maintain the chain of trust. (Todd, 2006, p. 6).

It can be argued that there is an inextricable link between corporate governance and trust in debt capital markets as well. This is particularly true since finance is 'the business of trust' (Knights et al., 2001), and trust has always been a central element wherever credit (lending) takes place (Kincaid, 2006). After major events such as the loss of trust in banks as a consequence of the 2007–2009 global financial crisis, it has been further suggested that corporate governance reforms are crucial in rebuilding or restoring trust in capital markets (Davey, 2010). However, as currently practised, the corporate governance/trust link tends to give way to Corporate Irresponsibility because the form of trust at work in global capital markets is faceless or 'system trust' which is deliberately produced as a means of expanding markets and increasing profits.

## THEORISING SYSTEM TRUST

Giddens (1990) offers system trust as a solution to the modern condition of risk and danger because of trust's ability to compress space and time. System trust is a faceless, impersonal form of trust which we, the public, place in money, and increasingly in expert systems such as finance. Giddens argues that people are able to trust large, abstract systems through a process of disembedding, in which social relations are lifted out of their local contexts of interaction and restructured across indefinite spans of time-space (1990, p. 21). Expert systems – networks of experts – are a disembedding mechanism, providing us with 'guarantees' of expectations across indefinite spans such as the financial system. The other principal disembedding mechanism identified by Giddens is money. It is here that the unique link between finance and trust is truly forged. Money works to reduce complexity and manage expectations, when traditional symbols of trust and authority have given way to competence in risk management (Gilbert, 2005). Credit ratings are themselves a disembedding mechanism, embodying both the symbolic qualities of money and the expertise offered by rating agencies.

Lapavitsas (2006) contends that it is the state which regulates money and imbues it with trust, ultimately 'lending' trust to financial institutions. These financial institutions have differing influence over money and the trust that goes with it, becoming layered in a 'pyramid of power' (Kincaid, 2006). The management of modern credit money draws on social power and trust invested in central banks (Lapavitsas, 2006). National central banks sit at the apex of this financial trust pyramid, providing guarantees to money and sustaining the trustworthiness of banks and financial companies at lower levels. Kincaid (2006, p. 41) refers to this provision of guarantees as "a socialisation of trust, backed by the power of the national state". Rating agencies add to this socialisation of trust, by providing health-checks for organisational debt.

The major US-based rating agencies are visibly backed by the state through legislation which identifies them as 'nationally recognised statistical rating organisations' or NRSROs (SEC, 2009). However, this US recognition has neither an international nor supranational equivalent. Meanwhile, structured finance vehicles which issue debt are unregulated, sitting outside of any nation's formal mantle of trust. Since structured finance vehicles lacked state-backed trust, rating agencies were encouraged to extend their voluntary governance mechanisms to this new growth area of financial markets. Rating symbols became devices for reducing the cost of trust formation in unregulated markets (Yandle, 2008). The trust placed in Triple A-rated structured finance created a thriving market for high-risk debt products, yielding profits for borrowers, lenders and rating agencies alike, thus contributing to the growth of a massive shadow banking system (McCulley, 2009) throughout the decade of the 2000s.

## THEORISING TRUST PRODUCTION

As the preceding section demonstrates, Giddens' presentation of system trust describes the drivers of trust production in capital markets. However, it does not shed light on the practices used by system actors to produce trust in corporate governance mechanisms. Here, it is useful to draw on insights from some of Foucault's extensive work on power produced through discourse (Foucault, 1969, 1976). Like Giddens, Foucault establishes a direct link between power and expertise, but Foucault makes expert systems the primary source of power, submitting that discursive strategies are forms of expert knowledge (Foucault, 1981). Foucault defined society by its multiplicity of fields of knowledge, highlighting the production of meanings, the strategies of power and the propagation of knowledge. Discourse is everything written or spoken about a specialist practice/knowledge, *controlling* those who lack specialist knowledge. Specialists produce statements about their practice, *regimes of truth* defined by the 'discursive rules' of their field (Faubion, 1994). In this way, the experts at rating agencies produced a discursive regime of truth about the trustworthiness of 'Triple A' rated structured finance debt, despite the inclusion of less trustworthy 'subprime' mortgages within many of these instruments.

Guided by Foucault's notion of the knowledge/power apparatus (Jäger, 2001), I have assembled a set of trust practices employed in financial systems in a framework illustrated in Table 2. Within this framework,

***Table 2.*** Five Trust Practices and Discursive Enactments.

| Trust Practice Framework | | | |
| --- | --- | --- | --- |
| 1. Protecting | 2. Guaranteeing | 3. Aligning | 4. Making visible |
| *'We represent our stakeholders' interests since they bear the risk'* | *'We are certain of delivering set results in a set time frame'* | *'We associate with other trust codes and systems'* | *'We are truthful, open and detailed about our expert practices'* |
| Building wealth or reducing debt | Keeping promises, honouring contracts, repaying money | Adopting standards and codes of 'best practice', e.g. auditing | Making and pricing accessible, transparent products and services |
| Managing risk while providing customers with exit strategies | Producing certification of competence, expertise | Complying with law and regulation | Making transparent contract terms |
| Assigning high/low trust actors, e.g. custodians to look after funds | Monitoring system soundness | Foregoing competitive imitation | Measuring financial performance, reporting frequently, honestly |
| Respecting property, e.g. monitoring, protecting customer data | Assessing effectiveness of policies | Recognising and supporting customer loyalty | Submitting or subscribing to monitoring and assessment |
| Treating all customer groups fairly | Enlisting third party endorsement, recommendation, ratings, warranties, seals of approval | Negotiating against stated expectations, with willingness to compromise | Giving customers a voice, listening to/acting on complaints |
| Adopting the role of industry or consumer 'champion' | | Supporting socially responsible behaviour | Apologising for failings, making amends |

←——————→ 5. Simplifying ←——————→

*'We are expert enough to explain what we do in plain terms'*
Codifying products and practices. Delineating 'good' from 'bad', 'opinion' from 'fact', 'myth' from 'reality'. Selecting/omitting messages, explaining technical jargon/occurrences, ranking providers, clarifying arguments or positions.

I propose five separate, but intertwined, activities which produce system trust – protecting, guaranteeing, making transparent, aligning and simplifying. *Protecting* is the first in the order of trust practices since it is through the act of protecting that financial institutions safeguard money and other assets. By protecting, financial institutions represent stakeholder interests. Borrowers/investors are crucial stakeholders because, typically, they are the ones who bear the lion's share of the risk by entrusting their money in the first place. The second trust practice is *guaranteeing*; in the act of guaranteeing, financial institutions show evidence of their certainty that they can produce concrete, and generally measurable, results within a specific timeframe.

The third trust practice is that of opening up or *making transparent*. Here financial institutions show evidence that they tell the truth, by opening up and making visible the way they conduct business. Transparency is a particularly sensitive issue for financial institutions, as they may need to shield certain practices which they do not want imitated by competitors. The fourth trust practice is that of *aligning* with other trust systems and codes such as governments and regulatory bodies, professional associations and certifications. Finally, there is the trust practice of *simplifying*: Here, a financial institution shows evidence that it is expert enough to explain, in simple terms, the way it conducts business in connection with finance. Each of these trust practices employs elements that are discursive and material, with the act of protecting being the most material while the act of simplifying is most discursive.

Of the five trust practices proposed in the framework, the one performed most visibly by rating agencies is the act of simplifying. Leading up to 2007, borrowers/issuers and lenders/investors leaned heavily on rating agencies to clarify and simplify the increasingly sophisticated and complex world of structured finance. The simple mnemonics 'AAA', 'BBB', 'CCC' and their meanings helped to produce trust in this expanding area of capital markets, while allowing rating agencies (and investment banks arranging debt issues) to control those who lacked specialist knowledge of complex debt structures. In the following case study, the trust practice framework is applied to discursive data deployed by or about S&P, the global rating agency. The aim is to determine whether rating agencies such as S&P produced trust through the act of simplifying and/or other practices outlined in the framework, thus forging a corporate governance ideology over structured finance prior to the 2007–2009 financial crisis.

## STANDARD & POOR'S: BACKGROUND

Of the five US-based rating agencies deemed to be NRSROs, only three were major players in the structured finance market in 2007 – S&P, Fitch and Moody's. S&P is a division of McGraw-Hill, Fitch is part-owned by French firm, Fimalac, while Moody's is a listed company which, in 2006, was the most profitable in the S&P 500 index (McRitchie, 2011). Rating structured finance deals had become big business for all three firms, yielding high fees and record profits (Deutsche Welle, 2010). Despite high profits accrued, the teams of rating analysts whose job it was to track credit quality had very heavy workloads, since agency staffing had not risen to match the rising volume of structured finance deals (SEC, 2009). Rating analysts were also paid relatively modest salaries and had limited upward mobility, resulting in high staff turnover (Partnoy, 1999); such internal weaknesses were bound to affect agencies' trust practices.

Furthermore, as a corporate governance mechanism, structured finance credit ratings were skewed. Firstly, the 'big three' rating agencies were effectively a 'government-mandated' cartel (Mutti, 2004; Yandle, 2008, p. 352). Secondly, the rating agencies' method of valuing complex financial instruments was so opaque and difficult to fathom, that few were in a position to contest the assigned ratings. Thirdly, rating agencies were paid not by lenders/investors, but by borrowers/issuers – often the investment banks which arranged the debt issues. In this issuer-paid structure, rating agencies had incentives to earn more fees by assigning higher ratings to as many debt issues as possible (Yandle, 2008). The degree of Corporate Irresponsibility inherent in this skewed system was exacerbated by the increasing lure of structured finance for mainstream investors, swayed by Triple A ratings assigned to these innovative, new financial products.

S&P is a US-based, global rating agency, which celebrated its 50th anniversary in 2007, though its history dates back more than 150 years. S&P played an integral role in developing global capital markets beginning with Henry Varnum Poor's publication of a 200-page book in 1868, containing operational and financial details on more than 120 railroad and canal companies. The company went on to supply credit ratings on corporate and government bonds in 1916 and municipal bonds during World War II (Standard & Poor's, 2011b). In equities markets, S&P became well-known for maintaining one of the most widely followed indices of large US firms: the S&P 500 (Standard & Poor's, 2011b). In debt markets, S&P's continued growth tracked the evolution of structured finance; and despite the 2007−2009 crisis, by 2011, S&P claimed to rate more than US $32 trillion in outstanding debt (Standard & Poor's, 2011b).

S&P has its own proprietary systems and models for analysing the complex structures of sophisticated debt instruments (Standard & Poor's, 2004). S&P's models are supposedly made more robust by hours of market research, scrutinised by third party market analysts, creating an aura of transparency. Yet, as with other rating agencies, the final credit rating assigned by S&P is subject to the opinion of an internal committee (Standard & Poor's, 2011a). So while the models are open to public scrutiny, the final decisions still take place behind closed doors. The case study focuses, not on communication 'behind closed doors' but, on discourses conducted in the public domain, with findings set out in the following section.

## STANDARD & POOR'S: FINDINGS

The findings are presented in five discursive excerpts. The first two excerpts were published by S&P, while the next three were published by various financial media, featuring direct quotes from material published and issued to the media by S&P's Ratings Direct service. The section begins with the first excerpt selected from 2004. By this time, the structured finance market and broader debt capital markets had been growing year on year since 2001 (SIFMA, 2007). S&P's structured finance team published a 98-page document outlining its criteria for rating Commercial Mortgage-Backed Securities (CMBS). As stated in its introduction, the document's purpose is to contribute to further growth of the CMBS market (and S&P's profits) by increasing understanding of S&P's rating criteria and process, some of which is set out below:

January 2004

Standard & Poor's Structured Finance

'CMBS Property Evaluation Criteria'

Standard & Poor's developed its criteria for the securitisation of commercial mortgages in the early 1990s... While criteria assumptions, perspectives, and outlook may change... the general approach to analysing commercial properties and rating CMBS has remained consistent.

The rating process usually begins with a request to conduct a preliminary assessment of a transaction... typically initiated by the issuer, borrower, or an investment banking firm...during a formal meeting [a] term sheet outlining the financial terms of the transaction, a data tape containing loan and property-level information needed to model the transaction, and a detailed presentation book may be provided.

[...] For proposals that entail a new property type or new financing structures, Standard & Poor's will typically hold internal meetings to determine the ratability of the proposed transactions. If they are determined to be ratable, Standard & Poor's proceeds with the preliminary assessment...

Preliminary assessments typically entail a desk review of the collateral [and could] entail an intensive review of the asset...a site visit, and discussions regarding the loan/deal structure...

The results of this preliminary assessment are communicated to the issuer/banker...If the preliminary results are accepted...an engagement letter outlining the terms of the rating process [is] prepared...

Upon receipt of the signed engagement letter, an analytical team is assigned to rate the transaction and the official rating process begins.

The rating process typically takes four to six weeks...During this period...analysts maintain a dialogue with the banker/issuer on issues concerning the collateral. This facilitates better understanding of the collateral and the motivations of the lender in structuring the loan [...] (Standard & Poor's, 2004, pp. 4–6).

This first discursive excerpt demonstrates two trust practices: Firstly, the document, 'CMBS Property Evaluation Criteria' produces system trust by opening up and simplifying S&P's process for rating commercial mortgage instruments, setting out this process step-by-step over 98 pages. S&P even 'opens up' examples of its engagement letters and ratings agreements in the document's appendices. It is difficult to ascertain real transparency levels produced, since much of the document will be understood only by specialists in commercial mortgage loan structures. Furthermore, the document focuses on processes connected with the initial transaction, offering no concrete view of ongoing surveillance after the debt is issued. The US regulator would later find that no rating agency had "consolidated and comprehensive written procedures" for rating complex financial instruments, while follow-up surveillance processes were less robust than initial ratings processes (SEC, 2009, p. 6).

The second discursive excerpt was published in 2005. S&P and other rating agencies had received heightened scrutiny, litigation and regulation following the collapse of Enron, the US energy company, in 2001. Together with its main competitors, S&P had given Enron a positive rating just four days before it collapsed in one of the largest bankruptcies in US history (Mutti, 2004). S&P successfully defended itself in the ensuing litigation. The next excerpt is taken from a 22-page memorandum setting out legal arguments for a constitutional guarantee recognising S&P's credit rating activity as 'freedom of the press' rather than commercial advice (Katz, Salinas, & Stephanou, 2009):

July 2005

Standard & Poor's Memorandum

'The First Amendment Protections Afforded to Rating Agencies'

In a wide array of circumstances, state and federal courts have consistently recognised that S&P and other rating agencies are entitled to the same First Amendment protections as other financial publishers such as *Business Week* and *The Wall Street Journal.*

These decisions have been based on widespread judicial recognition that, at their core, rating agencies perform First Amendment functions by gathering information, analysing it and disseminating opinions about it — in the form of credit ratings and commentary — to the general public... All of S&P's published rating actions are also made available to the public for free on its Web site, along with thousands of articles of fixed income-related commentary.

...Courts have consistently extended the protections of the First Amendment to S&P and other rating agencies. Most recently, the judge overseeing the multidistrict Enron litigation recognised that S&P's credit ratings deserve the 'constitutional breathing space' afforded by the First Amendment because they are 'opinions' about important public issues distributed 'to the world'.

...In recognising these full First Amendment protections, courts have concluded that rating agencies are fundamentally different from other market participants, such as public accountants, who do not enjoy the same First Amendment protections... (Standard & Poor's, 2005, pp. 6–11)

In this excerpt, S&P refutes the influential status accorded to it by litigants in Enron-related court cases. S&P's status as an NRSRO had long been enshrined in US legislation (US Senate, 2011). Now, by invoking legal precedent together with The First Amendment, S&P aligns with the trust code that is the US court system before aligning with an even higher authority — constitutional freedom of speech (Downing, 1999). In so doing, S&P discursively constructs itself as pro-American and its voluntary governance mechanisms as democratic ideology (Pesqueux, 2005). — It should be noted that every discursive excerpt can contain a host of meanings, which may shift with time. Re-reading the 2005 memo in the context of later events, S&P certainly appears to distance itself from the trust practices set out in Table 2. By arguing that it merely publishes opinions, S&P neglects the commercial impact of its credit ratings on issuers and waives any responsibility for protecting investors. S&P attempts to have the best of both worlds, invoking system trust without consequences.

The third discursive excerpt is taken from 2006, a year after the Enron litigation. This was a banner year for rating agencies, featuring unprecedented issuance of structured finance debt (SIFMA, 2007). S&P issued a ratings upgrade for Bear Stearns and two other global investment banks, an upgrade subsequently reported by Bloomberg, the specialist global news agency, in the excerpt below. The upgrade is significant as Bear Stearns[1] was associated with two highly levered investment vehicles that would spiral out of control just one year later:

27 October 2006

Bloomberg News

'Merrill Lynch, Goldman, Bear Stearns Ratings Boosted' (Update3)

Merrill Lynch & Co., Goldman Sachs Group Inc. and Bear Stearns Cos., three of the five biggest U.S. securities firms, had their long-term credit ratings raised by Standard & Poor's Corp. on improved risk management.

Merrill's and Goldman's ratings rose one level to AA−, the fourth highest on S&P's scale...Bear Stearns advanced to A +, one below its bigger rivals.

The rating changes will help reduce the companies' cost of borrowing as they use debt to boost trading with the firms' own money [. . .] The three firms have a combined $1.2 trillion in bonds, loans and other debt.

"Risk management at these firms has improved substantially," [said one market analyst]. "Still, are they taking on too much risk by relying on such unorthodox capital?"

[A second analyst] said he was "substantially" underweight the sectors, meaning that he held less than half the amount of brokerage bonds than are in investor indexes [. . .]. "We don't see a lot of upside," he said in an interview. "The ratings companies, by their nature, tend to validate what the market already knows"...

[A third analyst] said he agreed with S&P's decision on Merrill and Bear Stearns, [but] disagreed with Goldman Sachs's upgrade. "Goldman doesn't have a retail brokerage like Merrill or a credit card business like Morgan Stanley, which makes its earnings more vulnerable when markets fall", he said. "Goldman Sachs has become a private equity hedge fund practically", [the analyst] said. "Those don't deserve AA ratings"..." (Bloomberg, 2006)

Whenever S&P issues a ratings action it produces trust by guaranteeing the symbolic meaning attached to its familiar ratings symbols. At the same time, these guarantees are discursive and can be contested by other market experts, as illustrated in the Bloomberg excerpt, where third party analysts are called on to support or refute S&P's ratings upgrade. The first analyst expresses concern that all three firms are over-exposed to the wrong kind of risk. The second analyst states that he is 'underweight' the sector, effectively a lack of trust in what the future holds for the three firms. The third analyst particularly disputes S&P's AA rating for Goldman Sachs. Such market contestations are daily occurrences, yet S&P's institutionalised role as a state-backed voluntary governance mechanism means that its ratings actions tend to trigger the buying and selling of instruments whose ratings have been revised.

As 2006 unfolded, the asymmetry of market information available regarding the risk of structured finance vehicles was an increasing concern. Behind closed doors, rating agencies had discovered their models were not accurately predicting the performance of securities tied to risky mortgages (Nomura, 2006; US Senate, 2011). However, 2006 had yielded unprecedented profits from structured finance for S&P and its competitors (SIF-MA, 2007). Hence, despite deepening market concerns, S&P and the other rating agencies sent no early warning, waiting instead until July 2007 to begin a series of mass downgrades (US Senate, 2011), illustrated by the fourth discursive excerpt below:

3 August 2007

Bloomberg News

'Bear Stearns Cos Inc Outlook Revised to Negative'

... Standard & Poor's Ratings Services revised its outlook on Bear Stearns (BSC) to negative from stable. Standard & Poor's also said that it affirmed its A+/A−1 issuer credit rating on Bear Stearns as well as its ratings on various Bear Stearns affiliates.

Notwithstanding the challenges Bear Stearns currently faces, S&P believes the company's liquidity is strong. 'Still, the negative outlook reflects our concerns about recent developments and their potential to hurt Bear Stearns' performance for an extended period,' notes S&P credit analyst Diane Hinton. 'We believe Bear Stearns' reputation has suffered from the widely publicised problems of its managed hedge funds, leaving the company a potential target of litigation from investors who have suffered substantial losses.'

... The ratings could be lowered if large losses were to be incurred over the next few quarters or if earnings failed to stabilise at a satisfactory level beyond the next few quarters ... On the other hand, if Bear Stearns can overcome current challenges ... the rating outlook could be revised back to stable' (Bloomberg, 2007).

At first, the story appears to offer both good news and bad news − while S&P's has downgraded Bear Stearns, it maintains that the firm's liquidity is 'strong'. However, the intertextuality of this particular excerpt is important: In a climate of rising concern, S&P's review of Bear Stearns' creditworthiness served only to feed panic in the markets, illustrated by the next discursive excerpt from Dow Jones news wires:

6 August 2007

Dow Jones

'S&P says market overreacting to Bear Stearns outlook change'

...The stock market overreacted after Standard & Poor's lowered its long-term out-look on Bear Stearns Cos.' credit ratings to negative on Aug. 3, an S&P managing director said Monday.

Shares of Bear Stearns fell by as much as $8.60 Monday... after losing more than $7 on Friday, and are off about a third so far this year. The company failed to staunch the selloff despite holding a conference call Friday to defend its funding and earnings strength and firing one of its top executives over the weekend.

'We think it's all overplayed,' said Scott Sprinzen, an analyst at S&P's financial institu-tions rating group on Monday afternoon. 'Our thinking in making the change was pretty modest in comparison to the wholesale readjustment the market seems to be making.'

...Sprinzen said S&P adjusted its outlook negatively only on Bear Stearns because of the collapse of two subprime mortgage-dominated hedge funds and problems at a third fund...(Dow Jones, 2007)

S&P's attempt to play down the effect of its earlier downgrade, only underscores the discursive power − and potential harm − wrought by the agency's corporate governance ideology of 'freedom of speech' in financial markets. A simple discursive shift from 'stable' to 'negative' helped crystal-lise growing mistrust in Bear Stearns, helping to spell the firm's demise. By October, the 'big three' rating agencies had issued a slew of ratings down-grades. An entire structured credit edifice had been built on the assumption that Triple A was ultra-safe. Now the term 'AAA' had lost its discursive meaning. The cut in credit ratings acted as a 'trust solvent' (Yandle, 2008, p. 343), causing trust in structured finance and the shadow banking system to evaporate into thin air. As the summer of 2007 wore on, panic in the credit markets ensued. Institutions in both the mainstream and shadow banking systems lost trust in each other, and the entire structured finance system suddenly discovered that its lifeblood had been cut off (Tett, 2009).

## DISCUSSION AND IMPLICATIONS

The S&P discursive excerpts selected from 2004 to 2007 reveal several trust practices which form part of rating agencies' corporate governance mechanisms. From the outset, rating agencies produce trust by *aligning* with state regulatory systems, serving a vital, voluntary governance role where states seek to avoid excessive regulation. In this way, system trust produced by rating agencies is heavily intertwined with power; where rating agencies' discursive authority is not just backed by the state, it is further supported by powerful debt issuers and arrangers, including global investment banks. Rating agencies also engage in *simplifying*, producing trust in complex structured finance products by labelling them with well-known, long-established mnemonics. Until the summer of 2007, the term 'Triple A' told borrowers and lenders everything they needed to know at a glance.

Rating agencies also engage in the trust practice of *guaranteeing*, placing visible guarantees on many high-risk debt instruments through Triple A ratings. However, while rating agencies actively promoted their Triple A 'guarantees', they were unwilling to accept commercial responsibility for their ratings by providing the equivalent of a 'money back' offer if those guarantees proved wanting, thus rendering their 'guarantees' incomplete. Rating agencies also purport to balance the asymmetry in market information by offering *transparency*. However, any real transparency provided at the initiation of ratings coverage on structured finance debt was negated either by inconsistency and/or opacity in subsequent surveillance. Despite revising flawed models in 2006, S&P and other rating agencies failed to publicise these revisions until 2007, spreading and crystallising mistrust in high-risk debt instruments with global repercussions.

However, rating agencies make only a minimal contribution to producing trust by *protecting* investments in capital markets. First of all, rating agencies are paid not by the investors who risk their money, but by borrowers/issuers. It is with the latter that rating agencies are most closely aligned, together with investment banks which act as arrangers of debt. The trust practice framework suggests that protecting is usually carried out on behalf of customers. What the S&P analysis demonstrates is that customers are not always the vulnerable party in financial markets. Rating agencies' customers represent some of the market's most powerful actors, an acknowledged flaw in the rating agencies' voluntary governance mechanism (US Senate, 2011). It is worth underscoring that protecting assets together with protecting the most *vulnerable* parties in financial markets is the most powerful trust practice of all, and an integral part of achieving Corporate Responsibility.

# CONCLUSION

Discourse analysis is a highly subjective methodology and the selection of discursive excerpts and the decision to edit and excerpt them will always reflect some degree of bias. However, the trust practice framework provides a useful mechanism for reconsidering Corporate Responsibility versus Corporate Irresponsibility. The framework helps to shine a light on system trust as a deliberate form of trust production in financial markets, and forges a link between this form of trust production and the promotion of corporate governance as ideology. By using the trust practice framework to analyse discursive excerpts connected with Standard & Poor's, a clearer understanding is offered of credit ratings as a voluntary governance mechanism whose underlying role is to create an active market for trust in financial systems.

Rating agencies primarily operate at the discursive end of the trust practice framework guaranteeing, aligning, making visible and simplifying. They provide third party endorsement by guaranteeing a company's ability to pay its debt. They align the market by issuing credit rating standards. They make financial institutions more visible by publishing research on company performance. They translate and simplify the meaning of complex financial instruments by offering symbols that investors can easily identify. In some ways, these trust practices support Corporate Responsibility. However, rating agencies do not engage in the most powerful financial trust practice of all, that of protecting and safeguarding deposits of money, nor do they protect the most vulnerable parties in financial markets. This is an important point to take forward when assigning future trust roles in complex financial systems.

From a corporate governance perspective, the trust practice framework further indicates that *mis*trust can also be deliberately produced. While mistrust and trust are both necessary to the human condition, widespread mistrust can have powerful and deleterious repercussions. The discursive silence maintained by S&P and other rating agencies throughout 2006 when they uncovered defects in their structured finance models is an unmistakable example of Corporate Irresponsibility. However, this silence was conspiratorial, involving all those who stood to gain from the massive profits yielded by structured finance. If Corporate Responsibility is to be achieved, it will require an acknowledgement of market expansion and profits as the true drivers of trust/mistrust production in capital markets. Acknowledging these drivers would provide the appropriate context for implementing checks and balances on governance mechanisms market-wide.

# NOTE

1. N.B. As a fund manager and arranger of many structured finance vehicles, Bear Stearns had credit ratings attached to scores of entities containing the Bear Stearns name

# REFERENCES

Bhojraj, S., Sengupta, P. (2001). *Effect of corporate governance on bond ratings and yields: The role of insitutional investors and outside directors.* SSRN. Retrieved from http://www.ssrn.com/abstract = 291056. Accessed 20 April 2011.

Bloomberg, N. (2006). *Merrill Lynch, Goldman, Bear Stearns Ratings Boosted (Update3).* Bloomberg, 27 October 2006.

Bloomberg, N. (2007). *Bear Stearns: Behind S&P's negative call.* Bloomberg, 3 August 2007.

Child, J., & Rodrigues, S. B. (2004). Repairing the breach of trust in corporate governance. *Corporate Governance, 12,* 143–152.

Coval, J. D., Jurek, J., & Stafford, E. (2008). In H. B. School (Ed.), *The economics of structured finance.* Harvard: Harvard Business School.

Davey, E. (2010). Corporate governance reforms: Rebuilding trust, empowering shareholders and protecting long-term value. In Ministry For Employment Relations, C. A. P. A. (Ed.), *Association of British Insurers Investment Conference.* Grange St Paul's Hotel, London: Department for Business Innovation & Skills (BIS).

Deutsche Welle, D.W. (2010). *Credit rating agencies under a harsh spotlight again.* Retrieved from http://www.dw-world.de/dw/article/0,,5524523,00.html. Accessed on 21 June 2011.

Dow Jones, N. (2007). S&P says market overreacting to Bear Stearns outlook change. *Dow Jones,* 6 August 2007.

Downing, J. D. H. (1999). 'Hate Speech' and 'First Amendment Absolutism' Discourses in the US. *Discourse & Society, 10,* 175–189.

Faubion, J. D. (Ed.). (1994). *Michel Foucault: Power.* Penguin.

Foucault, M. (1969). *The archaeology of knowledge.* London: Routledge Publications.

Foucault, M. (1976). *The history of sexuality (Vol. 1): The will to knowledge.* London: Penguin Books.

Foucault, M. (1981). *The order of discourse. Untying the text: A poststructuralist reader-* London: Routledge & Keegan Paul.

Giddens, A. (1990). *The consequences of modernity. Polity Press in Association with Basil Blackwell*UK: Oxford.

Gilbert, T. P. (2005). Trust and managerialism: Exploring discourses of care. *Journal of Advanced Nursing, 52,* 454–463.

Hanlon, G., & Fleming, P. P. (2009). Updating the critical perspective on corporate social responsibility. *Sociology Compass, 3,* 937–948.

Jäger, S. (2001). Discourse and knowledge: Theoretical and methodological aspects of a critical discourse and dispositive analysis. In R. A. M. Wodak & Michael (Eds.), *Methods of critical discourse analysis.* London: Sage.

Jones, B., Bowd, R., & Tench, R. (2009). Corporate irresponsibility and corporate social responsibility: Competing realities. *Social Responsibility Journal, 5,* 300–310.

Katz, J., Salinas, E., & Stephanou, C. (2009). Credit rating agencies: No easy regulatory solutions. *Crisis Response: Public Policy for the Private Sector, 8,* 8pp.

Kincaid, J. (2006). Finance, trust and the power of capital: A symposium on the contribution of costas lapavitsas. Editorial Introduction. *Historical Materialism, 14*, 31–48.

Knights, D., Noble, F., Vurdubakis, T., & Willmott, H. (2001). Chasing shadows: Control, virtuality and the production of trust. *Organization Studies, 22*(2), 311–336.

Lapavitsas, C. (2006). Relations of power and trust in contemporary finance. *Historical Materialism, 14*, 129–154.

McCulley, P. (2009). The shadow banking system and Hyman Minsky's economic journey. In Pimco (Ed.), *Global Central Bank focus*. Newport Beach, CA: PIMCO.

McRitchie, J. (2011). *Breaking the hold on rating agencies*. CorpGov.net. Retrieved from http://corpgov.net/2011/06/breaking-the-hold-on-rating-agencies/. Accessed on 14 January 2012.

Mutti, A. (2004). The resiliency of systemic trust. *Economic Sociology, 6*, 13–19.

Nomura Fixed Income Research. (Ed.). (2006). CDO/CDS Update 06/26/06. Nomura Fixed Income Research. Nomura.

Partnoy, F. (1999). The Siskel and Ebert of financial markets? Two thumbs down for the credit rating agencies. *Washington University Law Quarterly, 77*, 617–712.

Pesqueux, Y. (2005). Corporate governance and accounting systems: A critical perspective. *Critical Perspectives on Accounting, 16*, 797–823.

Prieto-Carron, M., Lund-Thomsen, P., Chan, A., & Bhushan, C. (2006). Critical perspectives on CSR and development: What we know, what we don't kow, and what we need to know. *International Affairs, 82*, 977–987.

SEC. (2009). Written testimony concerning SEC Oversight of credit rating agencies. Retrieved from http://www.sec.gov/news/testimony/2009/ts080509sec.htm. Accessed 20 April 2011.

Shapiro, S. P. (1987). The social control of impersonal trust. *American Journal of Sociology, 93*, 623.

SIFMA, T. (Ed.). (2007). *Research Report November 2007*. Washington.

Skinner, D., & Spira, L. F. (2003). Trust and control – A symbiotic relationship? *Corporate Governance, 3*, 28–35.

Standard & Poor's. (2004). CMBS property evaluation criteria. In *Standard & Poor's Structured Finance. January 2004*. New York, NY: Standard & Poor's.

Standard & Poor's. (2005). Memorandum: Exhibit 2 prepared by Cahill Gordon & Reindel LLP re the "Credit Rating Agency Duopoly Relief Act of 2005." In Standard & Poor (Ed.). New York.

Standard & Poor's. (2011a). *About credit ratings*. New York, NY: Standard & Poor's. Retrieved from http://www.standardandpoors.com/aboutcreditratings/. Accessed on 25 June 2011.

Standard & Poor's. (2011b). *About Standard & Poor's*. New York, NY: Standard & Poor's. Retrieved from http://www.standardandpoors.com/about-sp/main/en/eu. Accessed on 5 June 2011.

Tett, G. (2009). *Fool's gold: How unrestrained greed corrupted a dream, shattered global markets and unleashed a catastrophe*. London: Abacus.

Todd, A. (2006). *Trust enabled corporate governance. 27th McMaster World Congress*. Hamilton, Ontario: Trust Enabling Strategies.

US Senate. (2011). *Wall Street and the financial crisis: Anatomy of a financial collapse*. US Senate Permanent Sub-Committee on Investigations (Ed.). Washington, DC. 650 pages

Yandle, B. (2008). Lost trust: The real cause of the financial meltdown. In George Mason University (Ed.), *Mercatus Center Working Papers*. Fairfax, VA: Mercatus Center.

Zucker, L. G. (1986). Production of trust: Institutional sources of economic structure, 1840–1920. *Research in Organizational Behavior, 8*, 53–111.

# ORGANISATIONS BEHAVING BADLY – THE ROLE OF COMMUNICATION IN UNDERSTANDING CSI AND CSR

Jennifer Bartlett, Steve May and Øyvind Ihlen

## ABSTRACT

Purpose – *Despite a long-standing interest in the responsibility of organisations, transgressions do occur. This raises questions about how these occur when there is so much focus on the legitimacy of organisations in being responsible. In this chapter, we draw on metaphors of communication as transmission and meaning making to consider the communicative approaches to CSR.*

Methodology/approach – *This chapter is a conceptual chapter drawing on literature review and cases to illustrate insights.*

Findings – *We suggest that while transmission models focus on highlighting responsibility, it is within the meaning making approaches that opportunities for responsibility and irresponsibility emerge as organisations and society negotiate the boundaries of organisational behaviours.*

Corporate Social Irresponsibility: A Challenging Concept
Critical Studies on Corporate Responsibility, Governance and Sustainability, Volume 4, 157–174
Copyright © 2012 by Emerald Group Publishing Limited
All rights of reproduction in any form reserved
ISSN: 2043-9059/doi:10.1108/S2043-9059(2012)0000004016

Implications — *We suggest implications for how the meaning and criteria of ethical corporate behaviour are constructed.*

Originality and value — *CSR has not been studied extensively through a communication lens. An extensive literature review of various communication approaches to CSR that forms the foundation of this chapter offers important insights into how responsibility and irresponsibility are constituted through communicative efforts of organisations.*

**Keywords:** CSR communication; responsibility; meaning making

CSR has a relatively long tradition rooted in notions of philanthropy, but also as a reaction against business' social transgression (Mitchell, 1989). Still, it is the 1953 book *Social Responsibility of the Businessman* by Howard R. Bowen that is most frequently credited as laying the foundation for CSR thinking (Carroll, 1999). Yet despite a long-standing interest in the responsibility of organisations, transgressions do occur. Crisisexperts.com for example suggests that more than half of corporate crises can be attributed to internal and management issues. Globalisation has brought much of the social responsibility and irresponsibility concerns to the fore as many Western companies have increased their presence in new provinces with democratic deficits, questionable human rights records and widespread corruption. This raises questions about whether the responsibility for these matters rests with the companies to root out such practices, or whether this should be left to civil society and the governments in the host countries? In addition, both large and small companies face increasing domestic challenges related to the environment, outsourcing and contracting, as well as corruption and other forms of economic crime.

Within this environment, the CSR movement has spawned a veritable flurry of communication activity to manage perceptions of corporations' social and environmental responsibility to society. Terms ranging from corporate social responsibility, social responsibility, sustainability and corporate citizenship have been coined to seek to articulate the phenomena (de Bakker, Groenewegen, & Den Hond, 2005). Corporations are increasingly spending substantial amounts to issue reports, engage with stakeholders and develop innovative social and environmental programmes to demonstrate their responsibility to society. It is estimated that almost 80% of the world's 250 largest corporations report and otherwise engage in CSR activities (KPMG, 2008). Yet at the same time, the world has witnessed some of the greatest cases of seemingly corporate irresponsibility with the global financial meltdown and bailouts, telephone hacking invading individual privacy, environmental disasters of endemic proportions and on-going examples of individual human abuses.

If there has ever been an institution that requires renewed scrutiny and critique, it is today's corporation. Undoubtedly, corporations are the most powerful and influential institution in many countries, often eclipsing the government, church and family in their impact (Deetz, 1992). As a result, and as we have seen recently, the ethical failures of business profoundly affect everyone. Ironically, however, irresponsible business corporations have received limited attention in the CSR literature.

This inevitably raises questions about what is ethical behaviour for organisations – including corporations with their massive economic clout, and social and environmental reach. We argue that communication plays a vital role where meaning is negotiated regarding what constitutes ethical behaviour. The notion of responsibility/irresponsibility necessarily has to be defined with the help of communication and there is a corridor of 'reality' that corporations must manoeuvre within. However, corporations can exploit the fact that the borders are unclear. This challenges the assumption that ethics is only an individual-level phenomenon or that ethics can be equated with legal compliance. Crises of irresponsibility can for example, be viewed as the result of corporations pushing the boundaries of what constitutes unethical behaviour or, in some cases, ignoring the tensions between profits and ethics. For example, the economic meltdown (in the United States and abroad) is, in many respects, a case of companies externalising their costs (and risks) onto others in ways that brought the whole system to its knees. Through this perspective, there are businesspersons who believe that repackaging bad loans so that others cannot see the risks inherent in them is 'just good business'. At the micro level, there are multiple examples of persons being either ignored or punished for raising ethical, business-related concerns (e.g. BP oil spill).

This chapter will explore the role of communication in negotiating realities that constitute corporate social irresponsibility (CSI) and responsibility. To do this, we explore these notions within a framework of organisational communication metaphors around transmission and meaning (Putnam & Boys, 2006). First, we will present this framework as a means to analyse relationship between communication and organising. Then we consider how corporate social responsibility and irresponsibility are considered within these perspectives. Finally we raise questions about how meaning making informs the discussion on corporate social irresponsibility.

# METAPHORS FOR ORGANISATIONAL
# COMMUNICATION

Organisational communication research provides a useful arena within which to consider the relationship between communication and organising as the underlying principle for understanding a contemporary organisational phenomena − corporate social irresponsibility. One such theoretical conceptualisation of the field of organisational communication was developed by Stan Deetz (2001) as a means to focus on the process of organising through symbolic interaction rather than merely on 'communication within an organisation'. Such an approach, according to Deetz, produces a focus not so much in theories of organisational communication but in "producing a communication theory of organisations" (p. 5). This directs scholars' attention to similarities and differences among research studies and, as such, can serve as an organising structure for exploring studies of organisational communication and CSR (see May, 2011).

As Deetz and others have noted (Krone, 2005), organisational communication scholars have made a significant paradigm shift over the past two decades from a transmission-based approach to one that emphasises interaction and meaning (Putnam & Boys, 2006). The transmission paradigm emphasises managerialism and decisions about how information is transmitted. In contrast, the meaning paradigm explores how meanings constitute organisations and organising patterns. It is through meaning making that notions of responsibility and irresponsibility can be constructed. Here we briefly discuss the transmission approach as well as meaning making processes that are useful for understanding CSR and CSI.

## Metaphors in the Transmission Paradigm

The earliest communication models, such as the one presented by Shannon and Weaver (1949), highlighted communication as a relatively simple process involving sender, receiver and message. While the complexity of this mechanism has evolved since that time, the role of the organisation, and of the manager within the organisation, remain prominent through the transmission paradigm.

Transmission paradigms encompass conduit, information processing and linkage frameworks that focus on the organisation as a central site through which communication travels, albeit in different ways. Conduit research emphasises the role of communication as tool or as transmission. As a tool, studies consider the outcomes of using various media or of their relative merits. Another strand focuses on the skill of the communicator in various situations. Communication as transmission models also discuss the amount and adequacy of communication. While originally transmission type models literally emphasised the role of the sender, the agency of senders and receivers are inherent (Putnam & Boys, 2006).

A second version of the conduit approach, the information processing approach, sees the organisation as a map for guiding choices about information flows. Often these studies have focused on employees in the organisation. For example, there has been emphasis on employee satisfaction, and positive and negative feedback (Geddes & Lineham, 1996). The third transmission approach concentrates on the linkages that communication facilitates in building relationships. Some studies concentrate on the role of communication in fostering relationships, such as organisational linkages, bringing similar individuals together (Monge & Contractor, 2001). Others however, focus on the social learning networks formed through communication-aided relationships as a form of contagion theory (Monge & Contractor, 2001). As such, communication through the transmission lens is viewed as a relatively mechanistic approach to considering messages, organisations and managerialism.

## Metaphors in the Meaning Paradigm

Another way to consider communication is through a paradigm of meaning. This perspective allows us to move away from the functionalist imperatives of the transmission paradigm and move into viewing communication and organisation in a constructionist mode of dynamic meaning making and interaction. Studies in this paradigm focus on social, rather than economic, assumptions about organising and, as a result, explore how organisational realities are created, maintained and transformed in and through informal stories, rituals and other daily practices. This approach draws on social metaphors and sees the organisation as a community that requires greater personalisation in order to strengthen a unified corporate culture, as well as personal commitment and satisfaction. Researchers from this orientation seek to understand the sense-making activities of the persons they study, as a kind of translation of participants' interests.

Two devices can be used to understand how meaning is constructed via communication. One device deals with the role of language in managing meanings around organisations (Grant & Hardy, 2004). Advocacy and issue formation by actors outside the organisation use language to create meaning around either the organisation itself or matters that will affect it (Metzler, 2001). Organisations themselves also use language in issue and crisis management within their boundaries and with key stakeholder groups (Bridges, 2004). Language is also used in impression management work to repair the legitimacy of the organisation should it be impaired, for example from the advocacy actions of outsiders or through meaning making around the consequences of organisational activities (Benoit, 1995).

Language studies draw on corporate rhetoric to construct shared zones of meaning to align corporate policies with the knowledge and opinions of those important for the organisation to influence (Heath & Coombs, 2006). These forms of advocacy draw heavily on language to persuade others to take on board the corporate message and positioning. The persuasive element of this communication is often concealed as informational messages by blurring text, receiver and context (Rogers, 2000). As such, advocacy can take place both by corporations and activist or interest organisations.

A second important element in understanding meaning is the device of voice which has been employed to understand which perspectives are heard within organisational and public discourses. Employee voice may occur within either formal mechanisms of organisations or informally through day-to-day communication practices. Formally, employees may participate in formalised decision processes, engage in labour—management negotiations, seek the counsel of an ombudsperson, initiate grievance proceedings or contribute to strategic plans, visions and values, among others. Informally, employees may provide constructive feedback, offer suggestions or champion ideas. Regardless of the nature of the voice, though, the intent is the same – to have some impact on how work gets done in organisations. Broader sets of publics, however, have somewhat limited opportunities for voice. Stockholders of publicly held companies may, for example offer ballot initiatives for stockholder meetings. Leaders of NGOs may engage in dialogue to promote positive organisational change. Activist groups may stage public protests. Citizens may pursue lawsuits or media publicity because of concerns about product quality, safety or cost. All, in some form or another, may seek to lobby corporate or political leaders.

As such, the metaphor of meaning involves multiple social actors using communication to actively promote particular interpretations of organisations and their practices. There is a distinctly political element to this approach as some actors and some views gain prominence over others in defining agreed meanings over time. As such, the meaning making perspective offers means to consider the agency of organisations, however, this is through a perspective which is not necessarily deterministic but instead relies on both intent and opportunity. As with other constructionist perspectives in creating meanings and cognitive and institutional rules around social life, there is an ongoing tension between agency and structure (Berger & Luckmann, 1967; Scott, 2001). However, as we will discuss later, this also provides the space for contradictions and paradoxes to occur.

## APPLICATION OF METAPHORS TO UNDERSTAND SOCIAL RESPONSIBILITY AND IRRESPONSIBILITY

The metaphors of communication as transmission and meaning making provide a lens through which to consider the notions of corporate responsibility and irresponsibility as they emerge. Firstly, we consider how CSR has been treated through the transmission lens. We then outline our case for the importance of meaning making to presenting insights on corporate responsibility and irresponsibility and the role of voice.

### CSR through the Transmission Lens

Overall, we suggest that many studies of communication and CSR view organisations as "naturally existing objects open to description, prediction, and control" (Deetz, 2001, p. 19). Described elsewhere as 'functionalist' (Burrell & Morgan, 1979), these transmission approaches draw on economic metaphors and view the organisation as a marketplace of ideas and practices that require intervention to produce structure and social order. Researchers from this perspective often accept the stated goals of the organisation and its leaders as taken for granted and pursue research that supports the efficient accomplishment of those goals. Communication and CSR, from such an approach, tends to be seen as an administrative function that includes information transfer, persuasion and control. When we consider the CSR and communication literature and the concepts revealed through the transmission metaphor, we suggest that this perspective is inherent in a number of normative studies on CSR. A number of these reside in the public relations (Bartlett, 2011), advertising (Pomering, 2011) and marketing (Brønn, 2011) literatures as arenas of applied strategic communication.

The public relations literature for example, has largely focused on how organisations, often through the work of public relations professionals, best identify and deal with specific publics who emerge in relation to organisational activity in the bid to achieve organisational success (Bartlett, 2011). Often these studies have focused on information dissemination and channels for achieving CSR goals (Capriotti & Moreno, 2007). The marketing literature has featured a strong emphasis on social marketing and cause-related marketing as means of dealing with social causes (Kotler, Roberto, & Lee, 2002). The marketing literature also considers brand building through making claims about an organisation's green or sustainability achievements (de Chernatony, 2001). So called 'green marketing' focuses on highlighting environmental initiatives undertaken by companies and associated with their brands. Advertising literature suggests that organisations deliberately utilise advertising to inform audiences of their desired image (Pomering, 2011). By doing so, they present the aspects of their brand which they wish stakeholders to incorporate into their image of the company and consider it more favourably than their competitors (Dowling, 2004).

The role of channels such as the Web and reports plays an integral role in transmission approaches. Studies relating to the role of the web in social responsibility highlight for example the role of the Internet as a tool for interaction (Capriotti, 2011). Some studies emphasise harnessing the Internet for achieving organisational goals (Capriotti, 2011). Since communicating CSR directly is fraught with mistrust (Morsing & Schultz, 2006), websites are also treated as a means for interested stakeholders to seek information about CSR. The focus on stakeholders and stakeholder engagement has been studied as a form of relationship linkage mechanism including inherent issues of who is a stakeholder to engage with (Mitchell, Agle, & Wood, 1997). Other transmission studies focus on reporting (Golob & Bartlett, 2007), its efficacy (Bortree, 2009) and usage (Birth, Illia, & Lurati, 2008).

These studies around corporate social responsibility retain an emphasis on a functionalist approach and organisational effectiveness outcomes through communication around CSR. The notion of responsibility is positioned as a norm which organisations emphasise to indicate their legitimacy by highlighting their socially and environmentally desirable actions.

What is apparent from our reading of the literature is that the notion of CSR has been the focus of much attention to articulate or reflect what constitutes responsibility against which organisations seek to strategically align their image. Some have seen it as a process of corporate social performance (Wood, 1991) with which organisations engage. Others have suggested that image building around CSR is a form of reputation building and restoration in a mediatised world (Eisenegger & Schranz, 2011). Another perspective again has viewed CSR as a compliance mechanism within the realm of governance (Kolk & Pinkse, 2010) or institutionalisation. Within these perspectives, communication has played an instrumental role in disseminating messages about corporate responsibility practices and compliance with institutionalised and socially accepted norms, to manage legitimacy. These transmission approaches can be seen as a reaction to claims of corporate irresponsibility, but do little to help us understand the phenomena of corporate social irresponsibility. Furthermore, these transmission approaches do not assist in considering how opportunities for irresponsibility emerge in a highly institutionalised environment that organisations seek to navigate.

## CSR through the Meaning Lens

We suggest that the meaning metaphor offers a richer way to understand corporate irresponsibility by allowing us to explore the ways and meanings of how responsibility and irresponsibility interrelate. Firstly, however, we consider interpretive studies which focus on corporate social responsibility.

In general, it appears that most interaction and meaning-based studies of CSR tend to focus on the attitudes (Burchell & Cook, 2006) and perceptions (Nielsen & Thomsen, 2009) about CSR among a range of employees, typically managers. Given the earlier emergence and stabilisation of CSR in many European countries, interpretive studies have emerged there more frequently than in the United States. In some cases, scholars (Swanson, 2008; Treviño, Hartman, & Brown, 2000) have sought to understand the role of ethical leadership in CSR-type efforts, although most of the data has been anecdotal rather than empirical. When interview or observation-based interpretive studies have been conducted, the focus has been largely on middle or upper-level managers. For example, Arvidsson (2010) studied the views of management teams in large companies, seeking to ascertain their understanding of, and response to, an emergent set of practices around CSR. Similarly, Hine and Preuss (2009) focused their research on a range of perceptions of CSR among different managerial groups. Not surprisingly, managers dichotomised what they saw as the critical operations of their companies and the discretionary actions of CSR.

Morsing, Midttun, and Palmas' (2007) research also focused on managers, whereby they explored the long history of Scandinavian companies' integration of issues of ethics and corporate social responsibility into corporate strategies. Drawing on companies such as SparNord, Novo Nordisk and Lego, they reported on the self-perceptions of CSR among managers in a range of companies. Although much of their discussion was a historical description of CSR's evolution they, nevertheless, also included an interpretive account of how managers viewed changes in CSR over the years. Using a more detailed case study approach, Seitanidi (2004) discussed the role of employees in developing accountable actions as they formed and delivered a CSR initiative in collaboration with non-profit business partnerships. The in-depth analysis also offered insight for how communication can strengthen participation and mutual responsibility for the success of joint CSR initiatives. This study, though, is among the few that includes the qualitative, emergent data-gathering methods common to interaction and meaning-based research.

## Work on Voice

Work on voice has a longer history in understanding social matters and the CSR construct. First conceived as a means for unhappy consumers to respond to concerns over products and services (Hirschman, 1970), voice has, over time, come to embrace a broader range of employee and public reactions to corporate actions (Gorden, 1988). Voice, for example is considered one of several responses to employee dissatisfaction with corporations. The others include exit, loyalty and neglect. Somewhat similar responses are likely to occur among other publics that express concerns about corporate irresponsibility. That is, consumers and citizens may boycott a company (or, at the least, choose another, preferred brand), continue to purchase, albeit with a lower sense of identification, or become increasingly apathetic, ignoring corporate irresponsibility − a kind of benign neglect.

An increasingly global economy has altered the nature and scope of how and when persons will voice concerns about corporate social irresponsibility. For example, as employees are geographically distributed, it may become more difficult to organise and gain a collective voice. Second, the threat of outsourcing or downsizing looms if employees express too much dissatisfaction with their employer. Furthermore, the employment contract has changed. Finally, the social contract between employer and employee has changed so that employees now are considered 'entrepreneurs' who create their own brand in an increasingly mobile economy.

Yet, globalisation has afforded other opportunities for voice, among which is understanding how corporate irresponsibility emerges. Citizens from around the world are now able to converge around common sets of concerns about corporate practices (e.g. environmental degradation, bribery, tax evasion, political influence, CEO salaries, labour practices and community impacts). In addition, the emergence of computer-mediated communication (e.g. blogs focused on irresponsible corporations and social media, e.g. Facebook and Twitter) has produced a migration of voice that extends beyond the corporate walls.

For the purposes of corporate social irresponsibility, voice could be differentiated along two dimensions (Gorden, 1988). It can be active or passive, constructive or destructive. As Kassing notes (2011), "making suggestions, expressing dissent, and providing critical feedback exemplify active constructive voice" (p. 36). He notes that these are active behaviours offered in the spirit of being constructive. By contrast, he explains, "listening, compliance, and cooperation are forms of passive constructive voice" (p. 36). These behaviours are still constructive, but are passive by comparison. On the destructive side of the continuum, active destructive voice includes "complaining, duplicity, and bad-mouthing, whereas passive destructive voice involves apathy, calculated silence, and withdrawal" (p. 37). Undoubtedly, such active behaviours are clearly destructive, particularly with an organisation. Not surprisingly, the passive behaviours are less destructive by comparison but can, nevertheless, be disruptive.

A more recent typology expands upon these differentiations by emphasising the motives that are behind employee and consumer/citizen voice (Van Dyne, Ang, & Botero, 2003). Pro-social voice, for example begins from a motive to improve the corporation in response to irresponsible actions. Defensive voice derives from fear — with the goal of protecting oneself, as when community members seek redress from companies that have harmed them. Finally, acquiescent voice emerges from a sense of resignation that little, if anything, will change as a result of voice. It is largely defeatist and creates apathy and indifference.

*Linking the Notions of Meaning Making and Voice*

We have suggested that by turning attention to the role of communication as meaning making around matters of responsibility, and irresponsibility, we can reach a more articulate understanding of what constitutes each of these dimensions. The concept of voice allows us to consider how various actors dominate or subside in the meaning making process. Meaning making helps construct and articulate shared meanings around the appropriateness of corporate activity and also has the possibility of blurring meaning where there are spaces of contradiction and organisations may advocate for particular perspectives to dominate. We present here three examples to demonstrate how this takes place.

When the Australian banking industry came under public scrutiny for alleged profiteering at the expense of the community, some organisations in the banking sector took an active role in shaping the national, and in some case international standards, of what constitutes responsible banking. Early in this crisis, the Australian Banking Association provided a detailed crisis response strategy providing a rationale for the banks' practices. Even so, the public, activists and eventually government continued to critique the banks and began framing their concerns in terms of social obligations and social responsibilities. Westpac Bank used this call to lead the way in defining the social responsibilities of banks. Among the devices used were policy statements, issuing social responsibility reports and developing links with prominent community and environmental advocacy and opinion leaders. In addition, they developed a series of practices that involved and engaged communities to deal with issues and in defining socially responsible banking. Areas of contention such as bank fees and branch closures were shaped in a way that defined the banks as responsible for only charging those who were not disadvantaged. As a result, this led to Australian, but also international, indices for being socially responsible as a corporation in the banking category, as well as corporations generally. In this way, Westpac developed a legitimation strategy for their sector, but in doing so, set the benchmarks for other organisations to follow. To this day, Westpac and the Westpac Foundation continue to be leaders in defining and articulating the notion of being a socially responsible organisation.

There are other cases where corporate irresponsibility becomes integrated and legitimated as appropriate. The recent 'economic meltdown' represents one of the most significant issues of the day, with people experiencing one of the most devastating downturns in the global economy in several decades. The roots of the crisis are complex, encompassing questionable organisational strategy and culture, innovations in the design and use of non-transparent financial instruments, and promotion of new attitudes toward investment and risk, as well as the globalisation of investment markets, among others. These questionable organisational practices produced a series of interdependent events, which culminated in severe investment losses for organisations and individuals, widespread mortgage failures, extensive job loss and the rapid development and deployment of government bailout packages.

The economic meltdown of 2008–2009, is not merely an economic issue; it is, more importantly, an ethical one as well. It has been argued, for example that the current economic crisis is the result of an on-going, systematic silencing of ethics and corporate social responsibility (May, 2009). Employees of the organisations that have failed – or have been bailed out by governments across the globe have lacked:

- requisite communication with stakeholders;
- appropriate transparency regarding financial risk;
- collaborative participation in key decision making;
- courage to raise concerns about misconduct and
- willingness to hold leaders accountable for behaviours that have harmed millions people.

Questionable business practices, however, have created an important set of concerns related to CSR and corporate irresponsibility. As Deetz (2008) explained:

> The concern ranges through important issues such as human rights, environmental protection, equal opportunity and pay for women and various disadvantaged minorities, and fair competition. Such broad issues are instantiated in activities such as using prisoners as workers, moving operations to environmentally less restrictive communities, offering and taking bribes and payoffs, creating unsound or wasteful products, closing economically viable plants in takeover and merger games; also, including concerns about income disparity, declining social safety-nets, malingering harassment, unnecessary and unhealthy effects on employees, involuntary migration patterns, and rampant consumerism. (p. 3460)

Over time, many of these corporate practices have become naturalised and taken for granted in ways that they are not necessarily questioned or critiqued. As such, the recent economic crisis may be legitimised as an anomaly or a matter of a few rogue companies, in other words, a 'few bad apples' that do not require regulation or restriction.

Another legitimation strategy is in shaping the nature of what is responsible and what is irresponsible, even in relation to mandated principles.

In an interview with a Norwegian business daily, the Norwegian Minister of the Environment and International Development declared: "We have got to stop making excuses for aid and private investment in undemocratic countries. I reject the idea that investment in a country is a support for the government. It is helping to create a middle class... and makes a transition towards democratic governance more likely" [author's translation] (Sundnes, 2011, pp. 28−29). The minister pointed to the uprisings in Egypt, Tunis and Libya as examples, to illustrate his analysis that economic relations are of the good in the long run. The premise, he argued, is that investments are made in such a manner that the rulers do not have direct access to the funds (Sundes & Sæter, 2011). Such a perspective certainly eases the role of CSR to include a focus on such aspects as no-tolerance for corruption. This is obviously in the interest of many companies. The Norwegian oil company Statoil for instance, defended its engagement in Libya arguing that "it is a political decision to introduce economic sanctions against countries, it is not the responsibility of individual companies like Statoil. Without international sanctions against Libya [there is no reason] for Statoil to not establish operations in the country. ... We run our operations according to international laws and sanctions. Statoil is open and responsible in Libya" [author's translation] (Therkelsen, 2011, p. 18).

This provides a clear example of how an organisation has strategically used communication to blur the lines of responsibility and irresponsibility by reshaping the nature of the debate but also broadening or shifting the context of the discussion. In doing so, they shift jurisdiction on one hand, but also attempt to move cognitive framing on the other.

## CONCLUSION

These examples highlight for us that organisations take a strategic role in building, normalising and reshaping what is legitimate and not legitimate using existing structures and rationales within the broader society. They are actively involved in using communicative practices to shape meaning making around what is responsible, and normalising or validating what might have otherwise been considered irresponsible. As such we believe that corporate social irresponsibility is more than a case of personal ethics.

We noted that there appear two significant areas within which irres-ponsibilities appear to occur. The first was in the internal management practices as noted by crisisexperts.com and the research that shows the majority of crises occur due to management decisions and internal practices. The other occurs at the macro level revealed through globalisation. It is here that shifting jurisdictions, weak governments and economic imbalances provide fertile ground for irresponsibility to emerge as organisations seek to negotiate business in less familiar territory.

It is within these spaces of contradictions that human praxis can engage and go beyond the institutionalised, legitimised, and taken for granted (Seo & Creed, 2002). The CSR agenda has opened up a contradiction between economic and shareholder rationales and the broader stakeholder, social, environmental and governance discourse. If such perspectives are socially constructed, then these are indeed corridors of reality which are open to multiple interpretations and to exploitation of the boundaries. They also provide spaces within which transgressions can be strategically reframed and normalised through communication. As such, while attention has been paid in the literature to articulating corporate responsibilities, there is also need for a counter movement to explicate irresponsibilities. This volume seeks to do this by focusing on the call that corporate social irresponsibility is in part a failure of CSR and therefore a remit of this book is to better understand violations, wrongdoings and poor business practices that impact negatively on society and the broader environment. By attempting to legitimise both ends of the spectrum, the corridors of reality which allow contradictions to emerge are reduced if not removed.

# REFERENCES

Arvidsson, S. (2010). Communication of corporate social responsibility: A study of the views of management teams in large companies. *Journal of Business Ethics, 96*(3), 339–354.

Bartlett, J. L. (2011). Public relations and corporate social responsibility. In O. Ihlen, J. L. Bartlett & S. May (Eds.), *Handbook of communication and corporate social responsibility* (pp. 67–86). Oxford, UK: Wiley Blackwell.

Benoit, W. L. (1995). *Accounts, excuses, and apologies: A theory of image restoration strategies.* Albany, NY: State University of New York Press.

Berger, P. L., & Luckmann, T. (1967). *The social construction of reality: A treatise in the sociology of knowledge.* New York, NY: Anchor Books.

Birth, G., Illia, L., & Lurati, F. (2008). Communicating CSR: Practices among Switzerland's top 300 companies. *Corporate Communications: An International Journal, 13*(2), 182–196.

Bortree, D. S. (2009). The impact of green initiatives on environmental legitimacy and admiration of the organization. *Public Relations Review, 35*(2), 133–135.

Bridges, J. A. (2004). Corporate issues campaigns: Six theoretical approaches. *Communication Theory, 14*(1), 51–77.

Brønn, P. S. (2011). Marketing and corporate social responsibility. In O. Ihlen, J. L. Bartlett & S. May (Eds.), *Handbook of communication and corporate social responsibility* (pp. 110–127). Oxford, UK: Wiley Blackwell.

Burchell, J., & Cook, J. (2006). It's good to talk? Examining attitudes towards corporate social responsibility dialogue and engagement processes. *Business Ethics: A European Review, 15*(2), 154–170.

Burrell, G., & Morgan, G. (1979). *Sociological paradigms and organizational analysis.* London: Heinemann Educational Books Ltd.

Capriotti, P. (2011). Communication corporate social responsibility through the internet and social media. In O. Ihlen, J. L. Bartlett & S. May (Eds.), *Handbook of communication and corporate social responsibility* (pp. 358–378). Oxford, UK: Wiley Blackwell.

Capriotti, P., & Moreno, A. (2007). Corporate citizenship and public relations: The importance and interactivity of social responsibility issues on corporate websites. *Public Relations Review, 33*, 84–91.

Carroll, A. B. (1999). Corporate social responsibility: Evolution of a definitional construct. *Business & Society, 38*(3), 268–295.

de Bakker, F. G. A., Groenewegen, P., & Den Hond, F. (2005). A bibliometric analysis of 30 years of research and theory on corporate social responsibility and corporate social performance. *Business & Society, 44*(3), 283–317.

de Chernatony, L. (2001). *From brand vision to brand evaluation.* Oxford, UK: Butterworth & Heinemann.

Deetz, S. A. (1992). *Democracy in an age of corporate colonization: Developments in communication and the politics of everyday life.* New York, NY: State University of New York Press.

Deetz, S. A. (2001). Conceptual foundations. In F. M. Jablin & L. L. Putnam (Eds.), *The new handbook of organizational communication. Advances in theory, research, and methods* (pp. 3–46). Thousand Oaks, CA: Sage.

Deetz, S. (2008). Engagement as co-generative theorizing. *Journal of Applied Communication Research, 36*(3), 288–296.

Dowling, G. R. (2004). Corporate reputations: Should you compete on yours? *California Management Review, 46*(3), 19–36.

Eisenegger, M., & Schranz, M. (2011). Reputation management and corporate social responsibility. In O. Ihlen, J. L. Bartlett & S. May (Eds.), *Handbook of communication and corporate social responsibility* (pp. 128–146). Oxford, UK: Wiley Blackwell.

Nielsen, A. E., & Thomsen, C. (2009). CSR communication in small and medium-sized enterprises: A study of the attitudes and beliefs of middle managers. *Corporate Communications: An International Journal, 14*(2), 176–189.

Geddes, D., & Lineham, F. (1996). Exploring the dimensionality of positive and negative feedback performance. *Communication Quarterly, 44*, 326–344.

Golob, U., & Bartlett, J. L. (2007). Communicating about corporate social responsibility: A comparative study of CSR reporting in Australia and Slovenia. *Public Relations Review, 33*(1), 1–9.

Gorden, W. I. (1988). Range of employee voice. *Employee Responsibilities and Rights Journal, 4*, 283–299.

Grant, D., & Hardy, C. (2004). Struggles with organizational discourse. *Organization Studies, 25*(1), 5–14.

Heath, R. L., & Coombs, T. (2006). *Today's public relations: An introduction.* Thousand Oaks, CA: Sage.

Hine, J., & Preuss, L. (2009). "Society is out there, organisation is in here": On the perceptions of corporate social responsibility held by different managerial groups. *Journal of Business Ethics, 88*(2), 381–393.

Hirschman, A. O. (1970). *Exit, voice and loyalty: Responses to decline in firms, organizations, and states.* Cambridge, MA: Harvard University Press.

Kassing, J. W. (2011). *Dissent in organizations.* Cambridge, UK: Polity Press.

Kolk, A., & Pinkse, J. (2010). The integration of corporate governance in corporate social responsibility disclosures. *Corporate Social Responsibility and Environmental Management, 17,* 15–26.

Kotler, P., Roberto, N., & Lee, N. (2002). *Social marketing: Improving the quality of life.* Thousand Oaks, CA: Sage.

KPMG. (2008). KPMG International survey of corporate responsibility reporting 2008. Amsterdam.

Krone, K. J. (2005). Trends in organizational communication research: Sustaining the discipline, sustaining ourselves. *Communication Studies, 56,* 95–105.

May, S. K. (2009). Silencing ethics in the U.S. financial crisis. Chapter presented at the annual meeting of the International Communication Association Conference, Chicago, IL.

May, S. K. (2011). Organizational communication and corporate social responsibility. In O. Ihlen, J. Bartlett & S. May (Eds.), *Handbook of communication and corporate social responsibility* (pp. 87–109). Boston, MA: Wiley-Blackwell.

Metzler, M. S. (2001). The centrality of organisational legitimacy to public relations practice. In R. L. Heath (Ed.), *The handbook of public relations* (pp. 321–334). Thousand Oaks, CA: Sage.

Mitchell, N. J. (1989). *The generous corporation: A political analysis of economic power.* New Haven, CT: Yale University Press.

Mitchell, R. K., Agle, B. R., & Wood, D. J. (1997). Toward a theory of stakeholder identification and salience: Defining the principle of who and what really counts. *Academy of Management Review, 22*(4), 853–886.

Monge, P. R., & Contractor, N. S. (2001). *Theories of communication networks.* New York, NY: Oxford University Press.

Morsing, M., & Schultz, M. (2006). Corporate social responsibility communication: Stakeholder information, response and involvement strategies. *Business Ethics: A European Review, 15*(4), 323–338.

Morsing, M., Midttun, A., & Palmas, K. (2007). Corporate social responsibility in Scandinavia. In S. May, G. Cheney & J. Roper (Eds.), *The debate over corporate social responsibility* (pp. 87–104). Oxford, UK: Oxford University Press.

Pomering, A. A. (2011). Communicating corporate social responsibility through corporate image advertising. In O. Ihlen, J. L. Bartlett & S. May (Eds.), *Handbook of communication and corporate social responsibility* (pp. 379–398). Oxford, UK: Wiley Blackwell.

Putnam, L. L., & Boys, S. (2006). Revisiting metaphors of organizational communication. In S. Clegg, C. Hardy, T. B. Lawrence & W. R. Nord (Eds.), *The Sage handbook of organization studies* (pp. 541–576). London, UK: Sage.

Rogers, P. S. (2000). CEO presentations in conjunction with earning announcements. *Management Communication Quarterly, 13*(3), 426–485.

Scott, W. R. (2001). *Institutions and organizations* (2nd ed.). Thousand Oaks, CA: Sage.

Seitanidi, M. M. (2004). Corporate social responsibility and the non-commercial sector. *New Academy Review, 3*(4), 60–72.

Seo, M. G., & Creed, W. E. D. (2002). Institutional contradictions, praxis, and institutional change: A dialectical perspective. *Academy of Management Review, 27*, 222–247.

Shannon, C. E., & Weaver, W. (1949). *The mathematical theory of information.* Urbana: IL: University of Illinois Press.

Sundnes, T. (2011, Mars). Må slutte å be om unnskyldning. *Dagens Næringsliv*, pp. 28–29.

Sundes, T., & Sæter, K. (2011, Mars) Holder fast på min tese. *Dagens Næringsliv*, p. 39.

Swanson, D. (2008). Top managers as drivers for corporate social responsibility. In A. Crane, A. McWilliams, D. Matten, J. Moon & D. Siegel (Eds.), *The Oxford handbook of corporate social responsibility* (pp. 227–248). New York, NY: Oxford University Press.

Therkelsen, H. (2011, Mars) Statoil burde aldri vært i Libya. *Dagsavisen*, pp. 18–19.

Treviño, L. K., Hartman, L. P., & Brown, M. (2000). Moral person and moral manager: How executives develop a reputation for ethical leadership. *California Management Review, 42*, 128–142.

Van Dyne, L., Ang, S., & Botero, I. C. (2003). Conceptualizing employee silence and employee voice as multidimensional constructs. *Journal of Management Studies, 40*(6), 1359–1392.

Wood, D. J. (1991). Corporate social performance revisited. *Academy of Management Review, 16*(4), 691–718.

# RECONSTRUCTING STAKEHOLDER RELATIONSHIPS USING 'CORPORATE SOCIAL RESPONSIBILITY' AS A RESPONSE STRATEGY TO CASES OF CORPORATE IRRESPONSIBILITY: THE CASE OF THE 2010 BP SPILL IN THE GULF OF MEXICO

Audra R. Diers

## ABSTRACT

Purpose – *When organisations behave irresponsibly, a question remains: Can they use a messaging strategy based in the organisation's commitment social responsibility to effectively respond to the crisis? The purpose of this chapter is to analyse stakeholder attitudes and their antecedents in such a case. Because of its scope, magnitude and use of a response strategy based on messages of social responsibility, the 2010 BP oil spill in the Gulf of Mexico serves as an excellent case for measuring the effectiveness of such a messaging strategy.*

Corporate Social Irresponsibility: A Challenging Concept
Critical Studies on Corporate Responsibility, Governance and Sustainability, Volume 4, 175–204
Copyright © 2012 by Emerald Group Publishing Limited
ISSN: 2043-9059/doi:10.1108/S2043-9059(2012)0000004017

Methodology/approach — *The present study drew from two data sources: a content analysis of interactions on BP's Facebook page (N = 1,515) as well as an image survey of BP (N = 749).*

Findings — *BP's messaging strategy had limited positive effects in terms of (1) being viewed as a 'socially responsible' organisation and (2) creating significant good will towards the company. However, these data also reveal that BP has effectively opened lines of communication between stakeholders and the company.*

Practical and social implications — *This study has two central implications. First, for both organisations and activists, personal investment and the relevance of issues are both critical in order to change stakeholder attitudes about organisations. Second, based on this research, we can begin to develop stakeholder profiles based on age, sex and political identity.*

Originality/value — *In the last couple of years, considerable attention has been paid to describing and analysing the response strategies that organisations deploy; however, scant attention has been paid to measuring stakeholder evaluations of those crisis response strategies.*

**Keywords:** Research chapter; BP; crisis communication; stakeholder evaluation; social construction

Media and industry evaluations of BP's response to the 2010 spill in the Gulf of Mexico have been largely negative (e.g. Bell, 2012; Shogren, 2011; Warner, 2010; Webb, 2010). Two years after the spill, the company's stocks had not returned to their pre-spill value, 'partly due to a lack of clarity about the scale of the potential damages and penalties the company may face' (Chazan & Crooks, 2012). The company has been criticised for its leaders' gaffes, but both applauded and critiqued for its use of social media (Beal, 2010; Shogren, 2011).

Yet, research analysing BP's central response strategies, leaders' messaging and communication of remorse (Diers & Donohue, 2011; Diers, Gurien, & Otten, 2011; Diers & Pang, 2011) revealed that during the five-month 2010 crisis, BP's central response strategy centred on messages of corporate social responsibility (CSR). Specifically, BP emphasised messages combining self-enhancement, messages to frame the company positively, accommodation as well as excellence in order to send a message that 'they cared and would make it right'. BP's messaging seemed to be focused on people rather than investors and the media. BP's response strategy seems to be an effort to define itself as a socially responsible company; however, there have yet to be any significant analyses measuring whether the company was successful in reconstructing itself as a member of the community. Hearit and Courthright (2003) argue that 'the reality of a crisis is socially constructed through language... Thus communication is not something that occurs by organisations in crises, but rather something that constitutes the meaning that participants in that crisis come to hold' (p. 307).

The question for BP, as well as any organisation facing a major transgression, is whether grounding its messaging in a CSR-based strategy is appropriate — that is whether organisations in crisis can credibly disseminate their versions of reality. In the last couple of years, considerable attention has been paid to describing and analysing the response strategies that organisations deploy (Oles, 2010; Piotrowski & Guyette, 2010; Samkin, Allen, & Wallace, 2010, p. 927; Seeger & Griffin-Padgett, 2010; Sung-Un, Minjeong, & Johnson, 2010; Weber, Erickson, & Stone, 2011); however, scant attention has been paid to measuring stakeholder evaluations of those crisis response strategies. In fact, there have been only a handful of studies analysing stakeholder evaluations of crises. For example, Claeys, Cauberghe, and Vyncke's (2010) experiment applying Coombs (2007) situational crisis communication theory (SCCT) found that the type and severity of the crisis along with a person's locus of control influenced organisational image and strategy preference. This research focused on a limited variety of response strategies, as SCCT fails to consider the effectiveness of an organisation's efforts to use crisis response as a tool to socially construct both the organisation and crisis for stakeholders. Another example of a recent study analysing stakeholder evaluations of crises is Piotrowski and Guyette's (2010) analysis of the Toyota recall focusing on stakeholder evaluations and recall of leadership, brand loyalty and ethics. These findings provide important information about Toyota's ineffectiveness in managing their crisis but are not theoretically grounded; it is exploratory. Thus, while issues related to corporate irresponsibility have been analysed, there remains no benchmark for CSR messaging as an effective tool to socially construct a crisis.

The dearth of research on the effectiveness of CSR messaging comes at a time when organisations are moving towards 'socially responsible' messaging as a cornerstone of their routine and crisis messaging strategies (Tengblad & Ohlsson, 2010; Uccello, 2009). Theoretical analyses posit that consumers will more positively evaluate companies engaging in socially responsible activities because the company is viewed as having higher moral standards (Kreng & May-Yao, 2011). Yet, these changes in governance that promote social and/or ecological sustainability must also be rewarded by financial markets, benchmarked, audited and subject to public scrutiny (Frankental, 2001). One of the few studies directly examining the efficacy of a CSR strategy studies in recent years found a significant relationship between CSR messaging and public intentions to engage in dialogue with the company (Hong, Yang, & Rim, 2010). These findings suggest that CSR messages positively influenced corporate image, both increasing stakeholder intentions to interact and their identification with the company. Hong et al.'s (2010) findings also reveal a positive relationship between stakeholder identification and behavioural feedback intentions − that is their intent to continue interacting with the company.

The oil industry is one of the few industries where research on the influence of CSR on corporate policy has been conducted. For example, Frynas (2005) found that oil companies are paying increased attention to the social and environmental implications of their work, are engaging more effectively with local companies and seem to support integrating CSR into their business models by making organisational changes. In particular, BP is keenly aware of the relationship between being perceived as socially responsible and their reputation, causing them to actively incorporate CSR activities into their business strategy (Anderson & Bieniaszewska, 2005). This is why the BP case represents an important benchmark for measuring the effectiveness of a company's social construction efforts after a major transgression − BP is an industry facing increasing pressure for socially responsible corporate behaviour, it is a company that has embraced CSR as a corporate strategy and it is a company that fully deployed the strategy in response to the 2010 spill in the Gulf of Mexico.

# RELATIONAL MODEL OF CORPORATE IMAGE ASSESSMENT

The present study examines antecedents of BP's image one year after the crisis in order to assess whether BP was successful in using its language of social responsibility to construct a more positive image after the 2010 spill. The study is grounded by a relational approach to evaluating corporate image first articulated by Haley (1996) after analysing consumer understanding of advocacy advertising. Haley described advocacy advertising as image advertising focusing on corporations taking 'appropriate stands on key issues' (p. 19) and found that three core relationships described effective and ineffective advocacy messages (see Fig. 1): (1) the relationship between organisations and stakeholders emphasising common values and a positive image; (2) the relationship between organisations and issues focusing on stakeholder evaluations of the company's positive intent and capabilities on the issue and (3) the relationship between stakeholders and the issue itself recognising that issues must be important and actionable to stakeholders if advocacy messages are likely to be effective. The model aligns with previous research establishing that stakeholder characteristics (e.g. Clayes et al., 2010), public pressure from interested stakeholders in the face of corporate irresponsibility (e.g. Piotrowski & Guyette, 2010; Uccello, 2009) and engagement (e.g. Hong et al., 2010) are all likely to influence stakeholder evaluations and behavioural intentions towards organisations.

As a benchmark case, BP's effort to define itself and its efforts after the 2010 spill in the Gulf of Mexico represents an important opportunity to evaluate factors that could influence whether a corporate strategy centred on CSR messaging after significant threat to that strategy's authenticity does affect public stakeholders views of the company and issues. Simply

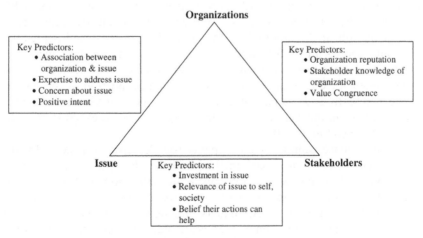

*Fig.1.* Relational Model of Stakeholder Evaluation of Advocacy Messages.

stated, BP has recognised and implemented CSR as an important component of their corporate strategy since at least 2005 (Anderson & Bieniaszewska, 2005) and that CSR approach was fully deployed in a multimedia response to the 2010 disaster that threatened the company (Diers & Donohue, 2011). Now, the questions remain – Is a CSR strategy effective when responding to a major crisis and for whom is the strategy most effective? To that end, I propose the following research questions based on the relational model of corporate image assessment:

**Research Question 1**: To what extent does the relationship between BP and the spill influence the relationship between stakeholders and BP?

**Research Question 2**: To what extent do stakeholder characteristics, investment with the Gulf spill, relevance of the Gulf spill and perceived ability to affect BP's actions influence the relationship between stakeholders and BP?

**Research Question 3**: To what extent do stakeholder characteristics, investment with the Gulf spill, relevance of the Gulf spill and perceived ability to affect BP's actions influence stakeholders' behavioural intent towards BP?

# METHODS

The present study triangulates findings by analysing stakeholder engagement on BP's Facebook page ($N = 1,515$) as well as an image survey of BP ($N = 749$). The Facebook messages were coded based on a random selection of the 9th of the month for May, June, July, August and September 2011 and coding all of BP's and member posts for those days. Approximately 45 people enrolled in an undergraduate advanced methods course were trained for one hour, given a codebook and a portion of the sample to independently code as part of a class project. Ten percent of the sample was coded by an independent coder and project leader to establish the reliability of the coding ($\alpha = 0.81$).

A convenience sample of participants was recruited via email by the same undergraduate advanced methods course. Prospective participants were given a link and asked to complete an anonymous online questionnaire. As a result, the sample had a relatively even distribution of men (42%) and women (58%), respondents ranging from 18 and 86 years old with a mean age of approximately 35 years old, were predominantly white (87%) and largely from the northeastern United States (80%).

## Variable Operationalisation

To operationalise the relationship between the organisation, spill and stakeholders using Facebook data, coders evaluated each Facebook member posts based on two personal interests communicated and two evaluations of BP. Member posts were analysed to look for a communication of personal interest in the Gulf coast — that is whether the member shared information like whether they lived, worked, vacationed, knew people in the region or felt so strongly about the issue that they seemed like they could be an activist. The other personal interest identified was their level of environmental interest based on their communication of the importance of environmental protection or issues. Each of these assessments was based on a rating from 1 to 7 (very low to very high). If the comment was unrelated to the variable, that was also noted.

In evaluating Facebook member attitudes towards BP, two other variables were coded on a 1−7 scale ranging from very negative to very positive. First, BP's image was coded based on the tone and content of the message about the company. Second, BP's connection to the Gulf coast was evaluated based on identification of assertions about whether BP cares about the Gulf coast, recovery and/or the spill. As with the personal interests, if the comment was unrelated that was also noted.

Using Haley's (1996) conceptualisation of advocacy advertising as the basis for assessing the key recovery relationships after a crisis, the survey analysed the influence of stakeholder characteristics, investment in the spill, relevance of the issue, and assessment of whether BP's actions can be influenced on measures of the relationships between organisation and issue as well as stakeholders and the organisation. Since this study includes new measures and operationalisations based on Haley's findings, Table 1 summarises the operationalisation of variables in this study. Exploratory principal components factor analyses with Varimax rotation were used to evaluate relevant items for each of the types of relationships tested. Emergent factors were then evaluated using Chronbeck's alpha for scale reliability.

Stakeholder characteristics were operationalised in three ways: age, gender and political identity. Age and gender were included both because there was a significant correlation between gender and environmental interest in the Facebook data ($r = -0.06$; $p < 0.05$). Political identity (i.e. conservativism vs. liberalism) was included because identity and the sociopolitical context has previously been identified as important influencers for organisational discourse (Finet, 2001; Mumby, 2001; Uccello, 2009).

*Table 1.*  Operationalisation of Study Variables.

| Relationship Tested | Variable | Questions | Factor Loading | Variance Explained | Alpha |
|---|---|---|---|---|---|
| Stakeholder to Gulf spill | Age | Age reported | N/A | N/A | N/A |
| | Gender | Gender reported | N/A | N/A | N/A |
| | Political identity | Tea party | 3.88 | 64.66 | 0.84 |
| | | Libertarian party | | | |
| | | Republican party | | | |
| | | Democratic party[a] | | | |
| | | Green party[a] | | | |
| | | Socialist party[a] | | | |
| | Relevance of issue | Personal relevance | 1.40 | 69.81 | N/A |
| | | Relevance to Americans | | | |
| | Ability to influence | Personal action | 1.81 | 59.14 | N/A |
| | | USFG action | | | |
| | Investment in spill | Knowledge of BP | 3.06 | 76.47 | 0.90 |
| | | Knowledge of spill | | | |
| | | Information seeking | | | |
| | | Accurately describe BP's response | | | |
| BP to Gulf spill | Ethic of CSR | BP setting good example for industry | 6.84 | 45.61 | 0.88 |
| | | BP demonstrates dedication to change | | | |
| | | BP demonstrates commitment to communities | | | |

| | | | | |
|---|---|---|---|---|
| | BP is trustworthy | | | |
| | BP is engaged in the community | | | |
| Commitment to clean-up | BP is focused on community responsibility | 6.84 | 45.61 | 0.87 |
| | BP communicates genuine concern | | | |
| | BP committed to fully restoring Gulf coast | | | |
| | BP's actions are sincere | | | |
| BP is self-serving | BP's actions are self-serving[a] | 1.03 | 6.84 | 0.76 |
| | BP's actions are only to manage their image[a] | | | |
| | BP's acting only because the USFG forced it[a] | | | |
| BP is corrupt | BP's corrupt | 2.12 | 14.10 | 0.86 |
| | BP's irresponsible | | | |
| | BP's deceptive | | | |
| Stakeholder to BP | | | | |
| Avoid patronising | Avoid buying gas from BP | 4.69 | 58.60 | N/A |
| Boycott BP | Willing to boycott BP | 4.69 | 58.60 | N/A |
| Advocate against BP | Post on BP's Facebook page | 4.69 | 58.60 | 0.90 |
| | Blog about BP | | | |
| | Join a BP watch campaign | | | |
| | Write a letter to my Congress person | | | |
| | Attend a demonstration against BP | | | |

[a]Reverse coded items.

Stakeholders' relationship between themselves and the spill was modelled after Haley's (1996) findings that the importance of the issue to themselves and society as well as stakeholder beliefs that their actions can help are key determinants of that relationship. It was assessed based on evaluations of the stakeholder investment, spill's relevance and ability to influence the crisis. These variables were assessed with 15 items and a total of four subscales.

Finally, the antecedents' influence was measured against stakeholder behavioural intentions towards BP. Although Haley's (1996) evaluation of the relationship between organisations and stakeholders focused on identifying the reputation, knowledge and value congruence of the organisation and stakeholders as important factors, these can be easily conceptually confused with stakeholder assessments of the company's relationship to the issue; therefore, as more direct measures of stakeholder assessments of reputation, their behavioural intent was evaluated. In campaign and persuasion research, behavioural intent is used as an important indicator of the effectiveness of a campaign's effectiveness (Yang, Liu, & Zhou, 2012). Because my goal is to evaluate the effectiveness of BP's CSR-based strategy, behavioural intent towards the company is a more direct measure of the relationship between stakeholders and BP. Intent was evaluated with two single-item measures of directly working to avoid buying gas at BP stations and more generally boycotting BP. Additionally, intent was measured in terms of stakeholders' willingness to advocate against BP.

### Analysis Methods

In order to evaluate each of the research questions, correlations and hierarchical regression analyses were used. First, a correlation analysis was performed in order to identify relationships between variables. Second, hierarchical multiple regression were performed to test the relationships. Collinearity tests revealed no significant multicollinearity problems.

# RESULTS

Broadly, these results demonstrate that a relational approach to evaluating CSR is a useful theoretical model indicating that relationships between stakeholders, issues and organisations are likely to influence the effectiveness of an organisation's CSR messaging (see Table 2). More directly, these results suggest that while negative evaluations of BP were not particularly high one year after the 2010 spill in the Gulf of Mexico, BP has not yet persuaded stakeholders that it is a company that values CSR.

## Influence of the Issue

Research questions one and two focused on the influence of the issue after a crisis, which is a moment of corporate irresponsibility. Findings for research question one (see Table 3) indicate that the more likely that BP was perceived as caring about the spill in the Gulf, the higher BP's image was among Facebook users interacting on BP's Facebook page $t$ (647) = 30.82; adjusted $R^2 = 0.59$.

Findings for research question two (see Tables 4–7) indicate that stakeholder characteristics, the relationship between stakeholders and the spill, and their perceived ability to influence BP's actions all consistently influence evaluations of the relationship between BP and the spill itself. Together, these findings indicate that political identity and investment are the two variables with the greatest overall influence on this relationship.

*Influence of stakeholder's relationship to the issue on perceptions that BP's intentions in the Gulf are corrupt.* Overall, while stakeholders' assessment of BP is slightly positive ($M = 3.84$), stakeholder characteristics, their investment, the relevance of the spill and the perceived ability to influence BP's actions predict approximately 10% of the variance in the relationship (see Table 4).

Stakeholder characteristics exercised the greatest influence on this measure. These data suggest that younger stakeholders are more likely to view BP as corrupt (adjusted $R^2 = 0.04$) and that the more conservative the stakeholder, the more likely to view BP as corrupt (adjusted $R^2 = 0.04$). Personal investment with the issue and its relevance each predicted about 1% of the variance. The greater the investment, the more likely respondents were to believe BP was corrupt. Similarly, the more personally relevant the spill was, the more likely BP was evaluated as corrupt, though in the final model, personal relevance was not significant. Finally, the more that stakeholders believed the United States Federal Government could influence BP's actions, the greater the perception that BP was corrupt (adjusted $R^2 = 0.01$).

*Influence of stakeholder's relationship to the issue on perceptions that BP's intentions in the Gulf are self-serving.* Overall, while assessments of BP suggest a moderate belief that BP is self-serving ($M = 4.40$), stakeholder

*Table 2.* Correlations for Survey Responses.

| Variable | 1 | 2 | 3 | 4 | 5 | 6 | 7 | 8 | 9 | 10 | 11 | 12 | 13 | 14 | 15 |
|---|---|---|---|---|---|---|---|---|---|---|---|---|---|---|---|
| 1. Gender | — | | | | | | | | | | | | | | |
| 2. Conservativism | 0.05 | — | | | | | | | | | | | | | |
| 3. Age | 0.08* | −0.09* | — | | | | | | | | | | | | |
| 4. Investment | −0.19** | 0.01 | 0.07 | — | | | | | | | | | | | |
| 5. Relevance: Personal | 0.16** | 0.08* | 0.15** | 0.17** | — | | | | | | | | | | |
| 6. Relevance: Americans | 0.09** | 0.03 | 0.20** | 0.09* | 0.40** | — | | | | | | | | | |
| 7. Response efficacy: Personal | 0.10** | −0.00 | −0.02 | 0.08* | 0.30** | 0.17** | — | | | | | | | | |
| 8. Response efficacy: USFG | 0.05 | 0.03 | −0.01 | 0.14** | 0.24** | 0.37** | 0.18** | — | | | | | | | |
| 9. BI: Avoid BP gas stations | −0.10** | 0.19** | −0.09* | −0.18** | −0.18** | −0.07 | −0.08* | −0.07 | — | | | | | | |
| 10. BI: Boycott BP | 0.14** | 0.28** | 0.03 | 0.11** | 0.27** | 0.20** | 0.09* | 0.27** | −0.49** | — | | | | | |
| 11. BI: Advocate against BP | 0.10** | 0.27** | −0.09* | 0.20** | 0.27** | 0.15** | 0.27** | 0.22** | −0.34** | 0.63** | — | | | | |
| 12. BP corrupt | −0.06 | 0.22** | −0.21 | 0.09** | 0.07* | 0.04 | 0.02 | 0.10** | −0.38** | 0.39** | 0.28** | — | | | |
| 13. BP self-serving | −0.08* | 0.22** | −0.07 | 0.21** | 0.09** | 0.12** | −0.05 | 0.17** | −0.40** | 0.41** | 0.31** | 0.54** | — | | |
| 14. BP quality action in Gulf | −0.02 | −0.30** | 0.04 | 0.07* | −0.04 | 0.07* | 0.11** | 0.09* | 0.37** | −0.35** | −0.21** | −0.39** | −0.42** | — | |
| 15. BP commitment to clean-up | −0.01 | −0.23** | 0.06 | −0.04 | −0.03 | 0.11** | 0.10** | 0.07** | 0.39** | −0.35** | −0.24** | −0.41** | −0.45** | 0.78** | — |

$N = 781$; *significant at the 0.05 level; **significant at the .01 level.

***Table 3.*** Correlations for Facebook.

| Variable | 1 | 2 | 3 | 4 | 5 |
|---|---|---|---|---|---|
| 1. Gender | – | | | | |
| | $n = 1,482$ | | | | |
| 2. Personal investment in Gulf | – 0.01 | – | | | |
| | $n = 1,390$ | $n = 1,411$ | | | |
| 3. Environmental interest | – 0.06* | 0.64** | – | | |
| | $n = 1,384$ | $n = 1,397$ | | | |
| 4. Image of BP | – 0.02 | – 0.04 | – 0.05 | – | |
| | $n = 717$ | $n = 703$ | $n = 707$ | | |
| 5. BP cares about the Gulf | 0.02 | 0.00 | – 0.07 | 0.77** | – |
| | $n = 677$ | $n = 672$ | $n = 673$ | $n = 649$ | |

$N = 1,515$; *significant at the 0.05 level; **significant at the 0.01 level.

characteristics, their investment, the spill's relevance and the perceived ability to influence BP's actions predict approximately 11% of the variance in the relationship (see Table 5).

Stakeholder characteristics (adjusted $R^2 = 0.05$) and investment (adjusted $R^2 = 0.04$) were the most powerful predictors of this perception. These data suggest that men were more likely to view BP as being self-serving with clean-up efforts. Further, conservatives were more likely to view BP's efforts as self-serving. The greater the personal investment in the issue, the more stakeholders believed BP's efforts were self-serving. While the relevance of the spill to respondents and Americans were significant when first introduced into the regression model, in the final model, they were not. Finally, the perceived ability of the USFG to positively influence BP's actions lead to conclusions that BP's actions were self-serving (adjusted $R^2 = 0.01$).

*Influence of stakeholder's relationship to the issue on perceptions that BP's intentions in the Gulf are rooted in an ethic of CSR.* Overall, while not a strong negative feeling, respondents do not believe BP's actions are grounded by CSR ($M = 3.31$). Political identity (adjusted $R^2 = 0.09$) and the perception that the USFG has positively influenced BP's actions (adjusted $R^2 = 0.01$) most influenced respondents' perceptions (see Table 6, adjusted $R^2 = 0.11$).

Though personal investment in the Gulf issue and the perceived relevance of the spill to Americans were significant when introduced into the model initially, once the perceived ability of the USFG to affect BP's actions positive was introduced, they were no longer influential. These data

**Table 4.** Regression Model for Corruption Measure.

| Regressor | Model 1 Beta | SE | t | Model 2 Beta | SE | t | Model 3 Beta | SE | t | Model 4 Beta | SE | t | Model 5 Beta | SE | t |
|---|---|---|---|---|---|---|---|---|---|---|---|---|---|---|---|
| Intercept | | 0.13 | 34.54 | | 0.22 | 16.14 | | 0.24 | 13.49 | | 0.25 | 12.22 | | .29 | 9.53 |
| Age | −0.21 | 0.00 | −5.95*** | −0.20 | 0.00 | −5.55*** | −0.20 | 0.00 | −5.78*** | −0.21 | 0.00 | −6.04*** | −.21 | .00 | −5.95*** |
| Conservatism | | | | 0.21 | 0.05 | 5.97 | 0.20 | 0.05 | 5.95*** | 0.20 | 0.05 | 5.72*** | .20 | .05 | 5.71*** |
| Investment | | | | | | | 0.11 | 0.04 | 3.13** | 0.10 | 0.04 | 2.76* | .09 | .04 | 2.54* |
| Spill relevance: Personal | | | | | | | | | | 0.07 | 0.03 | 2.12* | .06 | .03 | 1.58 |
| Response efficacy: USFG | | | | | | | | | | | | | .08 | .03 | 2.19* |
| F | 35.37*** | | | 36.31*** | | | 27.74*** | | | 22.02*** | | | 18.66*** | | |
| ΔF | | | | 35.67 | | | 9.78 | | | 4.49 | | | 4.80 | | |
| R² | 0.04 | | | 0.09 | | | 0.10 | | | 0.10 | | | .11 | | |
| R²adj | 0.04 | | | 0.08 | | | 0.09 | | | 0.10 | | | .10 | | |
| R² change | | | | 0.04 | | | 0.01 | | | 0.01 | | | .01 | | |
| df | 1,779 | | | 1,778 | | | 1,777 | | | 1,776 | | | 1,775 | | |

*p < 0.05, **p < 0.01, ***p < 0.001.

**Table 5.** Regression Model for Self-Serving Measure.

| Regressor | Model 1 | | | Model 2 | | | Model 3 | | | Model 4 | | | Model 5 | | |
|---|---|---|---|---|---|---|---|---|---|---|---|---|---|---|---|
| | Beta | SE | t | Beta | SE | t | Beta | SE | t | Beta | SE | t | Beta | SE | t |
| Intercept | | 0.17 | 28.05 | | 0.22 | 17.80 | | 0.25 | 12.73 | | 0.28 | 9.63 | | .29 | 8.40 |
| Gender | −0.08 | 0.10 | −2.27* | −0.09 | 0.10 | −2.66** | −0.06 | 0.10 | −1.60 | −0.07 | 0.10 | −1.96* | −.07 | .10 | −2.04* |
| Conservatism | | | | 0.22 | 0.04 | 6.30*** | 0.22 | 0.04 | 6.30 | 0.21 | 0.04 | 6.22*** | .21 | .04 | 6.21*** |
| Investment | | | | | | | 0.20 | 0.03 | 5.77 | 0.19 | 0.03 | 5.27*** | .18 | .03 | 4.96*** |
| Spill relevance: Personal | | | | | | | | | | 0.02 | 0.03 | .45 | .01 | .03 | .15 |
| Spill relevance: Americans | | | | | | | | | | 0.10 | 0.03 | 2.59** | .06 | .04 | 1.45 |
| Response efficacy: USFG | | | | | | | | | | | | | .12 | .03 | 3.34*** |
| F | 5.15* | | | 22.55*** | | | 26.74*** | | | 18.01*** | | | 17.06*** | | |
| ΔF | | | | 39.70 | | | 33.25 | | | 4.55 | | | 11.13 | | |
| R² | 0.01 | | | 0.06 | | | 0.09 | | | 0.10 | | | .12 | | |
| R²adj. | 0.01 | | | 0.05 | | | 0.09 | | | 0.10 | | | .11 | | |
| R² change | | | | 0.05 | | | 0.04 | | | 0.01 | | | .01 | | |
| df | 1,780 | | | 1,779 | | | 1,778 | | | 2,776 | | | 1,775 | | |

*p < 0.05, **p < 0.01, ***p < 0.001.

suggest that liberals were more likely to view BP's actions as being rooted in an ethic of CSR; further, the greater that the perception the USFG affected BP, the more that respondents believed BP's actions were rooted in CSR.

*Influence of stakeholder's relationship to the issue on perceptions that BP is committed to clean-up.* Overall, while not a strong negative feeling, respondents do not believe BP is committed to clean-up in the Gulf of Mexico ($M = 3.68$). Political identity, investment in the Gulf, the spill's relevance to Americans and the ability to influence BP's actions predict approximately 7% of the variance (see Table 7).

Liberals were more likely to view BP as being committed to clean-up (adjusted $R^2 = 0.05$). The more that respondents believed the spill was relevant to Americans, the more likely BP was perceived as being committed to clean-up. Finally, the more the USFG was perceived as able to influence BP, the more that BP was evaluated as committed to clean-up.

### Behavioural Intent Towards BP

Research question three evaluated three measures of behavioural intent regarding BP: stakeholders' intent to avoid buying gas from BP stations, their intent to boycott BP more generally and their intent to advocate against BP. These findings suggest that stakeholder characteristics, investment with the issue, relevance of the issue and perceived ability to affect BP were all significant predictors.

*Influence of stakeholder's relationship to the issue on their intent to avoid buying gas from BP stations.* Overall, respondents indicated they were moderately planning to avoid buying gas from BP ($M = 4.66$, adjusted $R^2 = 0.10$). Stakeholder characteristics, investment in the Gulf issue and perceived personal relevance of the spill all influenced behavioural intent (see Table 8).

All three measures of stakeholder characteristics significantly influenced this variable (adjusted $R^2 = 0.05$). Male, older and liberal respondents were all more likely to be willing to avoid BP stations. However, the more invested the respondent was in the issue, the less likely they were to avoid using BP gas stations (adjusted $R^2 = 0.04$). There was a similar negative relationship between the personal relevance of the spill and intent to avoid BP gas stations. The perceived ability to affect BP's actions was not a significant predictor.

Table 6. Regression Model for BP's Actions Rooted in CSR Measure.

| Regressor | Model 1 Beta | SE | t | Model 2 Beta | SE | t | Model 3 Beta | SE | t | Model 4 Beta | SE | t |
|---|---|---|---|---|---|---|---|---|---|---|---|---|
| Intercept | | 0.13 | 33.14 | | 0.16 | 27.07 | | 0.21 | 18.98 | | .22 | 16.83 |
| Conservativism | −0.30 | 0.04 | −8.64*** | −0.30 | 0.04 | −8.69*** | −0.30 | 0.04 | −8.76*** | −0.30 | .04 | −8.83*** |
| Investment | | | | 0.08 | 0.03 | 2.20* | 0.07 | 0.03 | 2.00* | 0.06 | .03 | 1.64 |
| Spill relevance: Americans | | | | | | | 0.08 | 0.03 | 2.19* | 0.04 | .03 | 1.03 |
| Response efficacy: Personal | | | | | | | | | | 0.06 | .03 | 1.64 |
| Response efficacy: USFG | | | | | | | | | | 0.09 | .02 | 2.60** |
| F | 74.68*** | | | 39.94*** | | | 28.36*** | | | 19.34*** | | |
| ΔF | | | | 4.83 | | | 4.82 | | | 5.35 | | |
| $R^2$ | 0.09 | | | 0.09 | | | 0.10 | | | 0.11 | | |
| $R^2_{adj.}$ | 0.09 | | | 0.09 | | | 0.10 | | | 0.11 | | |
| $R^2$ change | 0.01 | | | 0.01 | | | 0.01 | | | 0.01 | | |
| df | 1,780 | | | 1,779 | | | 1,778 | | | 2,776 | | |

$*p < 0.05$, $**p < 0.01$, $***p < 0.001$.

Table 7. Regression Model for BP Committed to Clean-Up Measure.

| Regressor | Model 1 Beta | SE | t | Model 2 Beta | SE | t | Model 3 Beta | SE | t |
|---|---|---|---|---|---|---|---|---|---|
| Intercept | | 0.15 | 30.70 | | 0.22 | 18.45*** | | 0.24 | 16.16 |
| Conservativism | −0.23 | 0.04 | −6.61*** | −0.23 | 0.04 | −6.75*** | −0.23 | 0.04 | −6.77*** |
| Spill relevance: Americans | | | | 0.12 | 0.03 | 3.48*** | 0.10 | 0.03 | 2.56** |
| Response efficacy: Personal | | | | | | | 0.03 | 0.03 | 0.84 |
| Response efficacy: USFG | | | | | | | 0.07 | 0.03 | 2.06* |
| F | 43.74*** | | | 28.22*** | | | 15.54*** | | |
| ΔF | | | | 12.08 | | | 2.74 | | |
| $R^2$ | 0.05 | | | 0.07 | | | 0.07 | | |
| $R^2$adj. | 0.05 | | | 0.07 | | | 0.07 | | |
| $R^2$ change | | | | 0.01 | | | 0.01 | | |
| df | 1,780 | | | 1,779 | | | 2,777 | | |

*$p < 0.05$, **$p < 0.01$, ***$p < 0.001$.

Table 8. Regression Model for Behavioural Intent: Avoid Buying Gas from BP Stations.

| Regressor | Beta | Model 1 SE | t | Beta | Model 2 SE | t | Beta | Model 3 SE | t | Beta | Model 4 SE | t |
|---|---|---|---|---|---|---|---|---|---|---|---|---|
| Intercept | | 0.30 | 16.59 | | 0.37 | 16.38 | | 0.40 | 17.69 | | .40 | 18.22 |
| Gender | −0.10 | 0.16 | −2.86** | −.09 | 0.15 | −2.59** | −0.13 | 0.15 | −3.78*** | −0.11 | .15 | −3.08** |
| Age | 0.10 | 0.01 | 2.79** | 0.08 | 0.01 | 2.36* | 0.10 | 0.01 | 2.92** | 0.12 | .01 | 3.42*** |
| Conservativism | | | | −0.18 | 0.07 | −5.07*** | −0.17 | 0.06 | −4.99*** | −0.16 | .06 | −4.68*** |
| Investment | | | | | | | −0.21 | 0.05 | −6.02*** | −0.18 | .05 | −5.22*** |
| Spill relevance: Personal | | | | | | | | | | −0.14 | .04 | −3.84*** |
| $F$ | 7.43*** | | | 13.68*** | | | 19.79*** | | | 19.06*** | | |
| $\Delta F$ | | | | 25.72 | | | 36.26 | | | 14.74 | | |
| $R^2$ | 0.02 | | | 0.05 | | | 0.09 | | | 0.11 | | |
| $R^2$ adj. | 0.02 | | | 0.05 | | | 0.09 | | | 0.10 | | |
| $R^2$ change | | | | 0.03 | | | 0.04 | | | 0.02 | | |
| df | 2,780 | | | 3,780 | | | 4,780 | | | 5,780 | | |

*$p < 0.05$, **$p < 0.01$, ***$p < 0.001$.

*Influence of stakeholder's relationship to the issue on their intent to boycott BP.* There was an important conceptual difference for stakeholders between avoiding buying gas and more generally boycotting BP as identified in these findings (see Table 9). While the desire to boycott was not strong ($M = 4.43$, adjusted $R^2 = 0.19$), the tested antecedents did substantially influence that behavioural intent.

Stakeholder characteristics (adjusted $R^2 = 0.09$), investment in the spill (adjusted $R^2 = 0.02$), perceived personal relevance of the spill (adjusted $R^2 = 0.05$) and perceived ability to influence BP's actions (adjusted $R^2 = 0.03$) were the most important predictors for the intent to boycott BP. In this case, women were more likely to boycott BP. Political identity accounted for about 7% of the variance on its own with a positive relationship between conservative identity and the intent to boycott BP. Additionally, the greater the personal investment with the spill, the more likely respondents were to support boycotting BP. Third, the greater the personal relevance of the Gulf spill, the more likely respondents reported being willing to boycott BP. Finally, the greater the perceived USFG influence on BP, the more likely that respondents were to support boycotting BP.

*Influence of stakeholder's relationship to the issue on their intent to advocate against BP.* While respondents indicated a moderately low level of intent to advocate against BP ($M = 3.39$), stakeholder characteristics, investment in the spill, relevance of the spill and perceived ability to influence BP significantly affected respondents' intent to advocate against BP predicting over one-fifth of the variance (see Table 10).

These data suggest that all three measures of stakeholder characteristics influence respondent intentions to advocate against BP one year after the Gulf spill (adjusted $R^2 = 0.08$). Women were more likely to report willingness to advocate against BP. Younger respondents were also more likely to report willingness to advocate against BP. However, the greatest influence was political identity (adjusted $R^2 = 0.07$) with conservatives reporting the greatest willingness to advocate against BP. In addition, the greater level of personal investment with the spill, the more willingness respondents reported for advocating against BP (adjusted $R^2 = 0.05$). Personal relevance of the spill and the relevance to Americans in general both significantly influenced willingness to advocate against BP (adjusted $R^2 = 0.05$); however, in the final model, relevance to Americans was not significant. Finally, the belief that BP's actions could be influenced significantly predicted whether respondents were willing to advocate against BP (adjusted $R^2 = 0.04$) with significant positive relationships for both personal influence as well as the USFG's influence.

Table 9.  Regression Model for Behavioural Intent: Boycott BP.

| Regressor | Model 1 Beta | SE | t | Model 2 Beta | SE | t | Model 3 Beta | SE | t | Model 4 Beta | SE | t | Model 5 Beta | SE | t |
|---|---|---|---|---|---|---|---|---|---|---|---|---|---|---|---|
| Intercept | | 0.26 | 13.44 | | 0.26 | 5.53 | | 0.37 | 2.80 | | 0.42 | -.09 | | .43 | -1.55 |
| Gender | 0.14 | 0.16 | 4.04*** | 0.13 | 0.15 | 3.76*** | 0.15 | 0.15 | 4.47*** | 0.11 | 0.15 | 3.21*** | .11 | .15 | 3.19** |
| Conservativism | | | | 0.27 | 0.06 | 7.86*** | 0.27 | 0.06 | 7.84*** | 0.25 | 0.06 | 7.62*** | .25 | .06 | 7.65*** |
| Investment | | | | | | | 0.14 | 0.05 | 3.97*** | 0.09 | 0.05 | 2.62** | .07 | .05 | 2.14* |
| Spill relevance: Personal | | | | | | | | | | 0.17 | 0.04 | 4.64*** | .16 | .04 | 4.23*** |
| Spill relevance: Americans | | | | | | | | | | 0.11 | 0.05 | 3.14** | .05 | .05 | 1.35 |
| Response efficacy: Personal | | | | | | | | | | | | | -.02 | .04 | -.58 |
| Response efficacy: USFG | | | | | | | | | | | | | .19 | .05 | 5.50*** |
| $F$ | 16.33*** | | | 39.66*** | | | 32.20*** | | | 30.35*** | | | 26.80*** | | |
| $\Delta F$ | | | | 61.72 | | | 15.77 | | | 24.64 | | | 15.15 | | |
| $R^2$ | 0.02 | | | 0.09 | | | 0.11 | | | 0.16 | | | .20 | | |
| $R^2_{adj.}$ | 0.02 | | | 0.09 | | | 0.11 | | | 0.16 | | | .19 | | |
| $R^2$ change | | | | 0.07 | | | 0.02 | | | 0.05 | | | .03 | | |
| $df$ | 1,780 | | | 1,779 | | | 1,778 | | | 2,776 | | | 2,774 | | |

*p < 0.05, **p < 0.01, ***p < 0.001.

**Table 10.** Regression Model for Behavioural Intent: Advocate against BP.

| Regressor | Model 1 Beta | SE | t | Model 2 Beta | SE | t | Model 3 Beta | SE | t | Model 4 Beta | SE | t | Model 5 Beta | SE | t |
|---|---|---|---|---|---|---|---|---|---|---|---|---|---|---|---|
| Intercept | | 0.23 | 13.94 | | 0.28 | 6.71 | | 0.31 | 3.32 | | 0.33 | 1.40 | | .34 | −.22 |
| Gender | 0.10 | 0.12 | 2.85** | 0.09 | 0.12 | 2.47* | 0.13 | 0.12 | 3.75*** | 0.09 | 0.12 | 2.60** | .07 | .11 | 2.20* |
| Age | −0.10 | 0.00 | −2.80** | −0.08 | 0.00 | −2.21* | −0.10 | 0.00 | −2.81** | −0.13 | 0.00 | −3.95*** | −.11 | .00 | −3.24*** |
| Conservativism | | | | 0.26 | 0.05 | 7.51*** | 0.25 | 0.05 | 7.50*** | 0.23 | 0.05 | 7.09*** | .24 | .05 | 7.46*** |
| Investment | | | | | | | 0.22 | 0.04 | 6.45*** | 0.18 | 0.04 | 5.22*** | .16 | .04 | 4.73*** |
| Spill relevance: Personal | | | | | | | | | | 0.20 | 0.03 | 5.42*** | .14 | .03 | 3.75*** |
| Spill relevance: Americans | | | | | | | | | | 0.07 | 0.04 | 1.87 | .02 | .04 | .42 |
| Response efficacy: Personal | | | | | | | | | | | | | .18 | .03 | 5.27*** |
| Response efficacy: USFG | | | | | | | | | | | | | .12 | .04 | 3.36*** |
| F | 7.41*** | | | 24.09*** | | | 29.42*** | | | 28.41*** | | | 27.79*** | | |
| ΔF | | | | 56.41 | | | 41.60 | | | 23.07 | | | 21.41 | | |
| $R^2$ | 0.02 | | | 0.09 | | | 0.13 | | | 0.18 | | | .22 | | |
| $R^2_{adj.}$ | 0.02 | | | 0.08 | | | 0.13 | | | 0.17 | | | .22 | | |
| $R^2$ change | | | | 0.07 | | | 0.05 | | | 0.05 | | | .04 | | |
| df | 2,778 | | | 1,777 | | | 1,776 | | | 2,774 | | | 2,772 | | |

*p < 0.05, **p < 0.01, ***p < 0.001.

# DISCUSSION

The purpose of this study was to use a relational model of impression management to evaluate two questions: Is a CSR-centred strategy effective when responding to a major crisis and for whom is it most effective? Aside from answering these questions, the findings demonstrate that a relational model of corporate image assessment, grounded in Haley's (1996) work on advocacy advertising (see Fig. 1), can effectively predict antecedents and outcomes associated with organisational advocacy. The model supports previous crisis research emphasising that crisis response is a contextually bound phenomenon (Carroll, 2009) and meaningfully develops our theoretical knowledge of the relationships between emergent issues (e.g. examples of corporate (ir)responsibility), organisations and stakeholder assessments. Applied in this case, the model affords us the opportunity to better evaluate an organisation's ability to construct a preferred reality after a crisis using CSR-based messaging.

## CSR Messaging, Limited Social Construction

Does CSR messaging construct a compelling reality after a major crisis? The answer to this question largely depends on BP's strategic goals. Previous research indicated that BP has long viewed CSR as an important component in their corporate strategy (Anderson & Bieniaszewska, 2005), with analyses of BP's response to the 2010 Gulf spill conclusively demonstrating that CSR-based messaging grounded BP's crisis response strategy (e.g. Diers & Donohue, 2011). If BP's goal was to be viewed as a socially responsible corporation one year after the spill, then these data suggest that BP's objective largely failed. The company's response to the spill is viewed as being moderately self-serving, moderately unlikely to be rooted in an ethic of CSR and moderately negatively committed to clean-up in the Gulf of Mexico. One weakness of this data is that there is no direct measure of BP's image in 2010 during or after the spill as a point of comparison for these findings. Repeating this assessment in the future could better evaluate if BP's image has changed and in which direction.

Similarly, if a goal of CSR messaging is to create good will towards the company, particularly in the face of a transgression, it also seems like BP has failed in this respect as well. These data suggest that behavioural intent is still negative towards BP as demonstrated by the respondents' moderate intent to either avoid buying gas from BP stations or boycott BP more generally. Because these two actions were predicted by opposite stakeholder characteristics (i.e. men, older respondents and liberals were more likely to be willing to avoid buying gas from BP stations and women and conservatives were more likely to be willing to boycott BP more generally), we can conclude that most people still view their relationship with BP as a negative.

Through these conclusions, it is important to note that there are some seemingly contradictory findings. For example, evaluations that when stakeholders perceive the US government as effectively influencing BP's actions, BP is viewed as significantly more self-serving paired with the finding that some stakeholders believe BP's actions are rooted in an ethic of CSR or even more clearly the findings that personal relevance of the issue can have both a positive and negative relationship with stakeholders' willingness to boycott BP. Given the strong influences of gender, age and political identity for each of these findings, I would argue that these findings demonstrate a limitation in the effectiveness of any response strategy – identity politics. In the United States, identity politics is ruling – in fact, Americans are probably more divided along gender, age and political identification now than at any point in the last three decades (Debevec, 2012). As such an influential component of the sociopolitical environment, it helps to explain these seemingly contradictory findings and demonstrate a significant limitation for any crisis response strategy.

*The silver lining for BP.* There may, however, be a silver lining as we evaluate BP's use of CSR as a response strategy. Though the relationships between BP and the Gulf of Mexico and stakeholders and BP are still generally negative, these data suggest there are three relatively positive outcomes for BP one year after the spill. First, the Facebook data have two important implications. Initially, there are a lot of people engaging BP on Facebook, confirming Hong et al.'s (2010) analysis that a CSR strategy can lead to important dialogue between a company and its stakeholders. Thus, while BP may not have created a new reality on its own, its consistent use of CSR as a messaging strategy seems to have opened the lines of communication between stakeholders and the company. That dialogue may lay the groundwork for an increasingly positive relationship between various stakeholder groups and BP in the future. Further, the analysis of member comments on Facebook indicates that when members perceive that BP cares about the spill in the Gulf, it predicts they will view BP more positively almost 60% of the time. That direct relationship between the perception of BP caring and a positive image suggests that when BP successfully persuades stakeholders they care, the relationship between the stakeholders and the company is going to improve.

The second positive indicator for BP and the utility of CSR as a message strategy is that one year after the spill, most respondents did not view BP as a fundamentally corrupt organisation. Though BP struggles with particular groups (i.e. younger participants and conservatives), these findings suggest that the negative association with BP is likely less about the fundamental character of the company and more about the evidence of their actions. In this way, BP was able to influence stakeholders' understanding of the company's character. Applying Haley's (1996) findings, these data suggest that while the BP's reputation is still negatively affected, it is not viewed as having values that are largely incongruous with most respondents. This suggests that the reputational problem can yet be addressed.

Finally, whilst stakeholders are still wary of patronising BP, these data suggest that most respondents were unlikely to be interested in actively advocating against BP one year after the spill. This, in combination with the dialogue evident on BP's Facebook page, is an indication that BP's CSR-based response strategy may have minimised the outrage towards BP. Though these data would indicate this may be true, I am wary about the causal connection between CSR and the interest in advocating against BP because of factors not tested in this study. For example, within one year after the spill, the environmental and economic effects of it seem to have been minimised. Thus, future research should analyse the influence of 'problems solved' as a mediating factor influencing the relationship between messaging and willingness to advocate against an organisation that has been irresponsible.

*Overall implications of a CSR strategy.* As one of the few direct measures of the use of CSR, these data suggest that while it may not be a solution to reputational problems, it may be strategically useful for an organisation trying to persuade stakeholders that it is a good company despite the transgression. Repeated measures of the changes in stakeholders' attitudes towards a company would substantially validate these findings. Absent the evaluations of changes in these outcome variables, these data can only describe the outcomes of BP's CSR-based response one year after the end of the Gulf spill. Yet, these cross-sectional data do suggest that there are reputational and dialogic benefits to this approach.

*Factors Influencing the Effectiveness of CSR as a Crisis Response Strategy*

By applying the relational model of corporate image assessment, we can better understand what influences both stakeholder evaluations of the quality of an organisation's actions as well as their behavioural intentions towards the organisation. These data suggest that the stakeholder's relationship to the issue and the organisation reveal new information about the effectiveness of CSR as a crisis response strategy. Equally important, these data tell a consistent story about who may be most susceptible to a company's use of the CSR crisis strategy. Thus, one of the strongest contributions this research makes is beginning to identify a profile of stakeholder characteristics, values and activism that should be pursued in future research.

*Moderator variables.* Moderator variables strengthen the direction or relationship between other independent variables and the dependent variables. Therefore, because personal investment – that is stakeholders' interest, information seeking behaviours and perceived knowledge about the issue – and the relevance of the issue to the stakeholder were consistently significant regardless of other stakeholder characteristic variables (i.e. they were significant regardless of the direction of the political identify, gender or age variables), these two variables are likely moderator variables in assessing the relationship between organisations, stakeholders and issues. For example, if we compare the findings from research question two assessing stakeholder intentions to avoid buying gas from BP and the willingness to advocate against BP, we find the exact opposite stakeholder characteristics predicting these behavioural intentions and similar influence of investment and relevance. Specifically, older, male and liberal stakeholders were more willing to avoid buying gas from BP stations where younger, female and conservative stakeholders were more willing to advocate against BP; yet, on both measures, investment and relevance were significant predictors as well.

These findings indicate for those populations interested in taking action for or against an organization, investment, and perceived relevance only strengthen those interests. Yet, in this moderator relationship is an opportunity for CSR messaging to affect the relationship because information-seeking behaviour is an essential component to investment. If an organisation is successful in reaching out to populations depending on their interests, then they have the opportunity to strengthen or even change the relationship between the stakeholders and organisation.

*Stakeholder profiles.* These data also suggest that understanding key stakeholder characteristics will help organisations reliably predict the probability that CSR messaging will be effective. Age and sex are certainly important demographic considerations for organisations trying to manage relationships, especially because younger demographics and women are much more likely to adopt an activist identity against organisations that have committed a transgression violating the public trust. In particular, younger demographics are more likely to view multinational corporations as corrupt organisations indicating CSR strategies may be less effective in changing the company's reputation.

However, the most striking finding was for the influence of political identity on assessments of BP's image and stakeholder behavioural intentions towards the company. The central arguments that BP made in their CSR messaging during the Gulf spill and in the year after were that they cared about the Gulf and its people (i.e. they had adopted an ethic of CSR) and were committed to fully restoring the Gulf. These data clearly suggest that liberals were more likely to view BP as adopting a CSR ethic and being committed to clean-up, suggesting that the messaging strategy was significantly more successful among liberals. Conversely, conservatives consistently evaluated BP more negatively. The negative evaluations seemed to be amplified with the perceived influence of the USFG on BP's actions. That is, for conservatives who were already inclined to evaluate BP negatively, when these respondents perceived BP as being swayed by the federal government's demands on the company, they evaluated BP even more negatively. For those who have followed American politics in the last several years, these findings are not surprising because they support a dominant theme communicated in the American conservative media − that taking money away from stockholders and cooperating with the democratic president are fundamental violations of 'conservative' values in the United States. These findings suggest that political dogmatism may make some stakeholders more susceptible to CSR messaging, likewise others less susceptible to CSR messaging. Future research should validate these conclusions with different organisations and contexts.

# CONCLUSIONS

There are two major contributions that this piece makes examining the effectiveness of the CSR strategy as a tool of crisis social construction after a major transgression. First, these data suggest that while strategies centred on social/environmental responsibility are not a panacea for transgressors, the CSR strategy is likely to improve dialogue between stakeholders and the organisation and separate evaluations of the transgression from the fundamental character of the organisation. These outcomes will likely help organisations move forward from irresponsible actions. Yet, organisations must create realistic objectives if they use CSR messaging as an integral part of their crisis response.

Second, the BP case confirms the utility of the relational model of image assessment to evaluate the effectiveness of CSR strategies. In so doing, these data reveal four important conclusions that should not only help develop future research but organisations to better apply CSR messaging to appropriate stakeholder groups. Initially, these data contributed to the conceptualisation of the relational model of image assessment by focusing on behavioural intentions as a key indicator of the relationship between stakeholders and the organisation. By doing so, it more effectively conceptually separates this relationship from reputational assessments of the organisation's actions. Second, these findings indicate that stakeholder characteristics are critical determinants of the relationships between stakeholders, organisations and emergent issues. Future research should focus on creating a more comprehensive typology of stakeholder characteristics that increase susceptibility to CSR messaging. Third, in line with Haley's (1996) arguments, perceived value congruence between stakeholders and organisations is an essential variable to evaluate the effectiveness of CSR messaging. This study only assessed political identity; however, that was the most consistently powerful predictor of respondent perceptions of BP. Future research needs to continue to identify important value congruence variables. Finally, the present research demonstrates the centrality of the issue itself in understanding the outcomes of CSR messaging strategies.

# REFERENCES

Anderson, C., & Bieniaszewska, R. (2005). The role of corporate social responsibility in an oil company's expansion into new territories. *Corporate Social Responsibility and Environmental Management*, *12*(1), 1–9.

Beal, A. (2010, June 23, 2010). BP's social media failure. *SoCon11 Archives*. Retrieved April 29, 2012.

Bell, J. (2012, April 20, 2012). The Gulf Spill: BP still doesn't get it. *Forbes*. Retrieved from http://www.forbes.com/sites/frederickallen/2012/04/20/the-gulf-spill-bp-still-doesnt-get-it/. Accessed on August 22, 2012.

Carroll, C. (2009). Defying a reputational crisis – Cadbury's salmonella scare: Why are customers willing to forgive and forget? *Corporate Reputation Review, 12*(1), 64–82.

Chazan, G., & Crooks, E. (2012, June 8). BP seeks $15bn spill settlement. *Financial Times*. Retrieved from http://www.ft.com/cms/s/0/69771938-b184-11e1-9800-00144feabdc0. html#axzz1yAOF1ZUW. Accessed on June 18, 2012.

Claeys, A., Cauberghe, V., & Vyncke, P. (2010). Restoring reputations in times of crisis: An experimental study of the situational crisis communication theory and the moderating effects of locus of control. *Public Relations Review, 36*(3), 256–262. doi: 10.1016/j. pubrev.2010.05.004

Coombs, W. T. (2007). Protecting organizational reputations during a crisis: The development and application of situational crisis communication theory. *Corporate Reputation Review, 10*(3), 163–176.

Debevec, N. (2012, June 10). Political identity deeply divisive. *United Press International*. Retrieved from http://www.upi.com/Top_News/US/2012/06/10/Politics-2012-Political-identity-deeply-divisive/UPI-12271339318920/. Accessed on June 18, 2012.

Diers, A. R., & Donohue, J. (2011). *Multi-media strategic crisis engagement: An analysis of BP's enacted crisis response to the Deepwater Horizon crisis in 2010*. Chapter presented at the EUPRERA Annual Congress, Leeds Metropolitan University, Leeds, UK.

Diers, A. R., Gurien, D., & Otten, R. (2011, October). *Lions or lambs? Analyzing the responsive role of BP's corporate leaders during the Gulf spill crisis*. Chapter presented at the 2nd International Research Group on Crisis Communication Conference Aarhus University, Aarhus Denmark.

Diers, A. R., & Pang, A. (2011, October). *Rhetoric of remorse: An analysis of BP's structure of apology in the Gulf Coast oil spill*. Chapter presented at the 2nd International Research Group on Crisis Communication Conference, Aarhus University, Aarhus Denmark.

Finet, D. (2001). Sociopolitical environments and issues. In F. M. Jablin & L. L. Putnam (Eds.), *The new handbook of organizational communication: Advances in theory, research, and methods* (pp. 270–290). Thousand Oaks, CA: Sage.

Frankental, P. (2001). Corporate social responsibility – A PR invention? *Corporate Communications: An International Journal, 6*(1), 18–23.

Frynas, J. (2005). The false developmental promise of corporate social responsibility: Evidence from multinational oil companies. *International Affairs, 81*(3), 581–598. doi: 10.1111/j.1468-2346.2005.00470.x

Hearit, K. M., & Courthright, J. L. (2003). A social constructionist approach to crisis management: Allegations of sudden acceleration in the Audi 5000. *Communication Studies, 54*(1), 79–96.

Haley, E. (1996). Exploring the construct of organization as source: Consumers' understandings of organizational sponsorship of advocacy advertising. *Journal of Advertising, 25*, 19–36.

Hong, S., Yang, S., & Rim, H. (2010). The influence of corporate social responsibility and customer–company identification on publics' dialogic communication intentions. *Public Relations Review, 36*(2), 196–198. doi: 10.1016/j.pubrev.2009.10.005

Kreng, V. B., & May-Yao, H. (2011). Corporate social responsibility: Consumer behavior, corporate strategy, and public policy. *Social Behavior and Personality: An International Journal, 39*(4), 529–541. doi: 10.2224/sbp.2011.39.4.529

Mumby, D. K. (2001). Power and politics. In F. M. Jablin & L. L. Putnam (Eds.), *The new handbook of organizational communication: Advances in theory, research, and methods* (pp. 585–623). Thousand Oaks, CA: Sage.

Oles, D. L. (2010). Deny, delay, apologize: The Oprah Winfrey image-defense playbook. *Northwest Journal of Communication, 39*(1), 37–63.

Piotrowski, C., & Guyette, R. W. (2010). Toyota recall crisis: Pubic attitudes on leadership and ethics. *Organizational Development Journal, 28*(2), 89–97.

Samkin, G., Allen, C., & Wallace, K. (2010). Repairing organisational legitimacy: The case of the New Zealand police. *Australasian Accounting Business & Finance Journal, 4*(3), 23–45.

Seeger, M. W., & Griffin-Padgett, D. R. (2010). From image restoration to renewal: Approaches to understanding postcrisis communication. *The Review of Communication, 10*(2), 127–141. doi: 10.1080/1535859090354526

Shogren, E. (2011, April 21). BP: A textbook example of how not to handle PR Morning. Retrieved April 29, 2012.

Sung-Un, Y., Minjeong, K., & Johnson, P. (2010). Effects of narratives, openness to dialogic communication, and credibility on engagement in crisis communication through organizational blogs. *Communication Research, 37*(4), 473–497. doi: 10.1177/00936502 10362682.

Tengblad, S., & Ohlsson, C. (2010). The framing of corporate social responsibility and the globalization of national business systems: A longitudinal case study. *Journal of Business Ethics, 93*, 653–669.

Uccello, C. (2009). Social interest and social responsibility in contemporary corporate environments. *Journal of Individual Psychology, 65*(4), 412–419.

Warner, J. (2010, June 18, 2010). The Gulf of Mexico oil spill is bad, but BP's PR is even worse. *The Telegraph.* Retrieved from http://www.telegraph.co.uk/finance/newsbysector/energy/oilandgas/7839136/The-Gulf-of-Mexico-oil-spill-is-bad-but-BPs-PR-is-even-worse.html. Accessed on August 22, 2012.

Webb, T. (2010, June 1, 2010). BP's clumsy response to oil spill threatens to make a bad situation worse. *The Guardian.* Retrieved from http://m.guardian.co.uk/business/2010/jun/01/bp-response-oil-spill-tony-hayward?cat = business&type = article

Weber, M., Erickson, S. L., & Stone, M. (2011). Corporate reputation management: Citibank's use of image restoration strategies during the U.S. banking crisis. *Journal of Organizational Culture, Communication and Conflict, 15*(2), 35–55.

Yang, H., Liu, H., & Zhou, L. (2012). Predicting young Chinese consumers' mobile viral attitudes, intents, and behavior. *Asia Pacific Journal of Marketing and Logistics, 24*(1), 59. doi: 10.1108/13555851211192704

# PART IV
# CSI IN PRACTICE: SYSTEMIC AND STRUCTURAL ISSUES

# THE STRUCTURAL DYNAMICS OF CORPORATE SOCIAL IRRESPONSIBILITY: THE CASE OF THE CANADIAN MINING INDUSTRY

Nicole Marie Lindsay

## ABSTRACT

Purpose − *This chapter examines how structural dynamics of the global mining industry condition and limit the positive impacts of corporate responsibility and sustainable development strategies, despite considerable efforts on the part of both the Canadian government and the global mining industry to promote the twin concepts.*

Methodology/approach − *The chapter reviews current literature highlighting the structural elements of corporate irresponsibility in the mining industry, arguing for a radical reconceptualization of governance in the mining industry based on four dimensions of responsibility and backed by a flexible and robust international legal framework.*

Research/practical implications − *This chapter presents practical implications for improving policy for and regulation of mining companies,*

Corporate Social Irresponsibility: A Challenging Concept
Critical Studies on Corporate Responsibility, Governance and Sustainability, Volume 4, 207−230
Copyright © 2012 by Emerald Group Publishing Limited
All rights of reproduction in any form reserved
ISSN: 2043-9059/doi:10.1108/S2043-9059(2012)0000004018

*Canadian or otherwise, with international operations. While further research needs to be undertaken to explore in more detail the ideal roles of different actors in a system of international governance, this chapter provides a theoretical framework for integrating four dimensions of responsibility into a governance framework that can address the systemic dynamics of organized irresponsibility in the mining industry.*

**Keywords:** Mining; corporate social responsibility (CSR); governance

In late September 2011, Canada's national news radio, CBC, aired a documentary focused on the conflict between a Canadian mining company, HudBay Minerals, and an indigenous Mayan Q'eqchi' community in Guatemala. In a forced eviction of the community in 2007, government and private security forces working on behalf of Skye Resources, the then-owner of a nickel mining concession, allegedly raped 11 women (Wells, 2011). In 2008, HudBay acquired Skye Resources and the El Estor (Fenix) mine, and in 2010, a Toronto law firm representing the 11 Mayan Q'eqchi' women filed a lawsuit against the company. The documentary recounts the legacy of conflict and violence surrounding the mine in Guatemala, a legacy for which the company claims it bears no responsibility. However, in the words of Rosa Elbira, one of the 11 women raped during the evictions,

> Not only did they rape me, but they destroyed my house. I'm pretty sure they will never pay me for any of the damage they did to me. And that's why we're seeking justice. We're tired of the fear that we live in. I want them to go home. Take the company, go home to its own country. All the investors in this company are from another country. I don't know who they are. I certainly can't go to their house and break their things. If I did something like that they would probably kill me. (Wells, 2011, np)

This story is only the latest to appear in the Canadian news as a growing awareness of violence and conflict at many foreign mines operated by Canadian companies raises concerns about not only the human rights and environmental risks of mining, but also of the reputation of Canadian companies who operate controversial mines abroad. In September 2011, Goldcorp, one of the largest gold mining companies in Canada, was removed from the Dow Jones North America Sustainability Index, and a shareholder resolution presented to the company's board in March 2012 highlighted concerns around the environmental contamination resulting from its Marlin mine in Guatemala as a factor (Goldcorp shareholders' resolution, 2012). The conflicts surrounding HudBay and Goldcorp's operations in Guatemala were also the subject of the television documentary *Lost Paradise* aired in April 2010 on Canada's CTV network. In June 2011, under the headline 'Scandals Piling up in the World of Canadian Business', a Canada.com news article recounted a violent clash between protestors and police over a Canadian-run mine in Peru which left five dead (Abma, 2011).

On the surface the mining industry seems an unlikely place to look for insights about the movement of corporate responsibility. However, the very nature of the mining industry makes some degree of social and environmental conflict almost a given at any mine site. Modern open-pit extraction processes consume enormous amounts of land and water, employ dangerous chemicals in mineral processing, and produce permanent deposits of toxic waste rock and water known as tailings. The risks inherent in large-scale mining projects have in many regards triggered the upsurge of activity around the idea of corporate social responsibility (CSR) in the industry. Mining industry groups and the Canadian government have taken seriously the call for improved social and environmental performance in the industry, resulting in a proliferation of social responsibility codes, guidelines and initiatives at both the national and international levels. However, while these initiatives represent a significant movement towards improving social and environmental responsibility among industry leaders, the voluntary nature of the initiatives, along with uneven participation rates, means that industry laggards remain largely unmonitored and free to act with impunity in jurisdictions with weak regulation for human rights and social and environmental protection.

This chapter takes the position that, given the complexities of the political economic context in which Canadian mining companies operate, mainstream policy approaches favouring voluntary self-regulation of the industry contribute to a 'recipe for irresponsibility' among industry laggards and a culture of complicity throughout the industry. Although rigid government command-and-control approaches to regulating business are clearly outdated, laissez-faire market solutions that have allowed corporations to define what constitutes 'responsibility' and encouraged them to monitor themselves have obvious limitations in an economic context defined by the imperative to maximize profit in a competitive global marketplace. This chapter argues that systemic limitations presented by the global economic context need to be understood and addressed in order to move beyond polarizations between hard and soft regulation of business and toward a more responsive, inclusive and robust mode of governing the business—society relationship in the mining industry.

# CANADA, MINING AND ITS CORPORATE RESPONSIBILITY INFRASTRUCTURE

Canada is considered by many to be the centre of the mining universe. The Toronto Stock Exchange (TSX) is one of the world's leading centres for mining finance, and Toronto is also the location of over 400 mining company offices, with 30 head offices and a multitude of suppliers, consultants and other service providers. Western Canada is a centre for junior and exploration companies, with most of British Columbia's 1,200 exploration companies headquartered in Vancouver (MAC, 2010, pp. 12–13). Combined, Canada's stock exchanges have seen 82% of the world's mining finance transactions over the past five years, providing 32% of the equity raised in these transactions (MAC, 2010, p. 68). Canada's long history of domestic mineral exploration and exploitation means that it is also a hub for experienced industry professionals ranging from geologists, engineers and consultants to finance and legal experts.

As one might expect, the mining industry figures prominently in the Canadian economy. In 2009 its contribution to the national economy was $32 billion, or 4.3% of GDP (MAC, 2010). This is consistent with a GDP contribution ranging from 3.0% to 4.5% over the past 20 years, making the mining and oil and gas extraction sector Canada's third-most important in the goods-producing sectors (behind only manufacturing and the construction industry) (Statistics Canada, 2012). The Canadian mining industry is also a major player internationally, with over 800 companies operating in 100 countries, together accounting for 40% of global exploration spending. The Mining Association of Canada reports that Canadian-listed firms have over 4,300 mineral projects outside of Canada, representing an estimated $56 billion of foreign direct investment as of 2009 (MAC, 2010).

*Industry Leadership: The Early Development of Canadian Mining CSR*

Canada can also claim leadership in the early development of CSR and sustainable development norms in the mining industry. Responding to a range of external pressures building in the early 1990s, a small handful of Canadian mining companies began to take seriously external calls to improve their social and environmental performance, largely from environmental and watchdog NGOs and church-based civil society organizations.

Dashwood (2007) documents these early developments in CSR norm-development in two Canadian mining companies that she identifies as CSR leaders: Noranda, which released its first CSR report in 1990, and Placer Dome, which released its first report in 1998. Dashwood points to three indicators which gauge the importance of CSR norms for these and other companies. The first indicator is a shift in thinking about CSR at the senior level of management, suggesting a cumulative learning process among mining companies based on 'persuasion and rational calculations of what is required to ensure [their] continued acceptance' (Dashwood, 2007, p. 135). The second indicator is the adoption of the language of sustainable development in framing CSR policies. The third indicator is industry-level cooperation to promote CSR policies, practices, rules and norms.

As Dashwood (2007) notes, a small number of Canadian mining companies were early movers in applying the concepts and language of CSR and sustainable development in the mining industry in the 1990s. However, by the end of the first decade of the 21st century, CSR and sustainable development had become well established in the lexicon of mining companies, industry associations and branches of government concerned with development of Canada's domestic and international mining industry. By 2003, annual reporting on CSR and sustainability on the part of mining companies had become standard practice in the industry (Jenkins and Yakovleva, 2006), not just in Canada but internationally as well. And as Dashwood (2011) points out, by the end of the decade, the majority of mining companies of all sizes were publishing annual CSR or sustainability reports, including 40 out of 56 major mining companies headquartered in Canada, the United States, the United Kingdom and Australia.

Much of the increase in CSR reporting in the mining industry could be attributed to industry association efforts to promote the same. An early example originated in Canada in 1991 with the establishment of the International Council on Mining and the Environment (ICME) which released its Sustainable Development Charter in 1998. The Global Mining Initiative (GMI) was launched in 1998 by a group of mining company executives concerned with promoting CSR in the industry, leading eventually to the creation of the International Council on Mining and Metals (ICMM) in 2001 and the publication of its Sustainable Development Principles in 2003.

Adding to these international industry initiatives are initiatives undertaken by industry associations at the national level in Canada. In 2004, the Mining Association of Canada (MAC) released the Towards Sustainable

Mining (TSM) initiative, and the Prospectors and Developers Association of Canada (PDAC) first released its *e3* Framework for Responsible Exploration in 2003 and significantly updated it as the *e3* Plus in 2009. These initiatives provide detailed guidelines for use of industry best practices regarding environmental and social performance and all three encourage annual reporting on performance. However, uptake is still incomplete, with industry leaders following and reporting to the fullest extent of recommendations while many other companies choose not to participate fully or at all. Given the voluntary approach, relatively underdeveloped verification measures and lack of meaningful sanction for under-performance, the power of these initiatives to hold industry laggards accountable and meaningfully raise standards for social and environmental performance in the industry is limited (Lindsay, 2011).

## The Canadian Government and Mining CSR

The Canadian government has also taken up CSR in the mining industry as an area of policy development. In 2005 a subcommittee of the Canadian government's Standing Committee of Foreign Affairs and International Trade (SCFAIT) submitted a report to the Parliament of Canada, presenting concerns about the lack of a clear regulatory environment for Canadian mining companies operating overseas. The report, entitled *Mining in Developing Countries — Corporate Social Responsibility*, urged the Canadian government to develop stronger monitoring and complaints mechanisms for Canadian mining companies operating overseas, as well as greater incentives for Canadian companies to adhere to international human rights standards (SCFAIT, 2005; Seck, 2008). However, the government response to the SCFAIT report rejected recommendations to create clear legal norms through which Canadian mining companies might be held accountable for human rights and environmental abuses at their overseas operations, arguing that to do so would raise problems around extraterritorial jurisdiction and potentially create conflict with the sovereignty of foreign states (Seck, 2008).

One recommendation that the government did implement, however, was the creation of a multi-stakeholder public consultation on the issue of Canadian mining companies with overseas operations. The government convened a steering committee to work with the multi-sectoral advisory group that was formed to submit a report based on public round-table discussions held in four Canadian cities during 2006. These roundtable discussions saw industry and NGO representatives, government, academics and members of mining-affected communities consider a broad range of issues related to Canadian mining CSR in developing nations. The resulting advisory group report submitted in 2007 was seen by many as the result of a 'hard-won' consensus among participants with widely varying perspectives and interests (Drohan, 2010). The report made recommendations, among others, that the Canadian government establish a robust CSR framework for Canadian extractives companies with overseas operations.

The CSR framework recommended by the advisory report included a number of different elements. Among these were ongoing development of CSR standards; CSR performance reporting requirements; an ombudsman to provide advisory and fact-finding services and to review and report on complaints; a compliance committee; development of appropriate sanctions for under-performance, including withdrawal of government financial and diplomatic support; and the creation of a multi-stakeholder advisory group to develop the framework further (National Roundtables on Corporate Social Responsibility and the Canadian Extractive Industry Advisory Group, 2007).

For many involved in the roundtable process, the Canadian government's response to the Advisory Report, which was released in 2009 after a lengthy wait, represented a profound disappointment insofar as it rejected most of the recommendations made by the advisory report. Rejected recommendations included those that would have presented the greatest risk to continuing 'business as usual' in the industry – the creation of an independent ombudsman to investigate complaints, implementation of a compliance committee to monitor firm behaviour and the development of sanctions for companies found to be in violation of CSR standards.

Instead, the official response, released in a document entitled *Building the Canadian Advantage: A Corporate Social Responsibility (CSR) Strategy for the Canadian International Extractive Sector*, announced the government's intention to support capacity building in host states through Canadian International Development Agency (CIDA) programmes, to promote existing CSR standards and guidelines, to create a CSR Centre for Excellence to promote industry-led best practices and to create the office of the Extractive Sector CSR Counsellor – a new arm's length office focused on dispute resolution between Canadian companies and civil society groups who claim to be negatively impacted by their operations.

Although very little time has passed in which to assess the impact of the new initiatives announced by the Canadian government, it is worth noting that all of these initiatives fall squarely within the 'soft' regulatory approach preferred by the mining industry. Even the dispute resolution process of the Office of the Extractive Sector CSR Counsellor is entirely voluntary. At any point during the dispute resolution process, either party may withdraw from the process without repercussions. Indeed, in the first case reviewed by the Counsellor, this is precisely the outcome. A dispute was brought to the CSR Counsellor by two unions and a civil society group representing workers at Excellon Resource's La Platosa mine in the state of Durango, Mexico, and although the company initially agreed to participate in the process, it later withdrew before reaching the dialogue stage of dispute resolution (Office of the CSR Counsellor, 2011).

Notwithstanding the specifics of the Excellon case referred to above, many critics of the government's preferred policy approach have argued that voluntary initiatives lacking in meaningful sanction hold little promise for improving performance among industry laggards. Drohan's (2010) assessment of the government's CSR strategy echoes these sentiments:

> Having rejected a hard-won consensus between mining companies and their critics on a workable accountability framework, the government has come forward with an inadequate response that still leaves people in developing countries vulnerable to abuse without redress, allows responsible companies to be tarred along with the guilty, and tarnishes Canada's image abroad. (Drohan, 2010, p. 1)

Drohan's point is underscored by the increasing recognition that, despite the government's stated commitment to promoting CSR and despite industry leadership in the development of frameworks and norms, egregious abuses of these norms on the part of Canadian mining companies continue to surface. A watchdog report released in 2010 focused primarily on the Latin American operations of Canadian mining companies writes that in the months before the release of the report, 'several critics of Canadian mining companies have been murdered in El Salvador, Guatemala, and Mexico' (Keenan, 2010, p. 30). In 2012, shortly before the publication of this book, conflict surrounding a Canadian owned and operated mine in the state of Oaxaca, Mexico, left two anti-mining activists dead and several injured. Although the direct lines of responsibility are unclear – in one case, municipal police were ordered to fire at a group of people protesting the laying of a pipeline to the mine, and in the other, the killing appears to have been a direct assassination – civil society and activist groups monitoring the conflict have little doubt that, ultimately, culpability lies with the company (Paley, 2012).

These and other examples of what most casual observers would consider obvious cases of corporate social irresponsibility abound, providing ample evidence for NGO watchdog, civil society groups and representatives of mining-affected communities to argue that CSR discourse coming from industry and government is in many cases little more than feel-good rhetoric.

## CSR, Law and Securities Regulation

While the CSR infrastructure offered by industry and government seems unlikely to move beyond soft regulatory approaches, many have looked to civil and securities law as mechanisms to increase accountability for social and environmental outcomes in mining. Webb (2011a) provides an overview of Canadian law related to social and environmental mining issues. His analysis shows that although the law holds considerable potential in addressing social and environmental issues, there still exist deficiencies in both the laws themselves and in their implementation. Webb (2011a) examines the use of private litigation, shareholder proposals and anti-bribery law in efforts to hold companies accountable for alleged abuses, and although these methods have thus far had limited success, he suggests that the increasing use of legal measures against mining companies should serve as a caution for companies to put in place stronger CSR policies which might prevent potential legal problems from arising in the first place.

Securities law offers another relatively untested ground for addressing CSR accountability. Under regulation designed to protect investors, all companies listed on Canadian stock exchanges are required by law to publicly disclose information regarding the financial health and security of their operations. Mining companies are required to adhere to a number of regulations regarding disclosure, including those specified in National Instrument 51–102, Continuous Disclosure Obligations (NI 51–102); Form 51–102F1, Managements' Discussion and Analysis (MD&A); Form 51–102F2, Annual Information Form (AIF); and National Instrument 43–101, Standards of Disclosure for Mineral Projects (National Instrument 43–101, n.d.). Each of these regulatory tools contains guidelines for the types of information companies must disclose and the manner in which this information is to be presented.

Most of the disclosure requirements contained in the regulations listed above are intended to standardize financial and technical reports in order to provide investors with full and accurate information regarding the value of potential and proven extractives operations. However, despite growing recognition that social, environmental and political risk factors can present significant operational costs for large-scale mining projects, particularly in developing nation contexts, reviews conducted by the Ontario Securities Commission (OSC) have identified a number of limitations in regards to environmental disclosure in current regulations (OSC, 2008, 2009).

In 2008, the OSC reviewed the continuous disclosure (CD) documents of 35 reporting issuers in a number of sectors: environmental services, industrial products, mining, oil and gas, steel, transportation services and utilities. The review found that, while some issuers presented detailed reports on environmental liabilities, costs and risks, a significant number still failed to present any disclosure on these issues, and others addressed issues using boilerplate language insufficient to meet disclosure requirements (OSC, 2008). Following from this review, the OSC conducted a further review of corporate governance and environmental disclosure standards and compliance, and presented a report to Ontario's Minister of Finance which contained recommendations to enhance disclosure. Recommendations included further compliance reviews, educational outreach and additional guidance to issuers, and improved training for OSC staff regarding disclosure of environmental matters (OSC, 2009).

In 2010, the Canadian Securities Administrators (CSA) released a staff notice entitled *Environmental Reporting Guidance*, which clarifies the regulations and provides guidance for reporting issuers in '(1) determining what information about environmental matters needs to be disclosed, and (2) enhancing or supplementing their disclosure regarding environmental matters' (CSA, 2010, p. 1). The guidance document provides an overview of a range of disclosure requirements regarding environmental risk, trends and uncertainties, environmental liabilities and costs of compliance with environmental protection regulations. However, despite the very real potential threat of social conflict around large-scale mining projects, a survey of applicable regulation by the author of this chapter found only two references to social or political risk disclosure. NI 43–101, Standards of Disclosure for Mineral Projects, states in section 3.4(d), Requirements Applicable to Written Disclosure of Mineral Resources and Mineral Reserves, that 'if an issuer discloses in writing mineral resources or mineral reserves on a property material to the issuer, the issuer must include in the written disclosure ... (d) the identification of any known legal, political, environmental, or other risks that could materially affect the potential development of the mineral resources or mineral reserves' (NI 43–101, nd 9). Similarly, in

Form 51–102F1 (Management's Discussion and Analysis) section 1.4(d) (Discussion of Operations), issuers are required to discuss 'any factors that have affected the value of the project(s) such as change in commodity prices, land use or political or environmental issues' (Form 51–102F1, 2011, p. 6).

While these disclosure requirements are steps in the right direction and should help to ensure that companies review social and environmental issues as a matter of due diligence, more research needs to be done to assess the potential for securities law to act as a meaningful mechanism in improving the social and environmental performance of mining companies. Although a complaint to the securities commission could trigger an investigation of a company's disclosure documents, a social or environmental issue is only considered 'material' if it has a direct impact on share values. Since virtually every mining project has opponents, potential conflict with an affected community, for example, might not be considered material until it resulted in operational disruptions. Thus, the definition of materiality is determined by the company according to the degree of probability that a given problem will impact share value, and oversight appears relatively limited in the absence of a formal complaint to the securities commission.

## Opportunities and Limitations of the Canadian CSR Infrastructure

There is little doubt that, for the majority of Canadian mining companies, CSR policies and programmes offer a flexible, efficient way to anticipate, address and avoid a significant number of potential social and environmental problems. Further, as many authors have demonstrated, the development and institutionalization of CSR norms in the mining industry exerts pressure for individual companies to seek conformity with rising expectations. Webb (2011b) refers to the emergence and institutionalization of CSR norms as a process of 're-responsibilization', arguing that the recent development of the ISO 26000 standard on social responsibility, for example, represents a paradigm-shifting event in institutionalizing the emerging expectations to which corporations must aspire as they negotiate a 'complex arrangement of government and market-based regulatory instruments' (p. 18).

However, the gap between the CSR policy and practice of industry leaders and the negative social and environmental outcomes of industry laggards is an ongoing problem for which current regulatory

instruments – either government or market-based – seem unable to meaningfully address. The problem is further exacerbated by a marked lack of
third-party empirical research documenting the relationship between CSR
policies/best practices in the industry and sustainable development outcomes in the medium to long term. Although such a body of research is
emerging, it has been slow to take shape and it is arguably limited in scope
by the practical problem of defining key issues across the divergent and
complex social, political, environmental and economic contexts which the
global mining industry spans. This chapter represents one attempt to widen
the scope of analysis in the interests of better understanding how and why,
while CSR guidelines, policies and programmes proliferate across the
industry, irresponsible behaviour on the part of many mining companies,
Canadian and otherwise, appears to be business as usual.

## THE POLITICAL ECONOMY OF RESPONSIBILITY

While questions about the responsibilities of corporations are not new, the
acceleration of economic globalization since the mid-20th century and con-
current increase in the size, geographic reach, and economic and political
power of corporations has lent a sense of urgency to debates regarding
their rights and social responsibilities. Quite simply, by the end of the 20th
century, the largest multinational corporations (MNCs) had begun to
eclipse some nations in their economic power, and global pressures from
powerful economic actors to open domestic markets to foreign investment
and reduce barriers to free trade and flow of goods, services and investment meant further that MNCs of all sizes were increasingly free to operate outside of their home state regulatory jurisdictions, often in countries
with thin rule of law and weak regulatory capacity.

### Protect, Respect and Remedy: The UN Framework for
### Business and Human Rights

Notwithstanding the serious environmental issues related to economic
globalization, the human rights abuses that have surfaced in the context of
global economic liberalization, or neoliberalism, have triggered the work
of the United Nations Special Representative of the Secretary-General
(SRSG) on the issue of human rights and transnational corporations and

other business enterprises. Over the course of his work on this issue, John Ruggie has noted the significance of economic globalization and associated governance gaps as a fundamental problem, writing in 2008 that:

> The root cause of the business and human rights predicament today lies in the governance gaps created by globalization - between the scope and impact of economic forces and actors, and the capacity of societies to manage their adverse consequences. These governance gaps provide the permissive environment for wrongful acts by companies of all kinds without adequate sanctioning or reparation. How to narrow and ultimately bridge the gaps in relation to human rights is our fundamental challenge. (Ruggie, 2008, p. 3)

In 2011, Ruggie released his final report, presenting a set of guiding principles on for implementation of the 'Protect, Respect and Remedy' framework. The framework sets out the responsibilities of governments and corporations as consisting of three pillars: government duty to protect against human rights abuse by third parties, corporate duty to respect human rights and the need for access to remedy for victims of human rights abuse (Ruggie, 2011, p. 4).

The framework and guiding principles together provide a clear and coherent summation of the core issues relating to business and human rights, presenting a set of normative and high-level policy recommendations to focus government and corporate aspirations. However, the framework falls short of recommending the creation of an international legal framework along the lines of multi-lateral free trade agreements, which regulate government and corporate behaviour regarding business and trade. Significantly, these norms are enforced through law, and mining companies may seek reparations for lost investment through a system of courts, as is demonstrated by the ongoing CAFTA (Central American Free Trade Agreement) lawsuit brought against the government of El Salvador by the Canadian mining company Pacific Rim, through its American subsidiary (see Collins, 2009).

Critics of voluntary or 'soft' legal approaches to regulating corporate responsibility have long argued for the creation of a similarly robust and binding legal mechanism whereby victims of abuse might seek access to remedy, irrespective of the willingness or ability for any national legal framework to do so. However, Ruggie's recommendations leave states with the discretion to 'consider a smart mix of measures − national and international, mandatory and voluntary − to foster business respect for human rights' (Ruggie, 2011, p. 8), although he also recommends that states 'take appropriate steps to ensure the effectiveness of domestic judicial mechanisms when addressing business-related human rights abuses' (*ibid.*, p. 23).

In the mining industry, Canada could be an excellent test site for assessing the impact of Ruggie's recommendations — it is a relatively strong state where currently mining companies working overseas are virtually unregulated and where 'non-nationals who are adversely affected by the overseas operations of Canadian extractive companies face daunting barriers in accessing the country's legal system' (Keenan, 2010, p. 31). Following Ruggie's recommendations, the Canadian government should be under increased pressure to improve access to remedy for victims of corporate abuse at foreign mining operations run by Canadian companies.

*The Meaning of 'Responsibility' in a Context of 'Organized Irresponsibility'*

Ruggie's recommendations and other forms of 'soft' regulation intend to counter what Giddens (1999), following Beck refers to as 'organized irresponsibility'. Characteristic of an era of manufactured risk in which human development has created a wide range of uncertainties — of which even the existence of manufactured problems are sometimes highly disputed — organized irresponsibility arises from the ambiguous nature of cause and effect in which 'responsibility can neither easily be attributed nor assumed' (Giddens, 1999, p. 8). Examples abound in the mining industry, but consider in particular issues relating to water use in an era of climate change. A large-scale mining operation uses enormous amounts of water each day to extract and process raw minerals, and as a result mines frequently dig wells to avoid affecting the water supply of surrounding areas. However, given a context of relative scarcity, as is the case in many more arid areas negatively impacted by climate change, and the interconnected nature of regional water tables, shortages of water in mining-affected regions are frequently attributed to the high volume use of mining companies. But given unclear cause and effect and the absence of technical or scientific evidence, companies may quite easily deny responsibility by attributing water shortages to broader climactic issues — a claim that would be difficult to either prove or disprove.

Furthermore, 'responsibility' is to begin with an ambiguous concept. Pellazzoni (2004) takes up the meaning of responsibility in the context of environmental governance in an era of radical uncertainty. In the literature on governance, Pellazzoni (2004) notes that

> the concept of responsibility is invoked with considerable frequency. However, it is also surprisingly underdeveloped. Governance, it is said, entails the enhancement or

a change in the relations of responsibility. However, there is hardly any attempt to deepen this statement and make the concept of responsibility analytically useful. (p. 542)

In searching for an analytically useful framework for better understanding responsibility, Pellazzoni identifies four ideal types of responsibility emerging from moral philosophy. The first two, 'care' and 'liability', refer to the push-factor elements of responsibility in which a normative or legal expectation exists for a person or entity to do something. For example, if the normative or legal expectation exists for a mining corporation to do no harm to the environment, then the company can be seen as having a responsibility to care for the environment, and, failing to do so, it might be held liable for any damages done. As Pellazzoni notes, these dimensions of responsibility can be seen in the functioning of the modern state – 'care' insofar as it expresses the relationship between government and its constituents, and 'liability' through a judicial system that aims to remedy transgressions of care. Indeed, in Ruggie's 'Protect, Respect and Remedy' framework the 'protect' pillar might be seen as embodying the 'care' dimension of responsibility insofar as it spells out the ex ante duties of a caring state, and likewise the 'respect' pillar as inferring ex post liability for corporations should they fail to adhere to standards regarding human rights.

While liability is still generally regarded as a core dimension of responsibility, it has obvious limitations in the context of economic globalization in which MNCs frequently operate outside the jurisdiction of a strong state authority. Further, the challenge of radical uncertainty in environmental matters alluded to above – in which either the links between events and outcomes are poorly understood, or significant time lags between events and outcomes make attribution more difficult – further undermines the possibility of legitimately inferring legal liability in many cases.

Pellazzoni points out that the shift away from command-and-control forms of government and movement toward looser, more horizontal and multi-lateral networks of governance corresponds with a shift from 'liability' to the third dimension of responsibility – 'accountability', in which ex post justification, evaluation and monitoring replaces legal and regulatory enforcement. In such a context, Pellazzoni (2004) writes that 'the focus of responsibility shifts from causal imputation to reasoned justification' (p. 550) – in other words, the rise of more flexible soft regulations is based on relations of answerability and justification through voluntary adherence to guidelines, self-assessment and disclosure. Current environmental governance, largely favouring a system of voluntary self-regulation and CSR, fits squarely within this dimension of responsibility. As Pellazzoni and many others have pointed out, however, this orientation towards soft regulation can be problematic for a number of reasons, including 'lack of transparency, free riding, self-definition of goals, self-accounting, and doubtful effectiveness' (p. 556). Further, it has 'not yet lived up to expectations as regards the improvement of environmental protection and the recovery of institutional and corporate legitimacy and social trust' (p. 560).

One possible remedy, Pellazzoni suggests, might be found in a fourth, and as of yet relatively neglected, dimension of responsibility – 'responsiveness'. For Pellazzoni, responsiveness entails a process of genuine listening, understanding and inclusion of perspectives not generally included in scientific–technological liability approaches or in self-referential accountability approaches. Integrating responsiveness into accountability and liability regimes means moving beyond standard processes of consultation, which are often exclusionary and entail one-way information sharing, and into the rather more radical terrain of deliberative democracy, citizen-empowerment and innovative experiments in participatory governance.

While Pellazzoni's typology of responsibility adds analytic clarity to debates about governance and CSR, many other critical observers might argue that current governance regimes are far from integrating the relatively radical notion of responsiveness in which 'precautionary approaches ... take into consideration an extended range of evidences, viewpoints and concerns' in environmental matters (Pellazzoni, 2004, p. 561). The Canadian government's weak response to the National Roundtables on CSR is a clear example of the failure for a governance regime based on accountability principles to respond meaningfully to the findings of a broad-based consultation process, showing a clear policy preference for the type of soft regulation favoured by industry.

### The Political Economy of CSR and Corporate Irresponsibility

Literature critical of the ability for corporations to meaningfully self-regulate frequently points to the structural elements of capitalism and the modern corporation that limit the depth and meaning of CSR policy and practice. Ireland (2010), for example, is very clear on both the origins and implications of the coupling of exclusive control rights and limited liability for corporate directors characteristic of the modern corporation:

> What needs to be kept constantly in mind is that the corporate legal form is a contingent legal construct, a complex structure of rights and privileges with many different

elements. Its emergence and development in its specific contemporary form was not the economically determined product of efficiency-driven evolution. It was, rather, in significant part the product of the growing political power and influence of the financial property owning class.. ... The way in which it is currently configured, with its coupling of limited (or no) liability and exclusive rights is a recipe for irresponsibility. (pp. 853–854)

The recipe for irresponsibility contains other crucial ingredients, however, which have been well documented in the tradition of critical political economy. The reorganization of global capitalism over the 20th century culminated in the realization of the neoliberal vision during the 1980s and 1990s in most parts of the world as states opened their markets to freer flows of trade and investment, decreased regulation of business and increased regulation *for* business (Newell, 2001; Peck & Tickell, 2002). The emergence of CSR during an era of structural change which saw a marked expansion in the global reach and influence of corporations has prompted many critics to see CSR as inherently limited insofar as its primary goal appears to be in legitimating rather than transforming the very structures that provide the permissive environment and economic imperatives at the root of corporate irresponsibility. As Newell (2008) writes,

CSR is ultimately and inherently a product of the neoliberal political economy from which it emerged and which it aims to legitimate and advance, re-producing its modalities, technologies of governance and failings. In this regard there is a preference for selective engagements in private arenas — discretionary, closed, lacking in sanctioning measures. (p. 1069)

Critical observers of corporate responsibility in the mining industry pay particular attention to the significance of structural transformations in the global political economy of mining in creating a new and extraordinarily permissive environment for mining MNCs. Consistent with transformations in other sectors of the global economy, the last two decades of the 20th century marked a period of profound structural shifts in regulation of mining investment and development in many countries around the world, but most significantly in developing nations. As Szablowski (2002) writes,

Spurred by reigning market and foreign investment-led development philosophies, states throughout the South liberalized mining and investment legislation, privatized state mining companies, and rewrote tax codes to encourage foreign participation and leadership within their mineral economies. This, together with technological advances in the industry and favourable metals prices in the early 1990s, opened up enormous new regions for mineral exploration and development by transnational mining companies. (p. 247)

Campbell (2003) refers to the same movement in structural relations in the mining industry on the African continent. She notes that, in many countries, mining sector reforms that were aimed to create investment-friendly climates entailed 'a redefinition of the role of local states which is so profound that it has no historical precedent' (p. 3). Major international institutions such as the World Bank were influential in mandating the restructuring of states in order to stimulate and facilitate foreign direct investment in the mining sector. This type of structural adjustment, as it has been called, was seen as crucial for economic development in regions affected by high levels of poverty and national debt.

The rapid expansion of mining exploration and development in Africa (Campbell, 2003, 2008) and Latin America (Szablowski, 2002, 2007) result-ing from structural adjustment policies has contributed to the 'recipe for irresponsibility' in the sector – particularly where Canadian (and other foreign) mining companies come into direct conflict with communities affected by legacies of poverty, marginalization and political violence. Hamann, Kapelus, and O'Keefe (2011) point out that the conflict-prone relationships between constitutional states and traditional leadership struc-tures in African countries dealing with the legacies of European colonial-ism can be exacerbated by the presence of a mine because 'the stakes in decision-making become so much higher with the onset of prospecting and mine development' (p. 261). Similarly, in countries with unresolved indige-nous land rights issues, such as Peru, Bolivia, Brazil and Guatemala, mining companies can become unwitting agents in historical conflicts between states and indigenous communities, risking complicity with human rights abuse when state and private security forces become involved in vio-lent confrontations, as the example of HudBay in Guatemala clearly demonstrates.

## CONCLUSION: RESPONSIVE GOVERNANCE FOR RESPONSIBLE MINING

There is little question that different and more effective modes of gover-nance are needed in the mining industry in order to prevent harm – to ecosystems, communities, local economies, and to future generations who must deal with the long-term ecological, social and political eco-nomic outcomes of the surge in both scale and numbers of extractives operations.

But who exactly can and should take responsibility for these issues remains a critical problem. As a leading mining country, Canada can and should take leadership in addressing the complex problems associated with mining, but as this chapter has argued, the CSR frameworks, guidelines and initiatives that proliferate in the Canadian mining sector fall short. However, the attention and resources invested in the development of CSR initiatives indicate that both industry and government recognize that irresponsibility in the mining industry is a problem that must be addressed. Despite this, both the private and public sectors seem either incapable or unwilling to move beyond voluntary approaches with weak (if any) sanctions for under-performance. In this chapter, I've argued that the structural limits of CSR as it is currently practised and the complexity of the political economic context in which mining companies, governments and communities engage in negotiations over mining development needs to be given more attention in order to address two crucial questions for the industry: first, what might responsible mining look like, particularly in contexts where governance is weak and the risk of harm is high and, second, how might responsible mining best be enabled by coordinating the capabilities of multiple actors?

Clearly, there is no simple or singular approach for addressing either question, and much more work is needed to begin to move towards meaningful answers. Although an enormous and growing body of work exists on the technical aspects of reducing the ecological harm associated with mining, the search for genuine 'responsibility' in the mining industry needs to move beyond the technical and management approaches preferred by industry to deal with the more fundamental questions of when, where and how mining ought to take place. This broader approach reflects the orientation taken by Miranda, Chamber, and Coumans (2005) in formulating a framework for responsible mining based on four themes: (1) deciding whether a mine is an appropriate use of land; (2) ensuring environmentally responsible mine development; (3) ensuring that mine development results in benefits to workers and affected communities; and (4) ensuring that appropriate corporate governance structures are in place (p. xv). A key element of the approach taken by the authors of this report is in recommendations for the active engagement with communities and workers through decision-making in all four theme areas, corresponding with Pellazzoni's (2004) fourth, neglected, dimension of responsibility discussed above — responsiveness.

In an era of increasing demands to respect both human rights and ecosystem limits, decisions about where and when to mine take on increased significance. However, at present both governments and companies are subject to the imperatives of capital accumulation and economic growth in a competitive environment —dynamics which stand in direct opposition to the slow, careful, informed and responsive deliberation that would be required for a truly responsible approach to mining. Such an approach — responsive governance based on respect for human rights and sustainable ecosystems — would require an enormous and coordinated shift in the priorities and principles at the basis of the global political economy, and must be backed by flexible yet robust international regulation, as well as civil society capacity building. As Idemudia (2010) writes,

> While the call for legally binding international regulations is a necessity and a reflection of socio-political realities in developing countries, if CSR is to contribute to development, the call for global regulation of TNCs should be situated within the broader context of efforts that seek to constrain the negative effects of capital accumulation. This means efforts to ensure corporate accountability must be undertaken in tandem with efforts to ensure state-society accountability.... Therefore, in places like Nigeria, global regulation should be backed by social and technical capacity building of civil society (i.e., social forces) to enhance its relative ability to contest issues, seek accountability, and influence the state. (p. 149)

At present, no such international or global regulatory framework exists, and the idea of creating one may seem to be a lofty goal. However, as Idemudia and others have argued, global regulation of transnational corporations is desperately needed in order to avoid escalations of the types of conflicts witnessed routinely around large-scale mining projects — not just in 'weak governance' zones in Latin American or African nations, but also in areas of supposedly strong governance like Canada, where exploration and resource extraction projects are creating conflict with First Nations around unsettled indigenous land claims.

By framing the problem of responsible mining as a systemic problem, it becomes clear that solutions must operate at a systemic level as well. Preliminary explorations of systemic approaches to governance such as Webb's (2005) sustainable governance and the social and environmental value governance ecosystem (SEVGE) view (Sagebien & Lindsay, 2011) emphasize the varying roles and capabilities that multiple actors can contribute in a context of collaborative governance. By necessity, in the case of international mining, this collaborative governance must be of an international, multi-lateral nature. Such efforts are not without precedent. For example, in the recent history of the global mining industry, coordinated efforts on the part of international development institutions, industry groups and national governments have resulted in an open and permissive regulatory operating environment for mining companies in many countries in Latin America and Africa (Campbell, 2003, 2008; Szablowski, 2002, 2007). While this approach has triggered an economic boom in the industry in many of these countries, the uneven distribution of economic benefits and social and environmental harms resulting from rapid mining expansion has frequently undermined hopes for inclusive and sustainable development in these regions. In a context where communities are arming themselves with knowledge, and, in many cases, civil disobedience tactics aimed to prevent harm, it would be highly irresponsible for either home or host governments, international development institutions or the global mining industry to continue to ignore the 'perversities' or 'externalities' created by permissive regulatory environments for large-scale mining projects, particularly where vulnerable communities are impacted by these projects.

A 'middle way' in the global mining industry between command-and-control regulation on the one hand and organized irresponsibility on the other would require compromise and collaboration among all system actors. Further, all four dimensions of responsibility – care, liability, accountability and responsiveness – should be represented in codes and guidelines, legal standards, reporting and transparency requirements, and ongoing inclusive dialogue. With a history of considerable policy development focused on enhancing CSR in the mining industry, Canada is uniquely positioned to lead international efforts at finding such a middle way. And given the importance of the mining industry to its national economy, it has much to gain by doing so. As Bonnie Campbell (2008) writes,

> It would be short-sighted for the [Government of Canada] not to advance the debate concerning accountability and responsibility in the mining sector. For the issue of reinforcing the legitimacy of the regulatory processes which govern mining activities, if these are to be sustainable, needs to be reset within the broader framework of ensuring resources are developed to contribute to the improvement of the livelihoods of the populations in the communities and countries concerned. The security of mining companies and their activities will never be assured if [that of] mining communities and countries where they operate is not also assured and the promise of social and economic development respected. These issues are inextricably linked. (Campbell, 2008, pp. 383–384)

Returning to the case of the lawsuit against HudBay Minerals for the alleged rape of 11 women in the evicted community in El Estor, Guatemala, the CBC documentary closes by noting that in the summer of 2011, HudBay withdrew from Guatemala and the mining concession was sold to a Russian company at a significant loss (Brown, 2011). Although the current court case against HudBay by the 11 Mayan Q'echi women will still proceed through the Canadian courts, the outcome of the case is uncertain and future claims will not be heard in Canada. Unfortunately they will not likely be heard anywhere else either, until there exists a system of international governance based on care, liability, accountability and responsiveness backed by the type of legal framework which upholds trade agreements and mirroring the flexible, adaptive and rapidly expanding international nature of the mining industry.

# REFERENCES

Abma, D. (2011). *Scandals piling up in world of Canadian business.* Retrieved from http://www.canada.com/business/Scandals + piling + world + Canadian + business/5033622/story.html

Brown, J. (2011). *Firm hopes to keep HudBay lawsuits alive despite sale.* Retrieved from http://www.canadianlawyermag.com/3823/firm-hopes-to-keep-hudbay-lawsuits-alive-despite-sale.html

Campbell, B. (2003). Factoring in governance is not enough: Mining codes in Africa, policy reform and corporate responsibility. *Minerals & Energy − Raw Materials Report, 18*(3), 2–13.

Campbell, B. (2008). Regulation and legitimacy in the mining industry in Africa: Where does Canada stand? *Review of African Political Economy, 35,* 367–385.

Canadian Securities Administrators (CSA) (2010). CSA Staff Notice 51−333: Environmental Reporting Guidance.Canadian Securities Administration, Montreal.

Collins, D. (2009). The failure of a socially responsive gold mining MNC in El Salvador: Ramifications of NGO Mistrust. *Journal of Business Ethics, 88,* 245–268.

Dashwood, H. (2007). Canadian mining companies and corporate social responsibility: Weighing the impact of global norms. *Canadian Journal of Political Science, 40*(1), 129–156.

Dashwood, H. (2011). Sustainable development norms and CSR in the global mining sector. In J. Sagebien & N. M. Lindsay (Eds.), *Governance ecosystems: CSR in the Latin American mining sector.* London: Palgrave MacMillan.

Drohan, M. (2010). *Regulating Canadian mining companies abroad: The ten-year search for a solution.* Ottawa: Centre for Policy Studies, University of Ottawa, Policy Brief No. 7.

Form 51−102F1. (2011). *Management's discussion and analysis.* Ottawa: Government of Canada.

Giddens, A. (1999). Risk and responsibility. *The Modern Law Review, 62*(1), 1–10.

Goldcorp shareholders' resolution. (2012). *Shareholders' resolution of Goldcorp Inc.* Submitted 16 March 2012. Retrieved from http://www.amnesty.ca/files/Shareholder%20Resolution%20and%20Background%20Goldcorp%202012.pdf.

Hamann, R., Kapelus, P., & O'Keefe, E. (2011). Mining companies and governance in Africa. In J. Sagebien & N. M. Lindsay (Eds.), *Governance ecosystems: CSR in the Latin American mining sector.* London: Palgrave MacMillan.

Idemudia, U. (2010). Corporate social responsibility and the Rentier Nigerian State: Rethinking the role of government and the possibility of corporate social development in the Niger Delta. *Canadian Journal of Development Studies, 30*(1–2), 131–153.

Ireland, P. (2010). Limited liability, shareholder rights and the problem of corporate irresponsibility. *Cambridge Journal of Economics, 34*, 837–856.

Jenkins, H., & Yakovleva, N. (2006). Corporate social responsibility in the mining industry: Exploring trends in social and environmental disclosure. *Journal of Cleaner Production, 14*, 271–284.

Keenan, K. (2010). Canadian mining: Still unaccountable. NACLA Report on the Americas, May/June, pp. 29–42.

Lindsay, N. M. (2011). Mining industry associations and CSR discourse: Mapping the terrain of sustainable development strategies. In J. Sagebien & N. M. Lindsay (Eds.), *Governance ecosystems: CSR in the Latin American mining sector*. London: Palgrave MacMillan.

Mining Association of Canada (MAC). (2010). *Facts and figures 2010*. Ottawa: Mining Association of Canada.

Miranda, M., Chambers, D., & Coumans, C. (2005). *Framework for responsible mining: A guide to evolving standards*. Bozeman, Montana: Center for Science in Public Participation (CSP2) and World Wildlife Federation.

National Instrument 43–101. (n.d.). *Standards of disclosure for mineral projects*. Ottawa: Government of Canada.

National Roundtables on Corporate Social Responsibility and the Canadian Extractive Industry Advisory Group. (2007). *Corporate social responsibility (CSR) and the Canadian extractive industry in developing countries. Advisory Group Report*. Ottawa: Government of Canada.

Newell, P. (2001). Managing multinationals: The governance of investment for the environment. *Journal of International Development, 13*(7), 907–919.

Newell, P. (2008). CSR and the limits of capital. *Development and Change, 39*(6), 1063–1078.

Office of the CSR Counsellor. (2011, November). *Closing report: Request for review* (file #2011-01-MEX). Toronto.

Ontario Securities Commission (OSC). (2008). *OSC staff notice 51–716 environmental reporting*. Toronto: Ontario Securities Commission.

Ontario Securities Commission (OSC). (2009). *Corporate sustainability reporting initiative: Report to minister of finance*. Toronto: Ontario Securities Commission.

Paley, D. (2012). *Another activist murdered for resisting a Canadian mine: Bernardo Vásquez killed in Oaxaca, two others wounded*. Vancouver Media Co-op. Retrieved from http://vancouver.mediacoop.ca/story/another-activist-murdered-organizing-against-canadian-mine/10243

Peck, J., & Tickell, A. (2002). Neoliberalizing space. *Antipode, 34*(3), 380–404.

Pellazzoni, L. (2004). Responsibility and environmental governance. *Environmental Politics, 13*(3), 541–565.

Ruggie, J. (2008). *Protect, respect and remedy: A framework for business and human rights*. Geneva: UN Human Rights Council.

Ruggie, J. (2011). *Guiding principles on business and human rights: Implementing the United Nations' 'Protect, Respect and Remedy' framework*. Geneva: UN Human Rights Council.

Sagebien, J., & Lindsay, N. M. (2011). Systemic causes, systemic solutions. In J. Sagebien & N. M. Lindsay (Eds.), *Governance ecosystems: CSR in the Latin American mining sector*. London: Palgrave MacMillan.

SCFAIT (Standing Committee on Foreign Affairs and International Trade). (2005, June). *Mining in developing countries—Corporate social responsibility*. Ottawa: Government of Canada.

Seck, S. (2008, March 8). Home state responsibility and local communities: The case of global mining. *Yale Human Rights & Development Law Journal*. Symposium, Corporate Social Responsibility in the Extractive Industries, Yale Law School.

Statistics Canada. (2012). *Gross domestic product, at base prices by industry*, Retrieved from http://www.statcan.gc.ca/tables-tableaux/sum-som/l01/cst01/econ41-eng.htm.

Szablowski, D. (2002). Mining, displacement and the world bank: A case analysis of campania minera antamina's operations in Peru. *Journal of Business Ethics, 39*, 247–273.

Szablowski, D. (2007). *Transnational law and local struggles, mining, communities, and the World Bank*. Oxford & Portland: Hart Publishing.

Webb, K. (2005). Sustainable governance in the twenty-first century: Moving beyond instrument choice. In P. Eliadis, M. M. Hill & M. Howlett (Eds.), *Designing government: From instruments to governance*. Montreal: McGill-Queen's University Press.

Webb, K. (2011a). CSR and the law: Learning from the experience of Canadian mining companies in Latin America. In J. Sagebien & N. M. Lindsay (Eds.), *Governance ecosystems: CSR in the Latin American mining sector*. London: Palgrave MacMillan.

Webb, K. (2011b, June). The global institutionalization of the social responsibility norm: From de-responsibilization to re-responsibilization. Unpublished paper presented at the International CRIMT Conference on Multinational Companies, Global Value Chains and Social Regulation, Montreal.

Wells, K. (2011). *Unfinished business*. Toronto: CBC Radio. Retrieved from http://www.cbc.ca/thesundayedition/documentaries/2011/09/26/unfinished-business/

# THE COMMUNITY OBLIGATIONS OF CANADIAN OIL COMPANIES: A CASE STUDY OF TALISMAN IN THE SUDAN

Trish Glazebrook and Matt Story

## ABSTRACT

Purpose – *This chapter examines Talisman Energy's operations in the Sudan, as part of the Greater Nile Petroleum Operating Company (GNPOC). It seeks to demonstrate that international corporate culture precludes ethical decision-making and practices by placing would-be ethical actors in untenable situations.*

Methodology/approach – *A case study approach is adopted. It analyses various lawsuits brought against Talisman by the Presbyterian Church of Sudan, who claim that Talisman aided and abetted the government of Sudan in genocide during the various protracted conflicts of a violent civil war.*

Findings – *By reviewing Talisman's corporate social responsibility reports, we find that locating corporate charters in the hands of nation-states entails an inherent tension that can only be resolved by either*

Corporate Social Irresponsibility: A Challenging Concept
Critical Studies on Corporate Responsibility, Governance and Sustainability, Volume 4, 231–261
Copyright © 2012 by Emerald Group Publishing Limited
All rights of reproduction in any form reserved
ISSN: 2043-9059/doi:10.1108/S2043-9059(2012)0000004019

*implementing an international corporate charter in the case of multina-*
*tionals, or abandoning the corporate charter altogether*

Practical implications – *We argue for immediate application of the*
*International Criminal Court in The Hague against corporate enablers*
*of government violence against its peoples.*

Originality/value – *In the case of Talisman in the Sudan, international*
*corporate culture and lack of support from its operating partners did*
*more than discourage Talisman from implementing ethical practices; it*
*prevented Talisman from acting ethically. In particular, it prevented*
*Talisman from using the economic importance of GNPOC to the gov-*
*ernment of Sudan to disallow the government from using Talisman's*
*infrastructure or oil revenues in military campaigns against the peoples*
*of Sudan.*

**Keywords:** International corporate culture; ethical decision-making;
government violence; corporate charter

On November 8, 2001 the Presbyterian Church of Sudan and a group of
Sudanese relocated to upstate New York filed a class action lawsuit
against Talisman Energy, Inc. and the Republic of the Sudan under the
Alien Tort Claims Act in the United States District Court for the Southern
District of New York (Business and Human Rights Resource Centre,
2009).

This Act (also called the Alien Tort Claims Statute) was part of the
Judiciary Act of 1789. Though its original intentions are unknown, it is
generally agreed to have been intended for the protection of diplomats
abroad. It lay largely dormant until 1980 when an appeals court ruled in
*Filartiga v. Pena-Arala* that its jurisdiction between two aliens was not
unconstitutional. It has since been used in dozens of cases by people living
in the United States as a basis for action concerning human rights violations abroad.

The Sudanese alleged that Talisman had aided and abetted the government of Sudan "in a brutal ethnic cleansing campaign against civilian
populations" (Klauszus, 2006, p. 22). This chapter examines the history
and outcomes of this suit as an argument for implementing systems of
international corporate accountability. We argue that the case of Talisman
in the Sudan demonstrates that corporate culture not only does not support ethical decision-making and practice in international business but,

more strongly, precludes them by placing would-be ethical actors in an untenable situation. First, we overview briefly the history of conflict in the Sudan, detail the structure of Talisman's corporate interest, and summarize the legal proceedings. We then examine Talisman's official position on corporate social responsibility (CSR). Next, we assess corporate culture in the international oil industry, and argue for immediate application of the International Criminal Court (ICC) in The Hague against corporate enablers of government violence against its peoples. Finally, we argue that locating the corporate charter in the hands of the nation-state entails an inherent tension that can only be resolved by either implementing an international corporate charter in the case of multinationals, or abandoning the corporate charter altogether.

## THE SUDAN CIVIL WAR AND DARFUR

Genocide erupted in the Darfur region of the Sudan late in the Second Sudanese Civil War that lasted from 1983 until early 2005. The Southern Sudan is one of the least developed places on the planet, and is substantially underdeveloped in comparison to the north. Tensions concerning disparate treatment of the region go back to the First Sudanese Civil War of 1955–1972. These civil wars have their origin in economic inequities in the struggle to meet daily living needs. Early in the 21st century, this resource-based conflict became "cultural cleansing" and genocide in Darfur.

As early as 1991, the Zaghawa people, who are non-Arab Muslims and village farmers, were complaining of a growing Arab campaign against non-Arabs (Johnson, 2011, p. 38). These conflicts began as land disputes that intensified as drought pushed semi-nomadic Arab herders onto non-Arab farmland (Johnson, 2011, p. 38). In 2001, a group of Zaghawa and other non-Arab Muslims swore on the Qur'an to defend themselves against government-sponsored attacks on Zaghawa, Fur, and Masalit villages. These attacks were perpetrated by the Janjaweed, a Sudanese, primarily Arab militia with membership coming from camel and cattle herding cultural groups[1] that the government of Sudan had been mobilizing against the Masalit since their 1996 uprising. The government originally denied supporting the Janjaweed, but were subsequently shown to have provided weapons and money to the militia, and to have organized joint attacks. In 2002, the Dafur Liberation Front, later renamed the Sudan Liberation Army (SLA), was formed and began conducting successful raids on police stations, army garrisons, and military convoys. The Justice and Equality Movement (JEM) had already been operating in the region since 2000, and in 2003, the JEM joined forces with the SLA. On April 25, 2003, carried by 33 Landcruisers, they attacked the al-Fashir garrison, destroyed several bombers and helicopter gunships,[2] killed 75 people, and captured 32 soldiers, technicians, and pilots (Flint & de Waal, 2006, pp. 99–100). The SLA then moved east, winning 34 of its subsequent 38 engagements. The government responded decisively by equipping the Janjaweed as a paramilitary force and setting it loose in the region.

In the next six months, a major humanitarian crisis of gang-rape, murder, and village-burning ensued. Several thousand non-Arabs were killed and a further million displaced. Clearly, non-Arab communities were being singled out. A UN fact-finding and assessment mission noted that Fur villages were razed to the ground, while nearby Arab villages were untouched. The Sudanese government could not have been unaware of the potential for human rights violations when they sent in the Janjaweed as a similar strategy in the 1990s had led to just such consequences (Flint & de Waal, 2006, p. 6).

None of this is relevant to oil – except that the Sudanese government was financing its military operations with revenues from petroleum exploration and extraction.

## THE GREATER NILE PETROLEUM OPERATING COMPANY

Southern Sudan sits on substantial oil deposits. The Greater Nile Petroleum Operating Company (GNPOC) was incorporated in the Sudan in 1997 to develop oil resources, and to construct the Greater Nile Oil Pipeline, a 1,540-km (932 mile) underground pipeline connecting GNPOC's 12 million-acre exploration and development concession with a marine terminal at Port Sudan. As soon as production began in 1999, money began flowing into government coffers. Oil revenues accounted for roughly 7% of total government revenue in that first year. In 2000, 43% of the government of Sudan's income was oil revenues.

The GNPOC is a joint operating company. The China National Petroleum Corporation (CNPC) – the largest state-owned fuel producer in the People's Republic of China – owns 40%, and Petronas Carigali Overseas, a Malaysian company, owns 30%. A meager 5% belongs to a Sudanese company, Sudapet. The remaining 25% belongs to India's Oil and Natural Gas Corporation (ONGC). They purchased this holding in 2003 from Talisman (Greater Nile) B.V., a subsidiary of Talisman Energy Inc. based in Calgary, Alberta. Talisman had acquired the 25% holding in GNPOC through a complex arrangement of auxiliaries in October 1998, when another Canadian company, Arakis Energy, sold its interest in GNPOC to State Petroleum Corporation B.V. State Petroleum was owned by Goal Olie-en-Gasexploratie B.V., a subsidiary of British companies that were themselves wholly owned subsidiaries of Talisman Energy (UK) Limited, which was a direct and wholly owned subsidiary of Talisman Energy Inc. in Calgary. Goal Olie-en-Gasexploratie changed the name of State Petroleum Corp. B.V. to Talisman (Greater Nile) B.V.[3] Upon acquiring their interest in GNPOC in 1998, Talisman opened an office in Khartoum, the capital of Sudan.

Talisman sold its shares to ONGC less than two years after the suit was launched in New York State, and in the same year that the Sudanese government responded to the consolidation of rebel groups into an effective fighting force by setting the Janjaweed on local non-Arab populations. Jim Buckee, then President and Chief Executive Officer of Talisman in Calgary, offered the following explanation as to why Talisman sold its stake in GNPOC:

> The time had come to turn the page on this controversial asset for a number of reasons. First and foremost we have always said that we would sell at the right price and I believe this price and the resulting gain benefits our shareholders. Secondly, our shares had been discounted based on perceived political risk in-country and in North America to a degree that was unacceptable for only 12 percent of our production. Finally, shareholders repeatedly told me that they were tired of continually having to monitor and analyze events related to Sudan and the divestment campaigns of special interest groups. (Talisman, 2002, p. 3)

The first and second reasons indicate the type of cost–benefit that is typical of decision-making in business. The third indicates pressure from shareholders and attention to their demands.

We suggest in fact, as hinted by the reference to political risk in the second reason, Talisman was extricating itself from an impossible situation. From 1998 onwards, Talisman, and in particular, Jim Buckee, appear to have tried to prevent their oil field infrastructure from being used to commit human rights violations, and to exert influence to prevent the Sudanese government from using oil revenues to further military aims against its peoples. These attempts failed. At the same time, they made it perfectly clear that Talisman knew that the government of Sudan was both using

Talisman's infrastructure, and financing the military offensive with oil revenues[4] (cf. Talisman 2007, and *Presbyterian Church of Sudan v. Talisman Energy Inc.*, 2003, p. 301). In criminal law, such accessory after the fact can be interpreted as complicity.


# THE SUIT

The Sudanese plaintiffs sued Talisman and the government of the Sudan in 2001 arguing that, in exchange for investment in oil field development and extraction by Talisman, the Sudanese government would "clear the surrounding areas" so as to make Talisman's investment more efficient and thereby more lucrative. The plaintiffs argued that this "protection" constituted a "genocidal campaign of ethnic cleansing" in the non-Arab areas surrounding Talisman's oil operations, and that "the Government's oil development policy and its violent campaign against ethnic and religious minorities were inextricably linked from the beginning" (*Presbyterian Church of Sudan v. Talisman Energy Inc.*, 2003, Summary Proceedings). They demanded that Talisman cease operations in the area and publicly declare that it had violated international law. They subsequently claimed that Arakis, from which Talisman had acquired the Sudanese oil rights, had a "well-known and established relationship with the Sudanese military," and that Talisman, through its subsidiary Talisman (Greater Nile) B.V., maintained that relationship fully aware that government "protection" of oil operations entailed "ethnic cleansing" or "genocide" (*Presbyterian Church of Sudan v. Talisman Energy Inc.*, 2003, Class Action Summary Judgment). As evidence, the plaintiffs cited a May 7, 1999 internal memorandum from the Government's Petroleum Security Office in Khartoum to a satellite office in Heglig, a highly contested area where GNPOC had an oil field containing a militarily significant airstrip that Talisman developed and maintained. The e-mail was marked "very urgent" and stated: "In accordance with directives of His Excellency the Minister of Energy and Mining and fulfilling the request of the Canadian Company...the armed forces will conduct cleaning up operations in all villages from Heglig to Pariang." The plaintiffs claimed that a few days afterward, "thousands of villages and at least seventeen churches were destroyed in the areas surrounding Talisman's oil fields, and that one, el-Toor, was located within walking distance of a Talisman site" (*Presbyterian Church of Sudan v. Talisman Energy Inc.*, 2003, Class Action Summary Judgment).

Talisman responded to the action with a series of motions to dismiss – 19 in total – that were eventually successful in 2006. First they argued that the Court lacked subject matter jurisdiction because corporations "are not legally capable of violating international law" (*Presbyterian Church of Sudan v. Talisman Energy Inc.*, 2003, Class Action Summary Judgment, ¶ 6). The court responded by citing the Nuremburg Trials. Talisman cited Christopher Greenwood, Professor of International law at London School of Economics and member of the International Court of Justice, the primary judicial organ of the United Nations, and other relevant scholarly work. The Court responded by citing a 2nd circuit decision on a Bosnian case under the Alien Torts Claims Act (ATCA) against a non-state entity, as well as a case between Coca-Cola and Egypt that sets jurisdictional precedent even though it was eventually dismissed because the crime was "not of universal concern" (*Presbyterian Church of Sudan v. Talisman Energy Inc.*, 2003, p. 313). Talisman then argued that the plaintiffs had not proved they assisted the Sudan government with intent to violate international law; the plaintiffs replied that they need not show assistance but only material aid and that Talisman benefited directly from the crimes. Talisman moved to arguing that it is a Canadian company not operating in the Sudan. The Court replied that since Talisman owns 25% of GNPOC, it does operate in the Sudan, and since it is traded on the New York Stock Exchange, it is a "present actor" in the case. Talisman then claimed that the Presbyterian Church suffered no direct injury, but only loss of property, which is "not of universal concern," and referred to the Court's previous citation of the Egyptian precedent. The Court rejected these arguments. Talisman then argued there were no grounds for a class action, but the Court found the class action in good standing. Talisman next sought to have the case moved, but the Court found this request unduly prejudicial against the non-Muslim plaintiffs as the Sudan will almost certainly introduce Shari'a law, which devalues non-Muslim rights, and a Canadian court is likely to do the same as Canada uses *lex loci delecti*, "law of the place." Talisman then appealed to the government of Sudan's authority to act as it desires during states of emergency. The Court denied this motion due to the severity of the charges. Talisman, in a last desperate argument, suggested that the trial is embarrassing for Canada and may affect international relationships and treaties.[5] The Court denied this motion, and found the CSR program put in place by Talisman irrelevant.

In the meantime, Talisman had written to the Canadian Prime Minister's senior foreign policy advisor asking the government to intervene on their behalf (Klauszus, 2006, p. 34).[6] In the summer of 2004, the Canadian

Embassy in the United States wrote to the US Department of State. On January 14, 2005, the former sent a further 6-page letter stressing Canada's opposition to the Alien Tort Claims Act, because the "assumption of extraterritorial jurisdiction by a U.S. court constitutes an infringement in the conduct of foreign relations by the Government of Canada" (Jones, 2005) and that the Talisman case "Creates a 'chilling effect' on Canadian firms engaging in the Sudan" (Klauszus, 2006, p. 34). Washington then filed a statement of interest with the Court stating that the case frustrates Canada's foreign policy, and that Canada's judiciary is capable of dealing with the case. Judge Cote rejected the arguments by Talisman, Ottawa, and Washington, and pointed out that the Court had already decided that the Canadian legal system was not able to deal with the case. Beyond the issue of *lex loci delecti*, Canada has nothing similar to the ACTA that would allow it to try civil suits for violations of international law. On September 12, 2006 the case was finally dismissed on the basis that the plaintiffs had failed to supply sufficient admissible evidence to permit the lawsuit to go to trial (Klauszus, 2006, p. 34). The plaintiffs appealed, but in 2009 the ruling was upheld by the Second Circuit Court of Appeals.

The appellate court affirmed three issues upon which the dismissal was upheld. First, the plaintiffs' original claims often involved indirect subsidiary companies rather than those with direct links to Talisman, and contained little admissible evidence beyond "hearsay." Second, after the 2006 dismissal, the plaintiffs attempted a third amended argument to the first class action suit of 2001 which "when stripped to its essentials, seeks to hold Talisman responsible for the actions of GNPOC." This third amendment would, if continued, have contradicted the previous two that were based on a direct relationship between Talisman Energy, Inc. and the government of Sudan. Finally, the court finds that the plaintiffs could not "pierce the corporate veil" between Talisman Energy and the GNPOC, thus Talisman Energy Inc. is not liable for the on-the-ground actions of the GNPOC (Appeal Summary *Presbyterian Church of Sudan v. Talisman Energy Inc.*, 2009), ¶ 6, 8), of which it operated only 25% through various levels of subsidiaries.

The appellate court's closing summary accepted that southern Sudanese were attacked by the Sudanese government, that the attacks facilitated the oil enterprise, and that the revenues generated through oil development enhanced the government's military capability to carry out the attacks. The court also acknowledged the "knotty" issues involved in the corporate "veiling" of Talisman and the GNPOC. But the court held that since only Talisman Energy Inc., in Calgary, was charged, there is no evidence that, from its Canadian Headquarters, Talisman Energy assisted in the construction of any infrastructure beyond the direct industry-accepted purposes of maximizing efficiencies and profits. Thus, even if the Calgary offices had knowledge of their military advantage for the Sudanese government, there is no evidence supporting the claim that the Canadian company built infrastructure for the purpose of extending said military advantage through one of its subsidiaries. The court held moreover that if "knowledge of those abuses coupled only with such commercial activities as resource development" (*Presbyterian Church of Sudan v. Talisman Energy Inc.*, 2003, Class Action Summary Judgment) established liability, then the Alien Tort Claims Act would "act as a vehicle for private parties to impose embargos or international sanctions through civil actions in United States Courts. Such measures are not the province of private parties but are, instead, properly reserved to governments and multinational organizations" (*Presbyterian Church of Sudan v. Talisman Energy Inc.*, 2003, Class Action Summary Judgment).

In a similar case, on September 17, 2010, in a 2-1 decision, the US Court of Appeals for the 2nd Circuit decided in favor of defendants in *Kiobel v. Royal Dutch Petroleum*. The plaintiffs from Kiobel, Nigeria sought damages under the same act the Sudanese plaintiffs used, the ATCA. They claimed that Royal Dutch Petroleum had violated customary international law by aiding and abetting the Nigerian government in human rights violations against them. A district court in 2006 had dismissed claims of aiding and abetting property destruction, forced exile, extrajudicial killing, and violation of the rights to life, liberty, security, and association on the basis that the ATCA did not adequately define these particular violations as under its jurisdiction. The Appeals Court dismissed the remaining claims concerning arbitrary arrest and detention, crimes against humanity, and torture or cruel, inhuman, and degrading treatment by reasoning that corporations cannot be held liable for violations of customary international law (*Kiobel v. Royal Dutch Petroleum Co.*, 2010, p. 191). The norms of international law must be "specific, universal, and obligatory" (*Kiobel v. Royal Dutch Petroleum Co.*, 2010, p. 121) and corporate liability is not universally recognized. Thus the ATCA has no jurisdiction in the case.

Yet on July 8, 2011, a ruling by the US Court of Appeals for the District of Columbia Circuit revived an ATCA case accusing Exxon of abetting murder and torture in Indonesia, in direct contrast to the Kiobel ruling, and the Kiobel plaintiffs have asked for a review of their hearing (Donovan, 2011). It is up to the Supreme Court to decide if it will consider the matter. The issue of whether corporations are liable for atrocities against foreign nationals was raised by the Supreme Court in a footnote to their 2004 decision in *Sosa v. Alvarez-Machian*, where they cited a 1984 and a 1995 case with contrasting outcomes, the latter reaching sufficient consensus that genocide committed by a "private actor such as a corporation or individual" violates international law, while the earlier case had not achieve consensus concerning torture (*Sosa v. Alvarez-Machain*, 2004). So the Supreme Court itself has been well aware of controversy with respect to the question of jurisdiction with respect to the ATCA since 2004.

In the Talisman case, the appellate court's 2009 ruling also makes a jurisdictional objection, arguing that a nation-state is free to do what it pleases with respect to its territory, so restricting settlement or commerce in its military buffer zones around oil extraction areas is not unlawful. Here the issue is not whether corporations are capable of violating international law. The Court rules rather that international law has not been broken. This seems patently false. The Sudanese government may be free to do as it pleases with its territory, but that does not mean that it can bring about the outcomes it pleases by violating human rights. "International law" here means "customary international law," which is a vague term. It is incorporated into the Charter of the United Nations in Article 92 that applies "international custom, as evidence of a general practice accepted as law." The ATCA seems itself to be the closest thing to an international law available, in the sense that it allows civil litigation across US borders into another nation, but the court's reference to international law here is the assertion that the court holds defendants under ATCA to the standard of customary international law, as noted also in the Nigerian case against Royal Dutch Petroleum discussed above. It is worth noting that each of the cases referred to here involves Big Oil. This particular industry is an egregious example of failure to exercise ethical constraint in the absence of legal enforcement.

The Court gives several further reasons for upholding the 2006 dismissal that in essence boil down to two. First, it wants to avoid allowing private parties in effect to impose a ban or sanction on trade through civil actions in US Courts when the trading company knew of abuses but their actions were nothing more than the regular conducting of business. In truth, however, tort law always entails such risks, and the argument seems far-fetched – as if, for example, damages should not have been awarded in the infamous Ford Pinto case as it might discourage car manufacturers from making cars (*Grimshaw v. Ford Motor Co.*, 1981). If the effect of awarding damages to the plaintiffs in the Talisman case were to lessen trade in contexts where there is a risk of similar law suits, this effect would be the outcome of complex patterns of risk-evaluation and corporate decision-making that are not at all like the externally imposed trade restrictions of an embargo. Moreover, why the qualification about the regular conducting of business? If the company had supported abuses by doing more than just "business-as-usual," would it then be appropriate for civil courts to impose trade embargos or sanctions against a national government? This explanation of the dismissal is perhaps an extremely poorly thought out and equally poorly worded version of the jurisdiction argument, as if the argument hinges on staying within or exceeding the bounds of normal business conduct (which is itself a fuzzy concept).

Second, the court established the validity of the common multinational practice of "corporate veiling" when it acknowledged the "knotty" issues of the corporate "veiling" of Talisman within GNPOC. The plaintiffs had filed a series of amendments in response to various motions to dismiss, and the Court notes contradiction between the third amendment and the first two: the latter were founded on direct relation between Talisman Energy, in Calgary, and the government of Sudan, while the third seeks to hold Talisman responsible for the actions of GNPOC. The Court argues that the plaintiffs were unable to "pierce the corporate veil" between the two companies, and as a result, Talisman Energy is not responsible for the actions of GNPOC. Indeed, Talisman Energy generated an extremely complex corporate relation when if first bought its interest in GNPOC from Arakis by going through a series of nested subsidiary corporations in Britain. Moreover, it was not Talisman Energy Inc. but Talisman (Greater Nile) B.V., a subsidiary of Talisman Energy, that held the interest in GNPOC. So various actors at Talisman Energy, like Jim Buckee for example, can play an active role in managing the interest in the Sudan, including managing the flow of oil revenues upstream to the Calgary head office, while any accompanying flow of liability remains with the subsidiary, whose liability is already limited by the corporate charter.

Preliminary conclusions that can be drawn from *Presbyterian Church of Sudan et al. v. Talisman Energy Inc.* are that corporate "business-as-usual" practices enable governments in the violation of human rights and committing of crimes against humanity; that corporations are prepared to turn a blind eye; and that justice systems in nation-states are not prepared to tackle the issue of international corporate accountability. The ACTA in the United States is one of the few, if not the only, avenue of recourse for survivors to fight back against corporate enablers of brutally oppressive regimes.

The ICC in the Hague, founded on the basis of the Rome Statute, might offer recourse, but technically it has jurisdiction only over individuals who are nationals of a state party. In the Darfur situation, it has indicted six Sudanese nationals, including its President.[7] Its jurisdiction may eventually be extended to corporate actors. On April 30, 2002, Kathleen Maloney, Professor of Law at the University of Calgary and Chair of Rights & Democracy (Canada), warned Talisman that the ICC "would not balk at bringing to justice accomplices in human rights crimes" (CorpWatch, 2002), although it noted it would be several years before there is significant, relevant jurisprudence. Canada is a signatory to the Rome Statute and has incorporated the Statute into Canadian law. The ICC is further limited in that it can only prosecute crimes that took place after it came into being on July 1, 2002. By October 30, 2002 the company had secured an agreement to sell its Sudan operations for $1.2 billion CAD.

In a news conference on the eve of the 2002 shareholders meeting, Maloney further noted Talisman's "timid efforts to address issues of social responsibility," and Judge Cote later found Talisman's CSR program irrelevant to the issue of liability in one of her rulings on a Talisman motion to dismiss. The ICC likewise might perhaps find Talisman's other activities in the Sudan and its CSR program in general no mitigation, compensation, or excuse for what went on in the regular course of its business practices.

## TALISMAN'S CORPORATE SOCIAL RESPONSIBILITY

The company generated its first CSR Reports at the instigation of a group of shareholders who presented a proposal at the May 2000 AGM that Talisman prepare an independently verified report on the company's compliance with the International Code of Ethics for Canadian Business. They also asked that the Board instruct the company to produce an annual report assessing such compliance in the Sudan that would be publicly accessible and made available to shareholders as part of their annual reports. *Corporate Social Responsibility Report 2000 Sudan Operations* was produced in 2001, verified by PricewaterhouseCoopers out of London, UK. The 2001 CSR Report includes discussion of operations in Columbia, and 2002 covers all Talisman operating locations. In 2003, "based on stakeholder feedback we've collected throughout the year and significant input on our reporting process from our independent reviewer, PricewaterhouseCoopers" (Talisman, 2003, p. 2). Each report makes abundantly clear that Talisman has worked hard to comply with the International Code of Ethics for Canadian Business, but the voluntary nature of this compliance is unclear as Talisman was instructed to implement the Code by Canada's Foreign Affairs Minister Lloyd Axworthy in a meeting he held with them in late 1999, just before he commissioned the Harker Report on conditions in the Sudan, subsequently published on January 26, 2000 and immediately provided to Talisman (Human Rights Watch, 2003a; esp. notes 1200–1204 and accompanying text). Thus by the times shareholders asked for CSR Reports, Talisman was well aware of human rights violations in the Sudan, and the potential for intervention by the Canadian government to impose sanctions that would impede if not shut down their operations. So it is not possible to establish whether or not individuals in upper management at Talisman were complicit actors in human rights abuses, but they were certainly well aware of the use of their infrastructure in perpetration of human rights violations and the increased capacity of the Sudanese government to conduct a war against its peoples due to the oil returns that made up 43% of the Sudanese government's revenue in the year the Harker Report came out. As detailed above, the court, on no occasion, recognized knowledge alone as sufficient to establish liability. The latter, the court claimed, required also intent.

The 2001 CSR was prefaced by a statement from a British independent analyst, John Bray, on business and conflict. He notes the tension which oil companies experience: "From a commercial point of view, companies cannot afford to shirk the challenge of operating in difficult areas. At the same time, they are unlikely to win a lasting 'license to operate' – either in host or home countries – unless they can demonstrate that they exercise a positive influence" (Talisman, 2006, Independent Opinion). He singles out four issues: labor and environmental standards; the need to consult local communities; relations to security forces; and dealing with regimes that use oil revenues to buy arms or support corrupt officials. Bray recommends transparency and independent verification (much of the kind, we assume, that he is engaged in by writing this prefatory comment). He notes that companies cannot afford to alienate host governments, or be perceived as supporting oppressive regimes. He also observes that corporations alone "lack the legitimacy to press for political reforms" but can "play a positive role that is internationally accepted...in alliance with other actors," that he has already indicated include NGOs, governments, and intergovernmental organizations. This observation reveals a tension with his thinking. Bray asserts that companies "should use their influence to prevent human rights abuses. If abuses do occur, they should raise their concerns at the highest level" because "NGOs and other critics expect [companies] to use what influence they have to ensure that the revenue they produce is used constructively." At the same time, companies have limited influence over governmental decision-making.

In actual fact, however, the claim that companies cannot afford to alienate host governments is stronger than references to limited influence indicate. The problem is that not that the government will not listen, but exactly that it will – and then withdraw its support of the company's continuing operations. That would mean not only a cease in the revenue flow from that country, but another company reaping the profits of the existing infrastructure investment. This could be perceived as a breach of fiduciary responsibility to shareholders. But of course, in Talisman's case, the shareholders have already made it clear that if the financial bottom line conflicts with ethics, they choose ethics. So Bray's comments look like a guarded and carefully worded gloss that states the issues but then reverts to overly generalizing policy-speak that either waffles or evades in inverse proportion to generosity of interpretation. Placement of his text – its primacy – prioritizes the message that Talisman had no control over events in the Sudan. Whereas it is already abundantly clear from the Harker Report and numerous other sources that GNPOC oil revenues were financing the Sudanese government's assaults on non-Arab southerners, whether Muslim or not, and that Talisman's infrastructure was directly enabling military operations. To what extent did this disturb Talisman's upper management at home in Calgary?

Put another way, to what extent was Talisman's "corporate social responsibility" as made explicit in its CSR Reports, authentic? For example, the 2000 CSR Report indicates an expenditure of $150,000 CAD (Talisman, 2006, p. 23) in disaster response during the Bentiu emergency and relief operation. Because of renewed and escalating conflict between armed groups in the region, approximately 45,000 people, mostly women and children, flooded into Bentiu and Rubkona in July and August 2000, adding to the 15,000 who had already fled there (ReliefWeb, 2000).[8] Talisman provided medical supplies and staff, veterinary supplies to help deal with the 100,000 cattle the internally displaced people brought with them, tents, mosquito nets, and logistical support. During the eight-week emergency, Talisman provided "community development updates" to "our stakeholders" on their Web site.

Talisman had arranged, as part of its verification process "to demonstrate compliance with respect to the International Code of Ethics for Canadian Business,"[9] that PricewaterhouseCoopers of London would conduct interviews with "stakeholders across a range of Sudan and Nairobi-based stakeholder groups." An unnamed person from an international NGO in Khartoum noted in one such interview, "We do not want to be associated with Talisman because, among other reasons, the SPLA has issued specific threats against anyone assisting with the production of oil in Sudan. This was a problem for many agencies when Talisman falsely reported a relationship with us" (Talisman, 2000, p. 40). Talisman reports,

> Unfortunately these statements were poorly worded and did not clearly identify the roles and relationships between the many groups participating in relief efforts. In particular, specific references were made to a number of humanitarian and development agencies who also provided assistance during the Bentiu emergency through the Government of Sudan's Emergency Committee. These references gave many readers the false impression that these organizations were working directly with Talisman to provide aid. This was not the case, nor was it our intention to misrepresent the situation in any way.
>
> Our attempt to acknowledge the efforts of groups providing much needed assistance in Bentiu was flawed because we failed to recognize the impact these statements might have on the groups named. We put them in an untenable situation and we apologize for any offence that may have been given. We will make every effort to avoid such miscommunications in the future.

Talisman here is transparent about having made mistakes, and openly acknowledges that few groups can work with them because of threats of violence (Talisman, 2000, p. 23). Jim Buckee, President and Chief Executive Officer, also points explicitly to this mistake in his introductory letter to the report (Talisman, 2000, p. 7). He claims to have learned from such mistakes.

Indeed, Talisman management was clearly at best naïve in their failure to understand the impacts of perceptions of collaboration or association with Talisman, even in humanitarian efforts. This is the naïvete of privilege – the failure to see how what one takes for granted is a life-and-death situation for someone else – and is typical in early stages of interventions from the global North into the global South.[10] Talisman had begun its community development and social impact efforts in the Sudan, they note explicitly in response to public concern, and out of accountability to "shareholders, employees, governments, interest groups and the general public [that] demand more from corporations than just profitability" (Talisman, 2000, p. 5). In effect, Talisman must publicize its humanitarian and community development work in the Sudan if it is to achieve the goal of publicly demonstrating compliance with the International Code of Ethics for Canadian Business. Yet it needs to be more careful about who it implicates in this process. So for example, in the following year's report, Talisman quotes the Director of a women's group in Bentiu who said "I am very happy that the oil companies are in southern Sudan as they are the first to help in times of crisis like earlier this year (August 2001). Talisman helped with food, blankets and tents for the IDPs [internally displaced peoples]" (Talisman, 2000, p. 42) without naming the group, and one hopes there are sufficient women's groups to preserve anonymity. Influence and impact must be carefully distinguished. Talisman may have extremely limited influence on the government of Sudan's domestic policies, but it has significant impact on the lives of the people, whether IDPs or NGO workers – and for villagers living near oil fields, their impact is horrific. Is it enough to provide $150,000 CAD in aid at Bentiu, against the government of Sudan's entitlement in 2000 of $3.5 million CAD (Talisman, 2000, p. 28), for a company that in the same year approved an employee training program of almost $6 million CAD for 2001 (Talisman, 2001, p. 32), and in 2002 posted "record cash flows of $2.6 billion" CAD (Talisman, 2002, p. 32)? To what extent is Talisman's CSR program, beyond "timid" and "irrelevant" as discussed above, nothing more than a strategic management program of a difficult public relations issue in order to maintain the flow of profits from the Sudan to Calgary?

We have no way of knowing what material has been excluded from Talisman's CSR Reports. Yet most of the qualitative data from interviews in this chapter is quoted from the Reports, and not all is laudatory. The 2001 Report provides a list of quotations (Talisman, 2001, p. 42). A villager states that "Oil production is a good thing because our children will be able to benefit from the things it will bring us, like medicines and food," and a community development partner states that "No other company has done what Talisman and its people are doing. Project Hope shows that the people of Talisman have good feelings about the people of the Sudan and that they want to help. While they are all business-minded people, they do care about social issues." Others have a different view. A senior staff member of an intergovernmental organization in Khartoum says, "they didn't listen when they were being given advice and constructive criticism. They do things in a typically arrogant business fashion," and a Southern Sudanese living in Khartoum says, "Oil companies are not a good thing. Politicians have told us that the fighting is because of the oil. This is the cause of the suffering of the people." The reality of the situation is perhaps best expressed by a farmer participating in one of Talisman's community projects: "we wish that the oil companies can really alleviate us from our current difficulties and make life better for us." If they cannot, should they stay on the area? An international NGO asks exactly this: "When there are problems, the primary responsibility is with the ones who commit the atrocities, not with the oil companies – but if we are talking about ethics, should we work or not in a place where there is war?"

Looking back to the May 1999 e-mail between government offices in Khartoum and Helig, where Talisman had a airstrip allegedly used in village bombings, that referred to "the request of the Canadian Company" that armed forces conduct "cleaning up operations" in villages, what are we to conclude? (cf. *Presbyterian Church of Sudan v. Talisman Energy Inc.*, 2003, p. 301). Talisman may have asked that people be removed, or that trash be taken away and their request misconstrued or deliberately manipulated; or they may have asked nothing at all. Certainly, implicating Talisman, as this e-mail does, would be an effective way for the Sudanese government to silence a problem for a government engaged in ethnic cleansing who must not have been pleased by the process and publication of the Harker Report. The question is not whether Talisman had malicious intent, which doesn't really make much sense, but rather, whether they are guilty of corporate irresponsibility through indifference, that is, of prioritizing profit over lives, human suffering, ethnic cleansing or genocide, and crimes against humanity. Talisman has after all noted explicitly and repeatedly that "Creating value for our shareholders is our first priority" (Talisman, 2002, p. 32).

Indeed, there is something further to be noted concerning the Bentiu experience. The problem in the Sudan is not Talisman per se. The problem rather, as identified by the representative of the NGO quoted above, is oil production. Talisman is in the Sudan to produce oil; not all the community development projects and glossy CSR Reports in the world can change that.

So Talisman stands in an untenable situation: genuine response to the ethical call entails not just treating symptoms, but getting to the cause of the problem – corporate multinationals enable oppressive governments. The case of Talisman in the Sudan shows that oil developers, whether actively or passively, enable oppressive governments through managed irresponsibility. In the 2000 CSR Report, Talisman notes that reported bombing of civilians and other issues, including child soldiers, have been raised with the government of Sudan, including the President and various Ministers, and Buckee claims to be widely reported in newspapers and on television in the Sudan and neighboring countries supporting the protection of human rights and the peace process (Talisman, 2000, p. 16). They note their intent to develop guidelines with GNPOC, and promote them to the government of the Sudan, for "the acceptable uses of oilfield infrastructure" (Talisman, 2000, p. 13). Talisman defined such uses in a security protocol that they encouraged GNOPC to adopt, and they clearly state their intent to "use our corporate influence to ensure that the GNPOC infrastructure is not used for offensive military purposes" (Talisman, 2000, p. 15). They say that "use of oilfield infrastructure for non-defensive military purposes is of great concern to Talisman" (Talisman, 2000, p. 15), and they note that they have made these concerns known to GNOPC and the government of Sudan, and will continue to do so. They define "defensive security support" as protection of personnel and property using a proportionate level of force by forces legitimately deployed in the concession area, while anything else is "offensive activity" (Talisman, 2000, p. 15). They note "at least four instances of non-defensive usage of the Heglig airstrip in 2000" (Talisman, 2000, p. 16). The airstrip was closed in December 2000 for upgrading, which included plans to install a computerized monitoring system that would record all usage. The four instances are explained as helicopters or planes landing for reasons Talisman could "not determine were related to oilfield security and their presence was considered non-defensive" (Talisman, 2000, p. 16). All of this is against a background of their stated commitment to transparency, but Georgette Gagnon, a member of the Harker delegation and deputy director in Africa for Human Rights Watch, notes that the day before visits to the Heglig airstrip the Antanovs and gunships were moved off the airstrip "somewhere else, so that when we got there, you didn't see anything" (Klauszus, 2006, p. 33).

Talisman accordingly would have us believe that they were not actively complicit, but had good intentions, at least in 2000. They clearly knew then that the government of the Sudan was violating human rights. They quote the Canadian Department of Foreign Affairs and International Trade on this point "(Talisman, 2000, p. 2), and Board Chairman Widdrington notes 'widespread reports of human rights violations' in his statement" (Talisman, 2000, p. 5). Jim Buckee, President and CEO, cites a "duty to advocate respect for human rights where there are abuses," and claims to have personally raised the issue in advocacy (Talisman, 2000, p. 7). Unfortunately, he there falls back on a Canadian government statement that "trade leads to development, and development leads to respect of human rights and leads to respect of democracy," from a *Calgary Herald* article on an official Canadian visit to Beijing in February 2001 – as if oil development can lead to these things in due course when simply left to itself. Talisman claims that one of its objectives is to "develop and implement a program to monitor and investigate human rights concerns arising from our own and GNPOC operations" (Talisman, 2000, p. 13), while another is to develop a framework for independent monitoring, exactly as noted by a human rights lawyer in Khartoum in 2001: "Talisman should put pressure on GNPOC to make the link between business in Sudan and human rights and they should make a special fund from GNPOC to be directly monitored by them to assist in resolving the problems faced by the IDPs [internally displaced peoples]" (Talisman, 2001, p. 42).

Talisman also expresses concern for compensating people whose homes or crops are affected by GNOPC activities. GNOPC funds a Pipeline Compensation Committee to the tune of over $1.8 million USD at the time of the report, with anticipated total compensation of $2.5 million USD (Talisman, 2000, p. 17). Talisman introduced a human rights monitoring program in 2000, overseen by a Field Coordinator responsible for seeking out information and maintaining records to provide a clear audit trail (Talisman, 2000, p. 18). In 2000, only seven cases were documented, all involving employee relations. A further 10 cases from November were opened on displaced persons, but there is no indication of outcomes. Moreover, the program is described as "in its start-up phase" (Talisman, 2000, p. 18), focusing only on documentation rather than resolution at this stage, and hope is expressed to increase Talisman's influence and ability to address resolution. Given what was going on in the Sudan at the time, we would rate this program a dismal failure. Yet what could it possibly have achieved; more to the point, what could the Field Coordinator achieve in such a risk-laden context of conflict? The program seems entirely unrealistic and loaded with denial.

To what extent can the CSR Report be taken as an authentic attempt to grapple with ethical issues rather than a PR smokescreen to cover over business-as-usual oil-, which is to say, profit-extraction? Talisman certainly understands what the issues are. They have addressed human rights violations, use of oil field infrastructure to facilitate attacks on civilians, and government deployment of oil revenues for arms acquisition and other military purposes. They even note throughout CSR Report (2000) intent to "exercise our corporate influence to promote a fair distribution of the economic benefits of the GNPOC operations" (Talisman, 2000, pp. 20–21).

Talisman did return some of their profits to the community. In 2000, they completed 15 development projects at a cost of $1 million CAD, and planned almost $3 million CAD (approximately $2 million USD) in community development projects in 2001. It kept that promise and allocated the $2 million (Talisman, 2001, p. 22), though its spending fell short by almost $600,000 that it apparently placed in trust, and almost $750,000 supported projects approved in 2001 but not actually an expense until they were implemented in 2002, and almost $200,000 was allocated in 2001 from the 2000 budget. So in 2001, only roughly $819,000 of what was described as $2 million was actually spent on community development. In 2002, Talisman claims to have spent 6.5 million CAD on community development in Sudan (approximately two-thirds of its global budget for community development) (Talisman, 2002, p. 33), but the only detail throughout the report of this spending is that $600,000 was spent on a community farm (Talisman, 2002, p. 11). That looks like a lot of money, but is trivial compared to the fact that on October 30, 2002, Talisman announced selling its Sudan operations for $1.2 billion to ONGC Videsh Limited (OVL) (Talisman, 2002, p. 32), a subsidiary of India's national oil company, though the sale was not completed until March 2003. At that time, Talisman pledged to continue to provide community investment to Sudan until 2005, but it in fact did so until 2008. In 2003, it spent 1.5 million; in 2004, $646,000; and in 2005, $389,000. In 2006, Talisman stopped disaggregating the Sudan data, noting only that data include the Sudan in the total. Subtracting the line data from the total leaves $359,000 that appears to have been spent on community development in 2006 (Talisman, 2006, p. 42). In 2007, it returns to reporting the Sudan data more clearly, and spent $262,000 (Talisman, 2007, pp. 37–38). In 2008, the last year it reported on community investment in the Sudan, it provided $217,000, against sales of over $12 billion, a net income of $648 million, $4 billion in capital and exploration expenditures, and an enterprise value of $25 billion (Talisman, 2008, p. 35). The total dollars returned for community development to host countries in 2008, $8.5 million, represents only 1.3% of the revenues it paid to governments of those countries (Talisman, 2008, p. 35). As noted by a Director of an International NGO operating in the Sudan in 2002, "Compared to the amount of oil being produced and the amount of profits being earned, the level of community development is rather modest" (Talisman, 2002, p. 42). The Sudan does not appear at all in the 2009 or 2010 Reports.


# BLESSING OR CURSE? BIG OIL AND HUMAN RIGHTS

It seems then that Talisman found itself in an increasingly difficult situation between 1998 and 2003, when they sold their interest in GNPOC.

Certainly, whatever good intention Talisman had appears to have been lost by the end of 2001. The 2002 CSR Report states that:

> The common international practice of national defense forces providing protection to local oil and gas operations, and the conduct of such forces, can pose one of the most critical challenges corporations deal with in respect to human rights issues. It is also an area where corporations have very little ability to apply any controls. This issue was one of the most problematic faced by the Sudan operations, and we were unsuccessful in our attempts to finalize a security protocol that endeavoured to address the provision of security and the appropriate use of oilfield infrastructure. (Talisman, 2002, p. 9)

This statement points out that Talisman is dependent on the Sudanese government for security in the Sudan. Loss of government support could easily put employees at risk – employees who were blamed by local populations for their suffering. These same populations were supported by militant rebels who began in 2003 to have significant battle victories that resulted in the Janjaweed being armed to the hilt and subsequently set loose to brutalize locals and pursue any anti-non-Arab or anti-non-Muslim campaign they or the government wished.

Jim Buckee in particular must have felt his situation in the Sudan to be impossible for him – he had publicly admitted knowledge of human rights violations enabled by oil revenues and Talisman's infrastructure in the course of attempting to negotiate for human rights inside GNPOC and with the Sudanese government. He had broadcast these activities in CSR Reports and in the Sudanese media. The 1999 e-mail claiming that "the Canadian company" had asked for "cleaning up operations" became widely known through the 2001 filing under the ATCA in New York. And in April of 2002, a Calgary law professor and human rights advocate suggested that the ICC would eventually prosecute individuals in corporations for human rights abuses that happened anytime after July 1, 2002. In the case of Talisman, if that meant anyone, it meant Jim Buckee. If he spoke out against the brutalities in the Sudan because he genuinely felt he was responding to the ethical call, he found himself unable to make any significant change, blamed for the brutalities because his advocacy efforts made it clear he know about them, and then facing the possibility of prosecution in the ICC. If his "corporate social responsibility" efforts in the Sudan were nothing more than the work of a CEO doing his job by managing a challenging public relations issue, then his job description probably did not include facing the ICC and possible conviction – for he had admitted knowing that Talisman infrastructure was being used in the government of Sudan's "ethnic cleansing" campaign. How is it possible that Buckee's efforts had so little impact? After all, the government of Sudan depended on the oil companies for development of its oil resources.

The Sudanese government did not depend on Talisman; rather, it depended on GNOPC, the corporation in the Sudan of which Talisman held a 25% interest. Production of 6.9 million barrels of oil in 2000 increased to almost 83 million in 2001, of which over 80 million was by GNPOC (United States Geological Survey Minerals Yearbook, 2000–2009). Talisman described the governance structure of GNPOC in its 2000 CSR Report: "Key management positions within GNPOC are occupied by representatives of each member of the consortium. Decisions made by committees within GNPOC require an affirmative vote of at least two consortium members holding at least 60% interest" (Talisman, 2000, p. 1). In the years that Talisman held 25% of GNPOC, Petronas Carigali Overseas owned 30%, and Sudapet owned 5%, while the CNPC owned 40%. Thus CNPC had only to secure the agreement of the Sudanese company to control GNPOC, while Talisman had to secure agreement of all remaining partners in cases where it did not have the support of the CNPC. China is the single largest investor in the Sudan because of its interest in GNPOC, and it relies on the Sudan to meet its oil needs. For example, in 2007, China purchased 40% of Sudan's 25-million-ton annual output of oil, which accounted for about 6% of China's oil imports (Herbst, 2008). China is also widely known for its arms trade with the Sudan, even in direct violation of the arms embargo imposed by the United Nations in 2005 (see in particular, Human Rights Watch, 2003b).[11] Talisman actually had little power in GNPOC decision-making, given that Sino-Sudan relation were likely to affect the 5% interest a Sudanese corporation held in the company, and even less power to make demands or impose constraints on the Sudanese government. GNPOC did pay compensation to those displaced or affected by construction of the pipeline. The GNPOC Pipeline Compensation Committee is reported on in the 2000 CSR Report, but no particular efforts on Talisman's part to instigate or implement the compensation scheme are indicated, and it seems likely that Talisman would have trumpeted such efforts loudly if it was responsible for the scheme, given its stated intent in the report to demonstrate that it "can be more than 'good neighbours'" to its shareholders and others (Talisman, 2000, p. 5). GNPOC's governance structure made it virtually impossible for Talisman to succeed with respect to CSR in the Sudan, even if its attempts were sincere. As long as it had no support from its partners, its hands were tied, regardless of how sincere its commitment to ethics was.

Indeed, Talisman is the "odd one out" for even attempting to support corporate accountability. In fact, as the court noted, it did nothing outside of regular business-as-usual. That is, demonstrating an attitude rampant in international oil development in Africa, it took a stance of corporate indifference – only adopting and formalizing compliance with the International Code of Ethics for Canadian Business after it was urged to do so by Minister Axworthy in 1999, only providing CSR Reports at the request of its shareholders in 2000, and getting out in 2002 when it faced the threat of liability becoming potentially enforceable through the ICC. Business ethics texts abound with instances of corporate irresponsibility, and the Talisman case is the tip of the iceberg with respect to big oil. The cases discussed above concerning litigation based on the ATCA involve Royal Dutch Petroleum, which operates as Shell, and Exxon, whose role in fabricating climate change denial, for example, has been well-documented (cf. Monbiot, 2006). Big oil is particularly indifferent to the suffering of people affected by its complicity and enabling of oppressive governments in Africa. Nigeria has led the way on corporate indifference to human rights impacts of oil development since the 1960s.

Nigeria has in fact much in common with the Sudan. It gained independence from Britain in 1960; Sudan was under British rule until 1956. As in the Sudan, little is spent on oil-producing areas in Nigeria that lack infrastructure like schools, running water, and electricity (Adenikinju, 2002). Nigeria's southern states in the Niger Delta have long protested their underdevelopment and resisted oil development, which accounts for 83% of federal government revenue, 95% of export earnings, and 40% of GDP (Economist Intelligence Unit report on Nigeria, 2002, p. 20). Delta inhabitants have access to less than 5% of the $340 billion USD of oil revenues generated since the 1960s (Gary & Karl, 2003, p. 25), which remains in the hands of only 1% of the population (Maier, 2000). In the Sudan and in Nigeria, "oil is more of a curse than a blessing."[12] Ironically, both countries are anticipated to be hit hard by anthropogenic climate change in consequence of global consumption of the oil wealth that is being stolen from under their feet.

Glazebrook and Kola-Olusanya (2011) argue that the peoples of the Niger Delta are subject to a logic of capital that doubly breaches distributive justice in that multinationals and the government fail to return oil profits to the communities that nonetheless pay the lived costs of extraction. Many of the people in the Delta as in southern Sudan live in "abject poverty" as defined by the World Bank, subsistence on less than $1 USD per day, and the Nigerian government has subjected the Delta region to "abject neglect" (Ojefia, 2006). Glazebrook and Kola-Olusanya argue further that people in the Delta are being treated as disposable, and note that "abject" etymologically means "thrown away." Worikuma Idaulambo,

Chairman of the Obioku Council of Chiefs confirms: "it is like we don't exist, as far as government is concerned."[13] Thus not only distributive but also recognition justice that supports both identity and citizenship is breached – the peoples of the Delta are not recognized as deserving human dignity, social investment, and infrastructure development. Glazebrook and Kola-Olusanya argue that this is how the "logic of capital" is ontological in force: affected citizens are formally identified as "externalities" in traditional economic analyses of costs and benefits, and thus can be ignored or disposed of. This logic is the basis of corporate indifference.

The case of the Sudan, in which the government has militarized in what has been identified as genocide by many sources, though denied such identification by the United Nations in 2005, and committed innumerable violations of human rights, is an unmistakable example of even more egregious breaches of distributive and recognition justice in which people are deprived of their livelihood, their right to a share in national wealth, their family, dignity, bodily integrity, and in hundreds of thousands of cases in the Sudan, their life. Understanding capital as a way of thinking embedded in lived experience provides a perspective for interpreting the experience of Talisman in the Sudan. Talisman quotes the World Bank that "Sudan has benefited from investment in oil production," while on the next page quoting the United States Energy Information Administration that "conflict has maintained the scarcity of national development resources, despite the increase in government oil revenues" (Talisman, 2000, p. 3). Traditional international economic reckoning is blind to the suffering of people that does figure in the bottom line. Indeed, one of the few effective strategies for resistance has been making oil development simply too costly. This is how the Ogoni women got Shell off Ogoni land in Nigeria (cf. Glazebrook & Kola-Olusanya, 2011).

In writing Glazebrook and Kola-Olusanya (2011), my co-author and I disagreed. I maintained that the corporations are accountable for human rights violations, while Dr. Kola-Olusanya, a Nigerian national, argued that the state is responsible. In the end, we agreed that both are ultimately responsible and accountable. The Talisman case shows that governments can continue with abuses regardless of a corporation's ethical intent. As a senior official of the Sudanese Ministry of Energy and Mining stated, "It is out of place for Talisman to look at the situation outside its sphere of influence. Talisman's concern is only in the area where it operates" (Talisman, 2000, p. 17). Domestic policy was simply none of Talisman's business. And a Sudanese academic in Khartoum moreover noted, "If Talisman were to leave, would the oil stop flowing? If the oil were to stop flowing, would this force the government to change, would it bring down the government? Oil exploration will not stop if Talisman left" (Talisman, 2000, p. 42). A director of an NGO operating in southern Sudan also asked, "If you pressure Talisman to leave Sudan then will the remaining actors take any action to address these critical issues" (Talisman, 2000, p. 12)? Talisman's attempts in the Sudan to enact corporate responsibility, whether sincere or not, represent a radial break from typical "business-as-usual" corporate approaches. Yet if they had been able to persuade their partners, they could likely have had enough economic power to oblige the government of Sudan to alter its attitude toward and practices in southern Sudan. This case demonstrates, however, that corporate irresponsibility cannot be understood simply in terms of rogue capitalists exploiting the system; rather, corporate irresponsibility is institutionalized in the corporate charter. Is capital the tool of government? Or is government the weapon of capital?

How could the corporation as institutionalized capital be changed such that oil is a blessing and not a curse in developing countries subject to oppressive, corrupt regimes?

## CONCLUSIONS AND RECOMMENDATIONS

In simple ethical terms, Talisman was irresponsible when it continued to practice business in breach of distributive and recognition justice. Distributive justice was breached when neither Talisman nor the government shared the profits of oil production with the peoples of the Sudan. Talisman's efforts at CSR are difficult to interpret as more than an attempt to placate shareholders committed to ethical investing. Moreover, they treated locals as disposable – in the way, and needing to be cleared out – while recognition justice requires that people be recognized as bearers of human rights and dignity. In the Sudan, however, population removal was ethnically focused on non-Arabs. Thus in the Sudan, unethical and irresponsible corporate attitudes contributed to ethnic cleansing – "cleaning up" not just the people in the way of oil production, but the non-Arabs. What Talisman shows as a case study is that corporate irresponsibility is systemic, and that the international system of corporate irresponsibility is robust enough to withstand even genocide.

Industry standards in big oil of corporate indifference and irresponsibility placed Talisman in an untenable situation in the Sudan, once shareholders asked for accountability, because its attempts to demonstrate responsible behavior implicated its corporate leaders in "cultural cleansing" and crimes against humanity. The first thing to be noted, then, is gratitude to shareholders who keep track of the activities of the companies in which they invest rather than turning a blind eye and complacently accenting their dividend cheques. Second, the ATCA has made possible the attempt to seek damages in civil court in an international venue, which brings attention to corporate activities that otherwise may have gone unnoticed. This strange and singular piece of legislation would be worth mirroring in other nations, and we urge human rights activists and NGOs to lobby for it. International corporate accountability could be encouraged and enforced in other ways.

Corporate culture and lack of support from its partners did more than discourage Talisman from implementing ethical practice; it prevented Talisman from acting ethically. In particular, it prevented Talisman from using the economic importance of GNPOC to the government of Sudan to disallow the government from using Talisman's infrastructure or oil revenues in military campaigns against the peoples of Sudan. There are several ways in which the desire for corporate leaders to behave ethically could be supported, and corporate accountability enforced in the absence of such desire. First, immediate extension of the jurisdiction of the ICC and clear mandating to include corporate enabling of the kind of crimes it prosecutes would put much more at stake for corporate leaders who are free to ignore justice issues given current corporate culture and the protections of corporate, international governance structures. In fact, if shareholders could be held financially accountable in civil court under legislation similar to the ATCA, the whole notion of corporate accountability would probably be radically altered, that is, would become an actuality, fairly quickly. Shareholders could no longer risk complacency. China would likely put up strong resistance, given that it has already argued that the ICC definition of "war crimes" exceeds customary international law (Jianping & Zhixiang, 2005). Others would also resist, and it would not take long for the argument to emerge that this legislation is disrupting international business. Analogously, however, effective prosecution of students for cheating does not stop people taking classes; it stops people from cheating. It may not stop everyone, but it creates a culture in which cheating is not par for the course. In corporate culture, accountability would not stop every corporation from acting unethically; but it would change corporate culture such that enabling genocide cannot possibly be construed as "business-as-usual."

Finally, locating the corporate charter in the hands of the nation-state generates an inherent tension. Because Talisman was incorporated under the corporate charter of Canada and separately in the Sudan, it established a corporate governance structure that figured importantly in the court's 2009 decision to uphold the 2006 dismissal. The plaintiffs could not "pierce the corporate veil," an issue the court found "knotty" and was unable to untie such that the Calgary company could be held liable. This is in a situation in which it is part of the partnership agreement in GNPOC that "key management positions within GNPOC are occupied by representatives of each member of the consortium" (Talisman, 2000, Preface) and Jim Buckee, for example, CEO and President of Talisman Energy, Inc. in Calgary, visited the Sudan on several occasions, and signed an entire CSR entitled "Sudan Operations." If the corporate charter was revoked under international agreement between nation-states, this kind of corporate veiling, that is in essence a nesting relationship to further limit liability, would no longer be possible. Alternately, the internationalization of corporate charters such that incorporation anywhere has global status would likewise preclude corporate nesting, though it would preserve the limited liability that is intended by and at the heart of the corporate charter. The Talisman experience in the Sudan demonstrates that when corporate responsibility attempts fail, however sincere, systems of incorporation in nation-states provide refuge for those whose corporations find themselves partnered with oppressive governments.

Between January 9 and 15, 2011, over 3.8 million people in the Sudan voted for the secession of southern Sudan by a landslide of almost 99%. South Sudan came into being on July 9, 2011. Given China's existing domination of the oil industry in South Sudan with respect to infrastructure, and the capacity of Sudan to make trade demands because it controls the pipeline that takes oil to Port Sudan in the north and has long-standing relations with China, it is entirely reasonable to anticipate that South Sudan's main trading partner for oil will be China. In fact, former rebel child-soldier and hip-hop star Emmanuel Jal comments, while at Chungking Mansions restaurant in Hong Kong, "There isn't a party in Africa that doesn't like [the Chinese]. Even if you're a rebel movement... The Chinese don't influence our politics. They don't comment on it, and what they want, they pay for – sometimes double" (Shadbolt, 2011). Alternately, a Sudanese political analyst, notes, "Chinese petroleum companies... do not care much about human rights, they care about investment and trade" (Abbas, 2011). Influence can be a good thing. Multinational corporations have the capacity to influence oppressive governments toward fair treatment of their peoples. International systems of corporate accountability can help them do this when they do not themselves favor human rights over profits.

# SUITS, SUMMARIES, AND JUDGMENTS

**Appeal Summary:**
*Presbyterian Church of Sudan v. Talisman Energy Inc.* (October 2, 2009) United States Court of Appeals, Second Circuit. [Docket No 07-0016-cv].

*Grimshaw v. Ford Motor Co.* (1981)
1 19 Cal.App. 3d 757, 174 Cal. Rptr. 348

*Kiobel v. Royal Dutch Petroleum Co.* (2010) United States Court of Appeals, Second Circuit. [Docket No. 06-4800-cv, 06-4876-cv].

*Presbyterian Church of Sudan v. Talisman Energy Inc.* (2003) United States Court of Appeals, Second Circuit. [Docket No. 07-0016-cv].

*Presbyterian Church of Sudan v. Talisman Energy Inc.* (March 19, 2003) United States Court of Appeals, Second Circuit. [Docket No. 01 CIV.9882 (AGS)].

*Presbyterian Church of Sudan v. Talisman Energy Inc.* (2009) United States District Court; New York. October 2, 2009.

*Sosa v. Alvarez-Machain* (03-339) 542 U.S. 692 (2004) 331 F.3d 604, reversed. Cf. Summary note 20.

# NOTES

1. This is the United Nations definition, though members of other cultural groups have on occasion had membership in the Janjaweed.
2. The government says four, the rebels say seven.
3. "B.V." stands for "Besloten Venootschap" and is the Dutch indication of a privately owned limited liability corporation in contrast to "Namloze Vernootschap" which indicates a publicly traded corporation. For extensive information regarding the subsidiary structure, see the Suit Summary of *Presbyterian Church of Sudan v. Talisman Energy Inc.*, United States Court of Appeals, Second Circuit. [Docket No. 07-0016-cv]. October 2, 2009.
4. From the 2003 Court Proceedings, p. 301: "[Talisman's] concerted actions are purportedly demonstrated by, inter alia, a May 7, 1999 communication from the Government's Petroleum Security Office in Khartoum to a satellite office in Heglig...This directive, denominated as "very urgent," reads as follows: In accordance with directives of His Excellency the Minister of Energy and Mining and fulfilling the request of the Canadian Company...the armed forces will conduct cleaning up operations in all villages from Heglig to Pariang. [Sudanese] Plaintiffs claim that thousands of villages and at least seventeen churches were destroyed in

the areas surrounding Talisman's oil fields, and that one, el-Toor, was located within walking distance of a Talisman site. See id. at ¶ 30. The same government troops assigned to protect Talisman's oil operations participated in the armed campaign against ethnic and religious minorities in the Unity and Ruweng areas... Talisman officials were and are aware of these military activities around its oil fields, and of the government's tactics of targeting civilians."

5. From 2003 Court Proceedings (p. 343):

> Talisman also urges deference to Sudan's ongoing peace negotiations. Talisman fails to point to any specific enactment or process, however, to which this Court purportedly ought to pay deference. Instead, Talisman states that Sudan is in the midst of intense negotiations to resolve an ongoing civil war. The implication is that adjudication of this matter will somehow hinder these peace efforts. Talisman does not specify how or why adjudication of this matter in this Court is a threat...[and] The Court also notes Sudan has already been declared a state sponsor of terrorism by the United States government, and that the United States Congress has declared that Sudan has been conducting acts of genocide...Any adjudication of private plaintiffs' rights in this Court would certainly have far less impact than either of these government pronouncements.

6. Originally reported by Rick Westhead in the *Toronto Star* (July 6, 2005).

7. The ICC has indicted Omar Hassan Ahmad Al-Bashir, the current President of Sudan, and Ahmed Mohammed Haroun, Sudan's Minister of State for Humanitarian Affairs until May 2009. A former senior Janjaweed commander has also been indicted, as well as three men prominent in the rebel movements. Proceedings were discontinued against another rebel leader, who was the first person ever to appear voluntarily before the ICC and the first in connection with Darfur. Sudan has "unsigned" the Rome treaty.

8. *Note*: Given the existing organization and infrastructure of UNICEF in this area, it is unclear why Talisman did not simply support these efforts rather than begin their own program.

9. See PricewaterhouseCoopers' letter to Talisman on March 6, 2001 within Talisman 2000, p. 11. Cf. pp. 8–9: "It is these Principles which make the Code 'come alive.'"

10. For those unfamiliar with the terms "global South" and "global North," note that these terms are not geographical but economic. Australia is in the global North, while Mexico is in the global South. Nor is the term "economic" here intended to reflect traditional economic indices like GDP; rather, these terms refer to levels of poverty. "Global South" stands in for lack of better phrasing for the much more problematic terms "third world" or "lesser developed countries" that appear to evaluate and/or hierarchize, and "emerging economies" that accords with the notion of "economic" just rejected that implies successful economies are players in the global market. We use "economy" etymologically rather, that is, to indicate "laws of the household" such that economic indices indicate indices of poverty and well-being in the context of lived experience for the majority of the population. These indicators would include several, but not be limited to the indicators specified by the Genuine Progress Index.

11. Cf. ReliefWeb's "Sudan: UN resolution for Darfur" (August 2007) [http://reliefweb.int/report/sudan/sudan-un-resolution-darfur-important-insufficient-first-step-towards-protecting]; Bloomberg's "Darfur Rebel Factions Begin Talks on

Charting Road to Peace" (August 2007) [http://www.bloomberg.com/apps/news? pid=newsarchive&sid=awEadP__uCEU&refer=Europe]; BBC News' "Darfur rebel head warns of split" (September 2007) [http://news.bbc.co.uk/2/hi/africa/ 6999959.stm].

12. Anyakwee Nsirimovu, Executive Director of the Institute of Human Rights and Humanitarian Law in the Delta, quoted in Lydia Polgreen (2006).

13. Worikuma Idaulambo, Chairman of Obioku Council of Chiefs, quoted in Polgreen (2006).

# REFERENCES

Abbas, R. (2011). *China could oil the peace process*. Retrieved from http://www.ipsnews.net/ news.asp?idnews=105321. Accessed on October 3, 2011.

Adenikinju, A. (2002). *Resource ownership, human development and economic growth.* Retrieved from http://ipn.lexi.net/images/uploaded/6-405c4d220aae4—adeola-_adeni- kinju_september2002.pdf. Accessed on November 21, 2010.

Business and Human Rights Resource Centre. (2009). *Case profile: Talisman law suit (re Sudan).* Retrieved from http://www.business-humanrights.org/Categories/Lawlawsuits/ Lawsuitsregulatoryactionon/LawsuitsSelectedcases/TalismanlawsuitreSudan?sort_on= publication&batch_size=10&batch_start=4. Accessed on October 1, 2011.

CorpWatch. (2002). *Holding corporations responsible, Talisman oil advised, further abuses could result in prosecution.* Retrieved from http://www.corpwatch.org/article.php?id=2478. Accessed on December 30, 2006.

Donavon, J. (2011) Will SCOTUS review Alien Tort Statute after D.C. circuit ruling? *Reuters Online*. Retrieved from http://royaldutchshellplc.com/2011/07/11/kiobel-v-royal-dutch- petroleum/. Accessed on September on 29, 2011.

Economist Intelligence Unit (EIU) Country Profile on Nigeria. (2002). London: EIU Ltd.

Flint, J., & de Waal, A. (2006). *Darfur: A short history of a long war.* London: Zed Books, pp. 99–100.

Gary, I., & Karl.T. (2003). *Bottom of the barrel: Africa's oil boom and the poor* (p. 26). Catholic Relief Services. Available at http://crs.org/publications/list.cfm?sector=26

Glazebrook, T., & Kola-Olusanya, A. (2011). Justice, conflict, capital, and care: Oil in the Niger Delta. *Environmental Ethics*, *33*(2), 163–184.

Herbst, M. (2008). Oil for China, guns for Darfur. *Bloomburg BusinessWeek*. Retrieved from http://www.businessweek.com/globalbiz/content/mar2008/gb20080314_430126.htm. Accessed on October 2, 2011.

Human Rights Watch. (2003a). *Sudan, oil, and human rights: Talisman And Canada, 1998– 2000.* Retrieved from. http://www.hrw.org/fr/node/12243/section/29. Accessed on Sep- tember 30, 2011. See esp. notes 1200–1204 and accompanying text.

Human Rights Watch. (2003b). *China's involvement in Sudan: Arms and oil.* Retrieved from http://www.hrw.org/reports/2003/sudan1103/26.htm. Accessed on October 2, 2011.

Jianping, L., & Zhixiang, W. (2005). China's attitude towards the ICC. *Journal of Interna- tional Criminal Justice*, *3*(3), 608–620.

Johnson, H. F. (2011). *Waging peace in Sudan: The inside story of the negotiations that ended Africa's longest civil war* (p. 38). Brighton: Sussex Academic Press.

Jones, J. (2005). *Canada asked U.S. to intervene in Talisman case.* Retrieved from http://www. globeinvestor.com/servlet/ArticleNews/story/ROC/20050706/2005-07-06T220728Z_01_ N06227802_RTRIDST_0_BUSINESS-ENERGY-TALISMAN-SUDAN-COL. Accessed on October 1, 2011.

Klauszus, J. (2006). Big oil on trial: The story nobody's telling. *Alberta Views, 9*(5), 28–34.

Maier, K. (2000). *This house has fallen: Midnight in Nigeria.* New York, NY: Public Affairs.

Monbiot, G. (2006). *Heat: How to stop the planet from burning.* Toronto: Doubleday Canada.

Ojefia, I.A. (2006) The Nigerian State and the Niger Delta question. 22nd annual conference of the Association of Third World Studies, Americus, GA. http://www.deltastate.gov. ng/oyefia.htm. Accessed on May 9, 2007.

Polgreen, L. (2006). Blood flows with oil in poor Nigerian villages. *New York Times,* January 1. Retrievable from http://www.nytimes.com/2006/01/01/international/africa/01nigeria. html?pagewanted=1&ei=5087&en=b52f381d85a3c523&ex=1187154000. Accessed on May 9, 2007.

ReliefWeb. (2000). *UNICEF emergency programmes: Sudan Northern Sector Donor Update,* September 25, 2000. Retrieved from http://reliefweb.int/node/69743. Accessed on September 26, 2011.

Shadbolt, P. (2011). *China, hip-hop and the new Sudan.* Retrieved from http://www.cnn.com/ 2011/WORLD/africa/02/02/sudan.jal/index.html. Accessed on October 2, 2011.

Talisman CSR Report. (2000). Retrieved from http://www.talisman-energy.com/responsibility/cr_report.html. Accessed on March 21, 2012.

Talisman CSR Report. (2001). *Independent opinion.* Retrieved from http://www.talisman-energy.com/responsibility/cr_report.html. Accessed on March 21, 2012.

Talisman CSR Report. (2002). Retrieved from http://www.talisman-energy.com/responsibility/cr_report.html. Accessed on March 21, 2012.

Talisman CSR Report. (2003). Retrieved from http://www.talisman-energy.com/responsibility/cr_report.html. Accessed on March 21, 2012.

Talisman CSR Report. (2006). Retrieved from http://cr.talisman-energy.com/2006. Accessed on October 2, 2012.

Talisman CSR Report. (2007). Retrieved from http://www.talisman-energy.com/responsibility/cr_report.html. Accessed on March 21, 2012.

Talisman CSR Report. (2008). Retrieved from http://www.talisman-energy.com/responsibility/cr_report.html. Accessed on March 21, 2012.

United States Geological Survey Minerals Yearbook. (2000–2009). Retrieved from http:// minerals.usgs.gov/minerals/pubs/country/africa.html#su. Accessed on October 2, 2011.

# IMPACT OF CORPORATE SOCIAL IRRESPONSIBILITY ON THE CORPORATE IMAGE AND REPUTATION OF MULTINATIONAL OIL CORPORATIONS IN NIGERIA

Olusanmi C. Amujo, Beatrice Adeyinka Laninhun, Olutayo Otubanjo and Victoria Olufunmilayo Ajala

## ABSTRACT

Purpose – *This chapter examines how irresponsible corporate activities (environmental pollution, human rights abuses, tax evasion, corruption and contract scandals) of some multinational oil companies in the Niger Delta influence stakeholders' perception of their image/reputation in Nigeria.*

Methodology – *The objective of this chapter is accomplished through the review of literature on the activities of multinational oil corporations in the Niger Delta, supported by qualitative interviews and analysis of archival materials.*

Corporate Social Irresponsibility: A Challenging Concept
Critical Studies on Corporate Responsibility, Governance and Sustainability, Volume 4, 263–293
Copyright © 2012 by Emerald Group Publishing Limited
All rights of reproduction in any form reserved
ISSN: 2043-9059/doi:10.1108/S2043-9059(2012)0000004020

Findings − *Three important findings emerged from this study. First, the participants were fully aware of the irresponsible behaviours of oil corporations in the Niger Delta, and some oil corporations were involved in these illicit acts. Second, the analysis of archival materials supports the participants' views with reference to the identities of the corporations involved in these criminal acts. Third, the absence of a strong corporate governance system in Nigeria makes it possible for the officials of oil corporations to tactically circumvent the law by involving in a maze of sophisticated corrupt acts.*

Research/practical implications − *The implication for the academics and practitioners is evident when a corporation implements corporate social responsibility dutifully; it generates positive impact on its corporate reputation rating. Conversely, when a corporation engages in irresponsible corporate misbehaviours, it attracts negative consequences on its reputation.*

Originality − *The originality of this chapter lies in the fact that it is the first empirical study to examine the impact of corporate social irresponsibility on the image/reputation of multinational oil corporations in Nigeria.*

**Keywords:** Corporate image; corporate reputation; corporate social irresponsibility; Niger Delta; Nigeria

# INTRODUCTION

A German company, the Nigerian Bitumen Corporation, began oil exploration activities in Nigeria way back in 1903 (Steyn, 2009). The company operated in the Araromi area of the present Ondo State. The outbreak of World War I in 1914 forced the company to abandon its dry, shallow wells. However, the discovery of oil in commercial quantity in 1956 at Oloibiri in the Niger Delta by Shell-BP heralded the birth of the Nigerian oil and gas industry. The group began production in 1958 at the rate of 5,100bld, the bulk of which was exported. Other oil companies, such as Mobil, Agip, Gulf Oil (now Chevron), SaFrap (now Elf), Amoseas (now Texaco) and Tenneco, began exploration activities onshore and offshore in 1961 (Udosen, Etok, & George, 2009). However, Shell group had the largest onshore fields in Nigeria.

Oil and gas exports account for more than 98 per cent of Nigeria's export earnings, forming at least 83 per cent of the federal government revenue, and generating more than 40 per cent of the country's GDP. Oil and gas exports also provide 95 per cent of the nation's foreign exchange earnings, and about 65 per cent of total government budgetary revenues. These probably explain why the nation's oil and gas industry is referred to as the nation's cash cow. Currently, with a daily output of about 2.6 million barrels, Nigeria is rated as the world's 10th oil-richest nation (Adeyemi & Chawai, 2011). However, the irony of petroleum wealth in Nigeria is that it has brought dire consequences on human, domestic and aquatic animals, and the environment. It has exacerbated the distribution of poverty and underdevelopment of the oil producing Niger Delta region, due to corporate irresponsible behaviours (Armstrong, 1977; Christensen & Murphy, 2004; Frooman, 1997).

The elements of corporate responsibility have been viewed as key drivers of corporate reputation (Hillenbrand & Money, 2007). Similarly, there is a close relationship between corporate social irresponsibility and reputation of a corporation (Duhe, 2009). Positive corporate behaviours are commended by stakeholders, whereas negative business behaviours are condemned by them, and they tend to have serious adverse effects on corporations (Frooman, 1997; Jones, 1995). Importantly they have negative effects on stakeholders perception of corporate image, reputation and brand identities of companies. In the mid-1990s, the Greenpeace International pressured Royal Dutch Shell Oil to stop the sinking of a decommissioned floating oil storage facility at Brent Spar in the North Sea (Sluyterman, 2010). During the crisis, Shell's reputation was hard hit by its technical arrogance to justify its deepwater disposal plan of the oil storage despite Greenpeace's consistent articulation of its likely adverse effects on the ocean environment and animals. Also, British Petroleum was accused of negligence in the Gulf of Mexico oil spill disaster, which claimed 11 lives and destroyed innumerable aquatic lives (Public Eye Awards, 2011; Urban Guerilla, 2011). The crisis threatened to destroy the firm's finances and corporate reputation (Krauss & Werdigier, 2012).

This chapter examines how the unwholesome activities of some multinational oil corporations (i.e. environmental pollution, irresponsible corporate lobbying, the use of armed forces to quell protests, tax evasion, bribery, corruption and contract scandals) influence stakeholders' perception of the image/reputation of these firms. It also investigates the involvement of some multinational oil corporations in tax evasion, bribery, corruption and contract scandals in Nigeria and how these affect stakeholders' perception of their corporate image/reputation. This empirical study was achieved through qualitative interview, archival analysis and theoretical literature on the activities some of multinational oil corporations in the Niger Delta, Nigeria.

# THEORETICAL FOUNDATION

## *Corporate Social Irresponsibility*

Corporate social irresponsibility cannot be discussed in isolation of stakeholder theory and corporate social responsibility. Freeman (1984) defines stakeholders as any group or individual who can affect or is affected by the achievement of the firm's objectives; those groups who are vital to the survival and success of the corporation (Freeman, 2002). In the context of our study, the stakeholders in the Niger Delta comprise oil producing communities and their opinion leaders, federal government, state and local governments in the Niger Delta, oil corporations, employees of oil corporations, social and environmental activists, media and others, that influence, directly and indirectly, the ability of a firm to achieve its objectives (Freeman & Velamuri, 2006). Additionally, Heal (2005) defines corporate social responsibility as a programme of actions to reduce externalised costs or to avoid distributional conflicts. Heal's definition is appealing because of its foundation in economic theory; the distributional conflicts in the Niger Delta over who gets what and how much they get are avoidable impasse. However, the state social irresponsibility on the part of the Nigerian government and corporate social irresponsibility on the part of some oil corporations in the Niger Delta, led to the escalation of conflicts in the region (Cayford, 1996; *Daily Trust Newspapers*, 2007; Ejibunu, 2007; Mouwad, 2007; Kretzman, 1995; *This Day*, 2007; The Vanguard, 2007). This unwholesome development was due to the failure of both the government and some oil corporations to conceive and accept the people of the Niger Delta as equal stakeholders in the Nigerian oil industry (Akinola, 2011). It is important to stress that corporate social responsibility is a situation where the firm goes beyond compliance and engages in some actions that appear to further some social good, beyond the interests of the firm and that which is required by law (McWilliams, Siegel, & Wright, 2006). Social responsibility of business encompasses the economic, legal, ethical and discretionary expectations that society has of all organisations at a given point in time (Carroll, 1979). Making contributions to society where a business corporation operates is considered social good or social investment which goes beyond the interests of the firm; it helps a corporation to gain a social licence to operate (Howard-Grenville,

Nash, & Coglianese, 2007; Gunningham, Kagan, & Thornton, 2004) peacefully and successfully without encumbrance among the host communities. Unfortunately, the state and some oil corporations failed to leverage on social capital investment in the Niger Delta; hence, they unwittingly reap the consequential attritional conflicts, insecurity and disruption of their operational and production infrastructures in the region.

The theory of corporate social irresponsibility is a contraposition of corporate social responsibility. Positive corporate behaviours are commended by stakeholders, whereas negative business behaviours are condemned by them, and they tend to have serious adverse effects on corporations (Frooman, 1997; Jones, 1995). The conflicts in the Niger Delta and the national and international solidarity enjoyed by the people of the region in their struggle against coordinated state–oil corporations' repression and oppression are clear condemnation of negative business behaviours of some oil corporations in the enclave. Corporate social irresponsible behaviours involve a gain by an organisation at the expense of society (Armstrong, 1977). According to Armstrong, one key parameter of corporate social irresponsibility is the exploitation of negative externalities. Negative externalities are the property rights problems, and they sometimes constitute some losses to society. However, a positive externality is something that benefits a society. While applying Coase Theorem (1960) on negative externalities in the Niger Delta, we argue that oil exploration and distribution of its wealth should be a situation of perfect competition among the three key stakeholders – Nigerian government, citizens of the Niger Delta and multinational oil corporations. That is, once a government has stipulated clearly defined property rights in contested resources, and as long as transactions costs are negligible, private parties that generate or are affected by externalities will negotiate voluntary agreements that lead to the socially optimal resource allocation and output mix regardless of how the property rights are assigned. In the Niger Delta context, if the people own the petroleum resource in the land, then the oil corporations drilling and distributing it, including the government that grants exploration licences to oil corporations, have to pay the people of the Niger Delta some royalties. Thus the negative externality is directly added to the oil corporations' marginal cost of oil production. It is important to stress that both the Nigerian state and some oil corporations failed to shoulder the cost of negative externalities rather they pushed them to the helpless people of the Niger Delta; and when the people of the region could not cope with the decimating and destructive costs of the negative externalities, they revolted against the state and some oil corporations in the region.

Frooman (1997) adds that socially irresponsible and illegal corporate behaviours cause substantial decreases in shareholders' wealth. Socially irresponsible corporate conducts are reflected in the negative scores of the KLD social ratings database on corporate social performance. In some corporations in the United States, where some CEOs and top executives were involved in unethical financial mismanagement and acted irresponsibly by indulging in either enterprise corruption, creative accounting system, flawed in board governance, jumbo CEO salary or stock market price manipulation, caused substantial decreases in shareholders' wealth and employees' compensations in their organisations.

In the mid-1990s, the Greenpeace International pressured Shell to stop sinking a decommissioned floating oil storage facility at Brent Spar in the North Sea. Recently, Yishau (2011) reported that residents of villages around Shell's Bonga oil field in the Niger Delta bitterly lamented the effect of the spill, which occurred on 21 December 2011, on their health and livelihood. Shell had, on Wednesday 21 December 2011, announced that some 40,000 barrels of crude had leaked into the Atlantic Ocean from 200,000 barrels per day at Bonga Deep Offshore Oil Fields which it operates. Also, the *Public Eye Awards 2011* for the most irresponsible company was awarded to the Finnish oil company, the Neste Oil, which has been tagged 'the world's most evil' corporation by the vote of more than 53,000 participants. Additionally, BP was accused of negligence in the Gulf of Mexico oil spill disaster (Cherry & Sneirson, 2010), which claimed 11 lives and destroyed innumerable aquatic lives. It is important to stress that some irresponsible corporate behaviours of some oil corporations in the Niger Delta had been documented by scholars (Frynas, 2000; Holzer, 2007; Iyayi, 2008; Jike, 2004; Kretzman, 1995; Ojakorotu, 2009).

## CORPORATE IMAGE AND REPUTATION

Some scholars believe reputation and image are synonymous, while others differ. For instance, Bromley (2000) considers reputation as the aggregate of identity and image, while Cornelissen and Thorpe (2002) assert that reputation is the collective representation of past images of an institution through communication or past experience accumulated over time. However, Dowling (2001) distinguishes image from reputation. Dowling argues that corporate image is the global evaluation a person has about an organisation, while corporate reputation is the attributed values evoked of the company. We argue that perception of corporate reputation is informed by aggregate of information, experiences, observable evidences, including distributed opinions, comments and viewpoints in the public sphere, available to networks of stakeholder groups inside and outside a corporation.

Corporate reputation has been conceived from corporate historical heritage perspective. It is believed that a company's reputation reflects the history of its past actions (Yoon, Guffey, & Kijewski, 1993). Reputation is a historical notion based on the sum of the past behaviours of the entity (Herbig & Milewicz, 1995). It is a perceptual representation of a corporation's past actions and future prospects and its overall appeal to key stakeholders (Roberts & Dowling, 2002). A review of literature shows scholars (Robertson & Gatignon, 1986; Tauber, 1988) conceive reputation as a set of economic and non-economic attributes ascribed to a corporation. Pruzan (2001) contends that corporate reputation is an attribute vital for stakeholder trust and competitive advantage. Importantly, Fombrun (1996) refers to it as reputational capital.

Nevertheless, this study is designed to investigate the impact of stakeholders' perception of corporate social irresponsible behaviours of some oil corporations in the Niger Delta on their image/reputation. In order to accomplish this task, the following research questions will be addressed in this study.

**Research Question 1:** What are the unethical corporate behaviours of some multinational oil corporations operating in the Niger Delta that stakeholders can recall?

**Research Question 2:** How responsive are oil corporations to managing environmental pollutions in the Niger Delta?

**Research Question 3:** Do oil corporations pursue corporate governance, financial accountability and transparency in Nigeria?

**Research Question 4:** To what extent do oil companies promote economic development, human and social rights in the Niger Delta?

**Research Question 5:** What attributes aid stakeholders' perception of image/reputation of oil corporations involved in unethical behaviours in the Niger Delta?

# METHODOLOGY

The authors employed qualitative interview in this study. Qualitative interview provides understanding of human perceptions, experiences and intentions based on naturalistic interpretation of a subject and their contextual setting. It enables a researcher understand and interpret social construction of reality (Husserl, 1965) from the perspectives of the social actors. It generates data which consist of direct quotations from the respondents' responses about their experiences, opinions, feelings and knowledge concerning the issues under investigation.

We administered an open-ended questionnaire based on the public sphere (Habermas, 1962) concept. We gathered data in Lagos, Ibadan, Asaba and Port Harcourt from men and women between the ages of 25 and 56. Data gathering took place in the public spheres (Burnett & Jaeger, 2008) such as community halls, universities, libraries, clubs, gyms, kiosks of newspaper vendors and others, where citizens gather to discuss salient public issues. The samples were drawn from educated professionals in banking, education, law, public service, health, medicine, media, advertising, public relations, marketing, insurance, manufacturing, foods and beverages, oil and gas, telecommunication and others. They cut across stakeholder groups such as investors, employees and suppliers of oil companies, rights activists, natives of oil producing communities, media professionals, bankers, health service professionals, postgraduate students, public service employees and other professionals, who were following developments and issues in the Nigerian oil industry. The citizens in the public sphere behave neither like business or professional people transacting private affairs, not like members of a constitutional order subject to the legal constraints of a state bureaucracy (Habermas, 1964). Some citizens that were sampled in this study behaved as a public body when they confer in an unrestricted fashion with the guarantee of freedom of assembly, association and expression, and publish their opinions about matters of general interest (Habermas, 1964) such as oil communities—oil corporations' crisis in the Niger Delta.

We adopted consecutive sampling, a non-probability sampling technique. We employed this by allowing all willing and accessible stakeholders at some of the public places used for data gathering to participate in the completion of the open-ended questionnaire, in order to ensure better representation of the entire population within a reasonable period of time (Lunsford & Lunsford, 1995). To generate qualitative data, we administered 250 copies of an open-ended questionnaire to some samples of the population on critical issues unfolding in the Nigerian oil industry, and 32 per cent of the questionnaires were completed and returned.

Scholars such as Hanson and Stuart (2001) have established a relationship between corporate misbehaviours and corporate reputation. The damage to the reputation of Broken Hill Propriety Ltd in Australia, resulted in sharp drop in its share price from around AUS$20 to AUS$12 in 1998. Against this background, our prime objective in this study was to find out the impact of corporate social irresponsibility on stakeholders' perception of corporate reputations of oil corporations in the Niger Delta. This was done through qualitative open-ended questionnaire used to gather data from some stakeholders of oil industry in Nigeria.

## DATA ANALYSIS

We adopted qualitative content analysis method (Elo & Kynga, 2008; Graneheim & Lundman, 2004) and narrative analysis method (Bletzer & Koss, 2006; Thomas et al., 2009) in this study. We applied qualitative content analysis method to the data generated, which enabled us to identify evolving themes through 'open coding' (Strauss & Corbin, 1990) system. Through open coding, the researchers undertook conceptual labelling and categorising of concepts/themes that evolved from the data. Some of the themes, categories and codes derived through qualitative content analysis of the data were given in Table 1.

We conducted axial coding by rearranging the data together to ensure there are meaningful connections between each category and its sub-

***Table 1.*** Themes, Categories, Sub-categories and Codes Derived From Data Analysis.

| Theme | Category | Sub-Category | Code |
|---|---|---|---|
| Corporate irresponsible behaviours | Oil spills | Gas flaring | Environmental pollution |
| Description of reputational attributes | Corporate characteristics | Corporate traits | Reputational indicators |
| Sustainable environmental management | Environmental destruction | Water and land pollution | Environmental degradation |
| Managing oil spills and gas flaring | Fuel contaminants | Toxicity | Environmental contamination |
| Oil contract scandals and corporate governance | Bribery | kickback | Contract scandals |
| Corporate financial accountability and transparency | Tax evasion | Profit concealment | Unaccountability |
| Community development initiatives | Infrastructural underdevelopment | Inadequate social investment | Underdevelopment |
| Promotion of human and social rights | Human rights abuse | Social rights abuse | Rights abuse |
| Bribery and corruption | Financial inducement | bribery | Corruption |

Developed by the authors from the qualitative data.

categories derived from the themes. Subsequently, we employed selective coding to integrate the categories that we identified to form the primary theoretical frameworks. Through narrative analysis method (Phoenix, Smith, & Sparkes, 2008), we used the thematic and theoretical frameworks that emerged from these coding processes to develop some descriptive narratives that enabled us conceptualise the central phenomena of the study under each theme below. The purpose of using an open-ended questionnaire was to elicit in-depth narrative description (Fisher, 1995) or story from some respondents rich with contextual information (Peterson, Jesso, & McCabe, 1999). We resolved inter-research differences through discussion and reference to the transcriptions (Miles & Huberman, 1994). Data analysis revealed the following patterns and themes:

**Research Question 1:** What are the unethical corporate behaviours of some multinational oil corporations operating in the Niger Delta that stakeholders can recall?

*Corporate Irresponsible Behaviours*

Gabb (2009) advises that choice of vocabulary and use of symbolic phrases are most enlightening in qualitative research. In an attempt to confirm whether the respondents understand and can identify corporate misbehaviours that constitute corporate social irresponsibility in the Niger Delta, they were asked to mention five unethical corporate behaviours of oil corporations in the region. Some of the phrases used by the participants included: '*Underdevelopment of oil communities*' (Participant 1); '*Poor handling of oil spills and constant gas flaring*' (Participant 3); '*Environmental pollution*' (Participant 9); '*Inadequate compensation for communities experiencing oil spills*' (Participant 5); '*Involvement of oil companies in oil contract scandals*' (Participant 12); '*Tax evasion*' (Participant 58); '*Arming and funding military and police to kill and maim protesters and militant youths*' (Participant 11). Identification of phrases above permits data to be understood in its textual context. It enables researchers to recognise and articulate emergent patterns, themes and explanations in this study.

# OIL CORPORATIONS INVOLVED IN CORPORATE MISBEHAVIOURS

Identification of oil corporations involved in corporate misbehaviours in the Niger Delta is paramount to establishing the presence of corporate social irresponsibility in the enclave. The participants were able to identify some oil corporations that had been involved in irresponsible corporate behaviours in the Niger Delta. Table 2 provides a summary of the frequency with which some respondents mentioned oil companies that are alleged to have been involved in irresponsible corporate behaviours in Nigeria.

It is revealing to note that Sola Omole, the spokesperson of Chevron-Texaco, admitted to some socially irresponsible behaviours of the company in the Niger Delta (Goodman & Scahill, 1998). Also, Paul Skinner, the CEO of Shell, during a talk at Manchester Business School in England, owned up to some corporate misdemeanours levelled against Shell in the Niger Delta (Torrance & Skinner, 2003). Furthermore, top management of other oil companies such as Mobil, Agip, TotalFinalElf admitted to charges of environmental irresponsibility in the region (Essential Action, 2001; The Niger Delta Solidarity, 2010). Their admittance to corporate misbehaviours of their corporations confirmed the presence of some unethical corporate misdemeanours enumerated against them by the participants in the survey. This shows that the participants were in good touch with reputational issues and developments in the Nigerian oil industry.

**Research Question 2:** How responsive are oil corporations to managing environmental pollutions in the Niger Delta?

*Table 2.* List of Oil Corporations Involved in Irresponsible Behaviour in the Niger Delta by the Interviewees.

| Oil Corporation | Frequency of Mention by the Respondents |
| --- | --- |
| Royal Dutch Shell/SDPC | 54 |
| ChevronTexaco | 44 |
| ExxonMobil | 33 |
| Agip | 16 |
| TotalfinaElf | 29 |
| NNPC | 4 |
| Halliburton | 7 |
| Schlumberger | 2 |
| Saipem | 2 |
| Eni | 3 |
| Stinnes | 1 |

Developed by the authors from the qualitative data.

## SUSTAINABLE ENVIRONMENTAL MANAGEMENT

Incessant oil spills and gas flaring have been identified as the two major sources of environmental pollution caused by oil corporations in the Niger Delta (Platform, 2006). In an attempt to investigate this claim, the participants were asked to explain oil companies' response to managing oil spills and gas flaring in the region. A participant observed: *'Managing oil spillage is very poor in the Niger Delta, the communities suffer severe environmental degradation as a result of oil spills and gas flaring. The net effects are destruction of human and aquatic lives, water pollution, and destruction of arable lands and farm products'* (Participant 9). Another respondent contended: *'Oil companies have been indifferent to oil spills in the Niger Delta.... Farmlands are destroyed which makes agricultural economy a daunting task for the teeming population of the zone .Water and environmental pollution have subjected people to ill health and terminal diseases such as asthmas, cancer among others'* (Participant 44). Nigeria is reported to have had over 300 oil spills per year in the early 1990s, more than in the developed world (Frynas, 2005, 2000). About 40 per cent of Shell's oil spills in 28 countries worldwide have occurred in the Niger Delta (Cayford, 1996), while there were 2,976 oil spills in the Niger Delta between 1976 and 1991 (Ellis, 1994). According to the Nigerian federal government statistics, there were over 7,000 recorded oil spillages between 1970 and 2000 in the Niger Delta. To corroborate this information, the UNDP (2006) estimates that between 1976 and 2001 there were about 6,800 oil spills amounting to 3,000,000 barrels of oil. A study reported the emergence of carcinogenic diseases in the Niger Delta caused by exposure of the people to the radioactive elements of gas flaring (Akoroda, 2000). The people of the region are beginning to develop symptoms of bronchial and respiratory diseases and other terminal diseases (Jike, 2004), including other terminal ailments resulting from long exposure to gas flaring.

Environmental sustainability is a critical index in measuring a company's reputation (Fombrun, Gardberg, & Sever, 2000); many multinational corporations have been criticised for their poor environmental management. In view of this, the participants were asked to describe the oil companies' operational activities in the Niger Delta. Some of the responses included: *'The exploration activities of some oil companies in Niger Delta have led to water pollution, environmental degradation, destruction of farmlands and rivers caused by persistent oil spills'* (Participant 43). A participant added, *'The explorations in the region have caused oil spills, acid rain, pollution, gas flaring, toxicity of agricultural land, killing of human, domestic and aquatic animals and exposure of the people to health hazards'* (Participant 21). Corporate environmental responsiveness is an important component of the sixth reputation quotient developed by Harris—Fombrun (Fombrun, 2001). Social responsibility comprises perceptions of the company as a good citizen in its dealings with communities, employees and the environment (Fombrun, 2001). However, some participants have identified some oil companies involved in oil spills, water pollution, poor waste disposal, deforestation, acid rain and destruction of animals and farmland in the Niger Delta (see Table 1).

**Research Question 3:** Do oil corporations pursue corporate governance, financial accountability and transparency in Nigeria?

# OIL CONTRACT SCANDALS AND CORPORATE GOVERNANCE

In the last decade, the Organisation for Economic Co-operation and Development (OECD) has been concerned with the malaise of bribery and corruption as major causes of poverty, underdevelopment and other social problems. The respondents were asked to explain all they know about oil companies' activities in oil contract awards in the country. One respondent stated: *'I read some media reports concerning the involvement of companies in oil contract bribery scandals in Nigeria'* (Participant 24). Another said, *'Recent media reports fingered some multinational oil companies in a bribery scandal in a bid to secure oil contracts'* (Participant 6). A respondent concluded, *'Oil companies pay kickbacks to government officials to secure lucrative oil contracts in Nigeria'* (Participant 53). The total lack or weak presence of corporate governance system in Nigeria provides an ideal environment for bribery and corruption involving multinational oil corporations to thrive. Anti-Bribery Convention establishes legally binding standards to criminalise bribery of foreign public officials in international business transactions. OECD Guidelines for Multinational Enterprises enforced in Nigeria will help minimise involvement of multinational corporations in bribery scandals (OECD, 2001).

## CORPORATE FINANCIAL ACCOUNTABILITY AND TRANSPARENCY

Payment of taxes is a fundamental way in which private and corporate organisations demonstrate good corporate citizenship and actively engage the broader spectrum of civil society. In this study, we asked the participants to explain oil companies' attitude to paying tax in the country. An interviewee observed, '*Most times oil companies exploited loopholes in our taxation system to remit more profits to their home countries*' (Participant 16). Another interviewee added, '*The oil companies' are highly engrossed in tax evasion. They manipulate figures, falsify documents and bribe government officials in order to evade payment of taxes*' (Participant 43). One respondent stated, '*Like most multinational corporations in Nigeria, oil companies often repatriate their revenue without paying the required tax to the nation. They engage in false declaration and tax evasion*' (Participant 24). Osagie (2010) reported that the Rivers State Government in Nigeria was locked in a dispute with an Italian oil and gas company, Saipem, over alleged tax evasion to the tune of N14 billion. On 12 October, 2010, Abdulah reported PGS Exploration Nigeria Limited was alleged to evade payment of tax amounting to N4.5 billion. Also, Oando plc, an indigenous oil company was alleged to be involved in a N3.1 billion tax evasion scam (Otusanya, 2011). Tax revenues serve as the lifeblood of the social contract (Christensen & Murphy, 2004), which governments the world over dutifully access to provide social development and maintenance of physical infrastructure in society.

## BRIBERY AND CORRUPTION

There are reports on increasing high profile corporate bribery and corruption involving big multinational companies in developing economies (Rose-Ackerman, 1998). There are two sides to bribery and corruption: the supply spectrum (giver) and the demand spectrum (receiver) of proceeds of corruption. At the demand side are public officials (RESIST, 2011), while the supply side involves captains and managers of business (OECD Anti-bribery Convention, 1997). In this study, we asked the participants to give their opinions on how oil companies have been involved in the reduction of bribery and corruption in Nigeria. Their responses included: '*Oil companies are the highest perpetrators of bribery and corruption in Nigeria. They manipulate financial figures, evade taxes and bribe their ways through in government quarters'* (Participant 43). An interviewee stated, *'I believe to a reasonable extent that oil companies in Nigeria are involved in bribery and corruption directly or indirectly. Officials of oil companies offer bribe to community elders in the Niger Delta to silence opposition and government representatives in order to get juicy oil contracts'* (Participant 59). Another one concluded, *'Oil companies really try to reduce bribery and official corruption because they are afraid of the laws in their home countries which make it an offence to give bribes to solicit for favours in foreign countries where they operate'* (Participant 51). Oil corporations have been indicted in bribery scandals in Nigeria. On 19 July 2007, a federal grand jury in Houston returned a four count indictment against Jason Steph, a US citizen and former manager of a subsidiary of Willbros Group Inc., an oil and gas engineering services in Nigeria. Steph was accused of bribing Nigerian officials to secure the Eastern Gas Gathering System (EGGS) contract (FCPA Advisor, 2007). Similarly, Jeffrey Tesler, a British solicitor, was accused of offering bribe to Nigerian officials in order to obtain a $6 billion contract for a natural gas plant on Bonny Island in Nigeria. Also an American company, Kelloff Brown and Root (KBR) Inc, the engineering subsidiary of Halliburton Company with interests in oil and gas reportedly paid $180 million bribe to some Nigerian government officials to secure lucrative oil contracts in Nigeria (Alechenu, 2010).

**Research Question 4:** To what extent do oil companies promote economic development, human and social rights in the Niger Delta?

# COMMUNITY DEVELOPMENT INITIATIVES

Corporate social responsibility involves contributing to local community development where business corporations make profit. In our attempt to investigate oil corporations' involvement in community development in the Niger Delta, we asked the participants to explain oil companies' contributions to community development in the region. One participant stated: *'Oil companies have contributed to the infrastructural development of the Niger Delta through provisions of roads, hospitals, schools, bridges, electricity, community centres, skill acquisition programmes and scholarships'* (Participant 21). Another added: *'Oil companies have been involved in some infrastructural development of oil producing communities, but what they are* giving back to these communities is not commensurate to the profits they are making there. The continued youth restiveness in the area is as a result of their inadequate contribution to community development in the region' (Participant 23). The World Business Council for Sustainable Development stresses that a socially responsible company contributes to economic development while improving the quality of life of the local community and society at large. Findings suggest that although oil companies have invested in infrastructural development of the Niger Delta, their social investment in the region is a tip of the iceberg when compared to the enormous wealth exploited from the region. Thus underdevelopment of the region by oil companies and the federal government has been the bane of increasing crisis in the region (Iyayi, 2008).

## PROMOTION OF HUMAN AND SOCIAL RIGHTS

One indication of a good corporate citizenship involves respecting the human, social and economic rights of host communities by oil companies. In our effort to investigate the progress made by oil corporations on this, we asked the participants to explain how they have been promoting human, social and economic rights of the people in the region. One respondent concluded: '*Oil companies don't promote human rights and social activism. They view these as inimical to their operations because they are involved in too many unethical practices, which rights activists have opposed*' (Participant 10). Another stated: '*Oil companies operating in the Niger Delta contribute to the oppression and suppression of human rights and social justice. They were implicated in the killing of Ken Saro Wiwa and other 8 Ogoniland activists*' (Participant 7). The violent suppression of non-violent demonstrations spearheaded by human rights activists between 1990 and 1996 leading to the killing of Ken Saro Wiwa and other eight Ogoni activists was a clear testimony that oil companies are intolerant of human rights activism in the region. It has been pointed out by the Human Rights Watch (1999) that multinational oil companies are accomplices in various rights' abuses committed by the Nigerian military and police in the enclave. Shell admitted funding of the military operation in Umeuchem village leading to the death of 80 people, and the destruction of houses and farmland in 1990. Shell conceded it paid the military twice to quell protests which resulted in deaths in Ogoni and Korokoro (Ellis, 1994; Rowell, Marriott, & Stockman, 2005). Also, Chevron was said to have conceded to funding and facilitating transportation of the Nigerian Navy and Mobile

Police that assaulted Ilajeland and killed Jola Ogungbeje and Aroleka Iro-waninu, wounded Larry Bowato and injured about 30 villagers (Goodman & Scahill, 1998).

**Research Question 5:** What attributes aid stakeholders' perception of image/reputation of oil corporations involved in unethical behaviours in the Niger Delta?

## DESCRIPTION OF REPUTATIONAL ATTRIBUTES OF SOME OIL CORPORATIONS

Saucier and Goldberg (1996b) argue that the most useful subset of single words is the set of adjectives that can be used to denote human propensities and qualities. Adjectives richly represent both the desirable and undesirable attributes applied to human and non-human (Saucier, 1997) entities. The authors asked the respondents to mention five adjectives that best describe their perception of irresponsible corporate behaviours of some oil corporations in the Niger Delta. Although, many adjectives were used by the respondents, the authors decided to exclude adjectives that were mentioned less than five times by different participants in Table 2.

Bromley (2000) supports the use of free description by stakeholders to construct reputation attributes. The lexical hypothesis states that (a) the most distinctive, significant and widespread phenotypic attributes tend to become encoded as single words in the conceptual reservoir of language, and (b) the degree of representation of an attribute in language tends to correspond with the relative importance of the attribute (Saucier, 1997; Saucier & Goldberg, 1996b). Therefore, the frequency of occurrence of some adjectival attributes listed above in a free description exercise indicates their relative saliency to stakeholders in their construction of reputational attributes of some oil corporations involved in some irresponsible activities in the Niger Delta.

## PERCEPTION OF IMAGES/REPUTATIONS OF SOME OIL CORPORATIONS OPERATING IN THE NIGER DELTA

Perceptual theory has been applied to reputation research by some scholars. For example, the impressional school sees reputation as a reflection of the accumulated perceptions of the single stakeholder, while the relational school sees reputation as an equal reflection of the internal and external views of the organisation (Chun, 2005 citing Hatch & Schultz, 2003; Davies & Miles, 1998). Based on the above, we asked the respondents to explain how they perceive the image/reputation of some oil corporations with records of irresponsible behaviours in the Niger Delta. Majority of the respondents used some of the negative adjectives (Table 3) to describe how they perceive some oil corporations in Nigeria. For example, a respondent stated: '*Based on what I have read and heard in the media concerning the activities of some oil companies in the Niger Delta, I perceive them as callous and inhuman*' (Participant 60). A participant said: '*The horrible pictures of environmental pollution, destruction of aquatic animals and birds in the Niger Delta accessed on the internet, and in the print media, made me perceive those oil companies involved as oppressive, inconsiderate and cruel*' (Participant 34). Wartick (2002) argues that reputation is purely perceptual. Following Wartick opinion, we argue that the perception of reputation by stakeholders is subjective and it is based on information available to stakeholders at a particular period of time. Given the adjectives used by the majority of the respondents, the collective constructs

*Table 3.* List of Adjectives Used by the Interviewees to Describe Corporate Misbehaviours of Some Oil Companies in the Niger Delta.

| Common Adjectives Used by the Participants to Describe Corporate Misbehaviours of Some Oil Companies | Frequency of Adjectives Mentioned up to Five Times in the Narratives of Different Participants |
| --- | --- |
| Irresponsible | 15 |
| Insensitive | 12 |
| Unethical | 11 |
| Uncaring | 10 |
| Inhuman | 9 |
| Exploitative | 9 |
| Selfish | 8 |
| Corrupt | 8 |
| Criminal | 7 |
| Cruel | 7 |
| Oppressive | 7 |
| Dishonest | 6 |
| Callous | 6 |
| Fraudulent | 6 |
| Inconsiderate | 6 |
| Dehumanising | 5 |

Developed by the authors from the qualitative data.

represent the aggregate perceptions of multiple stakeholders about some oil companies' irresponsible performance in Nigeria. We contend that based on a company's activities, the company can have different images held by different stakeholder groups. Bromley (2000) avers that commercial and industrial companies have as many reputations as there are distinct social groups (collectives) that take an interest in them. The media distribution and representation of socially irresponsible activities of some oil companies in the Niger Delta to some stakeholders in the country influenced the synthesis of their opinions, perceptions and attitudes about some oil organisations (Post & Griffin, 1997). The stakeholders' opinions and perceptions are formed as a consensus that results from their attention to information beyond the traditional boundaries (Gardberg, 2001), to include some narratives and pictorial messages accessed on the internet, websites of some environmental rights activist organisations, as well as some newspaper commentaries and articles of opinion leaders on the Niger Delta crisis. They often used these narratives and pictorial messages to communicate irresponsible activities of some oil companies in the region to the national and international stakeholder groups. Therefore, their perception of reputational attributes of some oil companies involved in the Niger Delta crisis is a fusion of a large collection of personal judgments about a standard set of corporate attitudes (Bromley, 2000).

Additionally, we asked the respondents to give their opinions on seeking employment in some oil corporations in the Niger Delta. One respondent replied: '*It is not my plan to work in oil companies involved in some irresponsible behaviours in Nigeria*' (Participant 55). Another added: '*I will like to work in an oil company, but I will never take an employment in oil companies linked with corporate misbehaviours in the Niger Delta*' (Participant 49). Good corporate reputation helps win the war for talents (Schwaiger, 2004) and plays an important role in attracting more qualified people in the labour market, retaining top talent (Fisher-Buttinger & Vallaster, 2011) and greater loyalty from employees. Helm (2007) contends that reputation is a potential signal that reduces uncertainty of future by employees concerning an employer's characteristics (Cable & Graham, 2000). Going by the opinions of the majority of the respondents, many jobseekers may not work in some oil companies in the country because of the rising ethical concerns. However, the rate at which this opinion can be generalised to young graduate jobseekers in the country remains a matter of conjecture. We observed that the rate at which young university graduates in Nigeria flock to write aptitude tests for employment opportunities in some oil companies in the country is very high. One undisputable fact is that oil industry is one of the best paying industries with good employee welfare system in Nigeria. It is possible that increasing poverty in the country might have influenced young graduate job-seekers to seek employment opportunities in some oil companies without minding their questionable ethical practices in the Niger Delta.

Helm (2007) argues that the reputation of a firm will increase its appeal as an investment choice (Chajet, 1997). Moreover, MacGregor, Slovic, Dreman, and Berry (2000) claim that in an initial public offer, corporate reputation and an affective evaluation provide the basis for investor buying decisions. In view of these positions, we asked the participants to explain if they will like to buy shares in some oil companies operating in the Niger Delta. A participant stated: '*I cannot invest my money in oil companies involved in atrocities in the Niger Delta*' (Participant 71). Also another respondent revealed: '*I will not buy shares of some oil companies that are engaged in the environmental destruction, human rights abuses, and killing of protesters in the Niger Delta*' (Participant 17). Another respondent added: '*I learnt that the United States and the United Kingdom have begun ethical investment screening, I will advise Nigerians to isolate stocks of some oil companies involved in social irresponsibility in the Niger Delta at the stock market*' (Participant 61). We observed that the opinions expressed by the majority of the respondents confirm Brown's (1998) argument that poor reputation signals to investors that disaster lurks in a company. Also stakeholders value associations and transactions with high-reputation firms (Roberts & Dowling, 2002). Furthermore, Shefrin (2001) and Goldberg and Nitzsch (2001) contend that representativeness effect in behavioural finance might lead investors to undertake premature selling of stock from badly reputed firms while inducing longer holding periods for shares from highly reputed firms. Representativeness effect is a form of representativeness bias which occurs among investors when they are assessing the probability of an object A originating from class B. According to heuristic rule, if object A is highly representative of class B, the probability of A originating from class B is judged as high. Therefore, low net worth investors may react to negative investment news if they perceive that it originates from high net worth investors, whose opinions are considered representative of the majority of investors. Studies reveal that the stock market reacts unfavourably to adverse news and criticism of a company's environmental impacts and positively when good environmental performance is recognised (Dasgupta, Laplante, & Mamingi, 2001). The available evidence suggests that some investors hold stocks of oil companies such as Agip Oil, ChevronTexaco, Mobil and others for a longer period in Nigeria. However, it is important to stress that since 2009 the Royal Dutch Shell Plc began divestment move by seeking buyers for 10 of its onshore oil production assets in the Niger Delta, which are valued between US$4 and US$5 billion. Also, the British Gas that invested about $500 million in Nigeria since 2004 has initiated a plan to end some of its business operations in March 2011. It is believed Shell's divestment activities were due to rising militant attacks on its facilities and mounting litigations affecting its operational activities in the region (Shell Nigeria, 2011; Nwankwo & Ayankola; 2011; Transparency for Nigeria, 2010).

Given the fact that our study focuses mainly on the social impact of operational activities of some oil corporations on the people and environment of the Niger Delta, we compared the data generated with the 2010 Corporate Social Responsibility Index (CSRI) proposed by the Reputation Institute and Boston College Center for Corporate Citizenship in their study. The CSRI consists of seven dimensions: the social impact (citizenship, governance and workplace) in addition to economic- and market-driven results (products/services, innovation, leadership and performance). The findings of this study reveal that the respondents were more concerned with the social impact dimensions of the index. The social impact dimension of the index encompasses corporate governance (15.7 per cent), corporate citizenship (14.2 per cent) and workplace (13.3 per cent). For stakeholders to trust, admire and support a corporation, it should promote *corporate governance*, that is become a responsibly-run company that behaves ethically and is open and transparent in its business dealings; foster *corporate citizenship*, that is the company is a good corporate citizen which supports good causes and protects the environment; and develop a conducive *workplace*, that is the company is an appealing place to work (Reputation Institute and Boston College, 2010). From the above analysis, majority of the respondents believed that some oil companies involved in social irresponsibility in the Niger Delta have poor corporate governance and corporate citizenship cultures. Based on these, many of the respondents were not willing to seek employment opportunities in them because of their negative image/reputation arising from some of their corporate misbehaviours in the Niger Delta.

## SUMMARY OF KEY FINDINGS

The findings of this study have shed more light on how corporate misbehaviours can impact corporate reputation adversely. First, we found that the participants were able to identify some corporate irresponsible behaviours of oil corporations in the Niger Delta and Nigeria. The phrases they used in describing these behaviours, which fit into realities in the region, show the participants were well aware of unethical operational activities of oil companies and they have negative perception of some oil corporations.

Decades of oil exploration in the Niger Delta have caused massive oil spills, gas flaring and acid rains, which resulted in water pollution, environmental degradation, destruction of farmlands and death of domestic and aquatic animals. The health effects of these include bipolar disorder, hypochrondriasis, convulsive stress disorder, neurosis, schizophrenia, skin rashes and sores, cancer of the stomach, skin and rectum, kidney, cervix and lymph nodes among others. The resulting economic problems include destruction of farming and fishing, low crops yields, starvation, change in subsistence lifestyle of natives, loss of life, contaminated water supplies, salmon and herring fisheries died out from the toxicity of the oil spill.

In addition, the respondents were able to mention some oil corporations involved in corporate misbehaviours in the Niger Delta. When we compared the companies listed by the participants with those that had been mentioned in media reports of Nigerian newspapers such as *The Punch*, *The Guardian*, *Nigeria Tribune*, *Thisday*, *Vanguard* and others, and archival materials obtained on the websites of the non-governmental organisations such as Human Rights Watch, Friends of the Earth International, Environmental Rights Action, Greenpeace International among others, we found that all the companies listed by the participants were equally mentioned by these organisations in some of their publications on negative impact of oil exploration on humans, animals and ecosystem of the Niger Delta.

Moreover, we discovered the absence of strong corporate governance in Nigeria. This makes it possible for some officials of oil corporations to tactically circumvent the law by involving in a maze of sophisticated, complex bribery and corruption in order to secure oil contracts in the country. Weak corporate and individual regulatory frameworks, lack of business ethical standards with control, compliance and monitoring mechanisms, abuse of shareholders' rights, inadequate commitment on the part of boards of directors to check executive abuses, poor political will on the part of government and its regulatory agencies to monitor ethical issues in oil industry and other sectors of the economy, provide rich opportunities to some foreign top executives of oil companies and their national compradors (i.e. supporters and loyalists), to engage in corporate malfeasance, financial impropriety and corruption in the oil industry.

# IMPLICATIONS FOR CORPORATE IMAGE/ REPUTATION MANAGEMENT

Findings of the study suggest that when a corporation implements corporate social responsibility dutifully, it will have positive impact on its corporate reputation rating among stakeholders. Conversely, when a corporation engages in irresponsible corporate misbehaviours, it will have negative consequences on its reputation rating among stakeholders.

Clandestine funding and arming of the Nigerian military and police establishments by oil corporations, and the ease with which they mobilise them into action to quell peaceful protests, have adversely affected the reputation of oil corporations as stakeholders perceive them as exploitative, oppressive, cruel, inhuman, inconsiderate and callous organisations.

The increasing rate of civil unrests, youths militancy, demonstrations organised at the facilities of oil corporations by the people of Niger Delta, and the retaliatory military and police actions unleashed by oil companies against the people affects their reputational capital. Hence, oil corporations enmeshed in corporate crisis and irresponsible behaviours resulting in damaged corporate reputations are more likely to experience a downward slide in their reputation indicators and a threat to their global brand as was the case of Shell in Nigeria in 1993 (Wheeler, Fabig, & Boele, 2002). For example, Paul Skinner, Group Managing Director of Shell admitted that Shell has learned the hard way the value of social awareness, ethics and trust in a world that appears to be finding less and less time for greed or corruption (Torrance & Skinner, 2003).

Effective implementation of corporate social responsibility and stakeholders' perception of an organisation as a good corporate citizen provide a store of goodwill and a wall of defence in a time of crisis. However, corporate social irresponsibility depletes goodwill, favour and prestige which a business acquires beyond the mere value of what it sells. Corporate managers should therefore guard against socially irresponsible behaviours that may take a toll on the reputation of their corporations and make their stakeholders perceive them as bad corporate citizens.

It is high time oil corporations took full responsibility for corporate misdemeanours such as oil spills and environmental destruction in the Niger Delta; this is a prelude to developing an effective and proactive strategy for sustaining favourable corporate reputation, goodwill, integrity and trustworthiness among oil producing communities. Also, top management of oil corporations involved should remorsefully tender public apology through news release or advertorial, and quickly devise tactics and strategies for minimising its negative impact. Those organisations identified by the participants should begin timely implementation of recovery plan, commence invitation of stakeholders on facility visit to inspect preventive mechanism against future re-occurrence and ensure prompt release of compensation package for the victims of the accident.

Corporate managers should be wary of spiral of reputational damage to entire industry reputation. Spiral of reputational damage in the Niger Delta context is a situation where some oil companies such as Shell, ChevronTexaco, ExxonMobil, Halliburton, Wilbros Group and others have suffered reputational damage due to their involvement in irresponsible acts in the region and failed to promptly address causes of their reputational damage overtime. Given the fact that the media have stigmatized the companies mentioned above because of their unethical practices, and some stakeholders have associated them with irresponsible behaviours in the Niger Delta overtime, some stakeholder groups transfer the negative perception of their reputation wholesale to other oil corporations in the oil industry that have positive reputational capitals.

Therefore, it is important for corporate managers to be proactive in identifying and managing reputational risks, such as corporate double speaks, irresponsible corporate lobbying, involvement in chains of lawsuits, disgruntled employees, refusal to pay adequate compensation for errors of judgment and accidents, corruption scandals and others, effectively before they snowball into big crisis.

## CONCLUSION

This study confirms the rising menace of corporate social irresponsibility in the Nigerian oil industry. The findings of the study point to the fact that corporate social irresponsibility affects corporate image/reputation of some oil corporations involved in unethical activities in the Niger Delta. Commitment to implementing corporate social responsibility will have a positive impact on a company's reputation: it will enable a corporation to establish favourable reputations among its stakeholders (D'Amato, Henderson, & Sue, 2009), attract socially responsible consumers (Lev, Petrovits, & Radhakrishnan, 2006; Bagnoli & Watts, 2003), prevent the threat of harsh regulation (Maxwell, Lyon, & Hackett, 2000) and reduce concerns of activists organisations (Lyon & Maxwell, 2006). Equally, corporate socially irresponsible behaviours leading to poor social and environmental ratings will detract substantially from a company's reputation and harm its performance (Chatterji, Levine, & Toffel, 2009). Based on the use of negative adjectives by some participants to describe their perceptions of some oil corporations in Table 3, the study confirms that socially irresponsible behaviours would have negative impact on a corporation's image/reputation as observed by Kinder, Lydenberg, Domini & Co., Inc. (1999). Following the findings of our study and some studies cited above, we argue that effective implementation of corporate social responsibility in the Niger Delta will cause a rise in reputation rating of some oil companies linked with irresponsible activities in the region, while socially irresponsible behaviours will cause a downslide in their reputation among stakeholders. The study substantially confirms Amujo, Otubanjo, Lanihun, and Adejo's (2010) view about the growing appreciation and understanding of corporate reputation as a strategic resource for conducting successful business in Nigeria's corporate landscape.

However, the limitation of this study is its inability to get the managements of some oil corporations alleged to be involved in corporate social irresponsibility in the Niger Delta to respond to the open-ended questionnaire. Nevertheless, some of their employees did partake in the exercise as individual citizens in the public sphere. Additionally, the authors were unable to obtain financial data from oil companies such as Shell, Chevron-Texaco, Mobil and others to ascertain the effects of corporate social irresponsibility on their corporate profitability by comparing their financial statements during the peak of crisis in the Niger Delta between 1995 and 2000 with during peace time between 2005 and 2010. We assumed Shell's and Chevron's outright suspension of operational activities in Ogoniland and Ilajeland between 1995 and 1997 must have affected their profitability adversely. We suggest further empirical study on this subject.

# REFERENCES

Abdulah, A. (2010). *Oil firm under investigation for N4.5bn tax evasion.* Retrieved from http://www.vanguardngr.com/2010/10/oil-firm-under-investigation-for-n4-5bn-tax-evasion/. Accessed on 12 October 2010.

Adeyemi, Y., & Chawai, E. (2011, March). Oil & gas in 55 years. NLNG, *10*(2), p. 4. Retrieved from http://www.nlng.com/publications/NLNG%20The%20Magazine%202nd%20Edition.pdf

Akinola, S.R. (2011) Polipreneurship and community exclusions in the Niger delta: Reinventing public service delivery through polycentric governance and poverty reduction strategy. Paper delivered at the International Academic Conference on Improving the Effectiveness of Public Services, 28–29 June 2011, Moscow, Russia.

Akoroda, M. (2000). *Remediation response in the Niger delta.* Jesse Fire Disaster Seminar Paper. Nigeria Institute of International Affairs, Lagos.

Alechenu, J. (2010, March 10). *Contract and financial scandals in Nigerian oil industry.* Retrieved from http://www.punchng.com/Ariel.aspx?

Amujo, O., Otubanjo, O., Lanihun, B., & Adejo, D. I. (2010). Corporate reputation and the news media in Nigeria. In C. E. Carroll (Ed.), *Corporate reputation and the news media: Perspectives from developed, frontier, and emerging markets.* New York, NY: Routledge.

Armstrong, J. S. (1977). Social irresponsibility in management. *Journal of Business Research, 5,* 185–213.

Bagnoli, M., & Watts, S. G. (2003). Selling to socially responsible consumers: Competition and the private provision of public goods. *Journal of Economics and Management Strategy, 12*(3), 419–445.

Bletzer, K. V., & Koss, M. P. (2006). After-rape among three populations in the southwest: A time of mourning, a time for recovery. *Violence Against Women, 12*(1), 5–29.

Bromley, D. B. (2000). Psychological aspects of corporate identity, image, and reputation. *Corporate Reputation Review, 3*(3), 240–252.

Brown, B. (1998). Do stock market investors reward companies with reputations for social performance? *Corporate Reputation Review, 1*(2), 271–280.

Burnett, G., & Jaeger, P. R. (2008). Small worlds, lifeworlds, and information: The ramifications of the information behaviour of social groups in public policy and the public sphere. *Information Research, 13*(2), 346. Retrieved from http://InformationR.net/ir/13-2/paper346.html

Cable, D., & Graham, M. E. (2000). The determinants of jobseekers' reputation perceptions. *Journal of Organizational Behaviour, 21*(8), 929–947.

Carroll, A. B. (1979). A three-dimensional conceptual model of corporate social performance. *Academy of Management Review, 4*(4), 497–505.

Cayford, S. (1996). The ogoni uprising: Oil, human rights and a democratic alternative in Nigeria. *Africa Today, 43*(2), 183–198.

Chajet, C. (1997). Corporate reputation and the bottom line. *Corporate Reputation Review, 1* (I), 19–23.

Chatterji, A. K., Levine, D. I., & Toffel, M. W. (2009). How well do social ratings actually measure corporate social responsibility? *Journal of Economics and Management Strategy, 18*(1), 125–169.

Cherry, M. A., & Sneirson, J. F. (2010). Beyond profit: Rethinking corporate social responsibility and greenwashing after the BP Oil disaster. *Tulane Law Review, 85*(4), 983.

Christensen, J., & Murphy, R. (2004). The social irresponsibility of corporate tax avoidance: Taking CSR to the bottom line. *Development, 47*(3), 37–44.

Chun, R. (2005). Corporate reputation: Meaning and measurement. *International Journal of Management Reviews, 7*(2), 91–109.

Cornelissen, P., & Thorpe, R. (2002). Measuring a Business School's reputation: Perspectives, problems and prospects. *European Management Journal, 20*(2), 172–178.

D'Amato, A., Henderson, S., & Sue, F. (2009). *Corporate social responsibility and sustainable business: A guide to leadership tasks and functions.* Greensboro, NC: CCL Press. Retrieved from http://www.ccl.org/leadership/pdf/research/CorporateSocialResponsibility.pdf

Dasgupta, S., Laplante, B., & Mamingi, N. (2001). Pollution and capital markets in developing countries. *Journal of Environmental Economics and Management, 42*(3), 310–335.

Davies, G., & Miles, L. (1998). Reputation management: Theory versus practice. *Corporate Reputation Review, 2*(1), 16–28.

Dowling, G. R. (2001). *Creating Corporate Reputations, Identity, Image, and Performance.* Oxford: Oxford University Press.

*Daily Trust Newspapers.* (2007). Niger Delta: Between violence and peace move. *Daily Trust Newspapers,* 12 July.

Duhe, S. C. (2009). Good management, sound finances, and social responsibility: Two decades of U.S. corporate insider perspectives on reputation and the bottom line. *Public Relations Review, 35*(1), 77–78.

Ejibunu, H.T. (2007). *Nigeria's Niger delta crisis: Root causes of peacelessness.* EPU Research Papers (pp. 1–6), European University Center for Peace Studies (EPU), Issue 07/07, Stadtschlaining/Austria.

Ellis, G. (Director), 1994. *The drilling fields* (text from film by Catma Films).

Elo, S., & Kynga, S. H. (2008). The qualitative content analysis process. *Journal of Advanced Nursing, 62*(1), 107–115.

Essential Action. (2001). *Shell in Nigeria: What are the issues?* Retrieved from http://www.essentialaction.org/shell/issues.html

FCPA Advisor. (October, 2007). A newsletter covering developments in criminal and civil enforcement of the Foreign Corrupt Practices Act (FCPA). Retrieved from http://www.steptoe.com/publications-5329.html. Accessed on 11 August 2010.

Fisher-Buttinger, C., & Vallaster, C. (2011). Corporate branding and corporate reputation: Divided by a shared purpose? *Management for Professionals, 2,* 59–73.

Fisher, R. P. (1995). Interviewing victims and witnesses of crime. *Psychology, Public Policy, and Law, 1*(4), 732–764.

Fombrun, C. J. (1996). *Reputation: Realizing value from the corporate image.* Boston, MA: Harvard Business School Press.

Fombrun, C. J., Gardberg, N., & Sever, J. (2000). The reputation quotient: A multistakeholder measure of corporate reputation. *Journal of Brand Management, 7*(4), 241–255.

Fombrun, C. J. (2001). Corporate reputation – Its measurement and management. *Thexis, 4,* 23–26.

Freeman, R. E. (1984). *Strategic management: A stakeholder approach.* Boston, MA: Pitman.

Freeman, R. E. (2002). A stakeholder theory of the modern corporation. In L. P. Hartman (Ed.), *Perspectives in business ethics* (pp. 171–181). Boston, MA: McGraw-Hill.

Freeman, E. R., & Velamuri, R. S. (2006). A new approach to corporate social responsibility: Company stakeholder responsibility. In A. Kakabadse & M. Morsing (Eds.), *Corporate social responsibility – Reconciling aspiration with application.* New York, NY: Palgrave MacMillan.

Frooman, J. (1997). Socially irresponsible and illegal behaviour and shareholder wealth. *Business & Society, 36*(3), 221–249.

Frynas, J. G. (2000). *Oil in Nigeria: Conflict and litigation between oil companies and village communities.* Hamburg: LIT Verlag.

Frynas, J. G. (2005). The false developmental promise of corporate social responsibility: Evidence from multinational oil companies. *International Affairs, 81*(3), 581–598.

Gabb, J. (2009). Researching family relationships: A qualitative mixed methods approach. *Methodological Innovations Online, 4*(2), 37–52.

Gardberg, N. (2001). *How do individuals construct corporate reputations?* Dissertation, New York University, New York, NY.

Goodman, A. & Scahill, J. (1998). Drilling and killing. *The Nation magazine*. Retrieved from http://www.democracynow.org/2003/7/11/drilling_and_killing_as_president_bush

Goldberg, J., & von Nitzsch, R. (2001). *Behavioral Finance*. New York, NY: Wiley.

Graneheim, U. H., & Lundman, B. (2004). Qualitative content analysis in nursing research: Concepts, procedures and measures to achieve trustworthiness. *Nurse Education Today, 24*, 105–112.

Gunningham, N., Kagan, R., & Thornton, D. (2004). Social license and environmental protection: Why businesses go beyond compliance. *Law & Social Inquiry, 29*, 307–341.

Habermas, J. (1962). *The structural transformation of the public sphere*. Cambridge, MA: MIT Press.

Habermas, J. (1964). The public sphere: An encyclopedia article. *New German Critique, 3*, 49–55.

Hanson, D., & Stuart, H. (2001). Failing the reputation management test: The case of BHP, the big Australian. *Corporate Reputation Review, 4*(2), 128–143.

Hatch, M. J., & Schultz, M. (2003). Bringing the corporation into corporate branding. *European Journal of Marketing, 37*(7/8), 1041–1064.

Heal, G. (2005). Corporate social responsibility: An economic and financial framework. *The Geneva Papers on Risk and Insurance – Issues and Practice, 30*(3), 387–409.

Helm, S. (2007). The role of corporate reputation in determining investor satisfaction and loyalty. *Corporate Reputation Review, 10*(1), 22–37.

Herbig, P., & Milewicz, J. (1995). The relationship of reputation and credibility to brand success. *Journal of Consumer Marketing, 12*(4), 5–10.

Hillenbrand, C., & Money, K. (2007). Corporate responsibility and corporate reputation: Two separate concepts or two sides of the same coin? *Corporate Reputation Review, 10*(4), 261–277.

Holzer, B. (2007). Framing the corporation: Royal Dutch/Shell and human rights woes in Nigeria. *Journal of Consumer Policy, 30*(3), 281–301.

Howard-Grenville, J.A., Nash, J. & Coglianese, C. (2007). Constructing the license to operate: Internal factors and their influence on corporate environmental decisions. *Scholarship at Penn Law*. Retrieved from http://lsr.nellco.org/upenn_wps/105

Human Rights Watch. (1999). *Oil companies complicit in Nigerian abuses: Rights group urges oil firms to help prevent Niger delta crackdown*. Retrieved from http://www.hrw.org/en/news/1999/02/23/oil-companies-complicit-nigerian-abuses. Accessed on 23 February.

Husserl, E. (1965). *Phenomenology and the crisis of philosophy*. New York, NY: Harper Torchbooks.

Iyayi, F. (2008, June 17). *Niger delta crisis: Development and socio-cultural implications*. Paper presented at the Forum organised by PENGASSAN at Gateway Hotel, Ijebu Ode.

Jike, V. T. (2004). Environmental degradation, social disequilibrium, and the dilemma of sustainable development in the Niger-delta of Nigeria. *Journal of Black Studies, 34*(5), 686–701.

Jones, T. M. (1995). Instrumental stakeholder theory: A synthesis of ethics and economics. *Academy of Management Review, 20*(2), 404–437.

Kinder, Lydenberg, Domini & Co., Inc. (1999). The Domini 400 social index: Statistical review, March.

Krauss, C. & Werdigier, J. (2012) BP strong 2 years after gulf oil spill. New York Times News Service, 8 February.

Kretzman, S. (1995). Nigeria's drilling fields: Shell oil's role in repression. *International Monitor, 16*, 1–2.

Lunsford, T. R., & Lunsford, B. R. (1995). Research forum: The research sample, Part I: sampling. *Journal of Prosthetics and Orthotics, 7*(3), 105–112.

Lyon, T. P., & Maxwell, J. W. (2006). *Greenwash: Corporate environmental disclosure under threat of audit.* Ann Arbor, MI: Ross School of Business.

Lev, B., Petrovits, C., & Radhakrishnan, S. (2006). *Is doing good good for you? Yes, charitable contributions enhance revenue growth.* Working Paper No 1. New York University Stern School of Business, New York, NY.

MacGregor, D. G., Slovic, P., Dreman, D., & Berry, M. (2000). Imagery, affect, and financial judgment. *The Journal of Psychology and Financial Markets, 1*, 104–110.

Maxwell, J. W., Lyon, T. P., & Hackett, S. C. (2000). Self regulation and social welfare: The political economy of corporate environmentalism. *Journal of Law and Economics, 43* (2), 583–618.

McWilliams, A., Siegel, D. S., & Wright, P. M. (2006). Corporate social responsibility: Strategic implications. *Journal of Management Studies, 43*(1), 1–18.

Miles, M. B., & Huberman, M. A. (1994). *Qualitative data analysis: An expanded sourcebook.* Thousand Oaks, CA: Sage.

Mouwad, J. (2007). Oil companies in Niger Delta face growing list of dangers. *International Herald Tribune.* Retrieved from http://www.iht.com/articles/2007/04/22/news/oil.php. Accessed on 9 June 2007.

Nwankwo, C. & Ayankola, M. (2011). Divestment: FG, NNPC threaten to deal with Shell. *The Punch newspaper,* 2 August.

Olusina, O. (2009) Willbros official admits bribing the country's politicians. *ThisDay Newspapers,* 13 November.

Organisation for Economic Co-operation and Development (1997) *Anti-bribery convention on combating bribery of foreign public officials in international business transactions.* Retrieved from http://www.oecd.org/document/21/0,3746,en_2649_34859_2017813_1_1_1_1,00.html. Accessed on 30 August 2011.

Organisation for Economic Co-operation and Development (2001, May 16). *Guidelines for multinational enterprises.* Retrieved from http://www.oecd.org/document/28/0,3746,en_2649_34859_2397532_1_1_1_1,00.html

Osagie, C. (2010) *Tax evasions by oil corporations in Nigeria.* Retrieved from http://allafrica.com/stories/201005120209.html

Otusanya, O. J. (2011). The role of multinational companies in tax evasion and tax avoidance: The case of Nigeria. *Critical Perspectives on Accounting, 22*(3), 316–332.

Ojakorotu, V. (Ed.). (2009). *Fresh dimensions on the Niger delta crisis of Nigeria.* South Africa: JAPSS Press, Inc.

Peterson, C., Jesso, B., & McCabe, A. (1999). Encouraging narratives in preschoolers: An intervention study. *Journal of Child Language, 26*, 49–67.

Phoenix, C., Smith, B., & Sparkes, A. C. (2008). Narrative analysis in aging studies: A typology for consideration. *Journal of Aging Studies, 24*, 1–11.

Platform (2006). *Oil pollution in the Niger delta.* Retrieved from http://www.platformlondon. org/carbonweb/showitem.asp?article=73&parent=7&link=Y&gp=3

Post, J., & Griffin, J. (1997). Corporate reputation and external affairs management. *Corporate Reputation Review, 1,* 165–171.

Pruzan, P. (2001). Can corporations have consciousness? Can they have values, visions, and virtues. *Journal of Business Ethics, 29,* 271–284.

Public Eye Awards. (2011 Jan 28). *Neste oil and anglogold in the public eye pillory in Davos.* Press Release. Retrieved from http://www.publiceye.ch/en/news/press-release-january-28th-2011/

Reputation Institute and Boston College. (2010). *The 2010 corporate social responsibility index.* Retrieved from http://www.bcccc.net/pdf/CSRIReport2010.pdf

RESIST. (2011, August 30). *Resisting extortions and solicitations in international transactions (RESIST).* Developed by the International Chamber of Commerce, United Nations Global Compact, Transparency International and World Economic Forum. Retrieved from http://www.transparency.org/publications/publications/resist

Roberts, P. W., & Dowling, G. R. (2002). Corporate reputation and sustained superior financial performance. *Strategic Management Journal, 23,* 1077–1093.

Robertson, T. S., & Gatignon, H. (1986). Competitive effects on technology diffusion. *Journal of Marketing, 50,* 68–78.

Rose-Ackerman, S. (1998). Corruption and the global economy. In G. Shabbir Cheema (Ed.), *Corruption and integrity improvement initiatives in developing countries.* Management Development and Governance Division, United Nations Development Programme: New York.

Rowell, A., Marriott, J., & Stockman, L. (2005). *The next gulf: London, Washington and the oil conflict in Nigeria.* London: Constable and Rebinson Ltd.

Saucier, G., & Goldberg, L. R. (1996b). The language of personality: Lexical perspectives on the five-factor model. In J. S. Wiggins (Ed.), *The five-factor model of personality: Theoretical perspectives.* New York, NY: Guilford.

Saucier, G. (1997). Effects of variable selection on the factor structure of person descriptors. *Journal of Personality and Social Psychology, 73*(6), 1296–1312.

Schwaiger, M. (2004). Components and parameters of corporate reputation: An empirical study. *Schmalenbach Business Review, 56,* 46–71.

Shell Nigeria. (2011 July 22). *SPDC restates commitment to Nigeria in divestment exercise.* News and Media Releases. Retrieved from http://www.shell.com.ng/home/content/nga/aboutshell/media_centre/news_and_media_releases/2011/divestment.html

Shefrin, H. (2001). Do investors expect higher returns from safer stocks than from riskier stocks? *The Journal of Psychology and Financial Markets, 2,* 176–181.

Sluyterman, K. (2010). Royal Dutch shell: Company strategies for dealing with environmental issues. *Business History Review, 84,* 203–226.

Steyn, P. (2009). Oil exploration in colonial Nigeria, c. 1903–1958. *The Journal of Imperial and Commonwealth History, 37*(2), 249–274.

Strauss, A., & Corbin, J. (1990). *Basics of qualitative research: Grounded theory procedures and techniques.* Newbury Park, CA: Sage.

Tauber, E. M. (1988). Brand leverage: Strategy for growth in a cost control world. *Journal of Advertising Research, 28,* 26–30.

The Niger Delta Solidarity. (2010, July 19). *Multinational oil companies.* Retrieved from http://nigerdeltasolidarity.wordpress.com/category/multinational-oil-companies/

The Vanguard. (2007). Restiveness in the Niger Delta: The long term role of NDDC.

This Day newspaper. (2007). Kidnapping is a child's play. *This Day newspaper*, 15 July.

Thomas, C., Reeve, J., Bingley, A., Brown, J., Payne, S., & Lynch, T. (2009). Narrative research methods in palliative care contexts: Two case studies. *Journal of Pain and Symptom Management, 37*(5), 788–796.

Torrance, & Skinner. (2003). Shell's bid to rebuild its reputation. *Strategic Direction, 19*(7), 3–9.

Transparency for Nigeria. (2010). *Shell continues to divest from Nigeria.* Retrieved from http://www.transparencyng.com/index.php?option=com_content&view=article&id=2605:shell-continues-to-divest-from-nigeria&catid=67:politics&Itemid=151

Udosen, C., Etok, A. S., & George, I. N. (2009). Fifty years of oil exploration in Nigeria: The paradox of plenty. *Global Journal of Social Sciences, 8*(2), 37–47.

Urban Guerilla. (2011). *Urban guerilla in activism news, environmental, informative, social activation.* Retrieved from http://urbanguerillaza.wordpress.com/2011/01/25/public-eye-awards-2011/

Wartick, S. (2002). Measuring corporate reputation. *Business & Society, 41*, 371–392.

Wheeler, D., Fabig, H., & Boele, R. (2002). Paradoxes and dilemmas for stakeholder responsive firms in the extractive sector: Lessons from the case of Shell and the Ogoni. *Journal of Business Ethics, 39*(3), 297–318.

Yishau, O. (2011). Bonga spill has turned us into debtors. *The Nation Newspapers.* Retrieved from http://www.thenationonlineng.net/2011/index.php/news/31339-%E2%80%98bonga-spill-has-turned-us-into-debtors%E2%80%99.html. Accessed on 28 December 2011.

Yoon, E., Guffey, H. J., & Kijewski, V. (1993). The effects of information and company reputation on intention to buy a business service. *Journal of Business Research, 27*, 215–228.

# THE IRRESPONSIBLE ENTERPRISE: THE ETHICS OF CORPORATE DOWNSIZING

Brad S. Long

## ABSTRACT

Purpose — *The purpose of this chapter is to recast downsizing as an act of corporate social irresponsibility by showing it to be contrary to ethical principles available to defend any course of action against the alternatives.*

Methodology — *Ethics theory is used to analyse the prevalent business practice of downsizing, drawing upon literature that examines downsizing and/or explains and demonstrates the application of ethical principles.*

Findings — *Downsizing, as defined in this chapter, is an unethical and irresponsible business practice because it reduces utility, ignores rights, creates injustice, breaks social contracts, creates agency relationships where none exist and fails to respond to the legitimate claims that employees, as a stakeholder, make upon corporations.*

Practical implications — *Change becomes necessary to the business practice of downsizing when it is carried out by profitable companies*

Corporate Social Irresponsibility: A Challenging Concept
Critical Studies on Corporate Responsibility, Governance and Sustainability, Volume 4, 295–315
Copyright © 2012 by Emerald Group Publishing Limited
ISSN: 2043-9059/doi:10.1108/S2043-9059(2012)0000004021

*without proper appeal to ethics principles for justification. Ethical principles may, instead, suggest alternative courses of action or techniques.*

Social implications — *Downsizing (and other forms of mass layoffs) is not a morally neutral activity, as it engenders significant social implications (i.e. harm) that necessitate ethical consideration. Moreover, when business actions have social consequences, the interests of other stakeholders may become legitimate.*

Value of the chapter — *This chapter illustrates the formulation and application of principles that help guide business people to take morally right courses of action. It also serves as a template for analysing other aspects of the employment relationship for a more critical approach to corporate responsibility. As shown in this chapter, ethics can have more than a peripheral role in business decision making.*

**Keywords:** Business ethics; corporate downsizing; corporate social irresponsibility

These are challenging economic times; our headlines frequently contain reference to 'crisis' and '(global) recession' along with their corollaries 'restructuring' and 'layoffs'. To be sure, companies are shedding jobs during the current slowdown in the global economy. Media treatment of this phenomenon is largely uncritical, the unfortunate consequence of economic necessity. According to Marens (2010, p. 743), scholarly treatment of corporate downsizing is equally unproblematic, for the corporate responsibility literature has "ignored an empirical record of corporate irresponsibility, especially in the area of employment relations." According to Rhodes, Pullen, and Clegg (2010, p. 535), the morality of downsizing has been subsumed within a hegemonic narrative in which 'managerial obligation' and 'business necessity' have been writ large, and "if people lose their jobs, then so be it — such matters are morally justified as being incidental to the pursuit of that duty."

In response, this chapter specifically acknowledges that the prevalent business practice of downsizing raises prescriptive questions of ethics (Cragg, 1998; Groarke, 1998). Prescriptive ethics is an attempt to formulate principles that will help guide business people to take morally right courses of action. According to the analysis contained herein, downsizing is contrary to the ethical principles to which we must appeal in order to defend any course of action against the alternatives available, and hence is recast as an act of corporate social irresponsibility. Although Cragg (1998) conceded that ethics is not the only consideration necessary for business leaders to ensure the success of their organizations, business ethics has the capacity to shape the definition of business success in the first place. The challenge in doing so is that we must appeal to ethical concepts that are at times abstract and lack the simplicity of appeals to that which is codified into law (VanBuren, 2000). By employing ethics to inform both the appropriateness and application of the particular business practice of downsizing, this chapter serves as an illustration of how ethics can have more than a peripheral role in governing business activity (Cragg, 1998). My intention, therefore, in writing this chapter is not to conduct a comprehensive literature review of how downsizing and restructuring has been subjected to ethical analysis, but rather how it can and should be. I am also not concerned with noting how downsizing techniques vary across global jurisdictions, and how some of these techniques may indeed be more enlightened than others, but to simply offer a set of universal ethical principles upon which these techniques should be evaluated. This chapter is, therefore, a template for analysing other aspects of the employment relationship for a more critical approach to corporate responsibility. The argument that results is inherently polemic, but appropriately so given the ethical lens through which I view downsizing. In the process, I highlight the mistreatment of business ethics by others, such as Hopkins and Hopkins (1999), for whom management's moral obligation is to act in the best interests of the firm.

The scope of my analysis will be limited to the private sector, although I appreciate how commonplace the application of downsizing is within the public sector as a technique to balance budgets and prevent deficit spending. Despite the fact that downsizing in either sector shares many of the same ethical problems, the social responsibilities of corporations are more debatable, leading some to find more support for downsizing in cases where private sector profitability expectations demand expense reductions. By making a case against downsizing within the private sector based on moral grounds, despite the many common defences offered for such practices, one could more easily condemn the use of such a practice in situations where the obligation to serve the interests of the public is more obvious.

The argument contained within this chapter unfolds as follows. First, boundaries are placed around downsizing to define the specific problem under study and examine its prevalence. Once done, I examine the consequences of downsizing to provide a foundation for the ethical critique that follows. The first component of the critique is to analyse the arguments in support of downsizing, flawed as they are by their misuse of the discourse of ethical theory to support a set of behaviours more apt to satisfy a corporate self-interest. The second component of the critique is to solidify the case against downsizing by showing its incompatibility with ethical principles more prescriptive of a morally right course of action.

# THE CONTEXT OF DOWNSIZING

## Defining Downsizing

The research of Baumol, Blinder, and Wolff (2003) exposed a two decade period of downsizing in the United States that had only been interrupted once, when the economy was experiencing low unemployment levels and labour shortages during the late 1990s. Even this lull was contradicted in a *New York Times* article claiming that the highest number of layoffs were experienced in 1998 "amid the economic boom" (Seglin, 2001). Statistics Canada (2007) more recently reported that 6.5% of workers with ages ranging from 25 to 49 were permanently laid off each year during the period of 1988 through 1997; 1.3% were displaced through what Statistics Canada narrowly defined as 'firm closures' or 'mass layoffs'. The Bureau of Labour Statistics in the United States similarly collects data on mass layoffs, triggered by 'layoff events' for which a minimum of 50 employees must file an unemployment claim against an organization over a five-week period. Such statistics are hence inevitably conservative, yet staggering, as evident in the 1996–2010 data reproduced in Table 1. News headlines remain peppered with ongoing downsizing announcements in industries ranging from paper mills to chocolate factories (chosen as they hit close to home) that are, for example, "shift[ing] production to Mexico to cut costs" (CBC, 2007).

The practice of downsizing is disguised by a number of aliases, such as 'reengineering', 'lean', 'rightsizing', 'restructuring', 'leveling' and 'retooling' (Hoffmaster, 1998; Miller, 2001). In all of these techniques, wherever there has been a focus on cost reduction, a loss of employees (whose wages comprise a significant expense) usually followed (Hoffmaster, 1998). In such a case, it is understood that the company has downsized. The dramatic personal consequences of downsizing are commented on shortly, as they give rise to the ethical concerns addressed in this chapter. For now, when defining downsizing, it is important to understand it as "the separation of individuals from the identity that provides the framework within which they

***Table 1.***　U.S. Mass Layoff Activity, 1996–2010.

| Period | Layoff Events | Separations |
| --- | --- | --- |
| 1996 | 4,760 | 948,122 |
| 1997 | 4,671 | 947,843 |
| 1998 | 4,859 | 991,245 |
| 1999 | 4,556 | 901,451 |
| 2000 | 4,591 | 915,962 |
| 2001 | 7,375 | 1,524,832 |
| 2002 | 6,337 | 1,272,331 |
| 2003 | 6,181 | 1,216,886 |
| 2004 | 5,010 | 993,909 |
| 2005 | 4,881 | 884,661 |
| 2006 | 4,885 | 935,969 |
| 2007 | 5,363 | 965,935 |
| 2008 | 8,259 | 1,516,978 |
| 2009 | 11,824 | 2,108,202 |
| 2010 | 7,158 | 1,213,638 |

*Source*: Bureau of Labour Statistics, United States Department of Labour. Retrieved from http://www.bls.gov/news.release/archives/mslo_02112011.pdf

make their living and relate to one another" (Miller, 2001, p. 148). Indeed, the language of downsizing obfuscates its devastating consequences for the downsized (Miller, 2001).

For some, the distinction between downsizing and restructuring is critical, for only the former necessarily implies shrinkage in the size of a workforce (Baumol et al., 2003). Indeed, there are many means by which a firm can be restructured, including through the acquisition of another company, but it is the component of restructuring that results in mass layoffs which raises the ethical red flags described in this chapter. Baumol et al. (2003) suggested that the replacement of some employees with others more able to meet the firm's needs is neither downsizing (because the firm size is not reduced) nor egregious. My understanding of downsizing is more nuanced than simply total headcount, however, and would include the moving of a factory to a location where cheap labour can be exploited. The following passage from a university textbook attempts to legitimize just such a management practice for its potential bottom-line benefit, and in doing so, lazily assumes moral neutrality or simply ignores the moral dimensions of their proposal.

> One obvious way of improving an operation's productivity is to reduce the cost of its inputs while maintaining the level of outputs...For example, a software developer may relocate its entire operation to India or China..." (Slack, Chambers, & Johnston, 2007, p. 51)

I do not wish, however, to diminish the sometimes necessary nature of layoffs, such as when firm survival is at stake. Even American social critic Michael Moore (1997) suggested layoffs can potentially be justified, presuming the techniques reviewed in the last section of this chapter are employed, when a company is losing money and is on the verge of being unable to pay its workers. The 'credit crisis' that has contributed to the severity of the current recession, for example, may surely mean that some companies have lost access to the funds necessary to meet their payroll obligations. I hence draw boundaries around morally problematic downsizing as *the form of restructuring done by profitable companies that results in a significant reduction to the size of a workforce within a community.*

## Why Companies Downsize

Given this period of downsizing prevalence, we can understand it as the common by-product of the management science techniques popularized from the latter part of the 1980s through today. These tools are seen as important mechanisms for sustaining corporate performance and competitiveness in the face of mounting global pressures. The problem is that within business models such as 'lean production' and 'total quality management', management decision making is increasingly reduced to technical terms, work is increasingly standardized and all sources of costs are seen as equally deserving targets of reduction efforts. "Lean thinking means identifying and eliminating waste in whatever form a business finds it" (Kennedy & Brewer, 2005). Technological innovations have resulted in the disassociation between the knowledge required to complete a task and the task itself, and hence workers have become degraded to simply factors of production, relegated to perform tasks that are increasingly predefined for them within a production process (Braverman, 1974). Principles of human resource management have thus regressed to embrace the scientific management principles popularized a century ago, and workforce cuts can be seen as entirely consistent with what McGregor coined as the Theory X approach to work (Di Norcia, 1998; Hoffmaster, 1998).

From this perspective, downsizing can be understood as a reactive response by management to change, executed in a manner that is more urgent, irresponsible and meaner. "Downsizing focuses very narrowly on costs, not people, skills or performance...When this happens, restructuring becomes a quick financial fix, not a long-term business plan" (Chrominska, 1998, p. 281). By placing blame upon the 'uncontrollable' economic and technical forces within the firm's environment as an excuse for downsizing, managers prove their own failure to be effective decision makers (Di Norcia, 1998). They mask their incompetence at enabling the organizations that they govern to be adaptive, creative and proactive in the context of global competitive pressures. "Massive downsizing is not a legitimate means of managing over the long term. It's irresponsible and it's damaging. It's short-term thinking for short-term, and often questionable, gains" (Chrominska, 1998, p. 283). Proactive cost containment requires managers to anticipate change and make strategic decisions to invest in areas (such as the hiring of employees) that will not expose themselves to future liabilities, and as we shall discuss later, to reduce expense obligations in the most responsible manner possible.

Returning to explanations for why companies downsize, Baumol et al. (2003) also described the changing nature of firm ownership. Not only has ownership shifted predominantly to large institutional shareholders, including pension and fund managers, but the demands of capital are also increasing (Baumol et al., 2003). Such new forms of ownership are solely focused on the bottom line and personal rewards and thereby have an impatient short-term horizon for receiving returns, are less relationship-oriented, and do not prioritize the interests of other firm stakeholders, such as workers (Baumol et al., 2003, p. 20). We shall come to see how all of these dynamics strain the social contract that exists between labour and capital in a morally problematic manner.

Broader ideological explanations have also been offered for why companies downsize, and in particular, the role of individualism in shaping the political and economic institutions in society (Watson, Shepard, Stephens, & Christman 1999). Through this lens, "individuals, not organizations, are ultimately responsible for their own life outcomes" (Watson et al., 1999, p. 661). Such a perspective leads naturally to laissez-faire political institutions and excuses private sector corporations from having to satisfy the demands of society. Although beyond the scope of this chapter, one could likely make the case (and some may have done so already) for how the period of downsizing has neatly coincided with a surging neo-conservative perspective in successive North American governments from the Reagan and Mulroney years through today, such that even the state's role in providing for the public welfare has been marginalized. "The free-market message has gotten through. Economic life is now imitating economic theory as never before" (Baumol et al., 2003, p. 21). The problem with individualism is that it fails to acknowledge the capacity of corporations to affect the public welfare, the historical role played by corporations in advancing the public good and the obvious important social role of employing people that has predominantly fallen upon private sector corporations (Orlando, 1999). In sum, "at a very basic level, the competitiveness of a company and the health of the communities around it are closely intertwined" (Porter & Kramer, 2011, p. 66). Failure to recognize this leads to too-easy excuses for practices such as downsizing without proper consideration of their moral deficiencies.

## The Consequences of Downsizing

Analysis of the consequences of downsizing upon workers makes apparent the serious ethical concerns with this business practice. The immediate impact of downsizing for workers is the partial or total loss of income they experience. "Workers displaced through firm closures or mass layoffs suffered earnings losses that not only were substantial but also persisted several years after displacement" (Statistics Canada, 2007). For example, five years after a termination that occurred within the period of 1988 through 1997, the average reduction in earnings remained as great as 31% of pre-displacement earnings; this specific depth was reached by high-seniority males displaced from manufacturing companies (Statistics Canada, 2007). Another common trend in the Canadian economy is the rise in part-time employment as a percentage of total employment. "Temporary work accounted for almost one-fifth of overall growth in paid employment between 1997 and 2003 despite a period of economic growth and favourable employment conditions" (Statistics Canada, 2005). Of note is the gap in hourly wages between part and full-time employment that consistently ranged between 16% and 19%, to the detriment of temporary workers, during this seven-year period (Statistics Canada, 2005).

Wage losses are only a component of the harm incurred by downsized workers. Additional negative consequences for individuals include escalating anxiety and depression that are often related to subsequent losses of one's property, spouse and even life (Orlando, 1999). Moreover, work is often central to who we are as human beings, and our identity is inseparable from what we do. Gini (2000, p. 187) argued that "work cannot go away because it underlies all that we are as human beings. Work is literally the foundation, the precondition for all that we do, acquire, and become. Neither the basic needs and necessities nor the highest intellectual and artistic achievements can be fulfilled without work." It is not just any work, but the promise that through our work we can feel as if we have realized our calling for how we can contribute to our world (Wrzesniewski, 2002). Such an existential quest is a central feature of the human condition, hence denying someone the opportunity to continue to work translates into the denial of one's sense of identity, and perhaps also of purpose.

When combined with increases in crime, abuse and addiction, entire communities are jeopardized. Moore (1997) further described how job blackmail is used to force numerous concessions from workers and pit communities against one another to extract the most corporate favours, hence removing funds available to municipalities to afford social programmes. Moore (1997) cited numerous examples where companies used their newly found profits to fund the relocation of entire plants to sites of cheaper labour. To widen the impact, secondary layoffs often accompany layoffs of a dominant firm. Entire societies eventually suffer from declining earnings, increasing wage gaps and the social disharmony generated by downsizing (Moore, 1997; Orlando, 1999).

Within the corporations, remaining employees "sense their dispensability" (Di Norcia, 1998, p. 145) and feel more overworked and insecure. Productivity may even decline, as the downsized firm not only has lost the knowledge and skills of dismissed workers, but a Hobbesian atmosphere is generated whereby employees work against one another to ensure they protect scarce remaining jobs (Baumol et al., 2003; Di Norcia, 1998). The spectre of age discrimination also rises, as the probability that one might be dismissed tends to be associated with worker tenure and age (Henry & Jennings, 2004).

Mainstream reporting of downsizing tends to accept without question the premise that downsizing is a means towards improved company productivity, mandated by the realities of global competition, insofar as output can be achieved using less input of labour hours. An example of this sentiment is contained in a recent commentary on the rash of layoffs in the North American automotive industry in *Business Week* (Welch, Foust, & Cowan 2006, p. 32): "The reality is that many of the layoffs at the Big Three were inevitable... Japanese auto makers have set the pace on productivity, forcing GM, Ford, and Chrysler to get in step." The analysis performed by Baumol et al. (2003) in the United States led them to conclude that there was little econometric support for the popular notion that downsizing resulted in enhanced productivity. Although there certainly has been an increase in profits as a result of corporate downsizing, the premise of increasing productivity is largely false (Baumol et al., 2003). Downsizing companies err in their calculations of productivity by allowing labour dollars to represent labour hours or effort, and hence are simply spending less on wages (Baumol et al., 2003). Furthermore, when TQM is used to usher in corporate layoffs, the promise of increasing quality fails to materialize (Hoffmaster, 1998). Bright, Cameron, and Caza (2006, p. 254) cite earlier research from Cameron to conclude that, owing to erosion in loyalty, trust, information sharing, flexibility and cooperation, companies "that do not downsize consistently outperform those that do, and restructured firms tend to decline in returns on investment after downsizing and do not recover enough to match non-downsizing firms three years later."

Given the damage it inflicts, it seems appropriate to consider who ultimately benefits from downsizing. Corporate executives, through their compensation packages, and corporate investors, through their share valuation and dividend payments, are among those who have profited nicely from downsizing in the short term, despite the absence of any fundamental change to the long-term competitiveness of the corporation. "The central effect of downsizing has apparently been a transfer of income from labor to capital – that is, from the workers to the owners" (Baumol et al., 2003, p. 261). There is surely evidence of increasing corporate profitability, just not its equal redistribution back to the workers whose efforts led to such spoils in the first place (Baumol et al., 2003). One can conclude, as did Miller (1998, p. 1693), that "beneath all the words and figures, lives are being deeply affected as a few become wealthier and the many become more anxious."

## FLAWED JUSTIFICATIONS FOR DOWNSIZING

As noted already, companies that downsize tend to discuss the imperative of improving firm performance within a competitive global economy; certainly firms that are neither productive nor capable of managing costs will be less able to sustain their business practices, let alone compete internationally. The justifications that are voiced in favour of the particular response of downsizing, as opposed to the alternatives available to management, are varied. Cragg (1998) found implicit in any restructuring decision a utilitarian assumption central to capitalism that the leanest, most efficient provision of goods and services is best able to benefit society through lower prices. "In the old, narrow view of capitalism, business contributes to society by making a profit, which supports employment, wages, purchases, investments and taxes. Conducting business as usual is sufficient social benefit" (Porter & Kramer, 2011, p. 66). Given the preceding account of the real consequences of downsizing, it seems a stretch to argue that the majority of citizens affected are recipients of any net gain in utility (Orlando, 1999). In this and other areas, caution is required when interpreting the defences of downsizing advocates, as the rhetoric of ethics is often employed to disguise unethical intentions (Cragg, 1998), including the desire to concentrate the rewards of profit maximization in the hands of a few. Utility must be maximized in scope, not scale, and more than simply financial rewards are necessary for its calculation (Orlando, 1999).

A more explicit defence of downsizing comes in the form of agency theory and its placement of fiduciary responsibilities upon managers to serve the interests of shareholders (Orlando, 1999). An agency relationship is thought to arise insofar as corporate managers are trustees of other people's money, namely, the firm's equity investors, as the provision of capital is a prerequisite for any business to operate. The inherent contradiction with the previous notion of utility should be observed, for if the utilitarian appeal is to maximize the benefits to society, how is it logical to say that managers then have an obligation only to shareholders (Evan & Freeman, 1988)? What results is the obvious oversight of other stakeholders, from employees to customers, which will be addressed later in this chapter. For now, let us resume the agency argument by acknowledging its additional claim that shareholder investments are inherently risky, and hence these individuals deserve the special consideration they receive as remuneration for this risk (Orlando, 1999). A belief in the primacy of shareholder interests is the consequence of agency theory, popularized by influential economists such as Friedman (1970).

Without ignoring entirely the interests of shareholders, three counterarguments can be raised in response to the practice of downsizing done as a response to the needs of owners to earn a return on their capital. First, agency does not inherently make an act one does on behalf of another morally right (Orlando, 1999). Indeed, it is generally accepted that "moral duties transfer through from principle to agent" (Orlando, 1999, p. 302), hence obligating corporate managers to adhere to ethical principles in their service to shareholder interests. Second, one cannot discount the risk assumed by workers and their opportunity to lose something of value when they agree to work for somebody (Orlando, 1999). Downsizing certainly exposes the losses that workers can incur. On the other hand, shareholders themselves have many levers available to them with which they manage their risk, itself limited to the amount of their initial investment, including the ability to buy and sell shares and to review information fully disclosed to them via a prospectus before purchase decisions are made (Boatright, 1994). Furthermore, limited liability legislation shields share-holders from the actions taken by corporate managers to make profits on their behalf (Glasbeek, 2002). Ireland's (2010, p. 837) historical analysis of limited liability led to the conclusion that it is simply a political construct developed to accommodate investors, not a product of any economic necessity, the result of which "institutionalizes irresponsibility." It seems unjustifiable, therefore, to note only one bearer of risk, that of share-holders, and pander exclusively to it. Third, and finally, the agency rela-tionship is an antiquated idea now strained by the behaviour of shareholders themselves who tend to not see themselves as owners of cor-porations (Orlando, 1999). Through such mechanisms as quarterly earn-ings reports, the investment horizon used within financial markets has contracted, and an over-emphasis on short-term returns prevails. Portfolio diversification means that many shareholders are no longer aware of each and every corporation in which they own a share. The kind of ownership that places fiduciary relationships upon corporate executives must be that which cares for the long-term viability of corporations they own while adhering to the moral principles necessary to maintain legitimacy.

Beyond utility and agency, the final common defence of downsizing rests upon managements' perceived prerogative and right to exercise their autonomy and do as they wish (VanBuren, 2000). From the management's perspective, it may seem appealing to claim a right to do whatever is neces-sary to make profits, including downsizing. Such a defence, however, is weakened by its failure to both clarify the source of the right and recognize the myriad of limitations to individual autonomy that already exist, whereby the exercise of one's right could cause harm to others (Moore, 1997). Since downsizing harms individuals and communities, limiting one's freedom to downsizing seems consistent with legal precedent (Moore, 1997). Government intervention is necessary for the free-market system to exist (Orlando, 1999), and hence demanding certain concessions from cor-porate actors seems entirely consistent. Miller (1998) reminded us that there are more restrictions governing the appropriate write-off of capital-ized assets than there are for the layoff of a corporation's most valuable assets. Orlando (1999) further clarified the likely source of the right to be property rights, but due to the separation between ownership and manage-rial decision making outlined in the preceding paragraph, property rights provide no added defence for the practice of downsizing. Workers are side-lined in this debate over managerial rights, for except where collective agreements are in place that dictate otherwise, workers cannot claim either a legal or common-law right to continued employment with a particular employer (VanBuren, 2000).

## RECASTING DOWNSIZING AS MORALLY PROBLEMATIC

The preceding section reviewed how the concepts of utility, agency and rights are employed within the most common defences of the business practice of downsizing, yet when subject to critical analysis, these arguments are consistently found wanting. This section begins with the premise that downsizing is ethically indefensible, and my purpose is to employ additional ethical theories to make this case. The acceptance of such a premise first is aided by assuming a communitarian ideological perspective in contrast to the individualist view, for whereas the latter seeks to disintegrate a collective society into its components, the former demands that "institutions exist largely to support social collectives" (Watson et al., 1999, p. 661). Surely one must acknowledge the social context within which all human activity takes place, and the potential therefore for this society to define a common good that may serve as a guide for individual behaviour. Once this lens is adopted, ethical notions of stakeholders, egalitarian justice and social responsibility become more readily embraced.

Properly understood, social responsibility rests upon implied social and psychological contracts that corporations have with both societal and individual level units of analysis respectively (VanBuren, 2000; Watson et al., 1999). Borrowing from Rousseau, VanBuren (2000) defined social contracts as reflective of the broader normative rules of the society in which the organization exists. Social contracts in turn establish the context for psychological contracts between individuals employees and their employer that reflect "each party's perceptions of the obligations that they have agreed to" (VanBuren, 2000, p. 208). Despite their implicit and unwritten nature, social and psychological contracts do give shape to the ethical obligations of employers to be socially responsible (Drinkwalter, 1998; VanBuren, 2000). Stakeholder theory, in particular, is a derivative of this social responsibility and is instructive to the critique of downsizing.

The term 'stakeholders' represents the collection of interest groups with a vested stake in, or claim upon, the activities of a corporation (Evan & Freeman, 1988). Even though stakeholders are necessary for the corporation to achieve its interests in the first place, their interests are typically treated as subservient to those of the corporation. In addressing this omission, stakeholder theory confers upon corporate managers an obligation to act in a manner consistent with the interests of all stakeholders (Evan & Freeman, 1988). By accepting that the interrelationships between a corporation and other entities in the community are salient, stakeholder theory is consistent with both the collectivist stance towards organizational responsibility (Watson et al., 1999) and the social contract a corporation has to act in a manner bound by the ethical norms of society. Acknowledging the legitimacy of stakeholders external to the organization also supports Porter and Kramer's (2011, p. 64) argument in favour of bridging the business versus society dichotomy and recognizing instead that "businesses must reconnect company success with social progress." As Jennings (1997) correctly pointed out, however, stakeholder theory is no panacea, since its definition is imprecise and it remains unclear what a corporation is to specifically do once a stakeholder interest is identified. Furthermore, the boundaries to this definition are broad (Groarke, 1998), hence diluting the degree to which the often conflicting interests of numerous stakeholders can be considered in a meaningful way. Evan and Freeman's (1988) 'narrow definition' is minimally contentious and grants 'stakeholder' status to those groups who are vital to the success of a corporation and whose interests are directly affected by corporate activity. This list includes owners, employees, customers, suppliers and the local community (including its natural environment). Since employees are a necessary prerequisite for corporations to obtain any benefit, and they clearly have interests that are affected by corporate decisions, their status as stakeholder is indisputable (Drinkwalter, 1998). Within the context of a downsizing decision, the consideration of employees' interests becomes obligatory according to stakeholder theory.

Greenwood (2007) reminded us of the importance of articulating the moral dimension of stakeholder engagement lest it simply serve to give the impression of corporate responsibility while masking the reality of corporate irresponsibility. Indeed, we must do well by stakeholders. For starters, the moral superiority of extending consideration to all stakeholders versus a shareholder-first approach in the context of corporate downsizing is based most particularly upon a Kantian idea that all individuals have a right not to be treated as a means to someone else's end (Evan & Freeman, 1988). This right obliges employers to give employees a say in determining the future direction of the firm in which they have a stake. Deontological arguments such as this do not justify the harming of some to benefit others, and bring into focus the individual injury that downsizing produces

(Lamsa & Takala, 2000; Orlando, 1999). As well, as previously mentioned, a correct application of the utilitarian argument requires one to maximize the scope of beneficiaries of the utility generated by corporate activity, and not to consolidate the benefits of downsizing into the hands of such few. Principles of care might additionally be relevant to stakeholder theory, as they encourage the consideration of such things as relationships that employees develop with their employers and one another (Evan & Freeman, 1988). Although care can be addressed in the techniques of dismissal, the act of downsizing inherently severs relationships.

Once we accept the notion that stakeholders are morally relevant, and that employees are legitimate stakeholders, the act of downsizing can be subject to a robust critique from the perspective of how unjust the practice is to employees. This notion was simply stated by Moore (1997, p. 285): "It is wrong to make money off people's labor and then fire them after you've made it." We can appeal to Rawl's egalitarian notion of justice for an explanation of why downsizing is morally wrong (Hoffmaster, 1998). Defining justice in more individualized terms simply grants license to one's desired actions. Egalitarianism requires, foremost, a principle of equality to which everyone would impartially accept (Poff, 2005). Management may be more apt to seek alternatives to layoffs should they share with all employees the same likelihood of being fired and not know in advance who would be so affected. Furthermore, the concentrated and personal benefits that corporate executives and institutional investors receive by downsizing their corporations fails to be just because the exercise of such discretion only serves to exacerbate social inequities. The equity principle central to egalitarianism requires greater consideration be given to those more vulnerable or in greater need, which in the case of downsizing are the victims and their communities, not their executioners. Perhaps this defence goes so far as to support a right to employment, and thus a reciprocal obligation on employers "for maintaining stability in life-sustaining activities such as work" (Watson et al., 1999, p. 662).

The preceding perspective on distributive justice also leads to the conclusion that downsizing is unfair insofar as "the individual does not deserve the rewards or punishments that come via things for which she is not responsible" (Orlando, 1999, p. 308). Using this logic, we can see how workers do not deserve their punishment of being dismissed, when the failure to anticipate change and lead with a long-term perspective belongs to management. Shareholders who receive short-term returns are equally undeserving of receiving such benefits, as they shoulder no responsibility to those who were downsized. We can conversely phrase the argument to say that justice requires consideration be given to those who were instrumental to capital's success, for "without labor, no capital would ever have been produced" (McCann, 1997 p. 65).

Lastly, downsizing can be deemed unjust by appealing to the psychological contract employees have with their employers. Examples include McCann's (1997) description of largely Catholic, blue-collar immigrant workers during the period of American industrialization, who offered discipline, loyalty and obedience in exchange, implicitly, for job security. Technical advancement fails to nullify this contract, but may further oblige corporations to ensure all workers have access to the specific knowledge needed to prevent their obsolescence. We may even derive a broader moral obligation upon corporations to ensure all individual participants in the economy have the opportunity to contribute, so they may achieve a sense of personal self-actualization while promoting the capacity of business to serve the social interests of families and communities (Childs, 1997; Miller, 1998). In another appeal to psychological contracts, Henry and Jennings (2004) suggested that because older workers are more often targets of downsizing, an employer who uses such a tactic is in violation of the implied promise to reward long and faithful service. Justice may require that employers assume a duty to act in the best interests of retirement-aged employees, as they are increasingly dependent upon the employer for the opportunity to remain employed and earn a retirement income (Henry & Jennings, 2004).

Although outside of the scope of this chapter, there are even self-interested arguments against the practice of downsizing. Popular contributors to management best practices, such as Demming, viewed the mandate of quality improvement as dependent upon job security to eliminate fear amongst employees (Darryl, 1999). Similarly, Pfeffer (1998) constructed job security as one of seven pillars to the successful management of human resources, critical to the creation of a productive and committed workforce. Pfeffer (1998) also noted that the costs of layoffs are prohibitive, and include not just the direct severance cost but also the indirect loss of talent to competitors and the inflationary wages demanded when rehiring in more prosperous times. Clearly the onus shifts to management to employ long-term thinking and apply lean thinking to hiring, not firing, practices (Champy, 1995; Pfeffer, 1998). In the midst of an earlier downsizing epidemic, Quigley (1992, p. 18) bravely concluded that "only by serving the interests of its employees can an organization ensure its own self-interest and financial viability." More recently, Porter and Kramer (2011) highlighted how decisions made based on short-term financial results often come at the expense of societal well-being, which in turn diminishes competitive advantage and long-term success. While there is no ethical basis to such a claim and hence no justification for the pursuit of one's self-interest per se, there may be practical benefits, including higher levels of productivity, quality, commitment and reputational capital that can accrue to employers by behaving morally.

## ARE ANY RESTRUCTURING TECHNIQUES ACCEPTABLE?

Given the weight of the critique against downsizing, it may seem unnecessary to consider whether there are any restructuring techniques that avoid the moral pitfalls presented herein. Indeed, the predominant theme in the literature is to pre-empt the necessity for downsizing through more proactive management (Cascio, 1998; Chrominska, 1998; Di Norcia, 1998). Proactive planning shifts the focus away from reductionary measures to "sales, market share, growth and stability, productivity, customer and employee satisfaction, technical development and environmental protection" (Di Norcia, 1998, p. 147). Numerous alternatives to mass layoffs become available to the proactive manager who sees opportunities to diversity product lines, better market existing product lines, (re)train existing employees and even sell-off underperforming business units to competitors who are better positioned to enable their success. This is consistent with the approach to strategy taken by Hamel and Prahalad (1994) whereby competitive advantage is built upon existing strengths and core competencies, and companies strive to achieve their own unique vision of the future. Effectiveness wins out over efficiency, and change occurs through the redeployment of existing employees in the most strategic manner possible (Cascio, 1998). Where necessary, reductions are surgically achieved through pruning poor investments, avoiding excess capacity, hiring freezes, trimming discretionary expenses and overtime, and in general focusing on unproductive non-labour costs in a proactive effort to improve business performance (Cascio, 1998; Di Norcia, 1998; Settles, 1988).

As I conceded earlier in this chapter, however, there are certainly instances where companies fail to cover their costs and must trim their workforce or face insolvency. As I also noted earlier, there is a wide range in techniques used internationally to achieve mass layoffs, and itemizing and analysing each against the set of ethical principles outlined in this chapter exceeds the scope of my intentions. It could simply be stated that where downsizing must occur, the principle of equity must remain a central tenet (Di Norcia, 1998). Equity first mandates the involvement of employees in the decisions about how costs can be reduced (Di Norcia, 1998; Settles, 1988), and so a policy of codetermination that is already commonplace in some jurisdictions seems a minimal starting point. Beyond governance, measures by which all employees share the burden of restructuring through reductions in pay and work hours should be considered (Di Norcia, 1998; Settles, 1988). Job retraining and the lateral redeployment of personnel within the context of job security, combined with voluntary and attractive early retirement programmes are means by which necessary restructuring can avoid some of the ethical concerns raised (Cascio, 1998; Settles, 1988). Finally, competent outplacement services should be made available to provide employees that are dismissed with comprehensive assistance through their transition from one employer to another (Drinkwalter, 1998). Readers interested in specific examples of codetermination policies are directed primarily to European jurisdictions, where the presence of works' councils and unions often provide a mechanism for giving voice to the interests of workers and establishing rules that govern the implementation of mass layoffs.

## CONCLUSION

As a teacher, I am concerned when the morally problematic nature of the now commonplace business activity of downsizing is not addressed, as this may lead current and future managers to incorrectly assume that 'lean' and its other incarnations are, at worst, morally neutral activities. My aim was to provide a more comprehensive account to back up Orlando's (1999, p. 303) assertion that "no philosophically sound argument has yet been advanced for privileging the interests of shareholders over those of workers." To do so, I have examined how rights, agency, utility, justice and social responsibility, when applied to the practice of downsizing, all coalesce around the same conclusion that it is an irresponsible and unethical business practice. Downsizing reduces utility, ignores rights, creates injustice, breaks social contracts, creates agency relationships where none exist and fails to respond to the legitimate claims that employees, as a stakeholder, make upon corporations. As with all forays into normative ethics, my aim in writing was "to prescribe how things ought to be" (Watson et al., 1999, p. 659). My ideal is for business executives to be informed by a communitarian ideology, a rich sense of social responsibility to stakeholders, and egalitarian notions of justice that together give rise to these conclusions. When this occurs, a new understanding of what it means to be a responsible and successful enterprise may be reached.

## ACKNOWLEDGEMENT

I would like to thank an anonymous reviewer of this chapter for providing me with valuable insights and suggestions.

## REFERENCES

Baumol, W. J., Blinder, A. S., & Wolff, E. N. (2003). *Downsizing in America: Reality, causes, and consequences*. New York, NY: Russell Sage Foundation.

Boatright, J. R. (1994). Fiduciary duties and the shareholder management relation: Or, what's so special about shareholders? *Business Ethics Quarterly, 4*(4), 393–408.

Braverman, H. (1974). *Labor and monopoly capital: The degradation of work in the twentieth century*. New York, NY: Monthly Review Press.

Bright, D. S., Cameron, K. S., & Caza, A. (2006). The amplifying and buffering effects of virtuousness in downsized organizations. *Journal of Business Ethics, 64*(3), 249–269.

Cascio, W. F. (1998). Responsible restructuring in the private sector. In L. Groarke (Ed.), *The ethics of the new economy* (pp. 61–73). Waterloo, ON: Wilfred Laurier University Press.

CBC (2007, December 21). Dartmouth chocolate factory closes. Retrieved from http://www.cbc.ca/canada/nova-scotia/story/2007/12/21/moirs-closing.html

Champy, J. (1995). Reengineering management: The mandate for new leadership. *Industry Week, 244*(4), 32–36.

Childs, J. M., Jr. (1997). Business in an age of downsizing. *Business Ethics Quarterly, 7*(2), 123–131.

Chrominska, S. D. (1998). The banking sector: Avoiding the pitfalls of restructuring. In L. Groarke (Ed.), *The ethics of the new economy* (pp. 279–283). Waterloo, ON: Wilfred Laurier University Press.

Cragg, W. (1998). Ethics and restructuring: Obstacles, challenges and opportunities. In L. Groarke (Ed.), *The ethics of the new economy* (pp. 287–299). Waterloo, ON: Wilfred Laurier University Press.

Darryl, L. (1999). Ethics and its place in business. *The Canadian Manager, 24*(4), 6.

Di Norcia, V. (1998). Downsizing, change and ownership. In L. Groarke (Ed.), *The ethics of the new economy* (pp. 143–154). Waterloo, ON: Wilfred Laurier University Press.

Drinkwalter, D. (1998). Discharging employer responsibilities to employees during mayor organizational change. In L. Groarke (Ed.), *The ethics of the new economy* (pp. 176–177). Waterloo, ON: Wilfred Laurier University Press.

Evan, W. E., & Freeman, R. E. (1988). A stakeholder theory of the modern corporation: Kantian capitalism. In T. L. Beauchamp & N. E. Bowie (Eds.), *Ethical theory and business* (pp. 75–93). Englewood Cliffs, NJ: Prentice Hall.

Friedman, M. (1970). The social responsibility of business is to increase its profits. *New York Times Magazine*, September 13.

Gini, A. (2000). What happens if work goes away? *Business Ethics Quarterly, 10*(1), 181–188.

Glasbeek, H. (2002). *Wealth by stealth: Corporate crime, corporate law, and the perversion of democracy*. Toronto, ON: Between the Lines.

Greenwood, M. (2007). Stakeholder engagement: Beyond the myth of corporate responsibility. *Journal of Business Ethics, 74*(4), 315–327.

Groarke, L., & Groarke, L. (Eds.). (1998). *The ethics of the new economy*, pp. 3–8. Waterloo, ON: Wilfred Laurier University Press.

Hamel, G., & Prahalad, C. K. (1994). *Competing for the future*. Boston, MA: Harvard Business School Press.

Henry, E. G., & Jennings, J. P. (2004). Age discrimination in layoffs: Factors of injustice. *Journal of Business Ethics, 54*, 217–224.

Hoffmaster, B. (1998). The ethics of restructuring. In L. Groarke (Ed.), *The ethics of the new economy* (pp. 25–40). Waterloo, ON: Wilfred Laurier University Press.

Hopkins, W. E., & Hopkins, S. A. (1999). The ethics of downsizing: Perceptions of rights and responsibilities. *Journal of Business Ethics, 18*(2), 145–156.

Ireland, P. (2010). Limited liability, shareholder rights and the problem of corporate irresponsibility. *Cambridge Journal of Economics, 34*, 837–856.

Jennings, M.M. (1997). Manager's journal: Trendy causes are no substitute for ethics. Wall Street Journal (Eastern Edition). December 1.

Kennedy, F. A., & Brewer, P. C. (2005). Lean: What's it all about? *Strategic Finance, 87*(5), 26–34.

Lämsä, A. M., & Takala, T. (2000). Downsizing and ethics of personnel dismissals – The case of Finnish managers. *Journal of Business Ethics, 23*(4), 389–399.

Marens, R. (2010). Destroying the village to save it: Corporate social responsibility, labour relations, and the rise and fall of American hegemony. *Organization, 17*(6), 743–766.

McCann, D. P. (1997). Catholic social teaching in an era of economic globalization: A resource for business ethics. *Business Ethics Quarterly, 7*(2), 57–70.

Miller, R. A. (2001). The four horsemen of downsizing and the tower of Babel. *Journal of Business Ethics, 29*(1/2), 147–151.

Miller, R. A. (1998). Lifesizing in an era of downsizing: An ethical quandary. *Journal of Business Ethics, 17*(15), 1693–1700.

Moore, M. (1997). *Downsize this!*. New York, NY: HarperPerennial.

Orlando, J. (1999). The fourth wave: The ethics of corporate downsizing. *Business Ethics Quarterly, 9*(2), 295–314.

Pfeffer, J. (1998). Seven practices of successful organizations. *California Management Review, 40*(2), 96–124.

Poff, D. (2005). Theories of justice and their relationship to business ethics. In D. Poff (Ed.), *Business ethics in Canada* (4th ed., pp. 1–13). Toronto, ON: Pearson Prentice Hall.

Porter, M. E., & Kramer, M. R. (2011). Creating shared value. *Harvard Business Review, 89*(1/2), 62–77.

Quigley, M. E. (1992). Ethical downsizing. *Executive Excellence, 9*(3), 18–19.

Rhodes, C., Pullen, A., & Clegg, S. R. (2010). 'If I should fall from grace...': Stories of change and organizational ethics. *Journal of Business Ethics, 91*(4), 535–551.

Seglin, J.L. (2001). The right thing: In a downsizing, loyalty is a two-way street. *The New York Times*, April 15.

Settles, M. F. (1988). Humane downsizing: can it be done? *Journal of Business Ethics, 7*(12), 961–963.

Slack, N., Chambers, S., & Johnston, R. (2007). *Operations management* (5th ed.). Harlow, UK: Pearson Education.

Statistics Canada (2007, January 16). Study: Earnings losses of displaced workers. *The Daily*. Retrieved from http://www.statcan.ca/Daily/English/070116/d070116a.htm

Statistics Canada (2005, January 26). Study: Earnings of temporary versus permanent employees. *The Daily*. Retrieved from http://www.statcan.ca/Daily/English/050126/d050126b.htm

VanBuren, H. J., III. (2000). The bindingness of social and psychological contracts: Toward a theory of social responsibility in downsizing. *Journal of Business Ethics, 25*(3), 205–219.

Watson, G. W., Shepard, J. M., Stephens, C. U., & Christman, J. C. (1999). Ideology and the economic social contract in a downsizing environment. *Business Ethics Quarterly, 9*(4), 659–672.

Welch, D., Foust, D. and Cowan, C. (2006). The good news about America's auto industry. *Business Week*, February 13, 32.

Wrzesniewski, A. (2002). 'It's not just a job': Shifting meanings of work in the wake of 9/11. *Journal of Management Inquiry, 11*(3), 230–234.